THE COMPLETE WORKS OF ROBERT BROWNING, VOLUME XIII

Portrait of Robert Browning (c. 1875) by Robert Barrett Browning. By courtesy of the Armstrong Browning Library.

The Complete works of Robert Browning

With Variant Readings & Annotations

Volume XIII

EDITED BY

ASHBY BLAND CROWDER

OHIO UNIVERSITY PRESS

ATHENS, OHIO

BAYLOR UNIVERSITY

WACO, TEXAS

1995

Ohio University Press, Athens, Ohio 45701
© 1995 by Ohio University Press and Baylor University
Printed in the United States of America
All rights reserved

99 98 97 96 95   5 4 3 2 1

Ohio University Press books are printed on acid-free paper ∞

Library of Congress Cataloging-in-Publication Data
(Revised for vol. 13)

Browning, Robert, 1812-1889.
The complete works of Robert Browning, with variant
readings & annotations. Editorial board.

Vol. 7-   : general editor, Jack W.Herring.
Vol. 8 has imprint: Waco, Tex. : Baylor University;
Athens, Ohio : Ohio University Press; v. 9, 13: Athens,
Ohio : Ohio University Press ; Waco, Tex. : Baylor
University Press.
Vol. 13 edited by Ashby Bland Crowder.
Includes bibliographical references and indexes.
I. King, Roma A. (Roma Alvah), 1914-   ed.
II. Herring, Jack W., 1925-   .   III. Crowder, A. B.
IV. Title.
PR4201.K5   1969   821'.8   68-18389
ISBN 0-8214-1111-X (v. 13)

CONTENTS

I CONTENTS

This edition of the works of Robert Browning is intended to be complete. It will comprise at least seventeen volumes and will contain:

1. The entire contents of the first editions of Browning's works, arranged in their chronological order of publication. (The poems included in *Dramatic Lyrics, Dramatic Romances and Lyrics,* and *Men and Women,* for example, appear in the order of their first publication rather than in the order in which Browning rearranged them for later publication.)

2. All prefaces and dedications which Browning is known to have written for his own works and for those of Elizabeth Barrett Browning.

3. The two prose essays that Browning is known to have published: the review of a book on Tasso, generally referred to as the "Essay on Chatterton," and the preface for a collection of letters supposed to have been written by Percy Bysshe Shelley, generally referred to as the "Essay on Shelley."

4. The front matter and the table of contents of each of the collected editions (1849, 1863, 1865, 1868 [70, 75], 1888-1889) which Browning himself saw through the press.

5. Poems published during Browning's lifetime but not collected by him.

6. Poems not published during Browning's lifetime which have come to light since his death.

7. John Forster's *Thomas Wentworth, Earl of Strafford,* to which Browning contributed significantly, though the precise extent of his contribution has not been determined.

8. Variants appearing in primary and secondary materials as defined in Section II below.

9. Textual emendations.

10. Informational and explanatory notes for each work.

II PRIMARY AND SECONDARY MATERIALS

Aside from a handful of uncollected short works, all of Browning's works but *Asolando* (1889) went through two or more editions during his lifetime. Except for *Pauline* (1833), *Strafford* (1837), and *Sordello* (1840), all the works published before 1849 were revised and corrected for the 1849 collection. *Strafford* and *Sordello* were revised and corrected for the collection of 1863, as were all the other works in that edition. Though no further poems were added in the collection of 1865, all the works were once again corrected and revised. The 1868 collection added a revised *Pauline* and *Dramatis Personae* (1864) to the other works, which were themselves again revised and corrected. A new edition of this collection in 1870 contained further revisions, and Browning corrected his text again for an 1875 reimpression. The printing of the last edition of the *Poetical Works* over which Browning exercised control began in 1888, and the first eight volumes are dated thus on their title-pages. Volumes 9 through 16 of this first impression are dated 1889, and we have designated them 1889a to distinguish them from the second impression of all 16 volumes, which was begun and completed in 1889. Some of the earlier volumes of the first impression sold out almost immediately, and in preparation for a second impression, Browning revised and corrected the first ten volumes before he left for Italy in late August, 1889. The second impression, in which all sixteen volumes bear the date 1889 on their title-pages, consisted of a revised and corrected second impression of volumes 1-10, plus a second impression of volumes 11-16 altered by Browning in one instance. This impression we term 1889 (see section III below).

Existing manuscripts and editions are classified as either primary or secondary material. The primary materials include the following:

1. The manuscript of a work when such is known to exist.

2. Proof sheets, when known to exist, that contain authorial corrections and revisions.

3. The first and subsequent editions of a work that preserve evidence of Browning's intentions and were under his control.

4. The collected editions over which Browning exercised control:

1849—*Poems*. Two Volumes. London: Chapman and Hall.

1863—*The Poetical Works*. Three Volumes. London: Chapman and Hall.

1865—*The Poetical Works*. Three Volumes. London: Chapman and Hall.

1868—*The Poetical Works*. Six Volumes. London: Smith, Elder and Company.

1870—*The Poetical Works*. Six Volumes. London: Smith, Elder and Company. This resetting constituted a new edition, which was stereotyped and reimpressed several times; the 1875 impression contains revisions by Browning.

1888-1889—*The Poetical Works*. Sixteen Volumes. London: Smith,

Elder and Company. Exists in numerous stereotype impressions, of which two are primary material:

1888-1889a—The first impression, in which volumes 1-8 are dated 1888 and volumes 9-16 are dated 1889.

1889—The corrected second impression of volumes 1-10 and a second impression of volumes 11-16 altered by Browning only as stated in section III below; all dated 1889 on the title pages.

5. The corrections in Browning's hand in the Dykes Campbell copy of 1888-1889a, and the manuscript list of corrections to that impression in the Brown University Library (see section III below).

Other materials (including some in the poet's handwriting) that affected the text are secondary. Examples are: the copy of the first edition of *Pauline* which contains annotations by Browning and John Stuart Mill; the copies of the first edition of *Paracelsus* which contain corrections in Browning's hand; a very early manuscript of *A Blot in the 'Scutcheon* which Browning presented to William Macready, but not the one from which the first edition was printed; informal lists of corrections that Browning included in letters to friends, such as the corrections to *Men and Women* he sent to D. G. Rossetti; verbal and punctuational changes Browning essayed in presentation copies of his works or in his own copies, if not used by his printers; Elizabeth Barrett's suggestions for revisions in *A Soul's Tragedy* and certain poems in *Dramatic Romances and Lyrics;* and the edition of *Strafford* by Emily Hickey for which Browning made suggestions.

The text and variant readings of this edition derive from collation of primary materials as defined above. Secondary materials are occasionally discussed in the notes and sometimes play a part when emendation is required.

III COPY-TEXT

The copy-text for this edition is Browning's final text: the first ten volumes of 1889 and the last six volumes of 1888-1889a, as described above. For this choice we offer the following explanation.

Manuscripts used as printer's copy for twenty of Browning's thirty-four book publications are known to exist; others may yet become available. These manuscripts, or, in their absence, the first editions of the works, might be considered as the most desirable copy-text. And this would be the case for an author who exercised little control over his text after the manuscript or first edition stage, or whose text clearly became corrupted in a succession of editions. To preserve the intention of such an author, one would have to choose an early text and emend it as evidence and judgment demanded.

With Browning, however, the situation is different, and our copy-text choice results from that difference. Throughout his life Browning continually revised his poetry. He did more than correct printer's errors and clarify previously intended meanings; his texts themselves remained fluid, subject to continuous alteration. As the manuscript which he submitted to his publisher was no doubt already a product of revision, so each subsequent edition under his control reflects the results of an ongoing process of creating, revising, and correcting. If we were to choose the manuscript (where extant) or first edition as copy-text, preserving Browning's intention would require extensive emendation to capture the additions, revisions, and alterations which Browning demonstrably made in later editions. By selecting Browning's final corrected text as our copy-text, emending it only to eliminate errors and the consequences of changing house-styling, we present his works in the form closest to that which he intended after years of revision and polishing.

But this is true only if Browning in fact exercised extensive control over the printing of his various editions. That he intended and attempted to do so is apparent in his comments and his practice. In 1855, demanding accuracy from the printers, he pointed out to his publisher Chapman, "I attach importance to the mere stops . . ." (DeVane and Knickerbocker, p. 83). There is evidence of his desire to control the details of his text as early as 1835, in the case of *Paracelsus*. The *Paracelsus* manuscript, now in the Forster and Dyce collection in the Victoria and Albert Museum Library, demonstrates a highly unconventional system of punctuation. Of particular note is Browning's unrestrained use of dashes, often in strings of two or three, instead of more precise or orthodox punctuation marks. It appears that this was done for its rhetorical effect. One sheet of Part 1 of the manuscript and all but the first and last sheets of Part 3 have had punctuation revised in pencil by someone other than Browning, perhaps J. Riggs, whose name appears three times in the margins of Part 3. In addition to these revisions, there are analogous punctuation revisions (in both pencil and ink) which appear to be in Browning's hand, and a few verbal alterations obviously in the poet's script.

A collation of the first edition (1835) with the manuscript reveals that a major restyling of punctuation was carried out before *Paracelsus* was published. However, the revisions incorporated into the first edition by no means slavishly follow the example set by the pencilled revisions of Parts 1 and 3 of the manuscript. Apparently the surviving manuscript was not used as printer's copy for the first edition. Browning may have submitted a second manuscript, or he may have revised extensively in proof. The printers may have carried out the revisions to punctuation, with or without the poet's point by point involvement. With the present evidence, we cannot be conclusive about the extent of Browning's control over the first edition of *Paracelsus*. It can be stated, however, in the light of the incompleteness of the pencilled revisions and the frequent lack or correspondence between the pencilled revisions and the lines as printed in 1835, that Browning himself may have been responsible for the punctuation of the first edition of *Paracelsus*. Certainly he was responsible for the frequent instances in the first and subsequent editions where the punctuation defies conventional rules, as in the following examples:

                   What though
    It be so?—if indeed the strong desire
    Eclipse the aim in me—if splendour break
              (Part I, 11. 329-331)

    I surely loved them—that last night, at least,
    When we . . . gone! gone! the better: I am saved
              (Part II, 11. 132-133)

    Of the body, even,)—what God is, what we are,
              (Part V, 1. 642, 1849 reading)

   The manuscripts of *Colombe's Birthday* (1844) and *Christmas-Eve and Easter-Day* (1850) were followed very carefully in the printing of the first editions. There are slight indications of minor house-styling, such as the spellings *colour* and *honour* for the manuscripts' *color* and *honor*. But the unorthodox punctuation, used to indicate elocutionary and rhetorical subtleties as well as syntactical relationships, is carried over almost unaltered from the manuscripts to the first editions. Similar evidence of Browning's painstaking attention to the smallest details in the printing of his poems can be seen in the manuscript and proof sheets of *The Ring and the Book* (1868-69). These materials reveal an interesting and significant pattern. It appears that Browning wrote swiftly, giving primary attention to wording and less to punctuation, being satisfied to use dashes to indicate almost any break in thought, syntax, or rhythm. Later, in the proof sheets for Books 1-6 of the poem and in the manuscript itself for Books 7-12, he changed the dashes to more specific and purposeful punctuation marks. The revised punctuation is what was printed, for the most part, in the first edition of *The Ring and the Book;* what further revisions there are conform to Browning's practice, though hardly to standard rules. Clearly Browning was in control of nearly every aspect of the published form of his works, even to the "mere stops."

Of still greater importance in our choice of copy-text is the substantial evidence that Browning took similar care with his collected editions. Though he characterized his changes for later editions as trivial and few in number, collations reveal thousands of revisions and corrections in each successive text. *Paracelsus,* for example, was extensively revised for the 1849 *Poems;* it was again reworked for the *Poetical Works* of 1863. *Sordello,* omitted in 1849, reappeared in 1863 with 181 new lines and short marginal glosses; Browning admitted only that it was "corrected *throughout*" (DeVane and Knickerbocker, p. 157). The poems of *Men and Women* (1855) were altered in numerous small but meaningful ways for both the 1863 and 1865 editions of the *Poetical Works* (See Allan C. Dooley, "The Textual Significance of Robert Browning's 1865 *Poetical Works,*" *PBSA* 71 [1977], 212-18). Michael Hancher cites evidence of the poet's close supervision of the 1868 collected edition ("Browning and the *Poetical Works* of 1888-1889," *Browning Newsletter,* Spring, 1971, 25-27), and Michael Meredith has traced Browning's attentions to his text in the 1870 edition and an 1875 reimpression of it ("Learning's Crabbed Text," *SBHC* 13 [1985], 97-107); another perspective is offered in Allan C. Dooley's *Author and Printer in Victorian England* (1992), Ch. 4-5. Mrs. Orr, writing of the same period in Browning's life, reports his resentment of those who garbled his text by misplacing his stops (*Life,* pp. 357-58).

There is plentiful and irrefutable evidence that Browning controlled, in the same meticulous way, the text of his last collected edition, that which we term 1888-1889. Hancher has summarized the relevant information:

> The evidence is clear that Browning undertook the 1888-1889 edition of his *Poetical Works* intent on controlling even the smallest minutiae of the text. Though he at one time considered supplying biographical and explanatory notes to the poems, he finally decided against such a scheme, concluding, in his letter to Smith of 12 November 1887, "I am correcting them carefully, and *that* must suffice." On 13 January 1888, he wrote, regarding the six-volume edition of his collected works published in 1868 which was to serve as the printer's copy for the final edition:
> "I have thoroughly corrected the six volumes of the Works, and can let you have them at once." . . . Browning evidently kept a sharp eye on the production of all sixteen of the volumes, including those later volumes. . . . Browning returned proof for Volume 3 on 6 May 1888, commenting, "I have had, as usual, to congratulate myself on the scrupulous accuracy of the Printers"; on 31 December he returned proofs of Volume 11, "corrected carefully"; and he returned "the corrected Proofs of Vol. XV" on 1 May 1889.

Throughout his long career, then, Browning continuously revised and corrected his works. Furthermore, his publishers took care to follow his directions exactly, accepting his changes and incorporating them into each successive edition. This is not to say that no one else had any effect whatsoever on Browning's text: Elizabeth Barrett made suggestions for revisions to *A Soul's Tragedy* and *Dramatic Romances and Lyrics*. Browning accepted some suggestions and rejected others, and those which he accepted we regard as his own. Mrs. Orr reports that Browning sent proof sheets to Joseph Milsand, a friend in France, for corrections (*Life,* p. 183), and that Browning accepted suggestions from friends and readers for the corrections of errors in his printed works. In some of the editions, there are slight evidences of minor house-styling in capitalization and the indication of quotations. But the evidence of Browning's own careful attention to revisions and corrections in both his manuscripts and proof sheets assures us that other persons played only a very minor role in the development of his text. We conclude that the vast majority of the alterations in the texts listed above as Primary Materials are Browning's own, and that only Browning's final corrected text, the result of years of careful work by the poet himself, reflects his full intentions.

The first impression of Browning's final collected edition (i.e., 1888-1889a) is not in and of itself the poet's final corrected text. By the spring or 1889 some of the early volumes of the first impression were already sold out, and by mid-August it was evident that a new one would be required. About this time James Dykes Campbell, Honorary Secretary of the London Browning Society, was informed by Browning that he was making further corrections to be incorporated into the new impression. According to Dykes Campbell, Browning had corrected the first ten volumes and offered to transcribe the corrections into Dykes Campbell's copy of 1888-1889a before leaving for Italy. The volumes altered in Browning's hand are now in the British Library and contain on the flyleaf of Volume I Dykes Campbell's note explaining precisely what happened. Of course, Dykes Campbell's copy was not the one used by the printer for the second impression. Nevertheless, these changes are indisputably Browning's and are those which, according to his own statement, he proposed to make in the new impression. This set of corrections carries, therefore, great authority.

Equally authoritative is a second set of corrections, also in Browning's hand, for part of 1888-1889a. In the poet's possession at the time of his death, this handwritten list was included in lot 179 of Sotheby, Wilkinson, and Hodge's auction of Browning materials in 1913; it is today located in the Brown University Library. The list contains corrections only for Volumes 4-10 of 1888-1889a. We know that Browning, on 26 July 1889, had completed and sent to Smith "the corrections for Vol. III in readiness for whenever you need them." by the latter part of August, according to Dykes Campbell, the poet had finished corrections for Volumes 1-10. Browning left for Italy on 29 August. The condition of the Brown University list does not indicate that it was ever used by the printer. Thus we surmise that the Brown list (completing the corrections through volume 10) may be the poet's copy of another list sent to his publisher. Whatever the case, the actual documents used by the printers—a set of marked volumes or handwritten lists—are not known to exist. A possible exception is a marked copy of *Red Cotton Night-Cap Country* (now in the Berg Collection of the New York Public Library) which seems to have been used by printers. Further materials used in preparing Browning's final edition may yet appear.

The matter is complicated further because neither set of corrections of 1888-1889a corresponds exactly to each other nor to the 1889 second impression. Each set contains corrections the other omits, and in a few cases the sets present alternative corrections of the same error. Our study of the Dykes Campbell copy of 1888-1889a reveals fifteen discrepancies between its corrections and the 1889 second impression. The Brown University list, which contains far fewer corrections, varies from the second impression in thirteen instances. Though neither of these sets of corrections was used by the printers, both are authoritative; we consider them legitimate textual variants, and record them as such. The lists are, of course, useful when emendation of the copy-text is required.

The value of the Dykes Campbell copy of 1888-1889a and the Brown University list is not that they render Browning's text perfect. The corrections to 1888-1889a must have existed in at least one other, still more authoritative form: the documents which Browning sent to his publisher. That this is so is indicated by the presence of required corrections in the second impression which neither the Dykes Campbell copy nor the Brown University list calls for. The significance of the existing sets of corrections is that they clearly indicate two important points: Browning's direct and active interest in the preparation of a corrected second impression of his final collected edition; and, given the high degree of correspondence between the two sets of corrections and the affected lines of the second impression, the concern of the printers to follow the poet's directives.

The second impression of 1888-1889 incorporated most of Browning's corrections to the first ten volumes of the first impression. There is no evidence whatever that any corrections beyond those which Browning sent to his publisher in the summer of 1889 were ever made. We choose, therefore, the 1889 corrected second impression of volumes 1-10 as copy-text for the works in those volumes. Corrections to the first impression were achieved by cutting the affected letters of punctuation out of the stereotype plates and pressing or soldering in the correct pieces of type. The corrected plates were then used for many copies, without changing the date on the title pages (except, of course, in volumes 17 [*Asolando*] and 18 [*New Poems*], added to the set by the publishers in 1894 and 1914 respectively). External evidence from publishers' catalogues and the advertisements bound into some volumes of 1889 indicate that copies of this impression were produced as late as 1913, although the dates on the title pages of volumes 1-16 remained 1889. Extensive plate deterioration is characteristic of the later copies, and use of the Hinman collator on early and late examples of 1889 reveals that the inserted corrections were somewhat fragile, some of them having decayed or disappeared entirely as the plates aged. (See Allan C. Dooley, "Browning's *Poetical Works* of 1888-1889," *SBHC* 7:1 [1978], 43-69.)

We do not use as copy-text volumes 11-16 of 1889, because there is no present evidence indicating that Browning exercised substantial control over this part of the second impression of 1888-1889. We do know that he made one correction, which he requested in a letter to Smith quoted by Hancher:

> I have just had pointed out to [me] that an error, I supposed corrected, still is to be found in the 13th Volume—(Aristophanes' Apology) page 143, line 9, where the word should be Opora—without an i. I should like it altered, if that may be possible.

This correction was indeed made in the second impression. Our collations of copies of volumes 11-16 of 1889a and 1889 show no other intentional changes. The later copies do show, however, extensive type batter, numerous scratches, and irregular inking. Therefore our copy-text for the works in the last six volumes of 1888-1889 is volumes 11-16 of 1888-1889a.

IV VARIANTS

In this edition we record, with a very few exceptions discussed below, all variants from the copy-text appearing in the manuscripts and in the editions under Browning's control. Our purpose in doing this is two-fold.

1. We enable the reader to reconstruct the text of a work as it stood at the various stages of its development.

2. We provide the materials necessary to an understanding of how

Browning's growth and development as an artist are reflected in his successive revisions to his works.

As a consequence of this policy our variant listings inevitably contain some variants that were not created by Browning; printer's errors and readings that may result from house-styling will appear occasionally. But the evidence that Browning assumed responsibility for what was printed, and that he considered and used unorthodox punctuation as part of his meaning, is so persuasive that we must record even the smallest and oddest variants. The following examples, characteristic of Browning's revisions, illustrate the point:

Pauline, 1. 700:
    1833: I am prepared—I have made life my own—
    1868: I am prepared: I have made life my own.
"Evelyn Hope," 1. 41:
    1855: I have lived, I shall say, so much since then,
    1865: I have lived (I shall say) so much since then,
"Bishop Blougram's Apology," 1. 267:
    1855: That's the first cabin-comfort I secure—
    1865: That's the first-cabin comfort I secure:
The Ring and the Book, Book 11 ("Guido"), 1. 1064:
    1869: What if you give up boys' and girls' fools'-play
    1872: What if you give up boy and girl fools'-play
    1889a: What if you give up boy-and-girl-fools' play

We have concluded that Browning himself is nearly always responsible for such changes. But even if he only accepted these changes (rather than originating them), their effect on syntax, rhythm, and meaning is so significant that they must be recorded in our variant listings.

The only variants we do not record are those which strongly appear to result from systematic house-styling. For example, Browning nowhere indicated that he wished to use typography to influence meaning, and our inference is that any changes in line-spacing, depth of paragraph indentation, and the like, were the responsibility of the printers of the various editions, not the poet himself. House-styling was also very probably the cause of certain variants in the apparatus of Browning's plays, including variants in stage directions which involve a change only in manner of statement, such as *Enter Hampden* instead of *Hampden enters;* variants in the printing of stage directions, such as *Aside* instead of *aside,* or [*Aside.*] instead of [*Aside*], or [*Strafford.*] instead of [*Strafford*]; variants in character designations, such as *Lady Carlisle* instead of *Car* or *Carlisle.* Browning also accepted current convention for indicating quotations (see section V below). Neither do we list changes in type face (except when used for emphasis), nor the presence or absence of a period at the end of the title of a work.

We have rearranged the sequence of works in the copy-text, so that they appear in the order of their first publication. This process involves the restoration to the original order of the poems included in *Dramatic Lyrics, Dramatic Romances and Lyrics,* and *Men and Women.* We realize, of course, that Browning himself was responsible for the rearrangement of these poems in the various collected editions; in his prefatory note for the 1888-1889 edition, however, he indicates that he desired a chronological presentation:

> The poems that follow are again, as before, printed in chronological order; but only so far as proves compatible with the prescribed size of each volume, which necessitates an occasional change in the distribution of its contents.

We would like both to indicate Browning's stated intentions about the placement of his poems and to present the poems in the order which suggests Browning's development as a poet. We have chosen, therefore, to present the poems in order of their first publication, with an indication in the notes as to their respective subsequent placement. We also include the tables of contents of the editions listed as Primary Materials above.

We have regularized or modernized the copy-text in the following minor ways:
1. We do not place a period at the end of the title of a work, though the copy-text does.
2. In some of Browning's editions, including the copy-text, the first word of each work is printed in capital letters. We have used the modern practice of capitalizing only the first letter.
3. The inconsistent use of both an ampersand and the word *and* has been regularized to the use of *and.*
4. We have eliminated the space between the two parts of a contraction; thus the copy-text's *it 's* is printed as *it's,* for example.
5. We uniformly place periods and commas within closing quotation marks.
6. We have employed throughout the modern practice of indicating quoted passages with quotation marks only at the beginning and end of the quotation. Throughout Browning's career, no matter which

publisher or printer was handling his works, this matter was treated very inconsistently. In some of the poet's manuscripts and in most of his first editions, quotations are indicated by quotation marks only at the beginning and end. In the collected editions of 1863 and 1865, issued by Chapman and Hall, some quoted passages have quotation marks at the beginning of each line of the quotation, while others follow modern practice. In Smith, Elder's collected editions of 1868 and 1888-1889, quotation marks usually appear at the beginning of each line of a quotation. We have regularized and modernized what seems a matter of house-styling in both copy-text and variants.

The remaining way in which the copy-text is altered is by emendation. Our policy is to emend the copy-text to eliminate apparent errors of either Browning or his printers. It is evident that Browning did make errors and overlook mistakes, as shown by the following example from "One Word More," the last poem in *Men and Women*. Stanza sixteen of the copy-text opens with the following lines:

> What, there's nothing in the moon noteworthy?
> Nay: for if that moon could love a mortal,
> Use, to charm him (so to fit a fancy,
> All her magic ('tis the old sweet mythos)
> She . . .

Clearly the end punctuation in the third line is incorrect. A study of the various texts is illuminating. Following are the readings of the line in each of the editions for which Browning was responsible:

MS:	fancy)	1855:	fancy)	1865:	fancy)	1888:	fancy
P:	fancy)	1863:	fancy)	1868:	fancy)	1889:	fancy,

The omission of one parenthesis in 1888 was almost certainly a printers error. Browning, in the Dykes Campbell copy corrections to 1888-1889a, missed or ignored the error. However, in the Brown University list of corrections, he indicated that *fancy* should be followed by a comma. This is the way the line appears in the corrected second impression of Volume 4, but the correction at best satisfies the demands of syntax only partially. Browning might have written the line:

> Use, to charm him, so to fit a fancy,

or, to maintain parallelism between the third and fourth lines:

> Use, to charm him (so to fit a fancy),

or he might simply have restored the earlier reading. Oversights of this nature demand emendation, and our choice would be to restore the punctuation of the manuscript through 1868. All of our emendations will be based, as far as possible, on the historical collation of the passage involved, the grammatical demands of the passage in context, and the poet's treatment of other similar passages. Fortunately, the multiple editions of most of the works provide the editor with ample textual evidence to make an informed and useful emendation.

All emendations to the copy-text are listed at the beginning of the Editorial Notes for each work. The variant listings for the copy-text also incorporate the emendations, which are preceded and followed there by the symbol indicating an editor's note.

VI APPARATUS

1. *Variants*. In presenting the variants from the copy-text, we list at the bottom of each page readings from the known manuscripts, proof sheets of the editions when we have located them, and the first and subsequent editions.

A variant is generally preceded and followed by a pickup and a drop word (example a). No note terminates with a punctuation mark unless the punctuation mark comes at the end of the line; if a variant drops or adds a punctuation mark, the next word is added (example b). If the normal pickup word has appeared previously in the same line, the note begins with the word preceding it. If the normal drop word appears subsequently in the line, the next word is added (example c). If a capitalized pickup word occurs within the line, it is accompanied by the preceding word (example d). No pickup or drop words, however, are used for any variant consisting of an internal change, for example a hyphen in a compounded word, an apostrophe, a tense change or a spelling change (example e). A change in capilalization within a line of poetry will be preceded by a pickup word, for which, within an entry containing other variants, the $<>$ is suitable (example f). No drop word is used when the variant comes at the end of a line (example g). Examples from *Sordello* (all from Book I except c[2] which is from Book 4):

a.   611| *1840:*but that appeared   *1863:*but this appeared

b.   variant at end of line: 109| *1840:*intrigue:"   *1863:*intrigue.
      variant within line: 82| *1840:*forests like   *1863:*forests, like

c.   132| *1840:*too sleeps; but   *1863:*too sleeps: but   77| *1840:*that night by
      *1863:*that, night by night,   *1888:*by night

d.   295| *1840:*at Padua to repulse the   *1863:*at Padua who repulsed the

e.   284| *1840:*are   *1863:*were
      344| *1840:*dying-day,   *1863:*dying day,

    f.   capitalization change with no other variants: ⁷⁴¹| *1840:*
retaining Will,   *1863:*will,
with other variants: ⁸⁴³| *1840:*Was < > Him back! Why *1863:*
Is < > back!'' Why *1865:*him
    g. ⁴²⁷| *1840:*dregs: *1863:*dregs.

Each recorded variant will be assumed to be incorporated in the next edition if there is no indication otherwise. This rule applies even in cases where the only change occurs in 1888-1889, although it means that the variant note duplicates the copy-test. A variant listing, then, traces the history of a line and brings it forward to the point where it matches the copy-text.

An editor's note always refers to the single word or mark of punctuation immediately preceding or following the comment, unless otherwise specified.

In Browning's plays, all character designations which happen to occur in variant listings are standardized to the copy-text reading. In listing variants in the plays, we ignore character designations unless the designation comes within a numbered line. In such a case, the variant is treated as any other word, and can be used as a pickup or drop word. When a character designation is used as a pickup word, however, the rule excluding capitalized pickup words (except at the beginning of a line) does not apply, and we do not revert to the next earliest uncapitalized pickup word.

2. *Line numbers.* Poetic lines are numbered in the traditional manner, taking one complete poetic line as one unit of counting. In prose passages the unit of counting is the type line of this edition.

3. *Table of signs in variant listings.* We have avoided all symbols and signs used by Browning himself. The following is a table of the signs used in the variant notes:

§ . . . §	Editor's note
< >	Words omitted
/	Line break
/ / , / / / , . . .	Line break plus one or more lines without internal variants

4. *Annotations.* In general principle, we have annotated proper names, phrases that function as proper names, and words or groups of words the full meaning of which requires factual, historical, or literary background. Thus we have attempted to hold interpretation to a minimum, although we realize that the act of selection itself is to some extent interpretive.

Notes, particularly on historical figures and events, tend to fullness and even to the tangential and unessential. As a result, some of the information provided may seem unnecessary to the scholar. On the other hand, it is not possible to assume that all who use this edition are fully equipped to assimilate unaided all of Browning's copious literary, historical, and mythological allusions. Thus we have directed our efforts toward a diverse audience.

Tables

1. *Manuscripts*. We have located manuscripts for the following of Browning's works; the list is chronological.
Paracelsus
    Forster and Dyce Collection,
    Victoria and Albert Museum, London
Colombe's Birthday
    New York Public Library
Christmas-Eve and Easter-Day
    Forster and Dyce Collection,
    Victoria and Albert Museum, London
"Love Among the Ruins"
    Lowell Collection,
    Houghton Library, Harvard University
"The Twins"
    Pierpont Morgan Library, New York
"One Word More"
    Pierpont Morgan Library, New York
Dramatis Personae
    Pierpont Morgan Library, New York
The Ring and the Book
    British Library, London
Balaustion's Adventure
    Balliol College Library, Oxford
Prince Hohenstiel-Schwangau
    Balliol College Library, Oxford
Fifine at the Fair
    Balliol College Library, Oxford
Red Cotton Night-Cap Country
    Balliol College Library, Oxford
Aristophanes' Apology
    Balliol College Library, Oxford
The Inn Album
    Balliol College Library, Oxford

Of Pacchiarotto, and How He Worked in Distemper
  Balliol College Library, Oxford
"Hervé Riel"
  Pierpont Morgan Library, New York
The Agamemnon of Aeschylus
  Balliol College Library, Oxford
La Saisaiz and The Two Poets of Croisic
  Balliol College Library, Oxford
Dramatic Idylls
  Balliol College Library, Oxford
Dramatic Idylls, Second Series
  Balliol College Library, Oxford
Jocoseria
  Balliol College Library, Oxford
Ferishtah's Fancies
  Balliol College Library, Oxford
Parleyings With Certain People of Importance in Their Day
  Balliol College Library, Oxford
Asolando
  Pierpont Morgan Library, New York

We have been unable to locate manuscripts for the following works, and request that persons with information about any of them communicate with us.

Pauline	*The Return of the Druses*
Strafford	*A Blot in the 'Scutcheon*
Sordello	*Dramatic Romances and Lyrics*
Pippa Passes	*Luria*
King Victor and King Charles	*A Soul's Tragedy*
"Essay on Chatterton"	"Essay on Shelley"
Dramatic Lyrics	*Men and Women*

    2. *Editions referred to in Volume XIII.* The following editions have been used in preparing the text and variants presented in this volume. The dates given below are used as symbols in the variant listings at the bottom of each page.

1875   *The Inn Album.* London: Smith, Elder, & Co.

1876   *Pacchiarotto and How He Worked in Distemper: with Other Poems.* London: Smith, Elder, & Co.

1889a   *The Poetical Works.*
          Volumes 9-16. London: Smith, Elder, & Co.

3. *Short titles and abbreviations.* The following short forms of reference have been used in notes for this edition:

Austin, *The Golden Age*	Alfred Austin. *The Golden Age: A Satire.* London: Chapman and Hall, 1871.
Austin, *My Satire*	Alfred Austin. *My Satire and Its Censors.* London: George Manwaring, 1861.
Austin, *Poetry of the Period*	Alfred Austin. *The Poetry of the Period.* 1870; rpt. New York: Garland, 1986.
Austin, *The Season*	Alfred Austin. *The Season: A Satire,* rev. ed. London: John Camden Hotten, 1869.
B	Browning
BMS	Balliol manuscript (used only when needed to distinguish between this MS and PMMS).
B's 1876	*Pacchiarotto and How He Worked in Distemper: with other Poems.* London: Smith, Elder, 1876. Copy owned by B and containing revisions in his hand.
Collins	Thomas J. Collins, ed. "Letters from Robert Browning to the Rev. J. D. Williams, 1874-89," *Browning Institute Studies,* 4 (1976), 1-56.
Crowell	Norton B. Crowell. *Alfred Austin: Victorian.* Albuquerque: Univ. New Mexico Press, 1953.
DeVane, *Hbk.*	William Clyde DeVane. *A Browning Handbook,* 2nd ed. New York: Appleton-Century-Crofts, 1955.
DeVane and Knickerbocker	*New Letters of Robert Browning,* ed. William Clyde DeVane and Kenneth L. Knickerbocker. London: John Murray, 1951.
Domett, *Diary*	*Diary of Alfred Domett, 1872-1885,* ed. E. A. Horsman. London: Oxford Univ. Press, 1953.
Drew	Philip Drew, *The Poetry of Robert*

	Browning: A Critical Introduction. London: Methuen, 1970.
EBB	Elizabeth Barrett Browning
Griffin and Minchin	W. Hall Griffin and H. C. Minchin. *The Life of Robert Browning*, rev. ed. London: Methuen, 1938.
Hood, "Classical Sources"	Thurman L. Hood. "Browning's Classical Sources," *Harvard Studies in Classical Philology*, 133 (1922), 78-180.
Hood, *Ltrs.*	*Letters of Robert Browning Collected by Thomas Wise,* ed. Thurman L. Hood. London: John Murray, 1933.
Irvine and Honan	William Irvine and Park Honan. *The Book, the Ring, and the Poet.* New York: McGraw-Hill, 1974.
Kelley and Coley	Philip Kelley and Betty A. Coley, comps. *The Browning Collections: A Reconstruction With Other Memorabilia.* Waco, Texas; New York; Winfield, Kansas; and London: Armstrong Browning Library, The Browning Institute, Wedgestone Press, Mansell, 1984
Korg	Jacob Korg. *Browning and Italy.* Athens: Ohio Univ. Press, 1983.
Landis and Freeman	*Letters of the Brownings to George Barrett,* ed. Paul Landis and Ronald E. Freeman. Urbana: Univ. of Illinois Press, 1958.
Laughter of the Muses	*Laughter of the Muses: A Satire on the Reigning Poetry of 1869.* Glasgow: Thomas Murray, 1869.
Dearest Isa	*Dearest Isa: Robert Browning's Letters to Isabella Blagden,* ed. Edward McAleer. Austin: Univ. of Texas Press, 1951.
Learned Lady	*Learned Lady: Letters from Robert Browning to Mrs. Thomas FitzGerald, 1876-1889,* ed. Edward McAleer. Cambridge: Harvard Univ. Press, 1966.

Orr, *Hbk.*	Mrs. Sutherland Orr. *A Handbook to the Works of Robert Browning,* 5th ed. London: George Bell, 1890.
Orr, *Life*	Mrs. Sutherland Orr. *Life and Letters of Robert Browning.* London: Smith, Elder, 1891.
Partridge	Eric Partridge. *A Dictionary of Slang and Unconventional English.* 7th ed. New York: Macmillan, 1970.
Peterson	*Browning's Trumpeter: The Correspondence of Robert Browning and Frederick J. Furnivall, 1872-1889,* ed. William S. Peterson. Washington, D.C.: Decatur House, 1979.
PMMS	Pierpont Morgan manuscript
RB-EBB, ed. Kintner	*The Letters of Robert Browning and Elizabeth Barrett Barrett, 1845-1846,* ed. Elvan Kintner. Cambridge, Mass.: The Belknap Press of Harvard Univ. Press, 1969.
Ryals	Clyde de L. Ryals. *Browning's Later Poetry, 1871-1889.* Ithaca: Cornell Univ. Press, 1975.
Vasari	Giorgio Vasari. *Le Vite de' Piu Eccelenti Pittori, Scultori e Architetti.* Firenze, 1846-57. 13 vols.
Watkins	"Robert Browning's 'The Inn Album' and the Periodicals," *Victorian Periodicals Newsletter,* 4 (December 1973), 11-17.

The King James Version is used for all Biblical references, and *The Riverside Shakespeare,* ed. G. B. Evans *et al.* (Boston: Houghton Mifflin, 1974) is used for all references to Shakespeare.

ACKNOWLEDGMENTS

For providing money and services which have made it possible for us to assemble the vast materials required for the preparation of this edition, the following institutions have our especial appreciation: the

Ohio University Press, the Ohio University Library, the Ohio University English Department, the Baker Fund Awards Committee of Ohio University; Baylor University and the Armstrong Browning Library of Baylor University; the American Council of Learned Societies; Kent State University's University Library, Research Council, English Department, and Institute for Bibliography and Editing; Hendrix College and its Computer Center; the National Endowment for the Humanities.

We also thank the following for making available to us materials under their care: the Armstrong Browning Library; the Balliol College Library, Oxford; the Beinecke Rare Book and Manuscript Library, Yale University; the British Library; the John Hay Library, Brown University; the Houghton Library, Harvard University; the Henry E. Huntington Library; the Department of Special Collections, Kent State University; Mr. Philip Kelley; Mr. John Murray; the Library of the Victoria and Albert Museum; the University of Kentucky Library; the Eastern Kentucky University Library; the University of London Library, Senate House; University College Library, London; Birkbeck College Library, London; the Bodleian Library, Oxford; the Pierpont Morgan Library, New York.

The editor of this volume also wishes to thank the many scholars, colleagues, family members, and friends who have assisted him, in particular the following: Jon Arms, Jerry Blackburn, Penelope Bulloch, Betty Coley, Ashby Crowder III, Lynn Crowder, John Farthing, Edward Glusman, John Grigg, Alice Hines, William and Dorothy Humphrey, Margaret Crowder Hutchinson, Daniel Karlin, Kenneth L. Knickerbocker, Marylou Martin, Jean Nunn, Suzanne Paris, E. V. Quinn, Lillian Ruff, Andrew Sanders, Michael Slater, Kenneth Story, David Teague, Dolores Thompson, Scot Walker, Francis Warner.

The frontispiece is reproduced by permission of the Armstrong Browning Library of Baylor University.

THE INN ALBUM

Edited by Ashby Bland Crowder

PACCHIAROTTO AND HOW HE WORKED IN
  DISTEMPER: WITH OTHER POEMS

Edited by Ashby Bland Crowder

For
Lynn, my wife
and
Ashby, my son

THE INN ALBUM

Edited by Ashby Bland Crowder

THE INN ALBUM

THE INN ALBUM

1875

I.

    "That oblong book's the Album; hand it here!
Exactly! page on page of gratitude
For breakfast, dinner, supper, and the view!
I praise these poets: they leave margin-space;
5   Each stanza seems to gather skirts around,
And primly, trimly, keep the foot's confine,
Modest and maidlike; lubber prose o'ersprawls
And straddling stops the path from left to right.
Since I want space to do my cipher-work,
10   Which poem spares a corner? What comes first?
'Hail, calm acclivity, salubrious spot!'
(Open the window, we burn daylight, boy!)
Or see—succincter beauty, brief and bold—
'If a fellow can dine On rumpsteaks and port wine,
15   *He needs not despair Of dining well here—'*
'Here!' I myself could find a better rhyme!
That bard's a Browning; he neglects the form:
But ah, the sense, ye gods, the weighty sense!
Still, I prefer this classic. Ay, throw wide!
20   I'll quench the bits of candle yet unburnt.
A minute's fresh air, then to cipher-work!

---

§MS in Balliol College Library, Oxford. Ed. 1875, 1889a.§　*Title*|　MS: *THE INN-ALBUM
1875: THE INN ALBUM*　　³|　MS:For <> view! §between 2-4§　　⁵|　MS:Beside,
§word and comma crossed out§ each §altered to§ Each stanza seems to §last two words
inserted above§ gathers §altered to§ gather　　⁶|　MS:keeps §altered to§ keep first
foot's　*1875:*keep the foot's　　⁷|　MS:maidlike: lubber　*1875:*maidlike; lubber
⁹|　MS:Since <> cipher-work, §between 8-10§　　¹²|　MS:window—we <> daylight,
sure! §last word and exclamation mark crossed out and replaced above by word and
exclamation mark§ boy!　*1875:* window, we　　¹⁴|　MS:*wine　1889a:wine,*
¹⁸|　MS:the thought §crossed out and replaced above by§ sense <> weighty thought!
§last word crossed out and replaced by§ sense!　　¹⁹|　MS:prefer my §crossed out
and replaced above by§ this §double quotation mark in R margin crossed
out§　　²¹|　MS:air—then the cipher-work!　*1875:*air, then to cipher-work!

7

Three little columns hold the whole account:
Ecarté, after which Blind Hookey, then
Cutting-the-Pack, five hundred pounds the cut.
25   'Tis easy reckoning: I have lost, I think.''

Two personages occupy this room
Shabby-genteel, that's parlour to the inn
Perched on a view-commanding eminence;
—Inn which may be a vertiable house
30   Where somebody once lived and pleased good taste
Till tourists found his coign of vantage out,
And fingered blunt the individual mark
And vulgarized things comfortably smooth.
On a sprig-pattern-papered wall there brays
35   Complaint to sky Sir Edwin's dripping stag;
His couchant coast-guard creature corresponds;
They face the Huguenot and Light o' the World.
Grim o'er the mirror on the mantelpiece,
Varnished and coffined, *Salmo ferox* glares
40   —Possibly at the List of Wines which, framed
And glazed, hangs somewhat prominent on peg.

So much describes the stuffy little room—
Vulgar flat smooth respectability:
Not so the burst of landscape surging in,
45   Sunrise and all, as he who of the pair
Is, plain enough, the younger personage
Draws sharp the shrieking curtain, sends aloft
The sash, spreads wide and fastens back to wall

22-23| MS:Three <> account:/*Ecarté*, <> which,—Blind Hookey,—then, §two lines
in R margin§   *1875:*which—Blind Hookey—then   *1889a:*which Blind Hookey,
then   24| MS:Cutting-the-Pack—Five <> cut: §between 21 and 26§
*1875:*Cutting-the-Pack, five <> cut.   25| MS:'Tis <> think §in R margin§
*1875:*think.''   25-26| MS: §marginal note that ¶ begins§   *1875:*§no ¶§
1889a:§¶§   27| MS:Shabby-genteel that's   *1875:*Shabby-genteel, that's
28| MS:an §altered to§ a eminence-commanding view- §transposed to§ a
view-commanding eminence   *1875:*eminence;   30| MS:pleased his §crossed
out and replaced above by§ good   31| MS:coigne   *1889a:*coign   39| MS:*salmo*
§altered to§ *Salmo* <> glares   *1875:*glares,   *1889a:*glares   40| MS:—Possibly
§dash in margin§   41-42| MS: §no ¶§   *1889a:*§¶§   46| MS:Is plain
enough the   *1875:*Is, plain enough, the   48| MS:wide with §crossed out§

Shutter and shutter, shows you England's best.
He leans into a living glory-bath
Of air and light where seems to float and move
The wooded watered country, hill and dale
And steel-bright thread of stream, a-smoke with mist,
A-sparkle with May morning, diamond drift
O' the sun-touched dew. Except the red-roofed patch
Of half a dozen dwellings that, crept close
For hill-side shelter, make the village-clump,
This inn is perched above to dominate—
Except such sign of human neighbourhood,
(And this surmised rather than sensible)
There's nothing to disturb absolute peace,
The reign of English nature—which means art
And civilized existence. Wildness' self
Is just the cultured triumph. Presently
Deep solitude, be sure, reveals a Place
That knows the right way to defend itself:
Silence hems round a burning spot of life.
Now, where a Place burns, must a village brood,
And where a village broods, an inn should boast—
Close and convenient: here you have them both.
This inn, the Something-arms—the family's—
(Don't trouble Guillim: heralds leave out half!)
Is dear to lovers of the picturesque,
And epics have been planned here; but who plan
Take holy orders and find work to do.
Painters are more productive, stop a week,
Declare the prospect quite a Corot,—ay,
For tender sentiment,—themselves incline

57| MS:village-clump *1875:*village-clump,   58| MS:inn was perched *1875:*inn
is perched   60| MS:And that surmised <> sensible,— §dash added in
pencil§ *1875:*And this surmised <> sensible, *1889a:*(And <> sensible)
62| MS:of English §inserted above§ <> which, be sure, §last two words and commas
crossed out§   66| MS:itself; *1875:*itself: 68| MS:Now, §word and
comma inserted above§ <> burns, there §crossed out§   69| MS village is,
an <> should be— *1875:*village broods, an <> should boast—
71| MS:something-arms §altered to§ Something-arms   72| MS:heralds don't
know §last two words crossed out an replaced above by two words§ leave out
74| MS:plan, *1875:*plan   75| MS:and have §crossed out and replaced above by§ find

Rather to handsweep large and liberal;
80   Then go, but not without success achieved
—Haply some pencil-drawing, oak or beech,
Ferns at the base and ivies up the bole,
On this a slug, on that a butterfly.
Nay, he who hooked the *salmo* pendent here,
85   Also exhibited, this same May-month,
'Foxgloves: a study'—so inspires the scene,
The air, which now the younger personage
Inflates him with till lungs o'erfraught are fain
Sigh forth a satisfaction might bestir
90   Even those tufts of tree-tops to the South
I' the distance where the green dies off to grey,
Which, easy of conjecture, front the Place;
He eyes them, elbows wide, each hand to cheek.

His fellow, the much older—either say
95   A youngish-old man or man oldish-young—
Sits at the table: wicks are noisome-deep
In wax, to detriment of plated ware;
Above—piled, strewn—is store of playing-cards,
Counters and all that's proper for a game.
100   He sets down, rubs out figures in the book,
Adds and subtracts, puts back here, carries there,
Until the summed-up satisfaction stands
Apparent, and he pauses o'er the work:
Soothes what of brain was busy under brow,
105   By passage of the hard palm, curing so
Wrinkle and crowfoot for a second's space;
Then lays down book and laughs out. No mistake,

79| MS:liberal: *1875:*liberal; 80| MS:go, and §crossed out and replaced above
by§ but 84| MS:pendent there, §altered to§ here, 90| MS:tree-top
*1875:*tree-tops 93-94| MS:§marginal note that ¶ begins§ 95| MS:oldish-young,
*1875:*oldish-young— 98| MS:strewn—good §crossed out and replaced above by§
is 101| MS:puts down §crossed out and replaced above by§ back 103| MS:work—
*1875:*work: 106| MS:crow-foot <> space— *1875:*space; *1889a:*crowfoot

Such the sum-total—ask Colenso else!

Roused by which laugh, the other turns, laughs too—
110 The youth, the good strong fellow, rough perhaps.

"Well, what's the damage—three, or four, or five?
How many figures in a row? Hand here!
Come now, there's one expense all yours not mine—
Scribbling the people's Album over, leaf
115 The first and foremost too! You think, perhaps,
They'll only charge you for a brand-new book
Nor estimate the literary loss?
Wait till the small account comes! 'To one night's
Lodging,'—for 'beds,' they can't say,—'pound or so;
120 Dinner, Apollinaris,—what they please,
Attendance not included;' last looms large
'Defacement of our Album, late enriched
With'—let's see what! Here, at the window, though!
Ay, breathe the morning and forgive your luck!
125 Fine enough country for a fool like me
To own, as next month I suppose I shall!
Eh? True fool's-fortune! so console yourself.
Let's see, however—hand the book, I say!
Well, you've improved the classic by romance.
130 Queer reading! Verse with parenthetic prose—
'Hail, calm acclivity, salubrious spot!'
(Three-two fives) 'life how profitably spent'
(Five-nought, five-nine fives) 'yonder humble cot,'

108–09| MS:§marginal note that ¶ begins§   110| MS:The < > perhaps. §between
109-11§   110–11| MS:§marginal note that ¶ begins§   114| MS:people's
album 1875:people's Album   115| MS:perhaps 1875:perhaps,
116| MS:bran-new 1889a:brand-new   118| MS:night's . . . 1889a:night's
119| MS:Lodging', for—'beds' 1889a:Lodging,'—for 'beds'   122| MS:album
§altered to§ Album late 1889a:Album, late   123| MS:Here at 1875:Here, at
126| MS:To < > month I < > shall! §between 125-27§ 1875:month, I 1889a:month
I   127| MS:fool's-fortune, so < > yourself! 1875:fool's-fortune! so < >
yourself.   128| MS:Let's < > say! §between 127-29§   129| MS:classic—by
romance, 1875:classic by romance.   130| MS:That's doubtful! §last two
words and exclamation mark crossed out and replaced above by two words and
exclamation mark§ Queer reading!   131| MS:spot! 1875:spot!'
133| MS:Five- §over illegible erasure§ nought, five- §first and third characters
over the two n's in nine§ nine §over illegible erasure§ fives §apparently over nine§

(More and more noughts and fives) *'in mild content;*
135 *And did my feelings find the natural vent*
In friendship and in love, how blest my lot!'
Then follow the dread figures—five! *'Content!'*
That's apposite! Are you content as he—
Simpkin the sonneteer? *Ten thousand pounds*
140 Give point to his effusion—by so much
Leave me the richer and the poorer you
After our night's play; who's content the most,
I, you, or Simpkin?"
　　　　　　　　So the polished snob.
The elder man, refinement every inch
145 From brow to boot-end, quietly replies:

"Simpkin's no name I know. I had my whim."

"Ay, had you! And such things make friendship thick.
Intimates I may boast we were; henceforth,
Friends—shall it not be?—who discard reserve,
150 Use plain words, put each dot upon each i,
Till death us twain do part? The bargain's struck!
Old fellow, if you fancy—(to begin—)
I failed to penetrate your scheme last week,
You wrong your poor disciple. Oh, no airs!
155 Because you happen to be twice my age

134| MS:*content;'* 1875:content; 138| MS:apposite!—are 1875:apposite!
Are 139| MS:Simpkin §partly over illegible erasure§ 140| MS:Give §partly over
illegible erasure§ pointed §altered to§ point to §inserted above§ 141| MS:Leaving
§altered to§ Leave me the §last word inserted above§ 142| MS:By §crossed out and
replaced above by§ After < > most 1875:most, 143| MS:or Simpkin?" §partly over
illegible erasure; marginal note that ¶ begins§ He's a §last two words crossed out and
replaced above by two words§ So the 144-45| MS:The < > inch/From < > replies
§two lines on one line between 143-46§ 1875:replies: 145-46| MS:§marginal note that
¶ begins§ 146| MS:Simpkin's §partly over illegible erasure§ no friend of mine. Well,
§last four words and comma crossed out and replaced above by three words§ name I
know 146-47| MS:§marginal note that ¶ begins§ 147| MS:you! And §inserted
above§ Such §altered to§ such < > make a §last word crossed out§ < >
thick; 1875:thick. 148| MS:Intimates, I < > were: henceforth, 1875:were;
henceforth, 1889a:Intimates I 149| MS:Friends,—shall it not §inserted above§ be?
Friends §last word crossed out and dash added above line§ 1875:Friends—
shall 153| MS:your plan §crossed out and replaced above by§ scheme

12

And twenty times my master, must perforce
No blink of daylight struggle through the web
There's no unwinding? You entoil my legs,
And welcome, for I like it: blind me,—no!
160 A very pretty piece of shuttle-work
Was that—your mere chance question at the club—
'Do you go anywhere this Whitsuntide?
I'm off for Paris, there's the Opera—there's
The Salon, there's a china-sale,—beside
165 *Chantilly; and, for good companionship,*
There's Such-and-such and So-and-so. Suppose
We start together?' 'No such holiday!'
I told you: *'Paris and the rest be hanged!*
Why plague me who am pledged to home-delights?
170 *I'm the engaged now; through whose fault but yours?*
On duty. As you well know. Don't I drowse
The week away down with the Aunt and Niece?
No help: it's leisure, loneliness and love.
'Wish I could take you; but fame travels fast,—
175 *A man of much newspaper-paragraph,*
You scare domestic circles; and beside
Would not you like your lot, that second taste
Of nature and approval of the grounds!
You might walk early or lie late, so shirk
180 *Week-day devotions: but stay Sunday o'er,*

158| MS:unwinding? They §crossed out and replaced above by§ You   161| MS:Was
<> the Club.— §between 160-62§ 1875:club—   163| MS: *for Paris;* §comma altered to
semi-colon by pencil§ 1875:*for Paris, there's*   164| MS:*a china-sale,—* §perhaps followed
by colon, which was erased and replaced by comma and dash§   165| MS:*Chantilly: and*
<> *companionship,* §between 164-66§ 1875:*Chantilly; and*   166| MS:So-and-so:
suppose 1875:So-and-so. Suppose   167| MS:*together?'* §originally double quotation
marks§   168| MS:I told <> hanged! §between 167-71§   169-70| MS:*Why* <>
home-delights,/I'm the Engaged now,—through <> *yours?* §two lines in R margin§
1875:*home-delights?/I'm the engaged now; through*   171| MS:*duty. And I told you.*
§last four words and full stop crossed out and replaced below by four words and full stop§
—as you well know. 1875:*duty. As*   174| MS:*'Wish* <> *you: but* <> *fast,—*
1875:*you; but* 1889a:*Wish* <> *fast,'—* §emended to§ *'Wish* <> *fast,—*§see
Editorial Notes§   175| MS:*newspaper-paragraph,* 1889a:*newspaper-paragraph*
§emended to§ *newspaper-paragraph,* §see Editorial Notes§   177| MS:lot, the <> day
§crossed out and replaced by§ taste 1875:lot, that   180| MS:*Week-day*
§inserted above in left margin§ *Devotions* §altered to§ *devotions: shabbily* §crossed out§

And morning church is obligatory:
No mundane garb permissible, or dread
The butler's privileged monition! No!
Pack off to Paris, nor wipe tear away!'
185 Whereon how artlessly the happy flash
Followed, by inspiration! *''Tell you what—*
Let's turn their flank, try things on t'other side!
Inns for my money! Liberty's the life!
We'll lie in hiding: there's the crow-nest nook,
190 *The tourist's joy, the Inn they rave about,*
Inn that's out—out of sight and out of mind
And out of mischief to all four of us—
Aunt and niece, you and me. At night arrive;
At morn, find time for just a Pisgah-view
195 *Of my friend's Land of Promise; then depart.*
And while I'm whizzing onward by first train,
Bound for our own place (since my Brother sulks
And says I shun him like the plague) yourself—
Why, you have stepped thence, start from platform, gay
200 *Despite the sleepless journey,—love lends wings,—*
Hug aunt and niece who, none the wiser, wait
The faithful advent! Eh?' 'With all my heart,'
Said I to you; said I to mine own self:
'*Does he believe I fail to comprehend*
205 *He wants just one more final friendly snack*
At friend's exchequer ere friend runs to earth,
Marries, renounces yielding friends such sport?'
And did I spoil sport, pull face grim,—nay, grave?
Your pupil does you better credit! No!
210 I parleyed with my pass-book,—rubbed my pair
At the big balance in my banker's hands,—

181| MS:*obligatory—* §dash in pencil over perhaps marked out colon§   *1875:obligatory:*
182| MS:*permissible or   1889a:permissible, or*   183| MS:*no!* §altered to§
No!   188| MS:*life—   1875:life!*   192| MS:*us—* §dash in pencil§
193| MS:*Aunt and* §inserted above§ <> *me: at night, arrive—   1875:me. At night
arrive;*   195| MS:*of Promise: then depart—   1875:of Promise; then depart.*
201| MS:*Hug Aunt and Niece   1875:Hug aunt and niece*   203| MS:Said I to you:
§last four words underlined and then underlining erased§ said <> self   *1875:* you;
said <> self: 205| MS:*friendly final* §transposed to§ *final friendly*
208| MS:*sport,—pull   1875:* sport, pull   210| MS:my pair §over illegible erasure§

Folded a cheque cigar-case-shape,—just wants
Filling and signing,—and took train, resolved
To execute myself with decency
215   And let you win—if not Ten thousand quite,
Something by way of wind-up-farewell burst
Of firework-nosegay! Where's your fortune fled?
Or is not fortune constant after all?
You lose ten thousand pounds: had I lost half
220   Or half that, I should bite my lips, I think.
You man of marble! Strut and stretch my best
On tiptoe, I shall never reach your height.
How does the loss feel! Just one lesson more!"

The more refined man smiles a frown away.

225   "The lesson shall be—only boys like you
Put such a question at the present stage.
I had a ball lodge in my shoulder once,
And, full five minutes, never guessed the fact;
Next day, I felt decidedly: and still,
230   At twelve years' distance, when I lift my arm
A twinge reminds me of the surgeon's probe.
Ask me, this day month, how I feel my luck!
And meantime please to stop impertinence,
For—don't I know its object? All this chaff
235   Covers the corn, this preface leads to speech,
This boy stands forth a hero. *'There, my lord!*
Our play was true play, fun not earnest! I
Empty your purse, inside out, while my poke
Bulges to bursting? You can badly spare

²¹⁴| *1875:*myselt *1889a:*myself ²¹⁵| MS:ten §altered to§ Ten ²¹⁶| MS:wind-up,
farewell *1889a:*wind-up-farewell ²¹⁹| MS:half— *1875:*half ²²³| MS:feel? Just
*1889a:*feel! Just ²²³⁻²⁴| MS:§marginal note that ¶ begins§ ²²⁴| MS:The <>
away. §between 223-25§ ²²⁴⁻²⁵| MS:§marginal note that ¶ begins§ ²²⁶| MS:at this
present *1875:*at the present ²²⁸| MS:never, full five minutes, §four words
transposed to§ full five minutes, never ²²⁹| MS:decidedly; and *1875:*decidedly:
and ²³⁰| MS:year's *1875:*years' ²³⁶| MS:hero 'There *1875:*hero.
'There ²³⁹| MS:*Bulks out* §two words crossed out and replaced above by§ *Bulges*

240   *A doit, confess now, Duke though brother be!*
  While I'm gold-daubed so thickly, spangles drop
  And show my father's warehouse-apron: pshaw!
  Enough! We've had a palpitating night!
  Good morning! Breakfast and forget our dreams!
245   *My mouth's shut, mind! I tell nor man nor mouse.'*
  There, see! He don't deny it! Thanks, my boy!
  Hero and welcome—only, not on me
  Make trial of your 'prentice-hand! Enough!
  We've played, I've lost and owe ten thousand pounds,
250   Whereof I muster, at the moment,—well,
  What's for the bill here and the back to town.
  Still, I've my little character to keep:
  You may expect your money at month's end."

  The young man at the window turns round quick—
255   A clumsy giant handsome creature; grasps
  In his large red the little lean white hand
  Of the other, looks him in the sallow face.

  "I say now—is it right to so mistake
  A fellow, force him in mere self-defence
260   To spout like Mister *Mild Acclivity*
  In album-language? You know well enough
  Whether I like you—*like*'s no album-word
  Anyhow: point me to one soul beside
  In the wide world I care one straw about!

240| MS:*now!—Duke* <> *be: 1875:now, Duke* <> *be!*   245| MS:*mouse!'*
§double quotation mark altered to single§   247| MS:not with §crossed out and replaced
above by§ on   248| MS:The §crossed out and replaced above by§ Make trial of the
§last word crossed out and replaced above by§ your prentice-hand *1875:*'prentice-hand
249| MS:pounds *1875:*pounds,   251| MS:town: *1875:*town.   252| MS:Still,
having, Sir, a character <> keep, §between 251-53§ *1875:*Still, I've my little character <>
keep: 253| MS:money in a §last two words crossed out and replaced below by one
word§ at month's §first two characters over illegible erasure§   253-54| MS:§marginal
note that ¶ begins§   255| MS:creature: takes §last word crossed out and replaced by§
grasps *1875:*creature; grasps   256| MS:In the large *1875:*In his large
257| MS:other §first letter over illegible erasure§   257-58| MS:§marginal note that ¶
begins§   261| MS:Well enough you know §four words transposed to§ You know
well enough   262| MS:album-word— *1875:*album-word, *1889a:*album-word
263| MS:beside— *1875:*beside   264| MS:world—I *1875:*world I

265 I first set eyes on you a year ago;
Since when you've done me good—I'll stick to it—
More than I got in the whole twenty-five
That make my life up, Oxford years and all—
Throw in the three I fooled away abroad,
270 Seeing myself and nobody more sage
Until I met you, and you made me man
Such as the sort is and the fates allow.
I do think, since we two kept company,
I've learnt to know a little—all through you!
275 It's nature if I like you. Taunt away!
As if I need you teaching me my place—
The snob I am, the Duke your brother is,
When just the good you did was—teaching me
My own trade, how a snob and millionaire
280 May lead his life and let the Duke's alone,
Clap wings, free jackdaw, on his steeple-perch,
Burnish his black to gold in sun and air,
Nor pick up stray plumes, strive to match in strut
Regular peacocks who can't fly an inch
285 Over the courtyard-paling. Head and heart
(That's album-style) are older than you know,
For all your knowledge: boy, perhaps—ay, boy
Had his adventure, just as he were man—
His ball-experience in the shoulder-blade,
290 His bit of life-long ache to recognize,
Although he bears it cheerily about,
Because you came and clapped him on the back,
Advised him 'Walk and wear the aching off!'
Why, I was minded to sit down for life
295 Just in Dalmatia, build a sea-side tower

267| MS:twenty five 1875:twenty-five   269| MS:abroad— 1875:abroad,
273| MS:think,—since 1875:think, since   274| MS:to think a 1875:to know a
279| 1875:millionnaire 1889a:millionaire   280| MS:his own §crossed out§
283| MS:Not pick 1875:Nor pick   284| MS:fly an §probably alteration of a§ yard
§crossed out and replaced by§ inch   285| MS:court-yard-paling 1889a:courtyard-paling
287| MS:boy—perhaps 1875:boy, perhaps   288| MS:man:— 1875:man—
290| MS:of life long §last two words inserted above§ 1875:life-long

High on a rock, and so expend my days
Pursuing chemistry or botany
Or, very like, astronomy because
I noticed stars shone when I passed the place:
300 Letting my cash accumulate the while
In England—to lay out in lump at last
As Ruskin should direct me! All or some
Of which should I have done or tried to do,
And preciously repented, one fine day,
305 Had you discovered Timon, climbed his rock
And scaled his tower, some ten years thence, suppose,
And coaxed his story from him! Don't I see
The pair conversing! It's a novel writ
Already, I'll be bound,—our dialogue!
310 *'What?' cried the elder and yet youthful man—*
So did the eye flash 'neath the lordly front,
And the imposing presence swell with scorn,
As the haught high-bred bearing and dispose
Contrasted with his interlocutor
315 *The flabby low-born who, of bulk before,*
Had steadily increased, one stone per week,
Since his abstention from horse-exercise:—
'What? you, as rich as Rothschild, left, you say,
London the very year you came of age,
320 *Because your father manufactured goods—*
Commission-agent hight of Manchester—
Partly, and partly through a baby case
Of disappointment I've pumped out at last—
And here you spend life's prime in gaining flesh
325 *And giving science one more asteroid?'*
Brief, my dear fellow, you instructed me,

296| MS:rock and *1875*:rock, and 301| MS:England—to §inserted above§ lay
it §last word crossed out§ 304| MS:repented, some §crossed out and replaced
above by§ one 305| MS:When you *1875*:Had you 307| MS:coaxed
my §crossed out and replaced by§ his 310–25| MS:§italics indicated
in L margin§ 315| MS:*The languid* §crossed out and replaced above by§
flabby 318| MS:*What? You 1875:you* 320| MS:*manufactured cloth*
§crossed out and replaced by word and dash§ goods— 321| MS:*Commission-agent*
<>*Manchester—* §between 320-22§ 324| MS:*here have* §crossed out and
replaced above by§ *you passed life's 1875:you spend life's* 326| MS:me *1875:*me,

18

At Alfred's and not Istria! proved a snob
May turn a million to account although
His brother be no Duke, and see good days
³³⁰ Without the girl he lost and someone gained.
The end is, after one year's tutelage,
Having, by your help, touched society,
Polo, Tent-pegging, Hurlingham, the Rink—
I leave all these delights, by your advice,
³³⁵ And marry my young pretty cousin here
Whose place, whose oaks ancestral you behold.
(Her father was in partnership with mine—
Does not his purchase look a pedigree?)
My million will be tails and tassels smart
³⁴⁰ To this plump-bodied kite, this house and land
Which, set a-soaring, pulls me, soft as sleep,
Along life's pleasant meadow,—arm left free
To lock a friend's in,—whose but yours, old boy?
Arm in arm glide we over rough and smooth,
³⁴⁵ While hand, to pocket held, saves cash from cards.
Now, if you don't esteem ten thousand pounds
(—Which I shall probably discover snug
Hid somewhere in the column-corner capped
With *'Credit,'* based on *'Balance,'*—which, I swear,
³⁵⁰ By this time next month I shall quite forget
Whether I lost or won—ten thousand pounds,
Which at this instant I would give . . . let's see,
For Galopin—nay, for that Gainsborough
Sir Richard won't sell, and, if bought by me,
³⁵⁵ Would get my glance and praise some twice a year,—)
Well, if you don't esteem that price dirt-cheap
For teaching me Dalmatia was mistake—

---

^{327|} MS:Istria—that a *1875:* Istria! proved a   ^{330|} MS:the wife §crossed out and
replaced above by§ girl <> some one *1889a:* someone   ^{332|} MS:touched Society,
1875: touched society,   ^{336|} MS:behold— *1875:* behold.   ^{339|} MS:and tassels
§altered to *tasseling*, then original reading restored§ gay §crossed out and replaced by§ smart
^{343|} *1875:* whose, but *1889a:* whose but   ^{344|} MS:glide we §over illegible word§
^{347|} MS:§parenthesis and dash added in margin§   ^{350|} MS:shall quite §inserted
above§   ^{351|} MS:or simply won the same,— *1875:* or won—ten thousand pounds,
^{352|} MS:give . . let's *1889a:* give . . . let's   ^{355|} MS:§dash and parenthesis added§

Why then, my last illusion-bubble breaks,
My one discovered phœnix proves a goose,
360 My cleverest of all companions—oh,
Was worth nor ten pence nor ten thousand pounds!
Come! Be yourself again! So endeth here
The morning's lesson! Never while life lasts
Do I touch card again. To breakfast now!
365 To bed—I can't say, since you needs must start
For station early—oh, the down-train still,
First plan and best plan—townward trip be hanged!
You're due at your big brother's—pay that debt,
Then owe me not a farthing! Order eggs—
370 And who knows but there's trout obtainable?''

The fine man looks well-nigh malignant: then—

"Sir, please subdue your manner! Debts are debts:
I pay mine—debts of this sort—certainly.
What do I care how you regard your gains,
375 Want them or want them not? The thing *I* want
Is—not to have a story circulate
From club to club—how, bent on clearing out
Young So-and-so, young So-and-so cleaned me,
Then set the empty kennel flush again,
380 Ignored advantage and forgave his friend—
For why? There was no wringing blood from stone!
Oh, don't be savage! You would hold your tongue,
Bite it in two, as man may; but those small
Hours in the smoking-room, when instance apt

358| MS:then—my *1875:* then, my   359| MS:proves §word illegibly crossed out and replaced above by§ a   363| MS:mornings' *1875:* morning's
367| MS:town-ward *1875:* townward   369| MS:Then—owe *1875:* Then owe
370-71| MS:§marginal note that ¶ begins§   371| MS:The <> well nigh <> then §between 370-72§ *1875:* then— *1889a:* well-nigh   371-72| MS:§marginal note that ¶ begins§   372| MS:Sir *1875:* "Sir   374| MS:What §over illegible erasure§
375| MS:thing I *1875:* thing *I*   378| MS:Young so-and-so—young so-and-so §three words altered to§ Young So-and-so—young So-and—so <> me *1875:* Young So-and-so, young <> me,   382| MS:tongue *1875:* tongue,
383| MS:may: but *1875:* may; but   384| MS:Hours i' *1875:* Hours in

385 Rises to tongue's root, tingles on to tip,
And the thinned company consists of six
Capital well-known fellows one may trust!
Next week, it's in the 'World.' No, thank you much.
I owe ten thousand pounds: I'll pay them!"

                                              "Now,—
390 This becomes funny. You've made friends with me:
I can't help knowing of the ways and means!
Or stay! they say your brother closets up
Correggio's long-lost Leda: if he means
To give you that, and if you give it me . . ."

395 "I polished snob off to aristocrat?
You compliment me! father's apron still
Sticks out from son's court-vesture; still silk purse
Roughs finger with some bristle sow-ear-born!
Well, neither I nor you mean harm at heart!
400 I owe you and shall pay you: which premised,
Why should what follows sound like flattery?
The fact is—you do compliment too much
Your humble master, as I own I am;
You owe me no such thanks as you protest.
405 The polisher needs precious stone no less
Than precious stone needs polisher: believe
I struck no tint from out you but I found
Snug lying first 'neath surface hair-breadth-deep!
Beside, I liked the exercise: with skill
410 Goes love to show skill for skill's sake. You see,
I'm old and understand things: too absurd
It were you pitched and tossed away your life,
As diamond were Scotch-pebble! all the more,
That I myself misused a stone of price.

388| MS:much! 1875:much.   389| MS:them!" §marginal note that ¶ begins§ "Now,—
393| MS:long lost 1889a:long-lost   394| MS:me". . §perhaps dash following me
erased§ 1875:me . . ."   394-95| MS:§marginal note that ¶ begins§
397| MS:court-vesture: still 1875:court-vesture; still   407| MS:tint out from you
which §crossed out and replaced above by§ but 1875:tint from out you   408| MS:Not
§crossed out and replaced above by§ Snug   410| MS:sake: you §colon and last word
altered to§ sake. You   412| MS:To see §last two words crossed out and replaced above
by two words§ It were you pitch and toss §last three words altered to§ pitched and tossed

415 Born and bred clever—people used to say
Clever as most men, if not something more—
Yet here I stand a failure, cut awry
Or left opaque,—no brilliant named and known.
Whate'er my inner stuff, my outside's blank;
420 I'm nobody—or rather, look that same—
I'm—who I am—and know it; but I hold
What in my hand out for the world to see?
What ministry, what mission, or what book
—I'll say, book even? Not a sign of these!
425 I began—laughing—*'All these when I like!'*
I end with—well, you've hit it!—*'This boy's cheque*
For just as many thousands as he'll spare!'
The first—I could, and would not; your spare cash
I would, and could not: have no scruple, pray,
430 But, as I hoped to pocket yours, pouch mine
—When you are able!"
                              "Which is—when to be?
I've heard, great characters require a fall
Of fortune to show greatness by uprise:
They touch the ground to jollily rebound,
435 Add to the Album! Let a fellow share
Your secret of superiority!
I know, my banker makes the money breed
Money; I eat and sleep, he simply takes
The dividends and cuts the coupons off,
440 Sells out, buys in, keeps doubling, tripling cash,
While I do nothing but receive and spend.

419| MS:stuff, the outside's   1875:stuff, my outside's   421| MS:it: but   1875:it;
but   422| MS:see—   1875:see?   423| MS:mission or   1875:mission, or
424| MS:—I'll §dash in margin§   426| MS:it!—'*This chap's cheque*   1875:it!—'*This
boy's cheque*   427| MS:*thousands as* I can." §last two words crossed out and replaced
above by two words§ *he'll spare!'* §double quotation mark altered to single§
428| MS:not: your   1875:not; your   429| MS:scruple, then §crossed out and replaced
above by§ pray   430| MS:But, pouch mine as <> yours— §transposed to§ But, as
<> yours—pouch mine   1875:yours, pouch   431| MS:—When §dash in
margin§ <> able!"/—"Which   1875:able!"/"Which   432| MS:heard—great
1875:heard, great   434| MS:*You* §crossed out and replaced above by§ *They*
435| MS:the album   1875:the Album   438| MS:Money; spontaneous
generation, §last two words and comma crossed out and replaced above
by six words§ I eat and sleep, he simply   440| MS:cash—   1875:cash,

But you, spontaneous generator, hatch
A wind-egg; cluck, and forth struts Capital
As Interest to me from egg of gold.
445 I am grown curious: pay me by all means!
How will you make the money?"

                    "Mind your own—
Not my affair. Enough: or money, or
Money's worth, as the case may be, expect
Ere month's end,—keep but patient for a month!
450 Who's for a stroll to station? Ten's the time;
Your man, with my things, follow in the trap;
At stoppage of the down-train, play the arrived
On platform, and you'll show the due fatigue
Of the night-journey,—not much sleep,—perhaps,
455 Your thoughts were on before you—yes, indeed,
You join them, being happily awake
With thought's sole object as she smiling sits
At breakfast-table. I shall dodge meantime
In and out station-precinct, wile away
460 The hour till up my engine pants and smokes.
No doubt, she goes to fetch you. Never fear!
She gets no glance at me, who shame such saints!"

443| MS:cluck and <> capital §altered to§ Capital   1875:cluck,
and   447| MS:affair: enough: <> money—or   1875:affair. Enough <>
money, or   449| MS:a week §crossed out and replaced above by§ month
450| MS:time: 1875:time;   451| MS:Your <> trap: §between 450-52§
1875:trap;   452| MS:down-train, stand arrived   1875:down-train, play the arrived
453| MS:platform and you'll have the   1875:you'll show the   1889a:platform, and
456| MS:them, and are §last two words crossed out and replaced above by one word§ being
457| MS:With thought's §probably over illegible word§ sweet §crossed out and replaced
above by§ sole   461| MS:she sends §crossed out and replaced above by§ goes
462| MS:me—who shame the §crossed out and replaced above by§ such   1875:me, who

II

So, they ring bell, give orders, pay, depart
Amid profuse acknowledgment from host
Who well knows what may bring the younger back.
They light cigar, descend in twenty steps
5   The *"calm acclivity,"* inhale—beyond
Tobacco's balm—the better smoke of turf
And wood fire,—cottages at cookery
I' the morning,—reach the main road straitening on
'Twixt wood and wood, two black walls full of night
10   Slow to disperse, though mists thin fast before
The advancing foot, and leave the flint-dust fine
Each speck with its fire-sparkle. Presently
The road's end and the sky's beginning mix
In one magnificence of glare, due East,
15   So high the sun rides,—May's the merry month.

They slacken pace: the younger stops abrupt,
Discards cigar, looks his friend full in face.

"All right; the station comes in view at end;
Five minutes from the beech-clump, there you are!
20   I say: let's halt, let's borrow yonder gate
Of its two magpies, sit and have a talk!
Do let a fellow speak a moment! More
I think about and less I like the thing—
No, you must let me! Now, be good for once!
25   Ten thousand pounds be done for, dead and dammed!

MS: §Roman numeral and period above first line and (in pencil) in R margin; marginal note that ¶ begins§　　1| MS:So, §word and comma added in R margin§ give the §crossed out§　　3| MS:Who <> back, §between 2-4§ *1889a:* back.　　4| MS:Light the cigar *1889a:* They light cigar　　5| MS:The *'mild acclivity'*, inhale *1875:* The *'calm acclivity,'* inhale *1889a:* The *"calm acclivity,"* inhale　　8| MS:straightening *1889a:* straitening　　10| MS:Still §crossed out and, first in pencil, then in ink, replaced by§ Slow <> disperse; the §changed to§ though *1875:* disperse, though　　12| MS:Each speck §inserted above§ <> its fire- §last word and hyphen inserted above§ sparkle; §semi-colon changed to full stop§ presently §altered to§ Presently　　13| MS:end and the *1875:* end with the §emended to§ end and the §See Editorial Notes§　　15-16| MS: §marginal note that ¶ begins§　　17| MS:face— *1875:* face.　　17-18| MS: §marginal note that ¶ begins§ *1889a:* §no¶; emended to restore ¶; see Editorial Notes§　　18| MS:end— *1875:* end;

We played for love, not hate: yes, hate! I hate
Thinking you beg or borrow or reduce
To strychnine some poor devil of a lord
Licked at Unlimited Loo. I had the cash
30   To lose—you knew that!—lose and none the less
Whistle to-morrow: it's not every chap
Affords to take his punishment so well!
Now, don't be angry with a friend whose fault
Is that he thinks—upon my soul, I do—
35   Your head the best head going. Oh, one sees
Names in the newspaper—great this, great that,
Gladstone, Carlyle, the Laureate:—much I care!
Others have their opinion, I keep mine:
Which means—by right you ought to have the things
40   I want a head for. Here's a pretty place,
My cousin's place, and presently my place,
Not yours! I'll tell you how it strikes a man.
My cousin's fond of music and of course
Plays the piano (it won't be for long!)
45   A brand-new bore she calls a *'semi-grand,'*
Rosewood and pearl, that blocks the drawing-room,
And cost no end of money. Twice a week
Down comes Herr Somebody and seats himself,
Sets to work teaching—with his teeth on edge—
50   I've watched the rascal. *'Does he play first-rate?'*
I ask: *'I rather think so,'* answers she—
'He's What's-his-Name!'—'Why give you lessons then?'—
'I pay three guineas and the train beside.'—
'This instrument, has he one such at home?'—

26| MS:love—not   1875:love, not   34| MS:Is just—he < > do,— §altered to§ do—
1875:Is that he   35| MS:going: oh   1875:going. Oh   37| MS:Gladstone, Carlyle,
Kenealy—much   1875:Gladstone, Carlyle, the Laureate:—much   38| MS:mine—
1875:mine: 39| MS:rights   1875:right   40| MS:for: here's §colon and last word
altered to§ for. Here's   43| MS:music, and   1875:music and   45| MS:bran-new
thing she < > 'semigrand'   1875:bran-new bore she < > 'semigrand'   1889a:brand-new
< > 'semi-grand,'   46| MS:Rose-wood < > drawing room,   1875:drawing-room,
1889a:Rosewood   47| MS:money: twice §colon and last word altered to§ money.
Twice   48| MS:himself, §comma in pencil, traced in ink§   50| MS:first rate?'
1875:first-rate?'   52| MS:He's What's-his-name'! Why < > lessons, then?'   1875:He's
What's-his-Name!'—'Why < > lessons then?'—   53| MS:beside.'   1875:beside.'—
54| MS:instrument—has < > home?'   1875:instrument, has < > home?'—

55　'He? Has to practise on a table-top,
　　When he can't hire the proper thing.'—'I see!
　　You've the piano, he the skill, and God
　　The distribution of such gifts.' So here:
　　After your teaching, I shall sit and strum
60　Polkas on this piano of a Place
　　You'd make resound with *Rule Britannia!*"

　　　　　　　　　　　　　　　　　　　"Thanks!
　　I don't say but this pretty cousin's place,
　　Appendaged with your million, tempts my hand
　　As key-board I might touch with some effect."

65　"Then, why not have obtained the like? House, land,
　　Money, are things obtainable, you see,
　　By clever head-work: ask my father else!
　　You, who teach me, why not have learned, yourself?
　　Played like Herr Somebody with power to thump
70　And flourish and the rest, not bend demure
　　Pointing out blunders—*Sharp, not natural!*
　　Permit me—on the black key use the thumb!'
　　There's some fatality, I'm sure! You say
　　'Marry the cousin, that's your proper move!'
75　And I do use the thumb and hit the sharp:
　　You should have listened to your own head's hint,
　　As I to you! The puzzle's past my power,
　　How you have managed—with such stuff, such means—
　　Not to be rich nor great nor happy man:
80　Of which three good things where's a sign at all?
　　Just look at Dizzy! Come,—what tripped your heels?

56|　MS:*proper music box* §last two words crossed out and replaced above
by one word§ *thing.' 'I　1875:thing.'—'I*　　　61|　MS:with *'Rule Britannia'!"* §¶§
*1889a:*with *Rule Britannia!"* §¶§　　　62|　MS:cousin's-place,　*1875:*cousin's place,
64–65|　MS: §marginal note that ¶ begins§　　　69|　MS:like < > Somebody who ought to
1875: like < > Somebody with power to　　　70|　MS:And rattle §crossed out and replaced
above by§ flourish　　　71|　MS:blunders—*'Sharp—not　1875:*blunders—*'Sharp, not*
74|　MS:*that's the* §crossed out and replaced above by§ *your*　　　76|　MS:Why not
§last two words crossed out and replaced above by two words§ You should
77|　MS:you: the §colon and last word altered to§ you! The < > power—　*1875:*power,
78|　MS:means,— §comma rubbed out§　　　79|　MS:rich and §crossed
out and replaced above by§ nor great and §crossed out and replaced above by§
nor　　　81|　MS:heels? §Probably word originally followed by comma§

Instruct a goose that boasts wings and can't fly!
I wager I have guessed it!—never found
The old solution of the riddle fail!
85 *'Who was the woman?'* I don't ask, but— *'Where*
I' the path of life stood she who tripped you?'"

                                        "Goose
You truly are! I own to fifty years.
Why don't I interpose and cut out—you?
Compete with five-and-twenty? Age, my boy!"

90 "Old man, no nonsense!—even to a boy
That's ripe at least for rationality
Rapped into him, as may be mine was, once!
I've had my small adventure lesson me
Over the knuckles!—likely, I forget
95 The sort of figure youth cuts now and then,
Competing with old shoulders but young head
Despite the fifty grizzling years!"

                          "Aha?
Then that means—just the bullet in the blade
Which brought Dalmatia on the brain,—that, too,
100 Came of a fatal creature? Can't pretend

82| MS:Tell a poor §three words crossed out and replaced by two words§ Instruct a
85| MS:*woman?'*— §dash in pencil§ I <> but—'Where   *1875:woman?* I <> but—
*Where   1889a:*but—'Where   86| MS:*you?"* §¶§ "Goose,   *1875:you?"* §¶§ "Goose
87| MS:You §in L margin§ Truly! §word and punctuation altered to§ truly are! §word and
exclamation mark inserted above§ Why, fool, §two words and punctuation crossed out§ <>
years!   *1875:* years.   88| MS:Why <> you, §between 87-89§   *1875:*you?
    89| MS:five and twenty? Age §over illegible erasure§ <> boy!" §exclamation mark in
pencil, traced in ink§   *1889a:*five-and-twenty   89-90| MS: §maginal note that ¶ begins§
*1889a:*no ¶; emended to restore ¶; see Editorial Notes§   90| MS:man,—no <> even
§inserted above§   *1875:*man, no   92| MS:Rapped §over illegible erasure§
93| MS:I §crossed out and, in L margin, replaced by§ I've <> small experience §crossed out
and replaced above by§ adventure   95| MS:then   *1875:*then,   96| MS:shoulders
and §crossed out and replaced above by§ but   97| MS:fifty grizzling §inserted above§
years!" §punctuation added, next three words crossed out§ of snow outside §¶§
"Aha—   *1875:* years!" §¶§ "Aha?   98| MS:Then §in L margin§ That §altered to§ that
means—just §inserted above§ the §followed by illegible erasure§   99| MS:that too,
1875: that, too,   100| MS:of the §crossed out and replaced above by§ a <> creature!—

Now for the first time to surmise as much!
Make a clean breast! Recount! a secret's safe
'Twixt you, me and the gate-post!"

        "—Can't pretend,
Neither, to never have surmised your wish!
105   It's no use,—case of unextracted ball—
Winces at finger-touching. Let things be!"

"Ah, if you love your love still! I hate mine."

"I can't hate."

        "I won't teach you; and won't tell
You, therefore, what you please to ask of me:
110   As if I, also, may not have my ache!"

"My sort of ache? No, no! and yet—perhaps!
All comes of thinking you superior still.
But live and learn! I say! Time's up! Good jump!
You old, indeed! I fancy there's a cut
115   Across the wood, a grass path: shall we try?
It's venturesome, however!"

        "Stop, my boy!
Don't think I'm stingy of experience! Life
—It's like this wood we leave. Should you and I
Go wandering about there, though the gaps
120   We went in and came out by were opposed

---

§dash smudged§ Can't   *1875:*creature? Can't   ¹⁰²| MS:breast! Recount! A secret
§altered to§ secret's   *1875:*breast! Recount! a   ¹⁰⁴| MS:to never §inserted above§
<> your modest §crossed out§   ¹⁰⁵| MS:unextracted shot §crossed out
and replaced above with§ ball   ¹⁰⁶⁻¹⁰⁷| MS: §marginal note that ¶ begins§
¹⁰⁷⁻¹⁰⁸| MS: §marginal note that ¶ begins§   ¹⁰⁸| MS:you—and   *1875:*you; and
¹⁰⁹| MS:You—therefore—what <> me   *1875:*You, therefore, what   *1889a:*me:
¹¹⁰⁻¹¹| MS: § marginal note that ¶ begins§   ¹¹¹| MS:My <> perhaps . . . §between
110-12§   *1875:*perhaps!   ¹¹²| MS:All out §crossed out and replaced above by§ comes
<> still!   *1875:*still.   ¹¹⁵| MS:grass-path   *1889a:*grass path
¹¹⁶| MS:venturesome, remember §crossed out and replaced above by§ however

28

As the two poles, still, somehow, all the same,
By nightfall we should probably have chanced
On much the same main points of interest—
Both of us measured girth of mossy trunk,
Stript ivy from its strangled prey, clapped hands
At squirrel, sent a fir-cone after crow,
And so forth,—never mind what time betwixt.
So in our lives; allow I entered mine
Another way than you: 'tis possible
I ended just by knocking head against
That plaguy low-hung branch yourself began
By getting bump from; as at last you too
May stumble o'er that stump which first of all
Bade me walk circumspectly. Head and feet
Are vulnerable both, and I, foot-sure,
Forgot that ducking down saves brow from bruise.
I, early old, played young man four years since
And failed confoundedly: so, hate alike
Failure and who caused failure,—curse her cant!''

"Oh, I see! You, though somewhat past the prime,
Were taken with a rosebud beauty! Ah—
But how should chits distinguish? She admired
Your marvel of a mind, I'll undertake!
But as to body . . . nay, I mean . . . that is,
When years have told on face and figure . . .''

                                    "Thanks,

Mister *Sufficiently-Instructed!* Such
No doubt was bound to be the consequence

_{121|} MS:poles, yet §crossed out and replaced above by§ still somehow   *1875:* still, somehow
_{125|} MS:ivy spiral §crossed out§ <> its strangled §inserted above§   _{126|}   MS:fir cone
1875: fir-cone   _{127|}   MS:—And §dash in margin§ <> forth, never   *1875:* And <>
forth,—never   _{130|}   MS:I §followed by illegible erasure, perhaps *still*§
_{132|} MS:from: as   *1875:* from; as   _{134|}   MS:circumspectly: head §colon and
last word altered to§ circumspectly. Head   _{135|}   MS:foot-sure, §comma in pencil,
traced in ink§   _{137|}   MS:man two years   *1875:* man four years   _{139-40|}   MS:
§marginal note that ¶ begins§   _{141|}   MS:beauty! Ah,—   *1875:* beauty! Ah—
_{144|} MS:body . . nay <> mean . . that   *1889a:* body . . . nay <> mean . . . that
_{145|} MS:figure . .'' §¶§ ''Thanks,   *1875:* figure . . .'' §¶§ ''Thanks,

29

To suit your self-complacency: she liked
My head enough, but loved some heart beneath
150 Some head with plenty of brown hair a-top
After my young friend's fashion! What becomes
Of that fine speech you made a minute since
About the man of middle age you found
A formidable peer at twenty-one?
155 So much for your mock-modesty! and yet
I back your first against this second sprout
Of observation, insight, what you please.
My middle age, Sir, had too much success!
It's odd: my case occurred four years ago—
160 I finished just while you commenced that turn
I' the wood of life that takes us to the wealth
Of honeysuckle, heaped for who can reach.
Now, I don't boast: it's bad style, and beside,
The feat proves easier than it looks: I plucked
165 Full many a flower unnamed in that bouquet
(Mostly of peonies and poppies, though!)
Good nature sticks into my button-hole.
Therefore it was with nose in want of snuff
Rather than Ess or Psidium, that I chanced
170 On what—so far from *'rosebud beauty'* . . . Well—
She's dead: at least you never heard her name;
She was no courtly creature, had nor birth
Nor breeding—mere fine-lady-breeding; but

148| MS:That suits *1876:*To suit   149| MS:loved a §crossed out and
replaced above by§ some   150| MS:A head *1875:*Some head   153| MS:
of fifty whom you *1875:*of middle age you   154| MS:A <> peer, two years ago?
§transposed to§ two years ago A <> peer? §then original restored§ *1875:*peer at
twenty-one?   157| MS:please! *1875:*please.   158| MS:My, fifty years, Sir <>
success! §between 157 and 159§ *1875:*My middle age, Sir   159| MS:occurred two
years *1875:*occurred four years   160| MS:just where §altered to§
while   164| MS:The thing proves <> looks: enough, §word and comma crossed out
and replaced by two words§ I plucked *1875:*The feat proves   165| MS:I plucked my
§last three words crossed out and replaced by three words§ My many a flowers §altered to§
flower unclasped §altered to§ unnamed *1875:*Full many   168| MS:Therefore §last four
characters inserted§   170| MS:what you call my §last three words crossed out and
replaced above by dash and three words§ —so far from <> *beauty'* . . Well—
1889a:beauty' . . . Well—   171| MS:dead: you never can have heard her
name: *1875:*dead: at least you never heard her name;   173| MS:breeding—that's

30

Oh, such a wonder of a woman! Grand
175   As a Greek statue! Stick fine clothes on that,
Style that a Duchess or a Queen,—you know,
Artists would make an outcry: all the more,
That she had just a statue's sleepy grace
Which broods o'er its own beauty. Nay, her fault
180   (Don't laugh!) was just perfection: for suppose
Only the little flaw, and I had peeped
Inside it, learned what soul inside was like.
At Rome some tourist raised the grit beneath
A Venus' forehead with his whittling-knife—
185   I wish,—now,—I had played that brute, brought blood
To surface from the depths I fancied chalk!
As it was, her mere face surprised so much
That I stopped short there, struck on heap, as stares
The cockney stranger at a certain bust
190   With drooped eyes,—she's the thing I have in mind,—
Down at my Brother's. All sufficient prize—
Such outside! Now,—confound me for a prig!—
Who cares? I'll make a clean breast once for all!
Beside, you've heard the gossip. My life long
195   I've been a woman-liker,—liking means
Loving and so on. There's a lengthy list
By this time I shall have to answer for—
So say the good folk: and they don't guess half—
For the worst is, let once collecting-itch
200   Possess you, and, with perspicacity,
Keeps growing such a greediness that theft
Follows at no long distance,—there's the fact!

---

fine-lady-breeding: but   *1875:* breeding—mere fine-lady-breeding; but   174| MS::Oh
such   *1875:* Oh, such   175| MS:statue!— §dash erased§   179| MS:Which
§apparently over§ That < > beauty: nay §colon and last word altered to§ beauty. Nay
183| MS:some fellow raised   *1875:* some tourist raised   187| MS:surprised me
§crossed out§ so much §apparently inserted§   189–91| MS:Down at my Brother's at
< > bust//Some cockney stranger. All < > prise— §transposed to§ Some cockney
stranger at < > bust//Down at my Brother's. All < > prise—   *1875:* The
cockney   192| MS:a fool!— §crossed out and replaced above by§ prig!—
198| MS:the parsons §crossed out and replaced above by two words§ good books: and
1875: the good folks: and   *1889a:* folk   200| perspicacity   *1889a:* perspicacity,

31

I knew that on my Leporello-list
Might figure this, that, and the other name
205 Of feminine desirability,
But if I happened to desire inscribe,
Along with these, the only Beautiful—
Here was the unique specimen to snatch
Or now or never. 'Beautiful' I said—
210 'Beautiful' say in cold blood,—boiling then
To tune of *'Haste, secure whate'er the cost*
This rarity, die in the act, be damned,
So you complete collection, crown your list!'
It seemed as though the whole world, once aroused
215 By the first notice of such wonder's birth,
Would break bounds to contest my prize with me
The first discoverer, should she but emerge
From that safe den of darkness where she dozed
Till I stole in, that country-parsonage
220 Where, country-parson's daughter, motherless,
Brotherless, sisterless, for eighteen years
She had been vegetating lily-like.
Her father was my brother's tutor, got
The living that way: him I chanced to see—
225 Her I saw—her the world would grow one eye
To see, I felt no sort of doubt at all!
'Secure her!' cried the devil: *'afterward*
Arrange for the disposal of the prize!'
The devil's doing! yet I seem to think—
230 Now, when all's done,—think with *'a head reposed'*
In French phrase—hope I think I meant to do
All requisite for such a rarity

204| MS:that and *1889a:*that, and   207| MS:these; §semi-colon altered to comma§
these,   208| MS:to sieze §crossed out and replaced by§ snatch   217| MS:discoverer:
let her once emerge *1875:*discoverer, should she but emerge   219| MS:Till I awake her,
country-parsonage *1875:*Till I stole in, that country-parsonage   223| MS:my brother's
§probably alteration of *Brother's*§   224| MS:him I went §crossed out and replaced
above by§ chanced   225| MS:would turn all §last two words crossed out and replaced
above by two words§ grow one eyes §altered to§ eye   226| MS:And §crossed out and
replaced above in pencil by§ To §which was subsequently inserted in the L margin in
ink§   227| MS:*'afterwards, 1875:'afterward*   230| MS:*reposed—' 1875:reposed'*

When I should be at leisure, have due time
To learn requirement. But in evil day—
235 Bless me, at week's end, long as any year,
The father must begin *'Young Somebody,*
Much recommended—for I break a rule—
Comes here to read, next Long Vacation.' 'Young!'
That did it. Had the epithet been *'rich,'*
240 *'Noble,' 'a genius,'* even *'handsome,'*—but
—'*Young*'!"

        "I say—just a word! I want to know—
You are not married?"

           "I?"

           "Nor ever were?"

"Never! Why?"

        "Oh, then—never mind! Go on!
I had a reason for the question."

           "Come,—
245 You could not be the young man?"

              "No, indeed!
Certainly—if you never married her!"

"That I did not: and there's the curse, you'll see!
Nay, all of it's one curse, my life's mistake
Which, nourished with manure that's warranted

233| MS:leisure, in good §two words crossed out and replaced above by two words§ have
due   236| MS:begin < > Somebody—   1875: begin < > Somebody,
237| MS:Rich, interesting,— §last two words and comma-dash crossed out
and replaced above by two words and dash§ Much recommended— for, I   1875:for
I   238| MS:read next 1875:read, next   239| MS:it! Had < > 'rich'
1875:it. Had < > 'rich,'   240| MS:'handsome,— but 1875:'handsome,'—
but   241| MS:—'Young!'" §¶§ "I 1875:—'Young'!" §¶§ "I
246-47| MS: §marginal note that ¶ begins§   247| MS:not—and 1875:not: and

250 To make the plant bear wisdom, blew out full
In folly beyond field-flower-foolishness!
The lies I used to tell my womankind,
Knowing they disbelieved me all the time
Though they required my lies, their decent due,
255 This woman—not so much believed, I'll say,
As just anticipated from my mouth:
Since being true, devoted, constant—she
Found constancy, devotion, truth, the plain
And easy commonplace of character.
260 No mock-heroics but seemed natural
To her who underneath the face, I knew
Was fairness' self, possessed a heart, I judged
Must correspond in folly just as far
Beyond the common,—and a mind to match,—
265 Not made to puzzle conjurers like me
Who, therein, proved the fool who fronts you, Sir,
And begs leave to cut short the ugly rest!
'*Trust me!*' I said: she trusted. '*Marry me!*'
Or rather, '*We are married: when, the rite?*'
270 That brought on the collector's next-day qualm
At counting acquisition's cost. There lay
My marvel, there my purse more light by much
Because of its late lie-expenditure:

252| MS:womankind *1875:*womankind,   255| MS:believed—I'll *1875:*believed,
I'll   256| MS:mouth:— §dash in pencil§ *1875:*mouth: 257| MS:Since
being §inserted above§ true < > constant—natural §crossed out§
258| MS:Alone seemed §last two words crossed out and replaced above by§ Found
< > the plain §probably last two words added when changes were made in
subsequent two lines§   259-260| MS:And < > character: / No mock-heroic
< > natural §two lines between 258-61§ *1875:*character. / No mock-heroics
263| MS:folly,—proved myself §comma-dash and last two words crossed out and replaced
above by three words§ just as far   265| MS:Not < > me §line inserted in right margin§
266| MS:Who, §word and comma in L margin§ Therein, §last word crossed out and then
restored§ the perfect §last two words crossed out and replaced below by two words§ proved
the *1875:*Who, therein   267| MS:Believe me, §last two words and comma crossed out
and replaced by three words§ And begs leave   269| MS:Or rather, '*Being
married—when* < > *rite?*'— §between 268-70§ *1875:*rather, '*We are married: when* < >
rite?'   270| MS:That came §crossed out and replaced below by§ brought < > next-day
fit *1875:*next-day qualm   271| MS:Of counting *1875:*At counting
272| MS:The marvel *1875:*My marvel   273| MS:of the late lie-dispenditure: *1875:*of

34

Ill-judged such moment to make fresh demand—
275 To cage as well as catch my rarity!
So, I began explaining. At first word
Outbroke the horror. *'Then, my truths were lies!'*
I tell you, such an outbreak, such new strange
All-unsuspected revelation—soul
280 As supernaturally grand as face
Was fair beyond example—that at once
Either I lost—or, if it please you, found
My senses,—stammered somehow—*'Jest! and now,*
Earnest! Forget all else but—heart has loved,
285 *Does love, shall love you ever! take the hand!'*
Not she! no marriage for superb disdain,
Contempt incarnate!''

    "Yes, it's different,—
It's only like in being four years since.
I see now!''

        "Well, what did disdain do next,
290 Think you?''

        "That's past me: did not marry you!—
That's the main thing I care for, I suppose.
Turned nun, or what?''

        "Why, married in a month
Some parson, some smug crop-haired smooth-chinned sort

---

its late lie-expenditure: 274| MS:judged the §crossed out and replaced above by§ such
275| MS:Bid cage *1889a:*To cage   276| MS:So I *1875:*So, I   280| MS:As
§crossed out and replaced above by§ So supernaturally *1875:*As supernaturally
282| MS:lost my §last word crossed out and replaced above by dash§ —or, if that §crossed
out and replaced above by§ it   284| MS:*Earnest! Forgive,* §last word and comma
crossed out§ *forget* §altered to§ *Forget* <> *else than* §last word crossed out and replaced by§
but   285| MS:*ever!* §exclamation mark over colon§   286| MS:marriage with
§crossed out and replaced below by§ for   287| MS:"Yes—it's *1875:*"Yes, it's
288| MS:It's <> being two years since. §between 287-89§ *1875:*being four years
290| MS:me: since she §last two words crossed out§   291| MS:That's <> suppose—
§between 290-92§ *1875:*suppose.   292| MS:nun or *1889a:*nun, or
293| MS:Some clergyman §crossed out and replaced above by§ parson, some smug §inserted

35

Of curate-creature, I suspect,—dived down,
295   Down, deeper still, and came up somewhere else—
I don't know where—I've not tried much to know,—
In short, she's happy: what the clodpoles call
'Countrified' with a vengeance! leads the life
Respectable and all that drives you mad:
300   Still—where, I don't know, and that's best for both."

"Well, that she did not like you, I conceive.
But why should you hate her, I want to know?"

"My good young friend,—because or her or else
Malicious Providence I have to hate.
305   For, what I tell you proved the turning-point
Of my whole life and fortune toward success
Or failure. If I drown, I lay the fault
Much on myself who caught at reed not rope,
But more on reed which, with a packthread's pith,
310   Had buoyed me till the minute's cramp could thaw
And I strike out afresh and so be saved.
It's easy saying—I had sunk before,
Disqualified myself by idle days
And busy nights, long since, from holding hard
315   On cable, even, had fate cast me such!
You boys don't know how many times men fail

---

above§ crop haired clean shaved kind §last three words crossed out and replaced above and
in R margin by two words§ smooth-chinned sort   *1875:*crop-haired   295| MS:deeper
even, came   *1875:*deeper still, and came   296| MS:I < > know— §between 295-97§
*1875:*know,—   297| MS:Out of the darkness, §last four words and comma crossed out
and replaced below by four words and colon§ In short she's happy:< > call—   *1875:*call
*1889a:*short, she's   298| MS:Countrified < > vengeance, leads   *1875:*'Countrified' < >
vengeance! leads   299| MS:drives man §crossed out and replaced above by§ you
300| MS:Still— §word and dash in margin§ Where < > that's the §crossed out§
*1875:*Still—where   300-01| MS:§marginal note that ¶ begins§   302| MS:know!"
*1875:*know?"   302-03| MS:§marginal note that ¶ begins§   305| MS:For §perhaps
over illegible erasure§ what < > you, lay §crossed out and replaced above by§
proved   *1875:*For, what < > you proved   309| MS:But §in margin§ More   *1875:*But
more   310| MS:cramp should §altered to§ could   312| MS:before,—   *1875:*before,
315| MS:even, should §crossed out and replaced above by§ though fate   *1875:*even, had fate
316| MS:times men §crossed out and replaced above by§ we fail   *1875:*times men

36

Perforce o' the little to succeed i' the large,
Husband their strength, let slip the petty prey,
Collect the whole power for the final pounce.
320 My fault was the mistaking man's main prize
For intermediate boy's diversion; clap
Of boyish hands here frightened game away
Which, once gone, goes for ever. Oh, at first
I took the anger easily, nor much
325 Minded the anguish—having learned that storms
Subside, and teapot-tempests are akin.
Time would arrange things, mend whate'er might be
Somewhat amiss; precipitation, eh?
Reason and rhyme prompt—reparation! Tiffs
330 End properly in marriage and a dance!
I said 'We'll marry, make the past a blank'—
And never was such damnable mistake!
That interview, that laying bare my soul,
As it was first, so was it last chance—one
335 And only. Did I write? Back letter came
Unopened as it went. Inexorable
She fled, I don't know where, consoled herself
With the smug curate-creature: chop and change!
Sure am I, when she told her shaveling all
340 His Magdalen's adventure, tears were shed,
Forgiveness evangelically shown,
'Loose hair and lifted eye,'—as someone says.

---

fail   318| MS:Husband your §altered to§ our   1875: Husband their
319| MS:whole man for <> pounce!   1875: whole power for <> pounce   1889a: pounce.
321| MS:boy's-diversion   1875: boy's diversion   322| MS:Of foolish hands had
frightened   1875: Of boyish hands here frightened   326| MS:Subside, this §crossed out
and replaced above by§ and teapot-tempests like its §last two words crossed out and replaced
above by§ are kin. §altered to§ akin.   329| MS:reparation:—all   1875: reparation! Tiffs
330| MS:Ends <> dance!' §single quotation mark erased§   1875: End   331| MS:I <>
blank'— §between 330-32§   332| MS:And, never   1875: And never
333| MS:interview, exposure of §last two words crossed out and replaced above
by three words§ that laying bare my sport, §crossed out and replaced above by§ game,
1875: my soul,   334| MS:last, the §comma and word crossed out and replaced above
by word and dash§ chance—one   335| MS:The §crossed out and replaced above by§
And only. Did I §last two words inserted above§ write? a letter §last two words
crossed out§ Back letter §over it§   339| MS:I, that §crossed out and replaced
above by§ when   341| MS:shewn   1889a: shown,   342| MS;says!   1875: says.

37

And now, he's worshipped for his pains, the sneak!"

"Well, but your turning-point of life,—what's here
345 To hinder you contesting Finsbury
With Orton, next election? I don't see . . ."

"Not you! But *I* see. Slowly, surely, creeps
Day by day o'er me the conviction—here
Was life's prize grasped at, gained, and then let go!
350 —That with her—may be, for her—I had felt
Ice in me melt, grow steam, drive to effect
Any or all the fancies sluggish here
I' the head that needs the hand she would not take
And I shall never lift now. Lo, your wood—
355 Its turnings which I likened life to! Well,—
There she stands, ending every avenue,
Her visionary presence on each goal
I might have gained had we kept side by side!
Still string nerve and strike foot? Her frown forbids:
360 The steam congeals once more: I'm old again!
Therefore I hate myself—but how much worse
Do not I hate who would not understand,
Let me repair things—no, but sent a-slide
My folly falteringly, stumblingly
365 Down, down and deeper down until I drop

343| MS:the snob!" *1875:* the sneak!"   343-44| MS:§marginal note that ¶
begins§   346| MS:see" . . . *1875:* see . . .' *1889a:* see . . ."
346-47| MS:§marginal note that ¶ begins§   347| MS:see—slowly §dash and last word
altered to§ see. Slowly   350| MS:—That §dash in margin§   351| MS:The §crossed
out§ ice §altered to§ Ice < > me melt— §word and dash inserted above§ grow
steam—drive *1875:* melt, grow steam, drive   354| MS shall hardly §crossed out and
replaced above by§ never   355| MS:Its §over perhaps *The*§ turning wherein §crossed
out and replaced above by word illegibly crossed out which was replaced by§ which we
likened life §altered to§ Life *1875:* which I likened   357| MS:visionary foot upon
§last two words crossed out and replaced above by two words§ presence on the crown
§crossed out and replaced above by§ goal *1875:* on each goal   358| MS:have
reached had *1875:* have gained had   359| MS:foot? Disdain §crossed out and
replaced above by two words§ The frown forbids! *1875:* foot? Her frown forbids:
360| MS:more; I'm < > again— *1875:* more: I'm < > again!   361| MS:much more
1875: much worse   363| MS:send §altered to§ sent   364| MS:folly, faulteringly
1875: folly faulteringly   365| MS:deeper still until *1875:* deeper down until

Upon—the need of your ten thousand pounds
And consequently loss of mine! I lose
Character, cash, nay, common-sense itself
Recounting such a lengthy cock-and-bull
370   Adventure—lose my temper in the act . . ."

"And lose beside,—if I may supplement
The list of losses,—train and ten-o'clock!
Hark, pant and puff, there travels the swart sign!
So much the better! You're my captive now!
375   I'm glad you trust a fellow: friends grow thick
This way—that's twice said; we were thickish, though,
Even last night, and, ere night comes again,
I prophesy good luck to both of us!
For see now!—back to *'balmy eminence'*
380   Or *'calm acclivity,'* or what's the word!
Bestow you there an hour, concoct at ease
A sonnet for the Album, while I put
Bold face on, best foot forward, make for house,
March in to aunt and niece, and tell the truth—
385   (Even white-lying goes against my taste
After your little story). Oh, the niece
Is rationality itself! The aunt—
If she's amenable to reason too—
Why, you stopped short to pay her due respect,
390   And let the Duke wait (I'll work well the Duke).

366| MS:Upon—this need   *1875:*Upon—the need   367| MS:mine. I *1875:*mine! I
368| MS:common sense *1889a:*common-sense   370| MS:Adventure, lose <> act,". .
§a third dot erased§ *1875:*act. . ." *1889a:* Adventure—lose <> act . . ."
270-71| MS:§marginal note that ¶ begins§   371| MS:besides *1875:*beside
376| MS:way and §crossed out and replaced above with two words and colon§ yourself said:
§*yourself* is then crossed out in pencil and *said* altered to *say*; these two words are then
crossed out in ink and replaced below with a dash, three words and a colon§ —that's twice
said: we <> thickish, friends before. §last two words and period crossed out and replaced
above by word and comma§ though, *1875:*said; we   378| MS:prophecy *1875:*prophesy
379| MS:I say §last two words crossed out and replaced above by two words in pencil, then
in ink§ For see   380| MS:Or <> *acclivity'* or <> word— §between
379-81§ *1875:*word, *1889a:acclivity,'* or <> word!   381| MS:hour—concoct
*1875:*hour, concoct   382| MS:album *1875:*the Album   384| MS:to Aunt <>
Niece *1875:*to aunt <> niece   386| MS:story.) Oh *1889a:*story).
Oh   389| MS:respect *1875:*respect,   390| MS:the Duke.) *1875:*the Duke).

If she grows gracious, I return for you;
If thunder's in the air, why—bear your doom,
Dine on rump-steaks and port, and shake the dust
Of aunty from your shoes as off you go
395 By evening-train, nor give the thing a thought
How you shall pay me—that's as sure as fate,
Old fellow! Off with you, face left about!
Yonder's the path I have to pad. You see,
I'm in good spirits, God knows why! Perhaps
400 Because the woman did not marry you
—Who look so hard at me,—and have the right,
One must be fair and own.''

                              The two stand still
Under an oak.

                     "Look here!" resumes the youth.
"I never quite knew how I came to like
405 You—so much—whom I ought not court at all:
Nor how you had a leaning just to me
Who am assuredly not worth your pains.
For there must needs be plenty such as you
Somewhere about,—although I can't say where,—
410 Able and willing to teach all you know;
While—how can you have missed a score like me
With money and no wit, precisely each
A pupil for your purpose, were it—ease
Fool's poke of tutor's *honorarium*-fee?
415 And yet, howe'er it came about, I felt
At once my master: you as prompt descried

392| MS:your fate, 1875:your doom, 393| MS:on the §crossed out and
replaced above by§ rump- 394| MS:from off §crossed out§ 398| MS:to
pace: §word and colon altered to§ pad. you §altered to§ You 399| MS:why—perhaps
1875:why! Perhaps 400| MS:you, 1875:you 402| MS:and say!'' §crossed out
and replaced above by§ own!'' §marginal note that ¶ begins§ The
1889a:own.'' §¶§ The 403| MS:oak. §marginal note that ¶ begins§ "Look
405| MS:at all: §apparently followed by a dash which was erased§ 407| MS:pains;
1875:pains 1889a:pains. 411| MS:score of §crossed out and replaced above by§ like
413| MS:purpose were 1875:purpose, were 414| MS:The poke < > honorarium-fee.
1875:Fool's poke < > *honorarium*-fee? 416| MS:master—you 1875:master: you

Your man, I warrant, so was bargain struck.
Now, these same lines of liking, loving, run
Sometimes so close together they converge—
420 Life's great adventures—you know what I mean—
In people. Do you know, as you advanced,
It got to be uncommonly like fact
We two had fallen in with—liked and loved
Just the same woman in our different ways?
425 I began life—poor groundling as I prove—
Winged and ambitious to fly high: why not?
There's something in 'Don Quixote' to the point,
My shrewd old father used to quote and praise—
'Am I born man?' asks Sancho: 'being man,
430 By possibility I may be Pope!'
So, Pope I meant to make myself, by step
And step, whereof the first should be to find
A perfect woman; and I tell you this—
If what I fixed on, in the order due
435 Of undertakings, as next step, had first
Of all disposed itself to suit my tread,
And I had been, the day I came of age,
Returned at head of poll for Westminster
—Nay, and moreover summoned by the Queen
440 At week's end, when my maiden-speech bore fruit,
To form and head a Tory ministry—
It would not have seemed stranger, no, nor been
More strange to me, as now I estimate,

420| MS:The two adventures <> mean— §between 419-21§ 1875: Life's great adventures
421| MS:people: do 1875: people. Do 423| MS:That §crossed out§ we §altered to§ We
two might §crossed out§ have §altered to§ had <> with,—liked §dash and last word inserted
above with apparently comma following which was erased and next word inserted above§
and 1875: with—liked 427| MS:point: 1875: point, 428| MS:My <> father
poked into me once— §between 427-29§ 1875: father used to quote and praise—
429| MS:'Am §over illegible erasure§ I born man? §apparently question mark is over
comma§ says §crossed out and replaced below by§ asks Sancho, 'being 1875: man?' asks
1889a: Sancho: 'being 430| MS:be pope §altered to§ Pope 431| MS:So, §word
and comma in margin§ Pope—I too §crossed out§ 1875: Pope I 432| MS:first was just
to 1875: first should be to 433| MS:woman,—and I'll tell 1875: woman; and I tell
434| MS:If what §first letter over illegible erasure§ 435| MS:undertakings, for
§crossed out and replaced above by§ as 436| MS:my shoe, 1875: my tread,
439| MS:—Nay §dash in margin§ 442| MS:no—nor 1875: no, nor

Than what did happen—sober truth, no dream.
445 I saw my wonder of a woman,—laugh,
I'm past that!—in Commemoration-week.
A plenty have I seen since, fair and foul,—
With eyes, too, helped by your sagacious wink;
But one to match that marvel—no least trace,
450 Least touch of kinship and community!
The end was—I did somehow state the fact,
Did, with no matter what imperfect words,
One way or other give to understand
That woman, soul and body were her slave
455 Would she but take, but try them—any test
Of will, and some poor test of power beside:
So did the strings within my brain grow tense
And capable of . . . hang similitudes!
She answered kindly but beyond appeal.
460 *'No sort of hope for me, who came too late.*
She was another's. Love went—mine to her,
Hers just as loyally to someone else.'
Of course! I might expect it! Nature's law—
Given the peerless woman, certainly
465 Somewhere shall be the peerless man to match!
I acquiesced at once, submitted me
In something of a stupor, went my way.
I fancy there had been some talk before
Of somebody—her father or the like—
470 To coach me in the holidays,—that's how
I came to get the sight and speech of her,—
But I had sense enough to break off sharp,

448| MS:sagacity §altered to§ sagacious wink, §last word and comma added§   *1875:* wink;
449| MS:marvel—not the §last two words crossed out and replaced above by two words§ no
least   450| MS:The §crossed out and replaced above by§ Least   451| MS:the
case,   *1875:* the fact,   452| MS:—Did §dash in margin§   *1875:* Did
454| MS:woman—soul   *1875:* woman, soul   455| MS:take—but   *1875:* take,
but   456| MS:will—and   *1875:* will, and   457| MS:within the
brain   *1875:* within my brain   459| MS:appeal—   *1875:* appeal.
460| MS:*me—who*   *1875:me, who*   462| MS:*someone* §first syllable over
illegible erasure§ *else—'*   *1875:else.'*   465| MS:shall hide the   *1875:* shall
be the   466| MS:once—submitted   *1875:* once, submitted   467| MS:stupor—went
< > way!   *1875:* stupor, went < > way.   469| MS:like   *1875:* like—

Save both of us the pain.''

"Quite right there!"

"Eh?
Quite wrong, it happens! Now comes worst of all!
475　Yes, I did sulk aloof and let alone
The lovers—*I* disturb the angel-mates?''

"Seraph paired off with cherub!"

"Thank you! While
I never plucked up courage to inquire
Who he was, even,—certain-sure of this,
480　That nobody I knew of had blue wings
And wore a star-crown as he needs must do,—
Some little lady,—plainish, pock-marked girl,—
Finds out my secret in my woeful face,
Comes up to me at the Apollo Ball,
485　And pityingly pours her wine and oil
This way into the wound: *'Dear f-f-friend,*
Why waste affection thus on—must I say,
A somewhat worthless object? Who's her choice—
Irrevocable as deliberate—
490　*Out of the wide world? I shall name no names—*
But there's a person in society,
Who, blessed with rank and talent, has grown grey
In idleness and sin of every sort
Except hypocrisy: he's thrice her age,
495　*A by-word for "successes with the sex"*
As the French say—and, as we ought to say,
Consummately a liar and a rogue,
Since—show me where's the woman won without

476| MS:angel-mates?—" *1875:* angel-mates?"　　476-77| MS:§marginal note that ¶ begins§　　477| MS:cherub?—" §¶§ "Thank *1875:* cherub!" §¶§ "Thank
479| MS:this— *1875:* this,　　481| MS:and §over illegible word§　　484| MS:Comes <> Ball, §between 483-85§　　486| MS:wound: 'dear §altered to§ 'Dear
f-f-friend *1875:* f-f-friend,　　491| MS:*a creature* §crossed out and replaced by§
person　　495| MS:*byeword for 'success* <> *sex'* *1889a:* by-word for "success" <> *sex"*

The help of this one lie which she believes—
That—never mind how things have come to pass,
And let who loves have loved a thousand times—
All the same he now loves her only, loves
Her ever! if by "won" you just mean "sold,"
That's quite another compact. Well, this scamp,
Continuing descent from bad to worse,
Must leave his fine and fashionable prey
(Who—fathered, brothered, husbanded,—are hedged
About with thorny danger) and apply
His arts to this poor country ignorance
Who sees forthwith in the first rag of man
Her model hero! Why continue waste
On such a woman treasures of a heart
Would yet find solace,—yes, my f-f-friend—
In some congenial'—fiddle-diddle-dee!"

"Pray, is the pleasant gentleman described
Exact the portrait which my *'f-f-friends'*
Recognize as so like? 'Tis evident
You half surmised the sweet original
Could be no other than myself, just now!
Your stop and start were flattering!"

                                        "Of course
Caricature's allowed for in a sketch!
The longish nose becomes a foot in length,
The swarthy cheek gets copper-coloured,—still,
Prominent beak and dark-hued skin are facts:

499| MS:*believed*— §altered to§ *believes*—   501| MS:*times,*—§comma erased§
502| MS:*same, he*   1875:*same he*   503| MS:by 'won' you <> mean 'sold,'   1889a:by
"won" you <> mean "sold,"   508| MS:*and betakes* §crossed out and replaced by§
apply   514| MS:*congenial'—fiddle-diddle-dee!"* §underlining for italic erased
for last three words§   1875:*congenial—fiddle-diddle-dee?'"*   1889a:*congenial—*
fiddle-diddle-dee?'" §emended to §*congenial'—fiddle-diddle-dee!"* §see Editorial
Notes§   514-15| MS:§marginal note that ¶ begins§   515| MS:pleasant
person here §last two words crossed out and replaced above by§
gentleman   516| MS:friends §altered to§ *f-f-friends*   1875:*'f-f-friends'*
520| MS:The stop <> course,   1875: Your stop <> course   521| MS:sketch:
1875:sketch!   523| MS:swarthy cheek §inserted above§   524| MS:Prominent
beak §over illegible erasure§ <> dark hued <> facts—   1875:dark-hued <> facts:

44

525 And *'parson's daughter'*—*'young man coachable'*—
'Elderly party'—*'four years since'*—were facts
To fasten on, a moment! Marriage, though—
That made the difference, I hope.''

                              "All right!
I never married; wish I had—and then
530 Unwish it: people kill their wives, sometimes!
I hate my mistress, but I'm murder-free.
In your case, where's the grievance? You came last,
The earlier bird picked up the worm. Suppose
You, in the glory of your twenty-one,
535 Had happened to precede myself! 'tis odds
But this gigantic juvenility,
This offering of a big arm's bony hand—
I'd rather shake than feel shake me, I know—
Had moved *my* dainty mistress to admire
540 An altogether new Ideal—deem
Idolatry less due to life's decline
Productive of experience, powers mature
By dint of usage, the made man—no boy
That's all to make! I was the earlier bird—
545 And what I found, I let fall; what you missed
Who is the fool that blames you for?''

                              "Myself—
For nothing, everything! For finding out
She, whom I worshipped, was a worshipper
In turn of . . . but why stir up settled mud?

525-26| MS:And <> *coachable'*— / *'Elderly party'*—these were facts enough §two lines
between 524-27§ *1875:party'—'four years since'*—were facts   527| MS:To fastened
§altered to§ fasten   529| MS:I never ma §two words and part of third mistakenly
written in space provided by broken line, then scratched out and three words
written on proper line below§ I never married: wish   *1875:*married; wish
530| MS:it—people <> sometime! §apparently colon altered to make exclamation
mark§ *1875:*it: people   531| MS:mistress—but I'm §above illegible
erasure§ *1875:*mistress, but   532| MS:case—where's *1875:*case, where's
533| MS:earlier bird §over illegible erasure, apparently beginning with
p§   535| MS:myself—'tis *1875:*myself! 'tis   544| MS:Yet §crossed out
and replaced above by§ That's   545| MS:fall: what <> missed, *1875:*fall;
what *1889a:*missed   549| MS:why rake up *1875:*why stir up

45

550 She married him—the fifty-years-old rake—
How you have teased the talk from me! At last
My secret's told you. I inquired no more,
Nay, stopped ears when informants unshut mouth;
Enough that she and he live, deuce take where,
555 Married and happy, or else miserable—
It's 'Cut-the-pack;' she turned up ace or knave,
And I left Oxford, England, dug my hole
Out in Dalmatia, till you drew me thence
Badger-like,—'Back to London' was the word—
560 'Do things, a many, there, you fancy hard,
I'll undertake are easy!'—the advice.
I took it, had my twelvemonth's fling with you—
(Little hand holding large hand pretty tight
For all its delicacy—eh, my lord?),
565 Until when, t'other day, I got a turn
Somehow and gave up tired: and 'Rest!' bade you,
'Marry your cousin, double your estate,
And take your ease by all means!' So, I loll
On this the springy sofa, mine next month—
570 Or should loll, but that you must needs beat rough
The very down you spread me out so smooth.
I wish this confidence were still to make!
Ten thousand pounds? You owe me twice the sum
For stirring up the black depths! There's repose
575 Or, at least, silence when misfortune seems
All that one has to bear; but folly—yes,

550| MS:She <> rake— §between 549-51§ 551| MS:teazed 1889a:teased
552| MS:enquired 1875:inquired 553| MS:But §crossed out and replaced
above by word and comma§ Nay, 554| MS:live, God knows where,
1875:live, deuce take where, 556| 1875:knave 1889a:knave,
558| MS:Dalmatia, had §crossed out and replaced above by§ till you draw
§altered to §drew 559| MS:Badger-like,—'back §altered to§ 'Back
to London' 1875:Badger-like,—'Back to London' 560| MS:hard—
1875:hard, 561| MS:advice, §altered to§ advice. 562| MS:my
two-year's fling 1875:my twelvemonth's fling 563| MS:Little
1875:(Little 564| MS:lord? 1875:lord?) 1889a:lord?), 565| MS:Until,
the other day 1875:Until when, t'other day 566| MS:and 'Rest' cried
§crossed out and replaced above by§ bade 1875:and 'Rest!' bade
568| MS:ease, by 1875:ease by 569| MS:the green sward §last two words
crossed out and replaced above by§ pleasant §crossed out and
replaced above by§ springy 576| MS:bear: but 1875:bear; but

Folly, it all was! Fool to be so meek,
So humble,—such a coward rather say!
Fool, to adore the adorer of a fool!
580   Not to have faced him, tried (a useful hint)
My big and bony, here, against the bunch
Of lily-coloured five with signet-ring,
Most like, for little-finger's sole defence—
Much as you flaunt the blazon there! I grind
585   My teeth, that bite my very heart, to think—
To know I might have made that woman mine
But for the folly of the coward—know—
Or what's the good of my apprenticeship
This twelvemonth to a master in the art?
590   Mine—had she been mine—just one moment mine
For honour, for dishonour—anyhow,
So that my life, instead of stagnant . . . Well,
You've poked and proved stagnation is not sleep—
Hang you!''

                    "Hang *you* for an ungrateful goose!
595   All this means—I who since I knew you first
Have helped you to conceit yourself this cock
O' the dunghill with all hens to pick and choose—
Ought to have helped you when shell first was chipped
By chick that wanted prompting *'Use the spur!'*
600   While I was elsewhere putting mine to use.
As well might I blame you who kept aloof,
Seeing you could not guess I was alive,
Never advised me *'Do as I have done—
Reverence such a jewel as your luck
605   Has scratched up to enrich unworthiness!'*
As your behaviour was should mine have been,

578| MS:So §S over either *T* or *F*§   582| MS:signet-ring— *1875:* signet-ring,
587| MS:the worship—know— *1875:* the coward—know—   589| MS:These two years
to *1875:* This twelvemonth to   591| MS:honor <> dishonor *1875:* honour <>
dishonour   592| MS:stagnant . . Well, *1875:* stagnant . . . Well,   593| MS:You
poke §last two words altered to§ You've poked and prove §altered to§ proved
597| MS:with the §crossed out and replaced above by§ all   599| MS:prompting— §dash
erased§   600| MS:And §crossed out and replaced above by§ While
602| MS:Seeing <> alive, §between 601-03§   606| MS:was, should *1889a:* was should

47

—Faults which we both, too late, are sorry for:
Opposite ages, each with its mistake!
'If youth but would—if age but could,' you know.
610 Don't let us quarrel. Come, we're—young and old—
Neither so badly off. Go you your way,
Cut to the Cousin! I'll to Inn, await
The issue of diplomacy with Aunt,
And wait my hour on *'calm acclivity'*
615 In rumination manifold—perhaps
About ten thousand pounds I have to pay!''

607| MS:Which both of us, too < > for— *1875:*—Faults which we both, too *1889a:*for:
608| MS:mistake, *1875:*mistake; *1889a:*mistake!   609| MS:know! *1889a:*know.
610| MS:quarrel! Come *1889a:*quarrel. Come   611| MS:off! Go < > way—
*1875:*way, *1889a:*off. Go   614| MS:hour or so §last two words crossed out§ on
eminence §last word crossed out and replaced above with two words and quotation marks§
'mild acclivity' *1875:*on *'calm acclivity'*

III

Now, as the elder lights the fresh cigar
Conducive to resource, and saunteringly
Betakes him to the left-hand backward path,—
While, much sedate, the younger strides away
5   To right and makes for—islanded in lawn
And edged with shrubbery—the brilliant bit
Of Barry's building that's the Place,—a pair
Of women, at this nick of time, one young,
One very young, are ushered with due pomp
10   Into the same Inn-parlour—*"disengaged*
Entirely now!" the obsequious landlord smiles,
"Since the late occupants—whereof but one
Was quite a stranger"—(smile enforced by bow)
"Left, a full two hours since, to catch the train,
15   *Probably for the stranger's sake!"* (Bow, smile,
And backing out from door soft-closed behind.)

Woman and girl, the two, alone inside,
Begin their talk: the girl, with sparkling eyes—

"Oh, I forewent him purposely! but you,
20   Who joined at—journeyed from the Junction here—

MS:§Roman numeral and period above middle of first line; marginal note, in pencil and
in ink, that Part III begins§   ¹| MS:Now as <> elder, having lit §last two words
crossed out and replaced above by three words§ lights the fresh   *1875:* Now, as <> elder
lights   ²| MS:resource, §next word illegibly crossed out§ all saunteringly
1875: resource, and saunteringly   ³| MS:left and backward   *1875:* left-hand backward
⁵| MS:and making §altered to§ makes for,—islanded   *1875:* for—islanded   ⁶| MS:And
§over illegible word, perhaps *That's*§ <> shrubbery,—the spark §crossed out and replaced
above by§ brilliant   *1875:* shrubbery—the   ⁸| MS:women at   *1875:* women,
at   ¹⁰| MS:same Inn-parlour—'disengaged   *1889a:* same Inn-parlour—"disengaged
¹¹| MS:*now*'! the <> smiles   *1875:now!'* the <> smiles,   *1889a:now!"* the
¹²| MS:'Since   *1889a:*"Since   ¹³| MS:*stranger*'—(smile   *1889a:stranger*'—(smile
§emended to§ *stranger"*—smile §see Editorial Notes§   ¹⁴| MS:'*Left* <> *since*, to catch
the train,   *1876:since, to* <> *train,*   *1889a:*"*Left*   ¹⁵| MS:*sake!'* (Bow   *1889a: sake!"*
(Bow   ¹⁶| MS:soft closed   *1889a:* soft-closed   ¹⁶⁻¹⁷| MS:§marginal note that ¶
begins§   ¹⁸⁻¹⁹| MS:§marginal note that ¶ begins§   *1889a:*§no ¶; emended to restore ¶;
see Editorial Notes§   ¹⁹| MS:"Oh, I escaped §crossed out and replaced above by§
forewent <> purposely,—but you—   *1875:* purposely! but you,   ²⁰| MS:Who
<> here— §between 19-21 and in R margin§   *1875:* here   *1889a:* here—

49

I wonder how he failed your notice. Few
Stop at our station: fellow-passengers
Assuredly you were—I saw indeed
His servant, therefore he arrived all right.
25   I wanted, you know why, to have you safe
Inside here first of all, so dodged about
The dark end of the platform; that's his way—
To swing from station straight to avenue
And stride the half a mile for exercise.
30   I fancied you might notice the huge boy.
He soon gets o'er the distance; at the house
He'll hear I went to meet him and have missed;
He'll wait. No minute of the hour's too much
Meantime for our preliminary talk:
35   First word of which must be—O good beyond
Expression of all goodness—you to come!"

The elder, the superb one, answers slow.

"There was no helping that. You called for me,
Cried, rather: and my old heart answered you.
40   Still, thank me! since the effort breaks a vow—
At least, a promise to myself."

                              "I know!
How selfish get you happy folk to be!

---

²¹| MS:how he failed §last two words inserted above§ <> notice! Few   *1889a:* notice. Few
²⁴| MS:arrived with you §last two words crossed out§ all right §over illegible erasure§
²⁷| MS:platform: that's   *1875:* platform; that's   ²⁸⁻²⁹| MS:To <> from Station <>
avenue / And <> exercise. §two lines between 27-30§   *1875:* from station
³⁰| MS:boy—   *1875:* boy.   ³¹| MS:He soon gets o'er §four words above illegible
erasure§ <> distance,—at   *1875:* distance; at   ³³| MS:wait: no   *1875:* wait. No
³⁶⁻³⁷| MS:§marginal note that ¶ begins§   ³⁷| MS:The <> slow §between 37-38§
1875: slow.   ³⁷⁻³⁸| MS:§marginal note that ¶ begins§   ³⁸| MS:that: you
1875: that. You   ³⁹| MS:rather,—and <> you—   *1875:* rather: and <> you.
⁴⁰| MS:me—since   *1875:* me! since   ⁴¹| MS:least, a §above word illegibly crossed out,
perhaps *such*§ <> myself . . . §¶§   *1875:* myself." §¶§   ⁴²| MS:What §crossed out

If I should love my husband, must I needs
Sacrifice straightway all the world to him,
45   As you do? Must I never dare leave house
On this dread Arctic expedition, out
And in again, six mortal hours, though you,
You even, my own friend for evermore,
Adjure me—fast your friend till rude love pushed
50   Poor friendship from her vantage—just to grant
The quarter of a whole day's company
And counsel? This makes counsel so much more
Need and necessity. For here's my block
Of stumbling: in the face of happiness
55   So absolute, fear chills me. If such change
In heart be but love's easy consequence,
Do I love? If to marry mean—let go
All I now live for, should my marriage be?"

The other never once has ceased to gaze
60   On the great elm-tree in the open, posed
Placidly full in front, smooth bole, broad branch,
And leafage, one green plenitude of May.
The gathered thought runs into speech at last.

"O you exceeding beauty, bosomful
65   Of lights and shades, murmurs and silences,
Sun-warmth, dew-coolness,—squirrel, bee and bird,
High, higher, highest, till the blue proclaims

---

and replaced above by§ How selfishness §altered to§ selfish gets §altered to§ get you
§inserted above§ happiness §altered to§ happy folks §inserted above§ *1889a:* folk
44| MS:straitaway *1875:* straightway   45| MS:leave home *1875:* leave house
47| MS:you— *1889a:* you,   49| MS:me—(fast *1875:* me—fast
50| MS:vantage)—just *1875:* vantage—just   53| MS:necessity: for *1875:* necessity.
For   56| MS:heart prove §crossed out and replaced by§ be   57| MS:means
§altered to§ mean   58| MS:for, shall §altered to§ should   58-59| MS:§marginal
note that ¶ begins§   61| MS:Placidly §inserted above word illegibly crossed out§
63| MS:The <> last §between 62-64§ *1875:* last.   63-64| MS:§marginal
note that ¶ begins§   67| MS:proclaims— *1875:* proclaims

'Leave earth, there's nothing better till next step
Heavenward!'—so, off flies what has wings to help!"

70   And henceforth they alternate. Says the girl—

"That's saved then: marriage spares the early taste."

"Four years now, since my eye took note of tree!"

"If I had seen no other tree but this
My life long, while yourself came straight, you said,
75   From tree which overstretched you and was just
One fairy tent with pitcher-leaves that held
Wine, and a flowery wealth of suns and moons,
And magic fruits whereon the angels feed—
I looking out of window on a tree
80   Like yonder—otherwise well-known, much-liked,
Yet just an English ordinary elm—
What marvel if you cured me of conceit
My elm's bird-bee-and-squirrel tenantry
Was quite the proud possession I supposed?
85   And there is evidence you tell me true.
The fairy marriage-tree reports itself
Good guardian of the perfect face and form,
Fruits of four years' protection! Married friend,

69-70| MS:§marginal note that ¶ begins§   70| MS:And <> girl §between 69-71§
1875:girl—   70-71| MS:§marginal note that ¶ begins§   71| MS:then—marriage
1875:then: marriage   71-72| MS:§marginal note that ¶ begins§   72| MS:"Two
years 1875:"Four years   72-73| MS:§marginal note that ¶ begins§
74| MS:life-long <> straight, from tent; §last two words and semicolon crossed out and
replaced above by two words§ you said, 1889a:life long   75| MS:You
said, §two words and comma crossed out and replaced above by two words§ From tent
which 1875:From tree which   76| MS:fairy tree with 1875:fairy tent with
78| MS:Blossom and bud, §three words and comma crossed out§ And those §crossed
out and replaced above by§ magic   79| MS:I, looking <> on a §above illegibly
crossed out word§ 1875:I looking   81| MS:Yet <> elm §between 80-82§
83| MS:That §in margin§ Elm §altered to§ Elm's with §crossed out§ bird bee and
squirrel 1875:My elm's 1889a:bird-bee-and-squirrel   84| MS:Was §over illegible
erasure§   85| MS:Yet there <> true 1875:And there <>
true.   86-87| MS:The fairy §inserted above§ <> itself §virgule inserted to divide
line§ in §crossed out and five words inserted above§ Good guardian of the perfect
88| MS:And form §last two words crossed out and replaced above by two words§ Fruit of

You are more beautiful than ever!"

                                                              "Yes:

90   I think that likely. I could well dispense
With all thought fair in feature, mine or no,
Leave but enough of face to know me by—
With all found fresh in youth except such strength
As lets a life-long labour earn repose
95   Death sells at just that price, they say; and so,
Possibly, what I care not for, I keep."

"How you must know he loves you! Chill, before,
Fear sinks to freezing. Could I sacrifice—
Assured my lover simply loves my soul—
100 One nose-breadth of fair feature? No, indeed!
Your own love . . ."

                                          "The preliminary hour—
Don't waste it!"

                              "But I can't begin at once!
The angel's self that comes to hear me speak
Drives away all the care about the speech.
105 What an angelic mystery you are—
Now—that is certain! when I knew you first,
No break of halo and no bud of wing!
I thought I knew you, saw you, round and through,

---

two years' *1875:* Fruits of four years'   89| MS:ever!" §¶§ "Yes— *1889a:* ever!" §¶§
"Yes: 91| MS:all §crossed out and replaced above by three words, the first of which
is partly over illegible erasure§ thought fair in feature, §next word, incomplete, crossed out§
93| MS:all found §above word illegibly crossed out§   94| MS:lets the due §last two
words crossed out and replaced above by§ a life-long §last half of hyphenated word
inserted above§ <> earn the rest §last two words crossed out and replaced by§ repose
95| MS:Death §first letter over illegible erasure§ <> say: §colon smeared§ and
1875: say; and   96-97| MS:§marginal note that ¶ begins§   98| MS:Fear gets
§crossed out and replaced above by§ sinks <> I spare my face, §last three words and comma
crossed out and replaced above by word and dash§ sacrifice—   99| MS:Assured
<> soul— §between 98-100§   101| MS:love . . " *1875:* love . . ."
106-07| MS:Now—that is certain— §last three words and dash inserted above§
<> first §virgule inserted to divide line§ no §altered to§ No touch §crossed out and
replaced above by§ break of it §crossed out and six words with exclamation
mark inserted above§ halo and no bud of wing! *1875:* certain! when <> first,

53

Like a glass ball; suddenly, four years since,
110   You vanished, how and whither? Mystery!
Wherefore? No mystery at all: you loved,
Were loved again, and left the world of course:
Who would not? Lapped four years in fairyland,
Out comes, by no less wonderful a chance,
115   The changeling, touched athwart her trellised bliss
Of blush-rose bower by just the old friend's voice
That's now struck dumb at her own potency.
I talk of my small fortunes? Tell me yours
Rather! The fool I ever was—I am,
120   You see that: the true friend you ever had,
You have, you also recognize. Perhaps,
Giving you all the love of all my heart,
Nature, that's niggard in me, has denied
The after-birth of love there's someone claims
125   —This huge boy, swinging up the avenue;
And I want counsel: is defect in me,
Or him who has no right to raise the love?
My cousin asks my hand: he's young enough,
Handsome,—my maid thinks,—manly's more the word:
130   He asked my leave to '*drop*' the elm-tree there,
Some morning before breakfast. Gentleness
Goes with the strength, of course. He's honest too,
Limpidly truthful. For ability—
All's in the rough yet. His first taste of life
135   Seems to have somehow gone against the tongue:

109| MS:ball: suddenly, two years   *1875:*ball; suddenly, four years
110| MS:vanished—how   *1875:*vanished, how   112| MS:Were §over illegible erasure§
<> and left §over illegible erasure§ <> course,—   *1875:*course: 113| MS:Lapped two
years   *1875:*Lapped four years   114| MS:Forth comes   *1875:*Out comes
115| MS:athwart the §crossed out and replaced above by§ her   116| MS:Of the
§crossed out§   117| MS:at its §crossed out and replaced above by§ her
118| MS:yours—   *1889a:*yours   123| MS:The §crossed out§ nature §altered to§
Nature, that's §inserted above§   124| MS:That §altered to§ The <> claims,
*1889a:*claims   125| MS:—This <> Avenue— §between 124-26§ *1875:*avenue;
126| MS:counsel: is   *1875:*counsel—is   *1889a:*counsel: is   127| MS:the ghost?
*1875:*the love?   128| MS:enough—   *1875:*enough,   129| MS:word—
*1875:*word: 132| MS:course: he's   *1875:*course. He's   133| MS:truthful:
for   *1875:*truthful. For   133-34| MS:§line, ending in a colon, inserted between
133-34, is illegibly crossed out§   135| MS:tongue—   *1875:*tongue:

He travelled, tried things—came back, tried still more—
He says he's sick of all. He's fond of me
After a certain careless-earnest way
I like: the iron's crude,—no polished steel
140 Somebody forged before me. I am rich—
That's not the reason, he's far richer: no,
Nor is it that he thinks me pretty,—frank
Undoubtedly on that point! He saw once
The pink of face-perfection—oh, not you—
145 Content yourself, my beauty!—for she proved
So thoroughly a cheat, his charmer . . . nay,
He runs into extremes, I'll say at once,
Lest you say! Well, I understand he wants
Someone to serve, something to do: and both
150 Requisites so abound in me and mine
That here's the obstacle which stops consent:
The smoothness is too smooth, and I mistrust
The unseen cat beneath the counterpane.
Therefore I thought *'Would she but judge for me,*
155 *Who, judging for herself, succeeded so!'*
Do I love him, does he love me, do both
Mistake for knowledge—easy ignorance?
Appeal to its proficient in each art!
I got rough-smooth through a piano-piece,
160 Rattled away last week till tutor came,
Heard me to end, then grunted *'Ach, mein Gott!*
Sagen Sie "easy"? Every note is wrong.

137| MS:of §next word, perhaps *it:*, and punctuation crossed out, replaced above by word
and period§ all. he's §altered to§ He's   139| MS:like—the *1875:* like: the
144| MS:of that §crossed out and replaced above by word and hyphen § face-
146| MS:cheat, this charmer—nay, *1875:* cheat, his charmer . . . nay,   148| MS:say!
§exclamation mark made from colon§ well §altered to§ Well   149| MS:do—and
1875: do: and   150| MS:Qualities so *1875:* Requisites so   151| MS:obstacle that
§crossed out and replaced above by§ which < > consent— *1889a:* consent:
152| MS:smooth—and *1875:* smooth, and   153| MS:the coverlet §crossed out and
replaced by§ counterpane.   154| MS:thought—'Would she but judge for me
1875: thought—*'Would she but judge for me, 1889a:* thought *'Would   155| MS:Who,
judging for herself, succeeded so! 1875:Who, judging for herself, succeeded so!'*
1889a:herself succeeded §emended to§ *herself, succeeded* §see Editorial
Notes§   158| MS:to the proficient *1889a:* to its proficient   162| MS:*Sagen sie
'easy'? Every* < > *wrong! 1875:Sagen Sie 1889a:Sagen Sie "easy"? Every* < > *wrong.*

All thumped mit wrist: we'll trouble fingers now.
The Fräulein will please roll up Raff again
165 *And exercise at Czerny for one month!'*
Am I to roll up cousin, exercise
At Trollope's novels for one month? Pronounce!"

"Now, place each in the right position first,
Adviser and advised one! I perhaps
170 Am three—nay, four years older; am, beside,
A wife: advantages—to balance which,
You have a full fresh joyous sense of life
That finds you out life's fit food everywhere,
Detects enjoyment where I, slow and dull,
175 Fumble at fault. Already, these four years,
Your merest glimpses at the world without
Have shown you more than ever met my gaze;
And now, by joyance you inspire joy,—learn
While you profess to teach, and teach, although
180 Avowedly a learner. I am dazed
Like any owl by sunshine which just sets
The sparrow preening plumage! Here's to spy
—Your cousin! You have scanned him all your life,
Little or much; I never saw his face.
185 You have determined on a marriage—used
Deliberation therefore—I'll believe
No otherwise, with opportunity
For judgment so abounding! Here stand I—
Summoned to give my sentence, for a whim,
190 (Well, at first cloud-fleck thrown athwart your blue)

163| MS:*wrists* §altered to§ *wrist—we'll* <> *now! 1889a:wrist:*
we'll <> *now.* 164| MS:*Fraulein 1875:Fräulein* 167| MS:On Trollope's novels
for §last three words inserted above words illegibly crossed out§ a month? Pronounce!"
§next word illegibly crossed out and double quotation mark erased§ *1875:* At Trollope's
1889a: for one month 167-68| MS:§marginal note that ¶ begins§ 170| MS:older:
am *1875:* older; am 171| MS:wife; advantages *1875:* wife: advantages
175| MS:these two years, *1875:* these four years, 179| MS:teach—to §crossed out
and replaced above by§ and *1875:* teach, and 180| MS:dazed— *1875:* dazed
183| MS:cousin: you §colon and last word altered to§ cousin. You
184| MS:much: I *1875:* much; I 189| MS:sentence—for *1875:* sentence, for
190| MS:—(Well <> blue)— §first dash in margin§ *1875:* (Well <> blue)

Judge what is strangeness' self to me,—say *'Wed!'*
Or *'Wed not!'* whom you promise I shall judge
Presently, at propitious lunch-time, just
While he carves chicken! Sends he leg for wing?
195 That revelation into character
And conduct must suffice me! Quite as well
Consult with yonder solitary crow
That eyes us from your elm-top!"

                                        "Still the same!
Do you remember, at the library
200 We saw together somewhere, those two books
Somebody said were noticeworthy? One
Lay wide on table, sprawled its painted leaves
For all the world's inspection; shut on shelf
Reclined the other volume, closed, clasped, locked
205 Clear to be let alone. Which page had we
Preferred the turning over of? You were,
Are, ever will be the locked lady, hold
Inside you secrets written,—soul-absorbed,
My ink upon your blotting-paper. *I—*
210 What trace of you have I to show in turn?
Delicate secrets! No one juvenile
Ever essayed at croquet and performed
Superiorly but I confided you
The sort of hat he wore and hair it held.
215 While you? One day a calm note comes by post:

191| MS:On what <> strangeness <> *'Wed'*   1875:strangeness' <> *'Wed!'*
1889a:Judge what   192| MS:*not'* whom   1875:*not!'* whom   193| MS:Presently
at <> lunch-time—just §between 192-94; last word over illegible erasure§
1875:Presently, at <> lunch-time, just   194| MS:chicken: sends
1875:chicken! Sends   198| MS:from his elm-top!" §¶§ <> same   1875:from
your elm-top!" §¶§ <> same   1889a:same!   199| MS:remember
at <> library,   1875:remember, at <> library   201| MS:notice-worthy
1889a:noticeworthy   202| MS:sprawled with painted   1875:sprawled
its painted   204| MS:other, §comma crossed out§ volume, §word and
comma inserted above§   206| MS:turning-over <> were   1875:turning
over <> were,   207| MS:—Are—ever <> the closed, clasped, §last
two words and commas crossed out§ locked   1875:Are, ever   208| MS:soul
absorbed,   1889a:soul-absorbed,   209| MS:blotting-paper: I—
1875:blotting-paper. *I—*   215| MS:While §in margin§ You?
One fine §crossed out§ <> post—   1875:While you   1889a:post:

'I am just married, you may like to hear.'
Most men would hate you, or they ought; we love
What we fear,—*I* do! *'Cold'* I shall expect
My cousin calls you. I—dislike not him,
220   But (if I comprehend what loving means)
Love you immeasurably more—more—more
Than even he who, loving you his wife,
Would turn up nose at who impertinent,
Frivolous, forward—*loves* that excellence
225   Of all the earth he bows in worship to!
And who's this paragon of privilege?
Simply a country parson: his the charm
That worked the miracle! Oh, too absurd
But that you stand before me as you stand!
230   Such beauty does prove something, everything!
Beauty's the prize-flower which dispenses eye
From peering into what has nourished root—
Dew or manure: the plant best knows its place.
Enough, from teaching youth and tending age
235   And hearing sermons,—haply writing tracts,—
From such strange love-besprinkled compost, lo,
Out blows this triumph! Therefore love's the soil
Plants find or fail of. You, with wit to find,
Exercise wit on the old friend's behalf,

217| MS:ought: we love—   *1875:*ought; we love   219| MS:you: I   *1875:*you.
I   220| MS:But—if < > means— §between 219-21§   *1875:*But (if < >
means)   221| MS:you—immeasurably   *1875:*you immeasurably   223| MS:at me
impertinent,   *1889a:*at who impertinent,   224| MS:forward—not §dash and word
crossed out and replaced above by dash and word§ —by that   *1875:*forward—*love*
that   *1889a:*forward—*loves* that   227-29| MS:Simply, a < > parson—his < > charm /
That < > absurd— / But < > stand! §three lines between 226-30§   *1875:*Simply a < >
parson: his   *1889a:*absurd   230| MS:But §crossed out and replaced in margin by§ Such
beauty goes for §last two words crossed out and replaced below by two words§ does
prove   231| MS:dispenses man §crossed out and replaced by§ eye   232| MS:what
may §crossed out and replaced above by§ has nourish §altered to§ nourished
233| MS:Dew < > place. §between 232-34§   234| MS:Enough, that out
of §last three words crossed out and replaced by§ from   235| MS:haply,
writing   *1875:*haply writing   236| MS:From such strange §three words in
L margin and above to replace illegibly crossed out word§ love-besprinkle
§altered to§ love-besprinkled compost—lo, §between 235-37§   *1875:*compost, lo,
237| MS:Out comes this < > Therefore, love's the flower §last two words
crossed out and replaced by two words§ for plant   *1875:*Out blows this
< > Therefore love's the soil   238| MS:To find   *1875:*Plants find

240 Keep me from failure! Scan and scrutinize
This cousin! Surely he's as worth your pains
To study as my elm-tree, crow and all,
You still keep staring at. I read your thoughts."

"At last?"

          "At first! *'Would, tree, a-top of thee*
245 *I winged were, like crow perched moveless there,*
And so could straightway soar, escape this bore,
Back to my nest where broods whom I love best—
The parson o'er his parish—garish—rarish—'
Oh I could bring the rhyme in if I tried:
250 The Album here inspires me! Quite apart
From lyrical expression, have I read
The stare aright, and sings not soul just so?"

"Or rather *so?* *'Cool comfortable elm*
That men make coffins out of,—none for me
255 *At thy expense, so thou permit I glide*
Under thy ferny feet, and there sleep, sleep,
Nor dread awaking though in heaven itself!' "

The younger looks with face struck sudden white.
The elder answers its inquiry.

                     "Dear,
260 You are a guesser, not a *'clairvoyante.'*

241| MS:he's as §inserted above§   242| MS:as yon elm tree
1875: as my elm-tree   243| MS:at! I <> thoughts!"   *1889a:* at. I <> thoughts."
243-44| MS:§marginal note that ¶ begins§   248| MS:*rarish—'*   *1889a:rarish—*
§emended to§ *rarish—'* §see Editorial Notes§   249| MS:rhymes <>
tried—   *1875:* rhyme <> tried: 250| MS:The album §altered to§ Album
252-53| MS:§marginal note that ¶ begins§   *1889a:* §no ¶; emended to restore ¶; see
Editorial Notes§   253| MS:rather, *so*   *1875:* rather *so*   255| MS:*permit me*
glide   *1875:permit I glide*   257| MS:*itself!"*   *1875:itself!"*
257-58| MS:§marginal note that ¶ begins§   258| MS:The other §crossed out and
replaced above by§ younger   259| MS:answers the §crossed out and replaced above by§
its enquiry. §marginal note that ¶ begins§ "Dear, *1875:* inquiry.
260| MS:guesser not a *'clairvoyant.'*   *1875:* guesser, not a *'clairvoyante.'*

I'll so far open you the locked and shelved
Volume, my soul, that you desire to see,
As let you profit by the title-page—"

"Paradise Lost?"

                "Inferno!—All which comes
265   Of tempting me to break my vow. Stop here!
Friend, whom I love the best in the whole world,
Come at your call, be sure that I will do
All your requirement—see and say my mind.
It may be that by sad apprenticeship
270   I have a keener sense: I'll task the same.
Only indulge me—here let sight and speech
Happen—this Inn is neutral ground, you know!
I cannot visit the old house and home,
Encounter the old sociality
275   Abjured for ever. Peril quite enough
In even this first—last, I pray it prove—
Renunciation of my solitude!
Back, you, to house and cousin! Leave me here,
Who want no entertainment, carry still
280   My occupation with me. While I watch
The shadow inching round those ferny feet,
Tell him *'A school-friend wants a word with me*
Up at the inn: time, tide and train won't wait:
I must go see her—on and off again—
285   *You'll keep me company?'* Ten minutes' talk,

262| MS:Volume <> soul that <> see, §between 261-63§ *1875:*soul, that
263-64| MS:§marginal note that ¶ begins§   266| MS:Dear §crossed out and replaced
above by§ Friend   268| MS:At your *1889a:*All your   270| MS:I own §crossed out
and replaced above by§ have <> same— *1875:*same.   271-73| MS:here be sight <>
speech! / I <> house again, *1875:*here let sight <> speech / Happen—this Inn is
neutral ground, you know! / I <> house and home,   274| MS:Engage §last four
letters crossed out and replaced above by seven letters forming§ Encounter
275| MS:ever: peril §colon altered to full stop and lower case *p* erased and replaced by
upper case§ ever. Peril   278| MS:Back, you, §last word and comma inserted above§
to the §crossed out§   281| MS:shadow inching §inserted above§ round those
§apparently alteration of *the*§   282| MS:him *'An old friend 1875:*him *'A school-friend*

With you in presence, ten more afterward
With who, alone, convoys me station-bound,
And I see clearly—and say honestly
To-morrow: pen shall play tongue's part, you know.

290 Go—quick! for I have made our hand-in-hand
Return impossible. So scared you look,—
If cousin does not greet you with *'What ghost
Has crossed your path?'* I set him down obtuse."

And after one more look, with face still white,
295 The younger does go, while the elder stands
Occupied by the elm at window there.

287| MS:who, alone, §last word and comma inserted above§   288| MS:And §in
margin§ I shall §crossed out§ see clearly and §crossed out and replaced above by dash and
word§—to say *1889a:* clearly—and say   289| MS:know! *1889a:* know.
290| MS:made a hand-in-hand *1875:* made our hand-in-hand   293-94| MS:§marginal
note that ¶ begins§   296| MS:Occupied <> there. §between 295 and 4.1§

IV

Occupied by the elm; and, as its shade
Has crept clock-hand-wise till it ticks at fern
Five inches further to the South, the door
Opens abruptly, someone enters sharp,
5   The elder man returned to wait the youth:
Never observes the room's new occupant,
Throws hat on table, stoops quick, elbow-propped
Over the Album wide there, bends down brow
A cogitative minute, whistles shrill,
10   Then,—with a cheery-hopeless laugh-and-lose
Air of defiance to fate visibly
Casting the toils about him,—mouths once more
"Hail, calm acclivity, salubrious spot!"
Then clasps-to cover, sends book spinning off
15   T'other side table, looks up, starts erect
Full-face with her who,—roused from that abstruse
Question, *"Will next tick tip the fern or no?"*,—
Fronts him as fully.

                    All her languor breaks,
Away withers at once the weariness
20   From the black-blooded brow, anger and hate

MS:§Roman numeral with period and note that Part IV begins§
²| MS:Had §altered to§ Has moved §crossed out and replaced above by§ crept
³| MS:Five seeming §crossed out§ <> South,—the   *1889a:* South, the
⁴⁻⁶| MS:sharp, / Never   *1875:* sharp, / The elder man returned to wait the youth— /
Never   *1889a:* youth: ⁸| MS:album §altered to§ Album   ⁹| MS:One cogitative
1875: A cogitative   ¹¹| MS:defiance of §crossed out and replaced above by§ to
¹²| MS:him,—yet §crossed out and replaced above by§ sings once   *1875:* him,—mouths
once   ¹³| MS:*'Hail, mild acclivity* <> *spot!'*   *1875:'Hail, calm acclivity*   *1889a:"Hail*
<> *spot!"*   ¹³⁻¹⁴| MS:§marginal note that ¶ begins§   *1875:* §no ¶§   ¹⁴| MS:He
clasps-to   *1875:* Then clasps-to   ¹⁷| MS:Question—*'Will* <> *no?'—*   *1875:* Question
'Will   *1889a:* Question, *"Will* <> *no?"*,—   ¹⁸| MS:fully. §no ¶§ All the languor
1875: fully. §¶§ All her languor   ¹⁹| MS:The weariness withers away at once
1875: Away withers at once the weariness   ²⁰| MS:From blood-black brow <> hate
convulse §perhaps a smudged *d* at end of last word§   *1875:* From the black-blooded brow

Convulse. Speech follows slowlier, but at last—

"You here! I felt, I knew it would befall!
Knew, by some subtle undivinable
Trick of the trickster, I should, silly-sooth,
Late or soon, somehow be allured to leave
Safe hiding and come take of him arrears,
My torment due on four years' respite! Time
To pluck the bird's healed breast of down o'er wound!
Have your success! Be satisfied this sole
Seeing you has undone all heaven could do
These four years, puts me back to you and hell!
What will next trick be, next success? No doubt
When I shall think to glide into the grave,
There will you wait disguised as beckoning Death,
And catch and capture me for evermore!
But, God, though I am nothing, be thou all!
Contest him for me! Strive, for he is strong!"

Already his surprise dies palely out
In laugh of acquiescing impotence.
He neither gasps nor hisses: calm and plain—

"I also felt and knew—but otherwise!
You out of hand and sight and care of me
These four years, whom I felt, knew, all the while . . .
Oh, it's no superstition! It's a gift
O' the gamester that he snuffs the unseen powers
Which help or harm him. Well I knew what lurked,

²¹| MS:Speech <> but it does §next word illegibly crossed out§ arrive.
*1875:*Convulse. Speech <> but at last—   ²¹⁻²²| MS:§marginal note that ¶ begins§
²³| MS:—Knew *1875:*Knew   ²⁴| MS:should snap his bait— *1875:*should,
silly-sooth,   ²⁶| MS:him once more *1875:*him arrears,   ²⁷| MS:on two years'
*1875:*on four years'   ²⁸| MS:bird's breast healed with §crossed out and replaced above
by§ of *1875:*bird's healed breast of   ³¹| MS:These two years *1875:*These four years
³³| MS:grave *1875:*grave,   ³⁴| MS:wait me, act the §last three words crossed out and
replaced above by two words§ disguised as   ³⁵| MS:evermore— *1875:*evermore!
³⁷| MS:for he is §last two words inserted above§   ³⁷⁻³⁸| MS:§marginal note
that ¶ begins§   ⁴⁰| MS:He <> plain— §between 39-41§   ⁴⁰⁻⁴¹| MS:§marginal
note that ¶ begins§   ⁴³| MS:These two years <> while . . *1875:*These
four years <> while . . .   ⁴⁶| MS:him! Well *1889a:*him. Well

Lay perdue paralysing me,—drugged, drowsed
And damnified my soul and body both!
Down and down, see where you have dragged me to,
50   You and your malice! I was, four years since,
—Well, a poor creature! I become a knave.
I squandered my own pence: I plump my purse
With other people's pounds. I practised play
Because I liked it: play turns labour now
55   Because there's profit also in the sport.
I gamed with men of equal age and craft:
I steal here with a boy as green as grass
Whom I have tightened hold on slow and sure
This long while, just to bring about to-day
60   When the boy beats me hollow, buries me
In ruin who was sure to beggar him.
O time indeed I should look up and laugh
'Surely she closes on me!' Here you stand!"

And stand she does: while volubility,
65   With him, keeps on the increase, for his tongue
After long locking-up is loosed for once.

"Certain the taunt is happy!" he resumes:
"So, I it was allured you—only I
—I, and none other—to this spectacle—
70   Your triumph, my despair—you woman-fiend

---

⁴⁹| MS:to, §comma replaced rubbed out exclamation mark§   ⁵⁰| MS:was, two years
1875: was, four years   ⁵¹| MS:Well < > creature: I became §altered to§ become < >
knave; *1875:*—Well < > creature! I < > knave.   ⁵²| MS:plumped §altered to§ plump
⁵³| MS:pounds; I < > play §over illegible erasure§ *1875:* pounds. I   ⁵⁴| MS:it: I
redoubled §last two words crossed out§ play turns labour now §last three words inserted§
⁵⁵| MS:sport; *1875:* sport.   ⁵⁷| MS:Nor §crossed out and replaced above by§ I
⁵⁹| MS:while just *1875:* while, just   ⁶³⁻⁶⁴| MS:§marginal note that ¶ begins§
⁶⁴| MS:does—while volubility *1875:* does: while volubility,   ⁶⁵| MS:With him, §last
two words and comma inserted in margin§ Keeps §altered to§ keeps < > for a silent §crossed
out§ tongue *1875:* for his tongue   ⁶⁶⁻⁶⁷| MS:§marginal note that ¶ begins§
1889a: §no ¶; emended to ¶; see Editorial Notes§   ⁶⁷| MS:happy!" §exclamation mark
made from colon; quotation mark apparently added later§ I allured §last two words crossed
out and replaced above by two words§ he resumes *1875:* resumes: ⁶⁸| MS:"So < > I"
§between 67-69§   ⁷⁰| MS:despair—the §crossed out and replaced above by§ you

That front me! Well, I have my wish, then! See
The low wide brow oppressed by sweeps of hair
Darker and darker as they coil and swathe
The crowned corpse-wanness whence the eyes burn black
75 Not asleep now! not pin-points dwarfed beneath
Either great bridging eyebrow—poor blank beads—
Babies, I've pleased to pity in my time:
How they protrude and glow immense with hate!
The long triumphant nose attains—retains
80 Just the perfection; and there's scarlet-skein
My ancient enemy, her lip and lip,
Sense-free, sense-frighting lips clenched cold and bold
Because of chin, that based resolve beneath!
Then the columnar neck completes the whole
85 Greek-sculpture-baffling body! Do I see?
Can I observe? You wait next word to come?
Well, wait and want! since no one blight I bid
Consume one least perfection. Each and all,
As they are rightly shocking now to me,
90 So may they still continue! Value them?
Ay, as the vendor knows the money-worth
Of his Greek statue, fools aspire to buy,
And he to see the back of! Let us laugh!
You have absolved me from my sin at least!
95 You stand stout, strong, in the rude health of hate,
No touch of the tame timid nullity
My cowardice, forsooth, has practised on!
Ay, while you seemed to hint some fine fifth act
Of tragedy should freeze blood, end the farce,

⁷¹| MS:fronts §altered to§ front < > then! There §crossed out and replaced above by§ See
⁷³| MS:they cord and   1875: they coil and   ⁷⁵| MS:now! Not   1875: now! not
⁷⁷| MS:time!   1875: time: ⁸⁰| MS:perfection—and   1875: perfection; and
⁸¹| My old cold enemy of lip and   1875: My ancient enemy, her lip and   ⁸³| MS:chin,
that's based   1875: chin, that based   ⁸⁸| MS:Whither §over partial erasure§ one < >
perfection! Each   1875: Consume one < > perfection. Each   ⁹¹| MS:money-worth,
1875: money-worth   ⁹²| MS:Say, of some statue   1875: Of his Greek statue
⁹⁷| MS:cowardice, §comma later inserted§ could stoop to §last three words crossed out and
replaced above by two words§ forsooth, has practise §altered to§ practised on! §last word
added§   ⁹⁸| MS:Even while you half threatened §last two words crossed out and
replaced above by three words§ seemed to hint some fine §inserted above§   1875: Ay,
while   ⁹⁹| MS:blood, and §crossed out§ end the §inserted above§

100   I never doubted all was joke. I kept,

May be, an eye alert on paragraphs,

Newspaper-notice,—let no inquest slip,

Accident, disappearance: sound and safe

Were you, my victim, not of mind to die!

105   So, my worst fancy that could spoil the smooth

Of pillow, and arrest descent of sleep

Was *'Into what dim hole can she have dived,*

She and her wrongs, her woe that's wearing flesh

And blood away?' Whereas, see, sorrow swells!

110   Or, fattened, fulsome, have you fed on me,

Sucked out my substance? How much gloss, I pray,

O'erbloomed those hair-swathes when there crept from you

To me that craze, else unaccountable,

Which urged me to contest our county-seat

115   With whom but my own brother's nominee?

Did that mouth's pulp glow ruby from carmine

While I misused my moment, pushed,—one word,—

One hair's breadth more of gesture,—idiot-like

Past passion, floundered on to the grotesque,

120   And lost the heiress in a grin? At least,

You made no such mistake! You tickled fish,

Landed your prize the true artistic way!

How did the smug young curate rise to tune

Of *'Friend, a fatal fact divides us. Love*

125   *Suits me no longer. I have suffered shame,*

100| MS:I hardly §crossed out and replaced above by§ never <> joke—perhaps §crossed out and replaced by two words§ I kept   *1875:* joke. I kept,   101| MS:I kept §last two words crossed out and replaced above by two words and comma§ May be,   103| MS:disappearance: all was §last two words crossed out and replaced above by two words§ sound and safe! §exclamation mark crossed out§   104| MS:Was she, my <> die! §between 103-05§ *1875:* Were you, my   105| MS:So my §possibly written over the§ *1875:* So, my   107| MS:Was— §dash crossed out§   108| MS:*wrong, the* §crossed out and replaced above by§ *her 1875:wrongs*   109| MS:*away?* Whereas <> swells! §exclamation mark possibly over a dash§ *1875: away?'* Whereas   111| MS:gloss so gay *1875:* gloss, I pray,   115| MS:With who §altered to§ whom   116| MS:Did the mouth's *1875:* Did that mouth's   117| MS:moment—pushed *1875:* moment, pushed   118| MS:One <> gesture,—like a boy,— §between 117-19§ *1875:* gesture,— idiot-like   120| MS:a laugh? At *1875:* a grin? At   123| MS:Did not the <> tune §between 122-24§ *1875:* How did the   124| MS:Of §in L margin§ *'Friend*—there's §crossed out§ *a* <> us! *Love* *1875:Friend, a* *1889a:us. Love*   125| MS:*For* §crossed out and replaced above by§ *Suits* <> *longer! I* *1889a:longer. I*

Betrayal: past is past; the future—yours—
Shall never be contaminate by mine.
I might have spared me this confession, not
—Oh, never by some hideousest of lies,
130 Easy, impenetrable! No! but say,
By just the quiet answer—"I am cold."
Falsehood avaunt, each shadow of thee, hence!
Had happier fortune willed . . . but dreams are vain.
Now, leave me—yes, for pity's sake!' Aha,
135 Who fails to see the curate as his face
Reddened and whitened, wanted handkerchief
At wrinkling brow and twinkling eye, until
Out burst the proper 'Angel, whom the fiend
Has thought to smirch,—thy whiteness, at one wipe
140 Of holy cambric, shall disgrace the swan!
Mine be the task' . . . and so forth! Fool? not he!
Cunning in flavours, rather! What but sour
Suspected makes the sweetness doubly sweet,
And what stings love from faint to flamboyant
145 But the fear-sprinkle? Even horror helps—
'Love's flame in me by such recited wrong
Drenched, quenched, indeed? It burns the fiercelier thence!'
Why, I have known men never love their wives
Till somebody—myself, suppose—had 'drenched

126| MS:*past: the* 1875:*past; the* 127| MS:*mine!* 1889a:*mine.* 128| MS:*confession—not* 1875:*confession, not* 129| MS:*—O <> lies—* 1875:*lies,* 1889a:*—Oh* 130| MS:*say—* 1875:*say,* 131| MS:*The* §crossed out and replaced above by three words§ *By just the <> answer—'I <> cold to you.'* §last two words crossed out; period and single quotation mark inserted after *cold* 1889a:*answer—"I <> cold."* 132| MS:*avaunt, the* §crossed out and replaced above by§ *each* 133| MS:*willed . . but <> vain!* 1889a:*willed . . . but <> vain.* 135| MS:the lover §crossed out and replaced above by§ curate 136| MS:Reddens and whitens, wants the handkerchief 1875:Reddened and whitened, wanted handkerchief 137| MS:At wrinkling §inserted above§ <> twinkling §inserted above§ 138| MS:bursts 1875:burst 139| MS:*Has thought to* §last two words inserted above§ smirched §altered to§ smirch in vain §last two words crossed out§ 141| MS:*task' . . and <>* Fool, said I? 1875:Fool? not he! 1889a:*task'* . . . and 143| MS:sweet? 1889a:sweet, 144| MS:what keep §crossed out and replaced above by§ stings 146| MS: §between 145 and 147; not underlined§ 1875:§italics§ 147| MS:*indeed?* §undetermined number of words illegibly crossed out and replaced below by five words§ *It burns the fiercelier thence!'* 149| MS:had drenched 1875:had 'drenched

And quenched love,' so the blockheads whined: as if
     The fluid fire that lifts the torpid limb
     Were a wrong done to palsy. But I thrilled
     No palsied person: half my age, or less,
     The curate was, I'll wager: o'er young blood
155   Your beauty triumphed! Eh, but—was it *he?*
     Then, it *was* he, I heard of! None beside!
     How frank you were about the audacious boy
     Who fell upon you like a thunderbolt—
     Passion and protestation! He it was
160   Reserved *in petto!* Ay, and *'rich'* beside—
     'Rich'—how supremely did disdain curl nose!
     All that I heard was—*'wedded to a priest;'*
     Informants sunk youth, riches and the rest.
     And so my lawless love disparted loves,
165   That loves might come together with a rush!
     Surely this last achievement sucked me dry:
     Indeed, that way my wits went. Mistress-queen,
     Be merciful and let your subject slink
     Into dark safety! He's a beggar, see—
170   Do not turn back his ship, Australia-bound,
     And bid her land him right amid some crowd
     Of creditors, assembled by your curse!
     Don't cause the very rope to crack (you can!)
     Whereon he spends his last (friend's) sixpence, just

150| MS:And quenched love so   *1875:And quenched love,'* so   152| MS:palsy! Him
§crossed out§ But   *1875:*palsy. But   153| MS:less!   *1875:*less   *1889a:*less,
154| MS:The < > blood §between 153-55§   155| MS:Tell how you §last three words
crossed out and replaced below by two words§ My beauty < > he? §question mark over
dash§   *1875:*Your beauty < > *he?*   160| MS:'rich' besides   *1875:'rich'* beside
161| MS:'Rich'—and how finely §last three words crossed out and replaced by two words§ as
supremely   *1875:'Rich'*—how supremely   162-63| MS:All < > 'wedded to a priest'; /
Friends §crossed out and replaced above by§ Informants sunk the §crossed out§ youth, and
§crossedout§ riches < > rest. §two lines between 161-64§   *1875:'wedded to a priest;'*
164| MS:disparted you §crossed out and replaced by§ friends   *1875:*disparted loves,
165| MS:That you §crossed out and replaced above by one word§ friends might   *1875:*That
loves might   166| MS:Oh, 'twas this < > dry   *1875:*Surely this < > dry:
167| MS:way the wits went! Mistress mine,   *1875:*way my wits went! Mistress-queen,
*1889a:*went. Mistress-queen   169| MS:Into the darkness! he's   *1875:*Into dark safety!
He's   173| MS:Don't §over illegible word§   174| MS:Whereon he §over
perhaps *I*§ spend §altered to§ spends my §crossed out and replaced above by§ his

¹⁷⁵   The moment when he hoped to hang himself!
    Be satisfied you beat him!''

                  She replies—

    "Beat him! I do. To all that you confess
    Of abject failure, I extend belief.
    Your very face confirms it: God is just!
¹⁸⁰   Let my face—fix your eyes!—in turn confirm
    What I shall say. All-abject's but half truth;
    Add to all-abject knave as perfect fool!
    So is it you probed human nature, *so*
    Prognosticated of me? Lay these words
¹⁸⁵   To heart then, or where God meant heart should lurk!
    That moment when you first revealed yourself,
    My simple impulse prompted—end forthwith
    The ruin of a life uprooted thus
    To surely perish! How should such spoiled tree
¹⁹⁰   Henceforward baulk the wind of its worst sport,
    Fail to go falling deeper, falling down
    From sin to sin until some depth were reached
    Doomed to the weakest by the wickedest
    Of weak and wicked human kind? But when,
¹⁹⁵   That self-display made absolute,—behold
    A new revealment!—round you pleased to veer,
    Propose me what should prompt annul the past,
    Make me *'amends by marriage'*—in your phrase,

---

^{175|} MS:when I §crossed out and replaced above by§ he hope §altered
to§ hoped <> hang myself! §altered to§ himself!   ^{176–77|} MS:§marginal
note that ¶ begins§   ^{177|} MS:"Beat you §crossed out and replaced
above by§ him   ^{180|} MS:eyes—in *1875:*eyes!—in   ^{181|} MS:say:
all-abjects's §colon and last word altered to§ say. All-abject's but §over illegible word§
^{182|} MS:all-abject all- §last word and hyphen crossed out and replaced above by§ knave
^{185|} MS:then—or <> lurk! §over be§ *1875:*then, or   ^{186|} MS:yourself
*1875:*yourself,   ^{189|} MS:perish. How <> such a tree *1875:*perish! How *1889a:*such
spoiled tree   ^{193|} MS:Doomed by §crossed out and replaced above by§ to
^{195|} MS:absolute,—again §crossed out and replaced above by§ behold
^{196|} MS:revealment! §exclamation mark over comma§ —round §followed
by three letters, *aga,* crossed out§   ^{198|} MS:phrase,— *1875:*phrase,

Incorporate me henceforth, body and soul,
200 With soul and body which mere brushing past
Brought leprosy upon me—'*marry*' these!
Why, then despair broke, re-assurance dawned,
Clear-sighted was I that who hurled contempt
As I—thank God!—at the contemptible,
205 Was scarce an utter weakling. Rent away
By treason from my rightful pride of place,
I was not destined to the shame below.
A cleft had caught me: I might perish there,
But thence to be dislodged and whirled at last
210 Where the black torrent sweeps the sewage—no!
'Bare breast be on hard rock,' laughed out my soul
In gratitude, *'howe'er rock's grip may grind!*
The plain rough wretched holdfast shall suffice
This wreck of me!' The wind,—I broke in bloom
215 At passage of,—which stripped me bole and branch,
Twisted me up and tossed me here,—turns back,
And, playful ever, would replant the spoil?
Be satisfied, not one least leaf that's mine
Shall henceforth help wind's sport to exercise!
220 Rather I give such remnant to the rock
Which never dreamed a straw would settle there.
Rock may not thank me, may not feel my breast,
Even: enough that *I* feel, hard and cold,
Its safety my salvation. Safe and saved,
225 I lived, live. When the tempter shall persuade
His prey to slip down, slide off, trust the wind,—
Now that I know if God or Satan be

199-201| MS:Incorporate <> / / <> me—marry these! §three lines added in R margin
between 198-202§ *1875*:me—'*marry*' these! 202| MS:Why then, despair *1875*:Why,
then despair 203| MS: Clearsighted *1875*:Clear-sighted 205| MS:scarce the
§crossed out and replaced above by§ an <> weakling! Rent *1875*:weakling. Rent
207| MS:below; *1875*:below. 208| MS:might wither there, *1875*:might perish there,
210| MS:sewage—No! *1875*:sewage—no! 212| MS:gratitude '*howe'er*
1875:gratitude, '*howe'er* 213| MS:*plain, rough, wretched* *1889a*:*plain rough*
wretched 216| MS:here—turns back *1875*:here,—turns *1889a*:back,
219| MS:help its sport *1875*:help wind's sport 221| MS:settle so. *1875*:settle there.
222| MS:It may *1875*:Rock may 225| MS:I live, live; when *1875*:I lived, live. When

Prince of the Power of the Air,—then, then, indeed,
Let my life end and degradation too!"

230 "Good!" he smiles, "true Lord Byron! *Tree and rock:*
'*Rock*'—there's advancement! He's at first a youth,
Rich, worthless therefore; next he grows a priest:
Youth, riches prove a notable resource,
When to leave me for their possessor gluts
235 Malice abundantly; and now, last change,
The young rich parson represents a rock
—Bloodstone, no doubt. He's Evangelical?
Your Ritualists prefer the Church for spouse!"

She speaks.

        "I have a story to relate.
240 There was a parish-priest, my father knew,
Elderly, poor: I used to pity him
Before I learned what woes are pity-worth.
Elderly was grown old now, scanty means
Were straitening fast to poverty, beside
245 The ailments which await in such a case.
Limited every way, a perfect man
Within the bounds built up and up since birth
Breast-high about him till the outside world
Was blank save o'erhead one blue bit of sky—

228| MS:Prince o' $<>$ o' the air   *1875:* Prince of $<>$ of the Air   229-30| MS:§no ¶§
1875: §¶§   230| MS:"Good, very like Lord Byron! Tree and rock—   *1875:* "Good!" he
smiles, "true Lord Byron! *'Tree and rock:'*   231| MS:Rock—there's $<>$ youth §between
231-36§   *1875:'Rock*'—there's $<>$ youth,   232-35| MS:Rich $<>$ therefore: next $<>$
priest, / Said riches $<>$ resource / When leaving me $<>$ / $<>$ change, §four lines in R
margin§   *1875:* therefore; next $<>$ priest: / Youth, riches $<>$ resource, / When to leave me
236| MS:And so §last two words crossed out§ The young rich §over illegible word§ parson
§inserted below§ represents the §crossed out§   238| MS:Your ritualist prefers §last two
words altered to §ritualists prefer   *1875:* Your Ritualists   238-39| MS:§marginal note
that ¶ begins§   *1889a:* §no ¶; emended to ¶; see Editorial Notes§   238-40| MS:spouse!" /
"There   *1875:* spouse!" / She speaks. "I have a story to relate. / There   *1889a:* speaks. §¶§ I
240| MS:a clergyman, §word and comma crossed out and replaced above by word and
comma§ parish-priest   242| MS:woe §altered to§ woes is §crossed out and replaced
above by§ are pity-worth: *1875:* pity-worth.   244| MS:straightening $<>$ beside—
1875: straitening $<>$ beside   249| MS:of sky.— §crossed out and replaced above
by perhaps *heaven*, which was crossed out and original reading restored§   *1875:* sky—

250 Faith: he had faith in dogma, small or great,
As in the fact that if he clave his skull
He'd find a brain there: who proves such a fact
No falsehood by experiment at price
Of soul and body? The one rule of life
255 Delivered him in childhood was 'Obey!
Labour!' He had obeyed and laboured—tame,
True to the mill-track blinked on from above.
Some scholarship he may have gained in youth:
Gone—dropt or flung behind. Some blossom-flake,
260 Spring's boon, descends on every vernal head,
I used to think; but January joins
December, as his year had known no May
Trouble its snow-deposit,—cold and old!
I heard it was his will to take a wife,
265 A helpmate. Duty bade him tend and teach—
How? with experience null, nor sympathy
Abundant,—while himself worked dogma dead,
Who would play ministrant to sickness, age,
Womankind, childhood? These demand a wife.
270 Supply the want, then! theirs the wife; for him—
No coarsest sample of the proper sex
But would have served his purpose equally
With God's own angel,—let but knowledge match
Her coarseness: zeal does only half the work.

---

²⁵⁰| MS:in Christianity §crossed out§ ²⁵²| MS:there: facts he §followed by illegible word§ would §last three words crossed out and replaced above by three words§ who would might prove *1875:*there: such a fact who proves *1889a:*there: who proves such a fact ²⁵³| MS:falsehoods *1875:*falsehood ²⁵⁴| MS:body. The *1875:*body? The ²⁵⁵| MS:Obey— *1875:Obey!* ²⁵⁶| MS:Labour < > has *1875:Labour* < > had ²⁵⁸| MS:have had §crossed out and replaced above by§ gained ²⁵⁹| MS:behind; some *1875:*behind. Some ²⁶⁰| MS:Springs' §over word illegibly crossed out§ ²⁶¹| MS:think: his January *1875:*think; but January ²⁶²| MS:as the year < > no May §over word illegibly crossed out§ *1875:*as his year ²⁶³| MS:snow-deposit,—old §altered to§ cold ²⁶⁵| MS:helpmate; duty *1875:*helpmate. Duty ²⁶⁶| MS:null, and §crossed out and replaced above by§ nor ²⁶⁸| MS:age *1875:*age, ²⁶⁹| MS:wife— *1875:*wife. ²⁷⁰| MS:wife—for him,— *1875:*wife; for him— ²⁷¹| MS:No §over illegible erasure§ ²⁷²| .MS:served the purpose *1875:*served his purpose ²⁷³| MS:angel let §over perhaps *had*§ but coarseness §crossed out and replaced above by§ knowledge matched §altered to§ match *1875:*angel,—let ²⁷⁴| MS:Coarseness, for naked §crossed out§ zeal *1875:*Her coarseness: zeal

275 I saw this—knew the purblind honest drudge
Was wearing out his simple blameless life,
And wanted help beneath a burthen—borne
To treasure-house or dust-heap, what cared I?
Partner he needed: I proposed myself,
280 Nor much surprised him—duty was so clear!
Gratitude? What for? Gain of Paradise—
Escape, perhaps, from the dire penalty
Of who hides talent in a napkin? No:
His scruple was—should I be strong enough
285 —In body? since of weakness in the mind,
Weariness in the heart—no fear of these!
He took me as these Arctic voyagers
Take an aspirant to their toil and pain:
Can he endure them?—that's the point, and not
290 —Will he? Who would not, rather! Whereupon,
I pleaded far more earnestly for leave
To give myself away, than you to gain
What you called priceless till you gained the heart
And soul and body! which, as beggars serve
295 Extorted alms, you straightway spat upon.
Not so my husband,—for I gained my suit,
And had my value put at once to proof.
Ask him! These four years I have died away
In village-life. The village? Ugliness
300 At best and filthiness at worst, inside.

275| MS:this—knew §over illegible erasure§   276| MS:simple blameless §inserted
above§ life, §words illegibly crossed out§   277| MS:And wanting help   1875:And
wanted help   279| MS:needed: §colon over erased comma§ <> myself,— §dash erased§
280| MS:so plain! §crossed out and replaced above by§ clear!   282| MS:perhaps,
of §crossed out and replaced above by§ from that dire   1875:from the dire
283| MS:napkin! No, 1889a:napkin? No: 285| MS:—In §dash in margin§ body? for
§crossed out and replaced above by word and comma§ since, all weakness of the   1875:since
of weakness in the   286| MS:Weariness of the heart—what fear <> these?
1875:Weariness in the   1889a:heart—no fear <> these!   287| MS:as the
§altered to§ these Arctic voyager §altered to§ voyagers   288| MS:Takes §altered
to§ Take <> to the toil <> pain—   1875:Take <> to their toil
<> pain: 290| MS:—Will §dash in margin§   293| MS:you got §crossed
out and replaced above by§ gained   294| MS:body which   1875:body!
which   297| MS:proof—   1875:proof.   298| MS:him! These two years   1875:him!
These four years   300| MS:worst—inside: 1875:inside.   1889a:worst, inside.

Outside, sterility—earth sown with salt
Or what keeps even grass from growing fresh.
The life? I teach the poor and learn, myself,
That commonplace to such stupidity
305 Is all-recondite. Being brutalized
Their true need is brute-language, cheery grunts
And kindly cluckings, no articulate
Nonsense that's elsewhere knowledge. Tend the sick,
Sickened myself at pig-perversity,
310 Cat-craft, dog-snarling,—may be, snapping . . ."

                                            "Brief:

You eat that root of bitterness called Man
—Raw: I prefer it cooked, with social sauce!
So, he was not the rich youth after all!
Well, I mistook. But somewhere needs must be
315 The compensation. If not young nor rich . . ."

"You interrupt."

                    "Because you've daubed enough
Bistre for background. Play the artist now,
Produce your figure well-relieved in front!
The contrast—do not I anticipate?
320 Though neither rich nor young—what then? 'Tis all
Forgotten, all this ignobility,
In the dear home, the darling word, the smile,

305| MS:all-recondite; being 1875:all-recondite. Being   306| MS:brute-language,—
cheery 1875:brute-language, cheery   307| MS:cluckings,—no 1875:cluckings, no
308| MS:knowledge: tend <> sick 1875:knowledge. Tend <> sick,
310| MS:dog-snarling—may <> snapping . ".§¶§ "Say— 1875:dog-snarling,—may <>
snapping . . ." §¶§ "Brief— 1889a:snapping . . ." §¶§ "Brief: 311| MS:called man
§altered to§ Man   313-15| MS:So <> all! / / The <> rich . ." §three lines inserted in
R margin§ 1875:rich . . ."   316| MS:§marginal note that ¶ begins§ "You interrupt!"
§marginal note that ¶ begins§ "Because <> enough of §erased§ 1889a:interrupt." §¶§
"Because   317| MS:background. play §altered to§ Play   318| MS:Produce the
§crossed out and replaced above by§ your figure's well-relieved <> front, §altered to§
front! 1875:your figure well-relieved   320| MS:Though <> all §between 319-21§

The something sweeter . . ."

                          "Yes, you interrupt.
I have my purpose and proceed. Who lives
325   With beasts assumes beast-nature, look and voice,
And, much more, thought, for beasts think. Selfishness
In us met selfishness in them, deserved
Such answer as it gained. My husband, bent
On saving his own soul by saving theirs,—
330   They, bent on being saved if saving soul
Included body's getting bread and cheese
Somehow in life and somehow after death,—
Both parties were alike in the same boat,
One danger, therefore one equality.
335   Safety induces culture: culture seeks
To institute, extend and multiply
The difference between safe man and man,
Able to live alone now; progress means
What but abandonment of fellowship?
340   We were in common danger, still stuck close.
No new books,—were the old ones mastered yet?
No pictures and no music: these divert
—What from? the staving danger off! You paint
The waterspout above, you set to words
345   The roaring of the tempest round you? Thanks!
Amusement? Talk at end of the tired day
Of the more tiresome morrow! I transcribed
The page on page of sermon-scrawlings—stopped
Intellect's eye and ear to sense and sound—
350   Vainly: the sound and sense would penetrate
To brain and plague there in despite of me

---

³²⁵| MS:beasts, assumes   *1875:* beasts assumes   ³²⁶| MS:And §in L margin§ < > more,
their §crossed out§ thought,—for   *1889a:* thought, for   ³³⁵| MS:culture, culture
1875: culture: culture   ³³⁷| MS:and man   *1875:* and man,
³³⁸| MS:now—progress   *1875:* now; progress   ³⁴³| MS:—What §dash in margin§
³⁴⁶| MS:Quite §crossed out and replaced above by word and question mark§ Amusement?
talk enough §crossed out§   *1875:* Amusement? Talk   ³⁴⁷| MS:morrow. §full stop
over illegibly erased punctuation§ I   *1875:* morrow! I   ³⁴⁹| MS:My intellectual
eye to   *1889a:* Intellect's eye and ear to   ³⁵⁰| MS:Vainly, the   *1875:* Vainly: the

Maddened to know more moral good were done
Had we two simply sallied forth and preached
I' the 'Green' they call their grimy,—I with twang
355   Of long-disused guitar,—with cut and slash
Of much-misvalued horsewhip he,—to bid
The peaceable come dance, the peace-breaker
Pay in his person! Whereas—Heaven and Hell,
Excite with that, restrain with this! So dealt
360   His drugs my husband; as he dosed himself,
He drenched his cattle: and, for all my part
Was just to dub the mortar, never fear
But drugs, hand pestled at, have poisoned nose!
Heaven he let pass, left wisely undescribed:
365   As applicable therefore to the sleep
I want, that knows no waking—as to what's
Conceived of as the proper prize to tempt
Souls less world-weary: there, no fault to find!
But Hell he made explicit. After death,
370   Life: man created new, ingeniously
Perfect for a vindictive purpose now
That man, first fashioned in beneficence,
Was proved a failure; intellect at length
Replacing old obtuseness, memory
375   Made mindful of delinquent's bygone deeds
Now that remorse was vain, which life-long lay
Dormant when lesson might be laid to heart;
New gift of observation up and down

353| MS:forth to §crossed out and replaced above by§ and   356| MS:of undervalued
§prefix crossed out and replaced above by word and prefix§ much misvalued   1889a: much-
misvalued   358| MS:person; whereas   1875: person! Whereas   359| MS:this,—so
§inserted above§ dealt out §crossed out§   1875: this!—so   1889a: this! So
360| MS:husband, as   1875: husband; as   361| MS:Drenching his   1875: He drenched his
363| MS:But what hand <> at would poison nose!   1875: But drugs, hand <> at, have
poisoned nose!   366-68| MS:That <> waking as whatever want / Soothes the world-
weary—there   1875: I want, that <> waking—as to what's / Conceived of as the proper prize
to tempt / Souls less world-weary: there   371| MS:purpose, now   1875: purpose now
373| MS:failure: intellect   1875: failure; intellect   374| MS:Replacing his obtuseness
1875: Replacing old obtuseness   375| MS:Mindful of the delinquent's   1875: Made
mindful of delinquent's   376| MS:vain, yet §crossed out and replaced above by§ which
377| MS:heart: 1875: heart;   378| MS:The §crossed out and replaced above by§ New

And round man's self, new power to apprehend
380   Each necessary consequence of act
In man for well or ill—things obsolete—
Just granted to supplant the idiocy
Man's only guide while act was yet to choose,
With ill or well momentously its fruit;
385   A faculty of immense suffering
Conferred on mind and body,—mind, erewhile
Unvisited by one compunctious dream
During sin's drunken slumber, startled up,
Stung through and through by sin's significance
390   Now that the holy was abolished—just
As body which, alive, broke down beneath
Knowledge, lay helpless in the path to good,
Failed to accomplish aught legitimate,
Achieve aught worthy,—which grew old in youth,
395   And at its longest fell a cut-down flower,—
Dying, this too revived by miracle
To bear no end of burthen now that back
Supported torture to no use at all,
And live imperishably potent—since
400   Life's potency was impotent to ward
One plague off which made earth a hell before.
This doctrine, which one healthy view of things,
One sane sight of the general ordinance—

379| MS:self, with §crossed out and replaced above by§ new   381| MS:ill—none
§crossed out and replaced above by§ things   382| MS:to §next word, incomplete,
crossed out and replaced above by§ supplant old idiotcy   1875: supplant the idiotcy
1889a: idiocy   383| MS:Bestowed for §last two words crossed out and replaced above by
two words§ Man's only < > was still§ crossed out and replaced above by§ yet
384| MS:And ill < > fruit: 1875:fruit;   1889a: With ill   385| MS:The §crossed out
and replaced above by§ A   386| MS:mind, before §crossed out and replaced above by§
erewhile   388| MS:slumber,—startled   1875: slumber, startled   389| MS:thro' < >
thro'   1875: through < > through   390| MS:that all §crossed out and replaced above
by§ the < > abolished; just   1875: abolished—just   395| MS:fell, the §crossed
out and replaced above by§ a   1875: fell a   396| MS:this same revived
1875: this too revived   397| MS:burthen did but back   1875: burthen
now that back   398| MS:Support the torture   1875: Supported torture
399| MS:potent—so   1875: potent—since   400| MS:potency be §crossed out and
replaced above by one word§ were impotent for plague §last two words crossed out and
replaced above by two words§ to ward   1875: potency was impotent   401| MS:One
plague of which < > before. §between 400-02§   1875: plague off which

Nature,—and its particular object,—man,—
405 Which one mere eye-cast at the character
Of Who made these and gave man sense to boot,
Had dissipated once and evermore,—
This doctrine I have dosed our flock withal.
Why? Because none believed it. *They* desire
410 Such Heaven and dread such Hell, whom every day
The alehouse tempts from one, a dog-fight bids
Defy the other? All the harm is done
Ourselves—done my poor husband who in youth
Perhaps read Dickens, done myself who still
415 Could play both Bach and Brahms. Such life I lead—
Thanks to you, knave! You learn its quality—
Thanks to me, fool!"

He eyes her earnestly,
But she continues.

"—Life which, thanks once more
To you, arch-knave as exquisitest fool,
420 I acquiescingly—I gratefully
Take back again to heart! and hence this speech
Which yesterday had spared you. Four years long
Life—I began to find intolerable,
Only this moment. Ere your entry just,
425 The leap of heart which answered, spite of me,

405| MS:With §altered to§ Which any eye-cast *1875:* Which one mere eye-cast
406| MS:gave no §crossed out and replaced above by§ man < > boot,— *1875:* boot,
408| MS:This precious doctrine, I have taught the §crossed out and replaced above by§ our
flock. §apparently full stop replaces semicolon§ *1875:* This doctrine I have dosed our flock
withal. 410| MS:hell §altered to§ Hell, whom, every day, *1875:* whom everyday
1889a: every day 411| MS:one—a dog fight *1875:* one, a dog-fight
412| MS:Despise the other: all §colon and last word altered to§ other? All *1875:* Defy the
413| MS:Ourselves—to §crossed out and replaced above by§ done 414| MS:Dickens, to
§crossed out and replaced above by§ done 415| MS:Can play *1875:* Could play
416| MS:quality, *1875:* quality— 417| MS:fool!" §marginal note that ¶ begins§ He
regards §crossed out and replaced above by§ eyes 418-20| MS:thanks again, §crossed
out and replaced above by two words§ once more, / I *1875:* §line 419 added§
421| MS:heart: and hence the §altered to§ this *1875:* heart! and 422| MS:Which
§partly in L margin§ < > you. Two years' *1875:* you. Four years
423| MS:intolerable. *1875:* intolerable, 424| MS:moment, ere *1875:* moment. Ere

A friend's first summons, first provocative,
Authoritative, nay, compulsive call
To quit, though for a single day, my house
Of bondage—made return seem horrible.

430 I heard again a human lucid laugh
All trust, no fear; again saw earth pursue
Its narrow busy way amid small cares,
Smaller contentments, much weeds, some few flowers,—
Never suspicious of a thunderbolt

435 Avenging presently each daisy's death.
I recognized the beech-tree, knew the thrush
Repeated his old music-phrase,—all right,
How wrong was I, then! But your entry broke
Illusion, bade me back to bounds at once.

440 I honestly submit my soul: which sprang
At love, and losing love lies signed and sealed
'Failure.' No love more? then, no beauty more
Which tends to breed love! Purify my powers,
Effortless till some other world procure

445 Some other chance of prize! or, if none be,—
Nor second world nor chance,—undesecrate
Die then this aftergrowth of heart, surmised
Where May's precipitation left June blank!

426| MS:A friend's §last two words inserted above§ First §altered to§
first summons, sample of §last two words crossed out and replaced above by one
word§ first provocative   1889a: provocative,   427| MS:Authoritative and §crossed
out and replaced above by§ nay compulsive   1875: Authoritative, nay, compulsive
428| MS:quit,—though < > a simple §inserted above§ day,—no more; such §last three words
crossed out and replaced above by§ my   1875: quit—though < > day—my   1889a: quit,
though < > day, my   429| MS:return too §crossed out and replaced above by§ seem
430| MS:a friend §crossed out§ human §inserted above illegible word§   431| MS:fear; I
§crossed out and replaced above by§ again saw the world §last two words crossed out and
replaced above by§ earth   432| MS:busy path §crossed out and replaced above by§ way
440| MS:soul which   1875: soul: which   442| MS:'Failure:' no §colon and last word
altered to§ 'Failure.' No   443| MS:Which tends to §last two words inserted above§
breeds §altered to§ breed love: purify §colon and last word altered to§ love! Purify
444-45| MS:other chance of prize §three words transposed to 1.445 and replaced by two words
from 1.445§ world procure / Some other world procure §last two words replaced by three
words transposed from 1.444§ chance of prize §next word illegibly crossed out§ ,— < > be—
§last word over dash§   1875: prize! < > be,—   446| MS:world and §crossed out and
replaced above by one word§ nor chance,—then §crossed out§ desecrate §altered to§
undesecrate   447| MS:Never §crossed out and replaced above by two words§ Die then
448| MS:Where Spring's §crossed out and replaced above by perhaps§ love's §crossed out

Better have failed in the high aim, as I,
450 Than vulgarly in the low aim succeed
As, God be thanked, I do not! Ugliness
Had I called beauty, falsehood—truth, and you
—My lover! No—this earth's unchanged for me,
By his enchantment whom God made the Prince
455 O' the Power o' the Air, into a Heaven: there is
Heaven, since there is Heaven's simulation—earth.
I sit possessed in patience; prison-roof
Shall break one day and Heaven beam overhead."

His smile is done with; he speaks bitterly.

460 "Take my congratulations, and permit
I wish myself had proved as teachable!
—Or, no! until you taught me, could I learn
A lesson from experience ne'er till now
Conceded? Please you listen while I show
465 How thoroughly you estimate my worth
And yours—the immeasurably superior! I
Believed at least in one thing, first to last,—
Your love to me: I was the vile and you
The precious; I abused you, I betrayed,
470 But doubted—never! Why else go my way,
Judas-like plodding to this Potter's Field
Were fate now finds me? What has dinned my ear
And dogged my step? The spectre with the shriek

---

and replaced by§ May's < > left the § crossed out and replaced above by perhaps§ love
§crossed out and replaced above by§ June   451| MS:As,—God 1875:As, God
452| MS:For beauty, truth §last three words crossed out and word, illegibly crossed out,
inserted above§ Had < > called—beauty 1875:called beauty   453| MS:My < > this
world's §crossed out and replaced above by§ earth's 1889a:—My   454| MS:who
§altered to§ whom   455| MS:heaven §altered to§ Heaven   456| MS:Heaven, for
§crossed out and replaced above by§ since < > is its §crossed out and replaced above by§
Heaven's < > earth— 1875:earth; 1889a:earth.   457| MS:sit there in my
senses—prison-roof 1875:sit possessed in patience; prison-roof   458-60| MS:Heaven be
§altered to§ beam overhead!" §marginal note that ¶ begins§ "Take 1875:overhead!" §¶;
1.459 added; §¶ "Take 1889a:overhead." / §no ¶; emended to restore ¶; see Editorial Notes§
462| MS:—Or §dash in margin§   466| MS:I— 1875:I   469| MS:precious,—I
1875:precious; I   471| MS:to my §crossed out and replaced above by§ the Potter's
1875:to this Potter's   473| MS:step? and §crossed out§ The §over illegible erasure§

'Such she was, such were you, whose punishment
Is just!' And such she was not, all the while!
She never owned a love to outrage, faith
To pay with falsehood! For, my heart knows this—
Love once and you love always. Why, it's down
Here in the Album: every lover knows
Love may use hate but—turn to hate, itself—
Turn even to indifference—no, indeed!
Well, I have been spell-bound, deluded like
The witless negro by the Obeah-man
Who bids him wither: so, his eye grows dim,
His arm slack, arrow misses aim and spear
Goes wandering wide,—and all the woe because
He proved untrue to Fetish, who, he finds,
Was just a feather-phantom! I wronged love,
Am ruined,—and there was no love to wrong!"

"No love? Ah, dead love! I invoke thy ghost
To show the murderer where thy heart poured life
At summons of the stroke he doubts was dealt
On pasteboard and pretence! Not love, my love?
I changed for you the very laws of life:
Made you the standard of all right, all fair.
No genius but you could have been, no sage,
No sufferer—which is grandest—for the truth!
My hero—where the heroic only hid
To burst from hiding, brighten earth one day!
Age and decline were man's maturity;
Face, form were nature's type: more grace, more strength,
What had they been but just superfluous gauds,

475
480
485
490
495
500

476| MS:There §crossed out and replaced above by§ She never was §crossed out and replaced above by§ owned   477| MS:For myself know 1875:For, myself 1889a:For, my heart knows   478| MS:always: why §colon and last word altered to§ always. Why   479| MS:Album—every 1875:Album: every   484| MS:so his 1875:so, his   488| MS:feather-phantom. I 1875:feather-phantom! I   489-90| MS:§marginal note that ¶ begins§   490| MS:"Mine, false? Ah, < > love—I 1875:"No love? Ah, < > love! I   491| MS:where the heart 1875:where thy heart   494| MS:life— 1875:life: 495| MS:fair: 1875:fair.   500| MS:The §crossed out§ age §altered to §Age and §inserted above§   501| MS:type—more < > strength 1875:type: more < > strength,   502| MS:had it §crossed out and replaced above by§ they < > but just §inserted above§ superfluity §altered to§ superfluous gauds, §word and comma added§

Lawless divergence? I have danced through day
On tiptoe at the music of a word,
505 Have wondered where was darkness gone as night
Burst out in stars at brilliance of a smile!
Lonely, I placed the chair to help me seat
Your fancied presence; in companionship,
I kept my finger constant to your glove
510 Glued to my breast; then—where was all the world?
I schemed—not dreamed—how I might die some death
Should save your finger aching! Who creates
Destroys, he only: I had laughed to scorn
Whatever angel tried to shake my faith
515 And make you seem unworthy: you yourself
Only could do that! With a touch 'twas done.
'Give me all, trust me wholly!' At the word,
I did give, I did trust—and thereupon
The touch did follow. Ah, the quiet smile,
520 The masterfully-folded arm in arm,
As trick obtained its triumph one time more!
In turn, my soul too triumphs in defeat:
Treason like faith moves mountains: love is gone!"

He paces to and fro, stops, stands quite close
525 And calls her by her name. Then—

                              "God forgives:
Forgive you, delegate of God, brought near
As never priests could bring him to this soul
That prays you both—forgive me! I abase—
Know myself mad and monstrous utterly
530 In all I did that moment; but as God
Gives me this knowledge—heart to feel and tongue

508| MS:The §crossed out and replaced above by§ Your   509| MS:to his §crossed out
and replaced above by§ your   512| MS:save his §crossed out and replaced above by§
your   519| MS:follow. §full stop made from colon§ see §crossed out and
replaced above by word and comma§ Ah, the calm, the smile,   *1875:* the quiet smile,
520| MS:masterfully fold of arm   *1875:* masterfully folded arm   *1889a:* masterfully-folded
521| MS:As §over perhap *The*§   522| MS:Ay, and §last two words crossed out and
replaced above by two words and comma§ In turn,   523-24| MS:§marginal note
that ¶ begins§   527| MS:never books could   *1875:* never priests could

82

To testify—so be you gracious too!
Judge no man by the solitary work
Of—well, they do say and I can believe—
535 The devil in him: his, the moment,—mine
The life—your life!"

He names her name again.

"You were just—merciful as just, you were
In giving me no respite: punishment
Followed offending. Sane and sound once more,
540 The patient thanks decision, promptitude,
Which flung him prone and fastened him from hurt,
Haply to others, surely to himself.
I wake and would not you had spared one pang.
All's well that ends well!"

Yet again her name.

545 "Had *you* no fault? Why must you change, forsooth,
Parts, why reverse positions, spoil the play?
Why did your nobleness look up to me,
Not down on the ignoble thing confessed?
Was it your part to stoop, or lift the low?
550 Wherefore did God exalt you? Who would teach
The brute man's tameness and intelligence
Must never drop the dominating eye:
Wink—and what wonder if the mad fit break,
Followed by stripes and fasting? Sound and sane,
555 My life, chastised now, couches at your foot.
Accept, redeem me! Do your eyes ask '*How?*'

532| MS:testify, so   *1875:*testify—so   534| MS:they do §inserted above§
536| MS:life!" §marginal note that ¶ begins§ He   536-37| MS:§marginal note that ¶
begins§   537| MS:were, *1875:*were   539| MS:offending: sane §colon and last
word altered to§ offending. Sane   541| MS:hurt *1889a:*hurt,   543| MS:spared
one §over perhaps *a*§ pang *1875:*pang.   544| MS:well!" §marginal note that ¶
begins§ Yet < > name— *1875:*name.   544-45| MS:§marginal note that ¶
begins§   546| MS:Parts, and §crossed out and replaced above by§ why
552| MS:eye; *1875:*eye: 553| MS:break— *1875:*break,   554| MS:sane
*1875:*sane,   555| MS:chastised, now couches *1875:*chastised now, couches

I stand here penniless, a beggar; talk
What idle trash I may, this final blow
Of fortune fells me. *I* disburse, indeed,
560 This boy his winnings? when each bubble-scheme
That danced athwart my brain, a minute since,
The worse the better,—of repairing straight
My misadventure by fresh enterprise,
Capture of other boys in foolishness
565 His fellows,—when these fancies fade away
At first sight of the lost so long, the found
So late, the lady of my life, before
Whose presence I, the lost, am also found
Incapable of one least touch of mean
570 Expedient, I who teemed with plot and wile—
That family of snakes your eye bids flee!
Listen! Our troublesomest dreams die off
In daylight: I awake, and dream is—where?
I rouse up from the past: one touch dispels
575 England and all here. I secured long since
A certain refuge, solitary home
To hide in, should the head strike work one day,
The hand forget its cunning, or perhaps
Society grow savage,—there to end
580 My life's remainder, which, say what fools will,
Is or should be the best of life,—its fruit,
All tends to, root and stem and leaf and flower.
Come with me, love, loved once, loved only, come,
Blend loves there! Let this parenthetic doubt
585 Of love, in me, have been the trial-test
Appointed to all flesh at some one stage
Of soul's achievement,—when the strong man doubts

568| MS:I the lost §two words inserted above§ am also §inserted above§   *1875:*I, the lost, am
571| MS:The family <> eye makes flee!   *1875:*That family <>   eye bids flee!
572| MS:Listen! §exclamation mark made from colon§ the §crossed out and replaced above by§ our <> dream dies §last two words altered to§ dreams die   *1875:*Listen! Our
573| MS:awake and   *1889a:*awake, and   575| MS:all there. I   *1875:*all here. I
578| MS:hand misdoubt its   *1875:*hand forget its   580| MS:remainder, that
§crossed out and replaced above by§ which   583| MS:Come <> come, §between
582-84§   584| MS:there: let §colon and last word altered to§ there! Let

His strength, the good man whether goodness be,
The artist in the dark seeks, fails to find
590 Vocation, and the saint forswears his shrine.
What if the lover may elude, no more
Than these, probative dark, must search the sky
Vainly for love, his soul's star? But the orb
Breaks from eclipse: I breathe again: I love!
595 Tempted, I fell; but fallen—fallen lie
Here at your feet, see! Leave this poor pretence
Of union with a nature and its needs
Repugnant to your needs and nature! Nay,
False, beyond falsity you reprehend
600 In me, is such mock marriage with such mere
Man-mask as—whom you witless wrong, beside,
By that expenditure of heart and brain
He recks no more of than would yonder tree
If watered with your life-blood: rains and dews
605 Answer its ends sufficiently, while me
One drop saves—sends to flower and fruit at last
The laggard virtue in the soul which else
Cumbers the ground! Quicken me! Call me yours—
Yours and the world's—yours and the world's and God's!
610 Yes, for you can, you only! Think! Confirm
Your instinct! Say, a minute since, I seemed
The castaway you count me,—all the more

588| MS:man, whether *1875:* man whether   589| MS:dark goes groping
for §last three words crossed out and replaced above by§ may §crossed out and next four
words and comma inserted above§ seeks, fails to §inserted above§ find, *1875:* find
590| MS:Vocation, and §crossed out and replaced above by illegible word, which was
itself erased and original reading restored§ < > saint divinity §crossed out and three words
added§ forswears his shrine.   592| MS:dark, and search *1875:* dark, must search
593| MS:star? but *1875:* star? But   594| MS:again,—I *1875:* again: I
595| MS:Tempted, I have not §last two words crossed out and replaced above by two
words§ fell: but fallen— fallen you, §last word and comma crossed out and replaced above
by§ lie *1875:* fell; but   596| MS:But §crossed out and replaced above by§ Here
600| MS:me, were such *1875:* me, is such   601| MS:as whom < > beside—
1875: as—whom < > beside,   604| MS:life-blood,—rains *1875:* life-blood: rains
608| MS:ground: quicken §colon and last word altered to§ ground! Quicken me! §last
word apparently over *the* and exclamation mark over a dash§ call §altered to§ Call
609| MS:God's— *1875:* God's!   611| MS:instinct! say you §last
two words and illegible word crossed out and replaced above by§ Say, a

85

Apparent shall the angelic potency
Lift me from out perdition's deep of deeps
615 To light and life and love!—that's love for you—
Love that already dares match might with yours.
You loved one worthy,—in your estimate,—
When time was; you descried the unworthy taint,
And where was love then? No such test could e'er
620 Try my love: but you hate me and revile;
Hatred, revilement—had you these to bear
Would you, as I do, nor revile, nor hate,
But simply love on, love the more, perchance?
Abide by your own proof! *'Your love was love:*
625 *Its ghost knows no forgetting!'* Heart of mine,
Would that I dared remember! Too unwise
Were he who lost a treasure, did himself
Enlarge upon the sparkling catalogue
Of gems to her his queen who trusted late
630 The keeper of her caskets! Can it be
That I, custodian of such relic still
As your contempt permits me to retain,

615| MS:light, and life, and *1875:* light and life and 616| MS:Love that §last two words inserted above in L margin§ already daring §altered to§ dares match its §crossed out§ 617| MS:For whom? §last two words and question mark crossed out and replaced above by two words§ You loved 618| MS:was; §semicolon apparently replaced dash§ 619| MS:test will e'er *1875:* test could e'er 620–21| MS:Try mine: but you have §last two words inserted above§ hate §altered to§ hated and §inserted above§ revile §altered to§ reviled; §next word illegibly crossed out and semicolon inserted above§ / §virgule inserted§ Hatred, revilement— §last two words and dash inserted above§ < > these returned, §word and comma added§ *1875:* Try my love: but you hate me and revile; / < > these to bear, *1889a:* bear 622| MS:As I do §last three words crossed out and five words and comma inserted above§ Would you, as I do, < > hate, again, §last word and comma crossed out§ 623| MS:love, see §inserted above word illegibly crossed out§ no return beside? *1875:* love on, love the more, perchance? 624| MS:Wait! there's one proof more: you §colon and last word altered to§ more. You loved well,— and why? *1875:* Abide by your own proof! *'Your love was love:* 625| MS:*'Your love knows 1875:Its ghost knows* 627| MS:lost the §crossed out and replaced above by§ a 629| MS:Of gem §altered to§ gems and gem §last two words crossed out§ to her his §last two words inserted above§ queen that §crossed out and replaced above by§ who trusted once *1875:* trusted late 630| MS:caskets: can §colon and last word altered to§ caskets! Can < > be I sit §last two words crossed out§ 631| MS:Only §crossed out and replaced above by two words and comma§ That I, < > relic now *1875:* relic still 632| MS:As her contempt permits that §crossed out and replaced above by§ me I§altered to§ to *1875:* As your contempt

All I dare hug to breast is—'How your glove
Burst and displayed the long thin lily-streak!'
635 What may have followed—that is forfeit now!
I hope the proud man has grown humble. True—
One grace of humbleness absents itself—
Silence! yet love lies deeper than all words,
And not the spoken but the speechless love
640 Waits answer ere I rise and go my way."

Whereupon, yet one other time the name.

To end she looks the large deliberate look,
Even prolongs it somewhat; then the soul
Bursts forth in a clear laugh that lengthens on,
645 On, till—thinned, softened, silvered, one might say
The bitter runnel hides itself in sand,
Moistens the hard grey grimly comic speech.

"Ay—give the baffled angler even yet
His supreme triumph as he hales to shore
650 A second time the fish once 'scaped from hook:
So artfully has new bait hidden old
Blood-imbrued iron! Ay, no barb's beneath
The gilded minnow here! You bid break trust,
This time, with who trusts me,—not simply bid
655 Me trust you, me who ruined but myself,

633| MS:All that I hug <> is 'How her glove   1875: All I dare hug
<> is— 'How your glove   636| MS:humble! there §crossed out§ True—
1889a: humble. True—   637| MS:The §crossed out and replaced above by§ One
638| MS:Silence: yet love speaks on, without a §last four words crossed out and replaced
above by four words§ lies deeper than all word §altered to§ words, §comma added§
1875: Silence! yet   639| MS:And <> love §between 640-42§   640| MS:ere I §over
illegible erasure§ <> go my §over illegible erasure§   640-41| MS:§marginal note that ¶
begins§   641| MS:time, the   1875: time the   641-42| MS:§marginal note that ¶
begins§   647| MS:the grimly comic §last two words transposed with next two words§
hard grey   647-48| MS:§marginal note that ¶ begins§   650| MS:fish once §inserted
above, next to illegible erasure§ <> hook—   1889a: hook: 652| MS:no barb §altered
to§ barb's   653| MS:here! Just breach of §last three words crossed out; illegible word
inserted above, cancelled and replaced by three words§ you bid break   1875: here! You
654| MS:time with—who <> simply me §crossed out and replaced by§ bid   1875: time,
with who   655| MS:Me <> myself §between 654-56§   1875: myself,

In trusting but myself! Since, thanks to you,
I know the feel of sin and shame,—be sure,
I shall obey you and impose them both
On one who happens to be ignorant
660 Although my husband—for the lure is love,
Your love! Try other tackle, fisher-friend!
Repentance, expiation, hopes and fears,
What you had been, may yet be, would I but
Prove helpmate to my hero—one and all
665 These silks and worsteds round the hook seduce
Hardly the late torn throat and mangled tongue.
Pack up, I pray, the whole assortment prompt!
Who wonders at variety of wile
In the Arch-cheat? You are the Adversary!
670 Your fate is of your choosing: have your choice!
Wander the world,—God has some end to serve
Ere he suppress you! He waits: I endure,
But interpose no finger-tip, forsooth,
To stop your passage to the pit. Enough
675 That I am stable, uninvolved by you
In the rush downwards: free I gaze and fixed;
Your smiles, your tears, prayers, curses move alike
My crowned contempt. You kneel? Prostrate yourself!
To earth, and would the whole world saw you there!''

680 Whereupon—"All right!" carelessly begins
Somebody from outside, who mounts the stair,
And sends his voice for herald of approach:

656| MS:Whose §crossed out and replaced below by§ And trust §altered to§ trusted was in
§last two words crossed out and replaced below by§ but   1875: In trusting but
661| MS:tackle, fisherman!   1875: tackle, fisher-friend!   663| MS:may yet §inserted
above§ <> but be §crossed out§   664| MS:Your §crossed out and replaced above by§ Be
helpmate, §comma crossed out§   1875: Prove helpmate   665| MS:hook, seduce
1889a: hook seduce   666-67| MS:Hardly the late §last three words inserted above§
Torn §altered to§ torn <> tongue. / §virgule inserted§ Pack up, §over illegible erasure§
I pray, the whole assortment prompt! §last four words inserted in R
margin§   671| MS:serve,   1889a: serve   672| MS:you: he §colon and last
word altered to§ you! He waits,— §dash erased§ I §altered to§ I'll endure,   1875: waits:
I endure,   676| MS:fixed—   1875: fixed;   679-80| MS:§marginal note that
¶ begins§   681| MS:who saunters up §last two words crossed out and replaced
above by three words§ mounts the stair,   682| MS:approach—   1875: approach:

88

Half in half out the doorway as the door
Gives way to push.

                    "Old fellow, all's no good!
685 The train's your portion! Lay the blame on me!
I'm no diplomatist, and Bismarck's self
Had hardly braved the awful Aunt at broach
Of proposition—so has world-repute
Preceded the illustrious stranger! Ah!—"

690 Quick the voice changes to astonishment,
Then horror, as the youth stops, sees, and knows.

The man who knelt starts up from kneeling, stands
Moving no muscle, and confronts the stare.

One great red outbreak buries—throat and brow—
695 The lady's proud pale queenliness of scorn:
Then her great eyes that turned so quick, become
Intenser: quail at gaze, not they indeed!

684| MS:push. §marginal note that ¶ begins§ "Old <> good! §apparently
dash erased before exclamation mark added§   685| MS:portion: lay §colon
and last word altered to§ portion! Lay <> me! 1875:me 1889a:me!   687| MS:aunt
§altered to§ Aunt   688| MS:had §altered to§ his §crossed out and replaced above
by§ world-   689| MS:stranger. Ah!—" 1875:stranger! Ah!—"
689-90| MS:§marginal note that ¶ begins§   690| MS:So §inserted above§ Changes the
voice §last three words transposed to§ the voice Changes to first §crossed out§ 1875:Quick
the voice changes   691| MS:Then, horror as the youth §inserted above§ stops, stands,
§last word and comma crossed out§ sees, and §crossed out and restored§ 1875:Then.horror,
as   691-92| MS:§marginal note that ¶ begins§   693-94| MS:§marginal note that ¶
begins§   694-95| MS:The <> scorn / Buries with one red outbreak throat <>
brow— 1889a:One great red outbreak buries—throat <> brow— / The <> scorn:
696| MS:Then §in L margin§ Her proud dark §last two words crossed out and replaced
above by§ great 1875:Then her   697| MS:Intenser—quail 1875:Intenser: quail

V

It is the young man shatters silence first.

"Well, my lord—for indeed my lord you are,
I little guessed how rightly—this last proof
Of lordship-paramount confounds too much
5   My simple head-piece! Let's see how we stand
Each to the other! how we stood i' the game
Of life an hour ago,—the magpies, stile
And oak-tree witnessed. Truth exchanged for truth—
My lord confessed his four-years-old affair—
10 How he seduced and then forsook the girl
Who married somebody and left him sad.
My pitiful experience was—I loved
A girl whose gown's hem had I dared to touch
My finger would have failed me, palsy-fixed.
15 She left me, sad enough, to marry—whom?
A better man,—then possibly not you!
How does the game stand? Who is who and what
Is what, o' the board now, since an hour went by?
My lord's 'seduced, forsaken, sacrificed,'
20 Starts up, my lord's familiar instrument,
Associate and accomplice, mistress-slave—
Shares his adventure, follows on the sly!

MS:§Roman numeral and period above first line; marginal note that Part V begins§
¹⁻²| MS:§marginal note that ¶ begins§   ³| MS:I never dreamed how justly—this
1875: I little guessed how rightly—this   ⁵| MS:head piece   *1875:* head-piece
⁶| MS:other! §perhaps exclamation mark over erased comma§   ⁸| MS:oak tree
witnessed—truth §dash and last word altered to§ witnessed. Truth   *1875:* oak-tree
⁹| MS:his two-years-old affair—§dash inserted after original punctuation illegibly erased§
1875: his four-years-old   ¹⁰| MS:seduced a girl §last two words crossed out and replaced
above by two words§ and then < > the girl §over illegible erasure§   ¹¹| MS:sad.
§perhaps period alteration of colon§   ¹⁴| MS:My §over *The*§ < > me palsy-fixed;
1875: me, palsy-fixed;   *1889a:* palsy-fixed.   ¹⁵| MS:She §over *Who*§   ¹⁶| MS:Then
certainly §crossed out and replaced above by§ possibly   ¹⁷| MS:stand,—who
§comma-dash and last word altered to§ stand? Who   ¹⁸| MS:since the §crossed
out and replaced above by§ an   ¹⁹⁻²⁰| MS:My lord's §last two words in
margin§ 'Seduced, forsaken, sacrificed,'— / §virgule inserted§ Starts < > my lord's familiar
instrument §last four words added in R margin§   *1875:* 'seduced, forsaken, sacrificed'—
1889a: sacrificed,'   ²¹| MS:The §crossed out§ associate §altered to§ Associate
²²| MS:Shares the §crossed out and replaced above by§ his < > sly,   *1889a:* sly!

90

—Ay, and since 'bag and baggage' is a phrase—
Baggage lay hid in carpet-bag belike,
25   Was but unpadlocked when occasion came
For holding council, since my back was turned,
On how invent ten thousand pounds which, paid,
Would lure the winner to lose twenty more,
Beside refunding these! Why else allow
30   The fool to gain them? So displays herself
The lady whom my heart believed—oh, laugh!
Noble and pure: whom my heart loved at once,
And who at once did speak truth when she said
'I am not mine now but another's'—thus
35   Being that other's! Devil's-marriage, eh?
'My lie weds thine till lucre us do part?'
But pity me the snobbish simpleton,
You two aristocratic tip-top swells
At swindling! Quits, I cry! Decamp content
40   With skin I'm peeled of: do not strip bones bare—
As that you could, I have no doubt at all!
O you two rare ones! Male and female, Sir!
The male there smirked, this morning, *'Come, my boy—*
Out with it! You've been crossed in love, I think:
45   *I recognize the lover's hangdog look;*
Make a clean breast and match my confidence,
For, I'll be frank, I too have had my fling,
Am punished for my fault, and smart enough!
Where now the victim hides her head, God knows!'
50   Here loomed her head life-large, the devil knew!
Look out, Salvini! Here's your man, your match!
He and I sat applauding, stall by stall,
Last Monday—*'Here's Othello'* was our word,

23| MS:—Ay §dash in margin§ <> is a §inserted above word illegibly crossed out§ phrase, *1875:*phrase—   24| MS:belike—   *1875:*belike,   29| MS:these: why §colon and last word altered to§ these? Why   *1875:*these! Why   33| MS:And who §apparently alteration of *whom*§   36| MS:*part'!*   *1875:part?'*
40| MS:of—do   *1875:*of: do   43| MS:there whined, this morning, §comma erased§ *'Come, old* §crossed out and replaced above by§ *my*   *1875:*there smirked, this morning, "Come   44| MS:*love, I know:*   *1875:love, I think:*   45| MS:*look:* *1875:look;*   50| MS:Here loomed §over illegible erasure§ <> head, life-large   *1889a:*head life-large   51| MS:man, and §crossed out and replaced above by§ your   52| MS:sat §erasure follows§   53| MS:word   *1875:*word,

'*But where's Iago?*' Where? Why, there! And now
55 The fellow-artist, female specimen—
Oh, lady, you must needs describe yourself!
He's great in art, but you—how greater still
—(If I can rightly, out of all I learned,
Apply one bit of Latin that assures
60 '*Art means just art's concealment*')—tower yourself!
For he stands plainly visible henceforth—
Liar and scamp: while you, in artistry
Prove so consummate—or I prove perhaps
So absolute an ass—that—either way—
65 You still do seem to me who worshipped you
And see you take the homage of this man
Your master, who played slave and knelt, no doubt,
Before a mistress in his very craft . . .
Well, take the fact, I nor believe my eyes,
70 Nor trust my understanding! Still you seem
Noble and pure as when we had the talk
Under the tower, beneath the trees, that day.
And there's the key explains the secret: down
He knelt to ask your leave to rise a grade
75 I' the mystery of humbug: well he may!
For how you beat him! Half an hour ago,
I held your master for my best of friends;
And now I hate him! Four years since, you seemed

---

[54] MS:there! §marginal note that ¶ begins§ And now, *1875:* there! §no ¶§ And now
[57] *1875:* grea *1889a:* great [58] MS:—(If §dash and parenthesis in L margin§
[60] MS:Art means just art's concealment *1875:* '*Art means just art's concealment*'
[62] MS:and cheat: while *1875:* and scamp: while [64] MS:absolute a
fool—that—anyway— *1875:* absolute an ass—that—either way— [65] MS:who
heard the §crossed out and replaced above by§ your lies *1875:* who worshipped you
[66] MS:And see §over *saw*§ <> man. *1875:* man, *1889a:* man [67] MS:knelt just now
1875: knelt, no doubt, [68] MS:Before the mistress <> craft— *1875:* Before a mistress
<> craft . . . [72] MS:Under <> day, §inserted between 71-73§ *1875:* day.
[73] MS:And that's the *1875:* And there's the [75-76] MS:humbug: well he may! §last
three words and exclamation mark inserted above; virgule inserted§ / For how you beat him!
§last five words and exclamation mark inserted above§ half <> ago, §word and comma
added *1875:* him! Half [77] MS:Ago §inserted in L margin and crossed out§ <> held
him §crossed out and replaced above by two words§ your master <> friends: *1875:* friends;
[78] MS:And now, §last two words and comma inserted in L margin§ I <> him: two §colon
and last word altered to§ him! Two years since,—you were *1875:* now I <> him! Four

My heart's one love: well, and you so remain!
What's he to you in craft?"

She looks him through.

"My friend, 'tis just that friendship have its turn—
Interrogate thus me whom one, of foes
The worst, has questioned and is answered by.
Take you as frank an answer! answers both
Begin alike so far, divergent soon
World-wide—I own superiority
Over you, over him. As him I searched,
So do you stand seen through and through by me
Who, this time, proud, report your crystal shrines
A dewdrop, plain as amber prisons round
A spider in the hollow heart his house!
Nowise are you that thing my fancy feared
When out you stepped on me, a minute since,
—This man's confederate! no, you step not thus
Obsequiously at beck and call to help
At need some second scheme, and supplement
Guile by force, use my shame to pinion me
From struggle and escape! I fancied that!
Forgive me! Only by strange chance,—most strange
In even this strange world,—you enter now,
Obtain your knowledge. Me you have not wronged
Who never wronged you—least of all, my friend,
That day beneath the College tower and trees,
When I refused to say,—'not friend but, love!'

years since, you seemed   79| MS:love—well 1875:love: well   80| MS:craft?"
§marginal note that ¶ begins§ She looks at §crossed out§ him. §period crossed out§ through.
§last word and period inserted above§   80-81| MS:§marginal note that ¶ begins§
84| MS:answer—answers 1875:answer! answers   85| MS:far—divergent 1875:far,
divergent   87| MS:him: as 1875:him. As   89| MS:report the §crossed out and
replaced above by§ your   91| MS:in the §over that§   93| MS:When < > since,
§between 92-94§   94| MS:—This §dash in L margin§ man's accomplice §crossed out
and replaced below by§ confederate: no < > not thus §over illegible word§
1875:confederate! no   98| MS:escape! I §apparently exclamation mark
over colon§   101| MS:knowledge; me 1875:knowledge. Me   103| MS:That
< > trees, §between 102-04§   104| MS:not, friend nay §crossed out and
replaced above by word and comma§ but, love'! 1875:not friend < > love!'

Had I been found as free as air when first
We met, I scarcely could have loved you. No—
For where was that in you which claimed return
Of love? My eyes were all too weak to probe
This other's seeming, but that seeming loved
110 The soul in me, and lied—I know too late!
While your truth was truth: and I knew at once
My power was just my beauty—bear the word—
As I must bear, of all my qualities,
To name the poorest one that serves my soul
115 And simulates myself! So much in me
You loved, I know: the something that's beneath
Heard not your call,—uncalled, no answer comes!
For, since in every love, or soon or late
Soul must awake and seek out soul for soul,
120 Yours, overlooking mine then, would, some day,
Take flight to find some other; so it proved—
Missing me, you were ready for this man.
I apprehend the whole relation: his—
The soul wherein you saw your type of worth
125 At once, true object of your tribute. Well
Might I refuse such half-heart's homage! Love
Divining, had assured you I no more
Stand his participant in infamy
Than you—I need no love to recognize
130 As simply dupe and nowise fellow-cheat!
Therefore accept one last friend's-word,—your friend's,

106| MS:you: no— *1875:* you. No— 107| MS:claimed §perhaps
alteration of *claims*§ 109| MS:that §apparently alteration of *the*§ 110| MS:know
§altered to§ knew *1875:* know 111| MS:But your <> truth—and *1875:* While your
<> truth: and 113| MS:As I must §inserted above§ bear, humbly §crossed
out§ of all §inserted above§ 115| MS:myself! so §colon and last word altered
to§ myself! So 119| MS:Soul must §inserted above perhaps *will*§ 120| MS:mine
now, would *1875:* mine then, would 122| MS:Missing mine, you <> man's.
1875: Missing me, you <> man. 125| MS:tribute. §full stop alteration of colon§
127| MS:Divines— §last word and dash altered in pencil, not in B's hand, to§ Divining, and
§crossed out in pencil§ 128| MS:Stand a §crossed out, first in pencil, gone over in ink,
and replaced above in pencil, gone over in ink, by§ his 129| MS:you—no need of §last
three words transposed in pencil to§ of need no *1875:* you—I need 130| MS:As
§inserted in L margin§ Simply the §crossed out§ <> and not the §last two words crossed out
and replaced above by§ nowise *1875:* As simply 131| MS:accept this §crossed out§ one

94

All men's friend, save a felon's. Ravel out
The bad embroilment howsoe'er you may,
Distribute as it please you praise or blame
135 To me—so you but fling this mockery far—
Renounce this rag-and-feather hero-sham,
This poodle clipt to pattern, lion-like!
Throw him his thousands back, and lay to heart
The lesson I was sent,—if man discerned
140 Ever God's message,—just to teach. I judge—
To far another issue than could dream
Your cousin,—younger, fairer, as befits—
Who summoned me to judgment's exercise.
I find you, save in folly, innocent.
145 And in my verdict lies your fate; at choice
Of mine your cousin takes or leaves you. *'Take!'*
I bid her—for you tremble back to truth.
She turns the scale,—one touch of the pure hand
Shall so press down, emprison past relapse
150 Father vibration 'twixt veracity—
That's honest solid earth—and falsehood, theft
And air, that's one illusive emptiness!
That reptile capture you? I conquered him:
You saw him cower before me. Have no fear
155 He shall offend you farther! Spare to spurn—

last friends' § last two words inserted above§ word more §crossed out§   *1875:*friend's-word
¹³²| MS:friend—save a felon's. Puzzle out   *1875:*friend, save a felon's. Ravel out
¹³³| MS:This §altered to§ The vile embroilment   *1875:*The bad
embroilment   ¹³⁵| MS:this fetish far— §dash over comma§   *1875:*this
mockery far—   ¹³⁶| MS:rag and feather   *1875:*rag-and-feather   ¹⁴¹| MS:Far
to another <> than she dreamed   *1875:*than could dream   *1889a:*To
far another   ¹⁴²| MS:Your <> fairer §next word illegibly crossed out§
<> befits— §between 142-44§   ¹⁴⁴| MS:And §crossed out and
replaced above by§ I   ¹⁴⁷| MS:I <> truth! §between 147-49§   *1889a:*truth.
¹⁴⁸⁻⁵²| MS:five lines underlined and then underlining crossed out§   ¹⁴⁸| MS:It §in
L margin§ Turns §altered to§ turns <> scale— §dash over *by*§ one <> the true
hand,—   *1875:*She turns <> scale,—one <> the pure hand   ¹⁴⁹| MS:And so weigh
§altered to§ weighs downward, prison §altered to§ prisons past escape   *1875:*Shall so press
down, emprison past relapse   ¹⁵⁰| MS:This §crossed out; next word illegibly
crossed out and replaced above by two words§ Night of vibration <> veracity,
*1875:*Farther vibration <> veracity—   ¹⁵¹| MS:That §altered
to§ That's   ¹⁵²| MS:emptiness. *1875:*emptiness!   ¹⁵³| MS:That
creature capture <> him—   *1875:*That reptile capture <> him:
¹⁵⁴| MS:me! Have   *1889a:*me. Have   ¹⁵⁵| MS:further *1875:*farther

Safe let him slink hence till some subtler Eve
Than I, anticipate the snake—bruise head
Ere he bruise heel—or, warier than the first,
Some Adam purge earth's garden of its pest
160 Before the slaver spoil the Tree of Life!

"You! Leave this youth, as he leaves you, as I
Leave each! There's caution surely extant yet
Though conscience in you were too vain a claim.
Hence quickly! Keep the cash but leave unsoiled
165 The heart I rescue and would lay to heal
Beside another's! Never let her know
How near came taint of your companionship!"

"Ah"—draws a long breath with a new strange look
The man she interpellates—soul a-stir
170 Under its covert, as, beneath the dust,
A coppery sparkle all at once denotes
The hid snake has conceived a purpose.

                                    "Ah—
Innocence should be crowned with ignorance?
Desirable indeed, but difficult!
175 As if yourself, now, had not glorified
Your helpmate by imparting him a hint
Of how a monster made the victim bleed
Ere crook and courage saved her—hint, I say,—

---

^{159|} MS:purge the §crossed out and replaced above by§ earth's   ^{160|} MS:Before
such §crossed out and replaced above by§ the slaver slime §crossed out
and replaced above by§ spoil   ^{160-61|} MS:§marginal note that ¶ begins§
^{161|} MS:You!—leave §dash erased and last word altered to§ Leave   ^{162|} MS:Leave
both §crossed out and replaced above by§ each: there's §colon and last word altered to§
each! There's   ^{163|} MS:Through kindness §crossed out and replaced above by§
conscience <> were too §over illegible erasure§ vain to claim: 1875: vain a
claim.   ^{164|} MS:quickly! Take §crossed out and replaced above by§ Keep
^{166|} MS:another's: never §colon and last word altered to§ another's! Never
^{167-68|} MS:§marginal note that ¶ begins§   ^{170|} MS:its covert §inserted
above perhaps *hiding*§   ^{172|} MS:The hid snake §last two words
inserted above perhaps *serpent*§ <> purpose. §marginal note that ¶
begins§ "Ah—   ^{173|} MS:ignorance? §question mark over exclamation
mark§   ^{176|} MS:The helpmate <> imparting any hint 1875: Your
helpmate <> imparting him a hint   ^{178|} MS: say— 1875: say,—

Not the whole horror,—that were needless risk,—
180 But just such inkling, fancy of the fact,
As should suffice to qualify henceforth
The shepherd, when another lamb would stray,
For warning 'Ware the wolf!' No doubt at all,
Silence is generosity,—keeps wolf
185 Unhunted by flock's warder! Excellent,
Did—generous to me, mean—just to him!
But, screening the deceiver, lamb were found
Outraging the deceitless! So,—he knows!
And yet, unharmed I breathe—perchance, repent—
190 Thanks to the mercifully-politic!"

"Ignorance is not innocence but sin—
Witness yourself ignore what after-pangs
Pursue the plague-infected. Merciful
Am I? Perhaps! The more contempt, the less
195 Hatred; and who so worthy of contempt
As you that rest assured I cooled the spot
I could not cure, by poisoning, forsooth,
Whose hand I pressed there? Understand for once
That, sick, of all the pains corroding me
200 This burnt the last and nowise least—the need
Of simulating soundness. I resolved—
No matter how the struggle tasked weak flesh—
To hide the truth away as in a grave
From—most of all—my husband: he nor knows

180| MS:Only §crossed out and replaced above by two words§ But
just   183| MS:To §altered to§ For warn §altered to§ warning §followed
apparently by illegible erasure§   184| MS:Silence is §inserted above word
illegibly crossed out§ generosity, —the §crossed out and replaced above by§ keeps
185| MS:Unhunted §over illegible erasure§ by the §crossed out§ <> warder! Excellent—
1875: warder! Excellent,   188| MS:deceitless: so §colon and last word altered to§
deceitless! So   190-91| §Marginal note that ¶ begins§   191| MS:is no §altered
to§ not   192| MS:Witness your ignorance what after-pangs 1875: Witness your
own ignoring after-pangs 1889a: Witness yourself ignore what after-pangs
193| MS:plague-infected. Merciful? 1875: plague-infected. Merciful   194| MS:Possibly:
for, the 1875: Am I? Perhaps! the 1889a: Am I? Perhaps! The   196| MS:cool §altered
to§ cooled   197| MS:I could not §two words inserted above perhaps cannot§
198| MS:press §altered to§ pressed   204| MS:From most of all my husband; he nor
knows §apparently last letter added later§ 1875: From—most of all—my husband: he

205   Nor ever shall be made to know your part,
     My part, the devil's part,—I trust, God's part
     In the foul matter. Saved, I yearn to save
     And not destroy: and what destruction like
     The abolishing of faith in him, that's faith
210   In me as pure and true? Acquaint some child
     Who takes yon tree into his confidence,
     That, where he sleeps now, was a murder done,
     And that the grass which grows so thick, he thinks,
     Only to pillow him is product just
215   Of what lies festering beneath! 'Tis God
     Must bear such secrets and disclose them. Man?
     The miserable thing I have become
     By dread acquaintance with my secret—*you*—
     That thing had he become by learning *me*—
220   The miserable, whom his ignorance
     Would wrongly call the wicked: ignorance
     Being, I hold, sin ever, small or great.
     No, he knows nothing!"

               "He and I alike
     Are bound to you for such discreetness, then.
225   What if our talk should terminate awhile?
     Here is a gentleman to satisfy,
     Settle accounts with, pay ten thousand pounds
     Before we part—as, by his face, I fear,
     Results from your appearance on the scene.
230   Grant me a minute's parley with my friend
     Which scarce admits of a third personage!

205| MS:ever could §crossed out and replaced above by§ shall   206| MS:I
trust §last two words circled apparently for transposition to end of line but directions
crossed out§   207| MS:matter: saved §colon and last word altered to§ matter.
Saved—I *1875:*Saved, I   210| MS:me the §crossed out and replaced above by§ as
214| MS:him, is *1875:*him is   218| MS:By understand §crossed out and replaced above
by two words§ dread acquaintance <> you— *1875:you*—   219| MS:me *1875:me*—
221| MS:Would wrong as wicked also—ignorance *1875:*Would wrongly call the wicked:
ignorance   222| MS:Being, I say, sin *1875:*Being, I hold, sin   229| MS:Results
<> scene. §between 229-31§   230| MS:Pray you, §last two words and comma crossed
out and replaced above by two words§ Grant me five minute's <> friend— *1875:*me a
minute's <> friend   231| MS:personage. *1875:*personage!

The room from which you made your entry first
So opportunely—still untenanted—
What if you please return there? Just a word
235 To my young friend first—then, a word to you,
And you depart to fan away each fly
From who, grass-pillowed, sleeps so sound at home!"

"So the old truth comes back! A wholesome change,—
At last the altered eye, the rightful tone!
240 But even to the truth that drops disguise
And stands forth grinning malice which but now
Whined so contritely—I refuse assent
Just as to malice. I, once gone, come back?
No, my lord! I enjoy the privilege
245 Of being absolutely loosed from you
Too much—the knowledge that your power is null
Which was omnipotence. A word of mouth,
A wink of eye would have detained me once,
Body and soul your slave; and now, thank God,
250 Your fawningest of prayers, your frightfulest
Of curses—neither would avail to turn
My footstep for a moment!"

                              "Prayer, then, tries
No such adventure. Let us cast about
For something novel in expedient: take
255 Command,—what say you? I profess myself

232| MS:made appearance §crossed out and replaced above by two words§ your
entry   235| MS:friend first §apparently over illegible erasure§ —then, the §crossed
out and replaced above by§ a   237-38| MS:§marginal note that ¶ begins§
242-43| MS:contritely—I refused assent §last three words inserted above and virgule
inserted§ /Just as to malice. §last four words and full stop inserted above with line
drawn to connect insertion with end of original line§   246| MS:Too well—the §last
two words crossed out and replaced above by two words§ much—prize knowledge
1875: much—the knowledge   247| MS:That §crossed out and replaced in
margin by§ Which < > was omnipotent. §full stop is alteration of colon§ one §crossed
out§ a §altered to§ A   1889a: was omnipotence. A   250-51| MS:Your very
utmost §last two words crossed out and replaced above by two words§ fawningest
of prayers, §comma inserted§ your frightfulest §last two words inserted
above§ /Of curses—neither §last three words inserted below and line drawn to
connect with rest of line§ would not §crossed out§   252| MS:for a §over illegible
erasure§   253| MS:adventure: let §colon and last word altered to§ adventure. Let

99

One fertile in resource. Commanding, then,
I bid—not only wait there, but return
Here, where I want you! Disobey and—good!
On your own head the peril!"

                              "Come!" breaks in
260   The boy with his good glowing face. "Shut up!
None of this sort of thing while I stand here
—Not to stand that! No bullying, I beg!
I also am to leave you presently
And never more set eyes upon your face—
265   You won't mind that much; but—I tell you frank—
I do mind having to remember this
For your last word and deed—my friend who were!
Bully a woman you have ruined, eh?
Do you know,—I give credit all at once
270   To all those stories everybody told
And nobody but I would disbelieve:
They all seem likely now,—nay, certain, sure!
I dare say you did cheat at cards that night
The row was at the Club: 'sauter la coupe'—
275   That was your 'cut,' for which your friends 'cut' you
While I, the booby, 'cut'—acquaintanceship
With who so much as laughed when I said 'luck!'
I dare say you had bets against the horse
They doctored at the Derby; little doubt,
280   That fellow with the sister found you shirk
His challenge and did kick you like a ball,
Just as the story went about! Enough:
It only serves to show how well advised,

257| MS:I say §crossed out and replaced above by§ bid   260| MS:his good §over
illegible erasure§   261| MS:here, 1875:here   262| MS:—Not §dash in L
margin§   265| MS:much: but 1875:much; but   270| MS:all the §altered to§
those   271| MS:disbelieve— 1875:disbelieve: 272| MS:now,— §dash
inserted above§ and §crossed out and replaced above by word and comma§ nay,
273| MS:daresay <> that day 1875:that night 1889a: dare say   274| MS:coupe',—
1875:coupe'—   275| MS:That <> 'cut', for <> you §between 275-77§ 1875: 'cut,'
for   276| MS:So cut you, §last three words and comma crossed out§ While I, the booby,
§last two words and comma inserted below§   277| MS:said §followed by illegible
erasure§   278| MS:daresay 1889a: dare say   279| MS:the Derby: little
1875:the Derby; little   282| MS:about! Enough— 1875:about! Enough:

Madam, you were in bidding such a fool
285 As I, go hang. You see how the mere sight
And sound of you suffice to tumble down
Conviction topsy-turvy: no,—that's false,—
There's no unknowing what one knows; and yet
Such is my folly that, in gratitude
290 For . . . well, I'm stupid; but you seemed to wish
I should know gently what I know, should slip
Softly from old to new, not break my neck
Between beliefs of what you were and are.
Well then, for just the sake of such a wish
295 To cut no worse a figure than needs must
In even eyes like mine, I'd sacrifice
Body and soul! But don't think danger—pray!—
Menaces either! He do harm to us?
Let me say 'us' this one time! You'd allow
300 I lent perhaps my hand to rid your ear
Of some cur's yelping—hand that's fortified,
Into the bargain, with a horsewhip? Oh,
One crack and you shall see how curs decamp!
My lord, you know your losses and my gains.
305 Pay me my money at the proper time!
If cash be not forthcoming,—well, yourself
Have taught me, and tried often, I'll engage,
The proper course: I post you at the Club,
Pillory the defaulter. Crack, to-day,
310 Shall, slash, to-morrow, slice through flesh and bone!
There, Madam, you need mind no cur, I think!''

"Ah, what a gain to have an apt no less

285| MS:hang: you 1875:hang. You   287| MS:topsy turvy:—no 1875:topsy-turvy:
no   288| MS:knows: and yet— 1875:knows; and yet   289| MS:that in
1875:that, in   290| MS:For—well 1875:For . . . well   293| MS:are. §full
stop alteration of comma§   296| MS:In foolish eyes 1875:In even
eyes   297| MS:soul: but §colon and last word altered to§ soul! But <>
pray— 1875:pray!—   298| MS:either: he <> us?— 1875:either! He <>
us?   299| MS:say "us" this 1889a:say 'us' this   303-04| MS:§marginal note that ¶
begins§ 1875:§no ¶§   307| MS:me—and 1875:me, and   309| MS:defaulter:
crack §colon and last word altered to§ defaulter. Crack   310| MS:slash to-morrow
<> flesh to bone! 1875:slash, to-morrow <> flesh and bone!   310-11| MS:§marginal
note that ¶ begins§ 1875:§no¶§   311-12| MS:§marginal note that ¶ begins§

Than grateful scholar! Nay, he brings to mind
My knowledge till he puts me to the blush,
315   So long has it lain rusty! Post my name!
That were indeed a wheal from whipcord! Whew!
I wonder now if I could rummage out
—Just to match weapons—some old scorpion-scourge!
Madam, you hear my pupil, may applaud
320   His triumph o'er the master. I—no more
Bully, since I'm forbidden: but entreat—
Wait and return—for my sake, no! but just
To save your own defender, should he chance
Get thwacked thro' awkward flourish of his thong.
325   And what if—since all waiting's weary work—
I help the time pass 'twixt your exit now
And entry then? for—pastime proper—here's
The very thing, the Album, verse and prose
To make the laughing minutes launch away!
330   Each of us must contribute. I'll begin—
'Hail, calm acclivity, salubrious spot!'
I'm confident I beat the bard,—for why?
My young friend owns me an Iago—him
Confessed, among the other qualities,
335   A ready rhymer. Oh, he rhymed! Here goes!
—Something to end with 'horsewhip!' No, that rhyme
Beats me; there's 'cowslip,' 'boltsprit,' nothing else!
So, Tennyson take my benison,—verse for bard,

---

³¹⁶| MS:whipcord! Whew!   *1889a:* whipcord! Whew §emended to§ Whew! §see Editorial
Notes§   ³¹⁸| MS:—Just §dash in margin§ <> weapons—my old scorpion-scourge?
§question mark erased and replaced by exclamation mark§   *1875:* weapons—some old
³¹⁸⁻¹⁹| MS:§marginal note that ¶ begins§   *1875:* §no ¶§   ³²¹| MS:Bully—since <>
forbidden I entreat—   *1875:* Bully, since <> forbidden: but entreat—   ³²²| MS:sake;
no   *1875:* sake, no   ³²³| MS:defender should   *1875:* defender, should
³²⁵| MS:since the waiting's   *1875:* since all waiting's   ³²⁸| MS:very thing, the §last
two words inserted above§ Album, full of §last two words crossed out§   ³²⁹| MS:the
minutes laughing §last two words transposed to§ laughing minutes   ³³⁰| MS:Each
of us §last two words inserted above§ <> contribute. §full stop added§ surely: §word and
colon crossed out§   ³³¹| MS:'Hail, calm   *1875:* 'Hail calm   *1889a:* 'Hail, calm
³³⁴| MS:Confessed <> qualities, §between 334-36§   ³³⁵| MS:The §crossed out
and replaced in margin by§ A <> rhymer! Oh   *1875:* rhymer. Oh
³³⁶| MS:—Something §dash in margin§ <> 'horsewhip'! No   *1875:* 'horsewhip!' No

Prose suits the gambler's book best! Dared and done!"

340 Wherewith he dips pen, writes a line or two,
Closes and clasps the cover, gives the book,
Bowing the while, to her who hesitates,
Turns half away, turns round again, at last
Takes it as you touch carrion, then retires.
345 The door shuts fast the couple.

---

³³⁹| MS:book, so—dared <> done!" *1875:* book best! Dared <> done!' *1889a:* done!'
§emended to§ done!" §see Editorial Notes§   ³³⁹⁻³⁴⁰| MS:§¶§ *1889a:*§no ¶; emended to
¶; see Editorial Notes§   ³⁴⁶| MS: couple. §¶called for in margin§

103

VI

                              With a change
Of his whole manner, opens out at once
The Adversary.

                         "Now, my friend, for you!
You who, protected late, aggressive grown,
5   Brandish, it seems, a weapon I must 'ware!
Plain speech in me becomes respectable
Henceforth, because courageous; plainly, then—
(Have lash well loose, hold handle tight and light!)
Throughout my life's experience, you indulged
10   Yourself and friend by passing in review
So courteously but now, I vainly search
To find one record of a specimen
So perfect of the pure and simple fool
As this you furnish me. Ingratitude
15   I lump with folly,—all's one lot,—so—fool!
Did I seek you or you seek me? Seek? sneak
For service to, and service you would style—
And did style—godlike, scarce an hour ago!
Fool, there again, yet not precisely there
20   First-rate in folly: since the hand you kissed
Did pick you from the kennel, did plant firm
Your footstep on the pathway, did persuade
Your awkward shamble to true gait and pace,
Fit for the world you walk in. Once a-strut
25   On that firm pavement which your cowardice
Was for renouncing as a pitfall, next
Came need to clear your brains of their conceit
They cleverly could distinguish who was who,
Whatever folk might tramp the thoroughfare.

MS:§Roman numeral and period inserted above first line§   ³| MS:adversary
§altered to§ Adversary §marginal note that ¶ begins§   ⁶| MS:speech §apparently
alteration of *speach*§   ⁷| MS:Therefore, because   *1889a:* Henceforth, because
¹⁴| MS:me: ingratitude §colon and last word altered to§ me. Ingratitude
¹⁷| MS:style   *1875:* style—   ¹⁸| MS:godlike scarce < > ago.   *1875:* godlike,
scarce < > ago!   ²⁰| MS:folly, since   *1875:* folly: since   ²⁶| MS:renouncing
as §over word illegibly crossed out§ a pitfall,—next   *1875:* pitfall, next

30 Men, now—familiarly you read them off,
    Each phyz at first sight! O you had an eye!
    Who couched it? made you disappoint each fox
    Eager to strip my gosling of his fluff
    So golden as he cackled 'Goose trusts lamb?'
35 *'Ay, but I saved you—wolf defeated fox—*
    Wanting to pick your bones myself!' then, wolf
    Has got the worst of it with goose for once.
    I, penniless, pay you ten thousand pounds
    (—No gesture, pray! I pay ere I depart.)
40 And how you turn advantage to account
    Here's the example. Have I proved so wrong
    In my peremptory *'debt must be discharged?'*
    O you laughed lovelily, were loth to leave
    The old friend out at elbows—pooh, a thing
45 Not to be thought of! I must keep my cash,
    And you forget your generosity!
    Ha ha, I took your measure when I laughed
    My laugh to that! First quarrel—nay, first faint
    Pretence at taking umbrage—*'Down with debt,*
50 *Both interest and principal!—The Club,*
    Exposure and expulsion!—stamp me out!'
    That's the magnanimous magnificent
    Renunciation of advantage! Well,
    But whence and why did you take umbrage, Sir?
55 Because your master, having made you know
    Somewhat of men, was minded to advance,

---

³⁰| MS:off— *1875:*off,   ³²| MS:it,— §comma altered to question mark§ it?—made
*1875:*it? made   ³⁴| MS:cackled 'Goose loves lamb?'   *1875:*cackled 'Goose trusts lamb?'
³⁵| MS:Ah, but I saved you,—wolf defeated fox,—   *1875:*'Ay, but I saved you—wolf
defeated fox—   ³⁶| MS:Wanting to pick your bones myself §altered above to§ himself?
§question mark in pencil, then inked in§ then   *1875:Wanting to pick your bones myself?'*
then   *1889a:myself!'* then   ³⁹| MS:(—No §parenthesis in L margin§ gestures,
pray—I <> depart—)   *1875:*gesture, pray! I <> depart!)   *1889a:*depart.)
⁴²| MS:*discharged'?*   *1875:discharged?'*   ⁴⁴| MS:pooh,—a   *1875:*pooh, a
⁴⁹| MS:umbrage—Down with debt,   *1875:*umbrage—*'Down with debt,*   ⁵⁰| MS:Both
interest and principal!—the Club,   *1875:Both interest and principal!—The Club,*
⁵¹| MS:Exposure and expulsion,—stamp me out,   *1875:Exposure and expulsion!—stamp*
me out!'   ⁵⁵| MS:Because my teaching §last two words crossed out and replaced above
by three words§ your master having   *1875:*master, having   ⁵⁶| MS:of §inserted in L
margin§ Men somewhat §altered to§ Somewhat §last three words transposed to§ Somewhat

105

Expound you women, still a mystery!
My pupil pottered with a cloud on brow,
A clod in breast: had loved, and vainly loved:
60 Whence blight and blackness, just for all the world
As Byron used to teach us boys. Thought I—
'Quick rid him of that rubbish! Clear the cloud,
And set the heart a-pulsing!'—heart, this time:
'Twas nothing but the head I doctored late
65 For ignorance of Man; now heart's to dose,
Palsied by over-palpitation due
To Woman-worship—so, to work at once
On first avowal of the patient's ache!
This morning you described your malady,—
70 How you dared love a piece of virtue—lost
To reason, as the upshot showed: for scorn
Fitly repaid your stupid arrogance;
And, parting, you went two ways, she resumed
Her path—perfection, while forlorn you paced
75 The world that's made for beasts like you and me.
My remedy was—tell the fool the truth!
Your paragon of purity had plumped
Into these arms at their first outspread—*'fallen*
My victim,' she prefers to turn the phrase—
80 And, in exchange for that frank confidence,
Asked for my whole life present and to come—
Marriage: a thing uncovenanted for,
Never so much as put in question. Life—

---

of men, he §crossed out§ < > advance   *1875:*of men < > advance,   57| MS:And teach
§last two words crossed out and replaced above by§ Expound   59| MS:breast—had
< > loved—   *1875:*breast: had < > loved: 63| MS:*a-pulsing!*—heart *1875:*
a-pulsing!—heart   65| MS:of man §altered to§ Man: now there's §crossed
out§ *1875:*of Man; now   67| MS:To woman-worship §altered to§ Woman-worship
69| MS:you avowed §crossed out and replaced above by§ described   71| MS:shows: her
scorn *1875:*showed: for scorn   72| MS:arrogance, *1875:*arrogance;
73| MS:So, parting *1875:*And, parting   76| MS:remedy is §altered to§ was
77| MS:purity had §over *was*; next word illegibly crossed out§ plumped §apparently
added§   78| MS:Inside §altered above to§ Into < > *fell* §altered to§
fallen   79| MS:phrase— §dash over colon§   82| MS:Marriage—a
thing—uncovenanted for? *1875:*Marriage: a thing uncovenanted for!
*1889a:*for,   83| MS:question! life— §altered to§ Life— *1889a:*question. Life—

106

Implied by marriage—throw that trifle in
85 And round the bargain off, no otherwise
Than if, when we played cards, because you won
My money you should also want my head!
That, I demurred to: we but played *'for love'*—
She won my love; had she proposed for stakes
90 *'Marriage,'*—why, that's for whist, a wiser game.
Whereat she raved at me, as losers will,
And went her way. So far the story's known,
The remedy's applied, no farther: which
Here's the sick man's first *honorarium* for—
95 Posting his medicine-monger at the Club!
That being, Sir, the whole you mean my fee—
In gratitude for such munificence
I'm bound in common honesty to spare
No droplet of the draught: so,—pinch your nose,
100 Pull no wry faces!—drain it to the dregs!
I say *'She went off'*—*'went off,'* you subjoin,
'Since not to wedded bliss, as I supposed,
Sure to some convent: solitude and peace
Help her to hide the shame from mortal view,
105 *With prayer and fasting.'* No, my sapient Sir!
Far wiselier, straightway she betook herself
To a prize-portent from the donkey-show
Of leathern long-ears that compete for palm
In clerical absurdity: since he,
110 Good ass, nor practises the shaving-trick,

84| MS:trifle too *1875:* trifle in   89| MS:won the stakes §last two
words crossed out and replaced above by two words§ my love: had <> proposed
the §crossed out and replaced above by§ for *1875:* love; had   90| MS:Marriage,—Why,
§last word and comma inserted above§ <> game! *1875:* 'Marriage,'—why <> game.
92| MS:Then goes §crossed out and replaced above by§ went <> way: so *1875:* And went
<> way. So   93| MS:farther—which *1889a:* farther: which   96| MS:Which
§crossed out and replaced above by§ Such being *1875:* That being   97| MS:In <>
munificence §between 96-98§   100| MS:Pull §over illegible erasure§
100-01| MS:§marginal note that ¶ begins§ *1875:* §no ¶§   101| MS:say 'She goes
§crossed out and replaced above by§ *went off'*—'goes §crossed out and replaced
above by§ *went off'* you subjoin *1875:* off,' you subjoin,   106| MS:betakes §altered
above to§ betook   107| MS:To this §crossed out and replaced above by§ a
109| MS:absurdity §perhaps alteration of *absurdities*§   110| MS:nor
goes in for §last three words crossed out and replaced above by§ practises

The candle-crotchet, nonsense which repays
When you've young ladies congregant,—but schools
The poor,—toils, moils and grinds the mill nor means
To stop and munch one thistle in this life
115 Till next life smother him with roses: just
The parson for her purpose! Him she stroked
Over the muzzle; into mouth with bit,
And on to back with saddle,—there he stood,
The serviceable beast who heard, believed
120 And meekly bowed him to the burden,—borne
Off in a canter to seclusion—ay,
The lady's lost! But had a friend of mine
—While friend he was—imparted his sad case
To sympathizing counsellor, full soon
125 One cloud at least had vanished from his brow.
'Don't fear!' had followed reassuringly—
'The lost will in due time turn up again,
Probably just when, weary of the world,
You think of nothing less than settling-down
130 *To country life and golden days, beside*
A dearest best and brightest virtuousest
Wife: who needs no more hope to hold her own
Against the naughty-and-repentant—no,
Than water-gruel against Roman punch!'
135 And as I prophesied, it proves! My youth,—
Just at the happy moment when, subdued

112| MS:schools, *1875:*schools   113| MS:poor,—he §crossed out and replaced
above by three words§ toils, moils and <> the parish §crossed out§   115| MS:him
with §over *in*§ roses—just *1875:*roses: just   116| MS:purpose: him §colon and last
word altered to§ purpose! Him she strokes §altered to§ stroked   117| MS:muzzle:
into mouth slides §crossed out and replaced above by§ with *1875:*muzzle; into
118| MS:back slips §crossed out and replaced above by§ with saddle, there he stands §altered
to§ stood *1875:*saddle,—there <> stood,   120| MS:And meekly §inserted above§ <>
burden—borne *1875:*burden,—borne   121| MS:Off to seclusion in a canter §last
five words transposed to§ in a canter to seclusion   122| MS:But short as sweet:
for had *1875:*The lady's lost! But had   123| MS:was, imparted
*1875:*was—imparted   124| MS:counsellor, full §inserted above§ soon §next
word illegibly crossed out§   126| MS:*fear,'* had <> reassuringly *1875:fear!'*
had <> reassuringly—   127| MS:*again 1875:again,*   132| MS:*Wife*
§over illegible erasure§ *—who need* §altered to§ *needs 1875:Wife: who*
133| MS:*Against our naughty-and-repentant 1875:Against the naughty-and-repentant*
134| MS:*water gruel 1875:water-gruel*   135| MS:youth, *1875:*youth,—

To spooniness, he finds that youth fleets fast,
That town-life tires, that men should drop boys'-play,
That property, position have, no doubt,
140 Their exigency with their privilege,
And if the wealthy wed with wealth, how dire
The double duty!—in, behold, there beams
Our long-lost lady, form and face complete!
And where's my moralizing pupil now,
145 Had not his master missed a train by chance?
But, by your side instead of whirled away,
How have I spoiled scene, stopped catastrophe,
Struck flat the stage-effect I know by heart!
Sudden and strange the meeting—improvised?
150 Bless you, the last event she hoped or dreamed!
But rude sharp stroke will crush out fire from flint—
Assuredly from flesh. *"Tis you?' 'Myself.'*
'Changed?' 'Changeless.' 'Then, what's earth to me?' 'To me
What's heaven?' 'So,—thine!' 'And thine!' 'And likewise mine!'
155 Had laughed *'Amen'* the devil, but for me
Whose intermeddling hinders this hot haste,
And bids you, ere concluding contract, pause—
Ponder one lesson more, then sign and seal
At leisure and at pleasure,—lesson's price
160 Being, if you have skill to estimate,
—How say you?—I'm discharged my debt in full!

137| MS:he finds §over illegible erasure§   138| MS:And town-life tires, and men <>
boys'-play, 1875: That town-life tires, that men <> boy's-play, 1889a: boys'-play
§emended to§ boys'-play, §see Editorial Notes§   139| MS:And property 1875: That
property   141| MS:And when we, wealthy, wed 1875: And if the wealthy wed
142| MS:The §crossed out and replaced above by§ Our double 1875: The double
143| MS:Our §last two letters crossed out and first letter altered to§ A long-lost 1875: Our
long-lost   146| MS:But, standing §crossed out§ by you §altered to§ your all §crossed
out§ un §prefix crossed out§ side instead of §last three words inserted above§
148| MS:The fine old §last three words crossed out and replaced above by three words§
Struck dumb the <> heart! §exclamation mark over dash§ 1875: Struck flat the
150| MS:she hoped or §last two words inserted above§   151| MS:Such rude <>
stroke would crush <> flint,— 1875: But rude <> stroke will crush <> flint—
152| MS:'Tis <> Myself!' 1875:"'Tis 1889a: Myself.'   153| MS:'Changed?'
'Changeless!' 'Then 1889a: 'Changed?' 'Changeless.' 'Then   154| MS: mine'
1875: mine!'   155| MS:laughed Amen the 1875: laughed *'Amen'* the
161| MS:Something like §last two words crossed out and replaced above by three words

Since paid you stand, to farthing uttermost,
Unless I fare like that black majesty
A friend of mine had visit from last Spring.
165 Coasting along the Cape-side, he's becalmed
Off an uncharted bay, a novel town
Untouched at by the trader: here's a chance!
Out paddles straight the king in his canoe,
Comes over bulwark, says he means to buy
170 Ship's cargo—being rich and having brought
A treasure ample for the purpose. See!
Four dragons, stalwart blackies, guard the same
Wrapped round and round: its hulls, a multitude,—
Palm-leaf and cocoa-mat and goat's-hair cloth
175 All duly braced about with bark and board,—
Suggest how brave, 'neath coat, must kernel be!
At length the peeling is accomplished, plain
The casket opens out its core, and lo
—A brand-new British silver sixpence—bid
180 That's ample for the Bank,—thinks majesty!
You are the Captain; call my sixpence cracked
Or copper; *'what I've said is calumny;*
The lady's spotless!' Then, I'll prove my words,
Or make you prove them true as truth—yourself,
185 Here, on the instant! I'll not mince my speech,
Things at this issue. When she enters, then,
Make love to her! No talk of marriage now—

---

and punctuation§ —How say you?—payment of my < > full—   *1875:*you?—I'm discharged
my < > full!   162| MS:Full value unto §last three words crossed out and replaced
above by five words§ Since paid you stand, to   169| MS:over ship-side, for §crossed out
and replaced above by§ says   *1875:*over bulwark, says   170| MS:The cargo—being
able §crossed out and replaced above by two words§ rich and   *1875:*Ship's cargo
171| MS:The §crossed out and replaced above by§ A < > purpose: see! §colon and last word
altered to§ purpose. See!   172| MS:same,   *1875:*same   173| MS:round: the hulls,
a multitude,   *1875:*round: its hulls, a multitude,—   174| MS:goats'-hair cloth,
*1875:*goat's-hair cloth   175| MS:board,   *1875:*board,—   179| MS:—A §dash in
margin§ bran-new   *1889a:*brand-new   180| MS:Sufficient §crossed out and replaced
above by two words§ That's ample < > Majesty!   *1875:*majesty!   181| MS:the
Captain!—call   *1875:*the Captain; call   182| MS:copper; what I've said is calumny'
*1875:*copper; *'what I've said is calumny;*   183| MS:The lady's spotless! Then, I
§altered to§ I'll   *1875:The lady's spotless!'* Then   186| MS:then,—   *1875:*then,

The point-blank bare proposal! Pick no phrase—
Prevent all misconception! Soon you'll see
190 How different the tactics when she deals
With an instructed man, no longer boy
Who blushes like a booby. Woman's wit!
Man, since you have instruction, blush no more!
Such your five minutes' profit by my pains,
195 'Tis simply now—demand and be possessed!
Which means—you may possess—may strip the tree
Of fruit desirable to make one wise.
More I nor wish nor want: your act's your act,
My teaching is but—there's the fruit to pluck
200 Or let alone at pleasure. Next advance
In knowledge were beyond you! Don't expect
I bid a novice—pluck, suck, send sky-high
Such fruit, once taught that neither crab nor sloe
Falls readier prey to who but robs a hedge,
205 Than this gold apple to my Hercules.
Were you no novice but proficient—then,
Then, truly, I might prompt you—Touch and taste,
Try flavour and be tired as soon as I!
Toss on the prize to greedy mouths agape,
210 Betake yours, sobered as the satiate grow,
To wise man's solid meal of house and land,
Consols and cousin! but my boy, my boy,
Such lore's above you!

Here's the lady back!

188| MS:proposal: pick §colon and last word altered to§ proposal! Pick
193| MS:Because you <> more, 1875:more! 1889a:Man, since you   194| MS:After
§crossed out and replaced above by dash and two words§ —Such the five <> pains—
1875:Such your five <> pains,   196| MS:you might §crossed out and replaced above
by§ may possess—strip bare the 1875:possess—may strip the   197| MS:wise!
1889a:wise.   198| MS:More I don't wish <> act, §between 197-99§ 1875:More I nor
wish   202| MS:sky-high, 1875:sky-high   203| MS:Once the truth taught you
that nor crab 1875:Such fruit, once taught that neither crab   205| MS:Than <>
Hercules. §between 204-06§   208| MS:as soon §over perhaps much§   209| MS:to
greedy §inserted above§   210| MS:Get §crossed out and replaced above by§
Betake you §altered to§ yours, sober §altered to§ sobered   211| MS:To the man's
1875:To wise man's   213| MS:you! §marginal note that ¶ begins§ Here's
<> back— 1875:you! §no ¶§ Here's <> back! 1889a:you! §¶§ Here's

So, Madam, you have conned the Album-page

215 And come to thank its last contributor?

How kind and condescending! I retire

A moment, lest I spoil the interview,

And mar my own endeavour to make friends—

You with him, him with you, and both with me!

220 If I succeed—permit me to inquire

Five minutes hence! Friends bid good-bye, you know."

And out he goes.

---

²¹⁴⁻¹⁵| MS:So, madam <> Album-page/And <> thank the last contributor? §two
lines inserted between 213-16§ *1875:*So, Madam <> / <> thank its last
²¹⁷| MS:interview— *1875:*interview, ²²¹| MS:hence. Friends <>
good bye <> know!" *1875:*hence! Friends <> good-bye <> know." ²²²| MS:
goes.§¶called for in margin§

VII

She, face, form, bearing, one
Superb composure—

"He has told you all?
Yes, he has told you all, your silence says—
What gives him, as he thinks the mastery
5   Over my body and my soul!—has told
That instance, even, of their servitude
He now exacts of me? A silent blush!
That's well, though better would white ignorance
Beseem your brow, undesecrate before—
10   Ay, when I left you! I too learn at last
—Hideously learned as I seemed so late—
What sin may swell to. Yes,—I needed learn
That, when my prophet's rod became the snake
I fled from, it would, one day, swallow up
15   —Incorporate whatever serpentine
Falsehood and treason and unmanliness
Beslime earth's pavement: such the power of Hell,
And so beginning, ends no otherwise
The Adversary! I was ignorant,
20   Blameworthy—if you will; but blame I take
Nowise upon me as I ask myself
—*You*—how can you, whose soul I seemed to read
The limpid eyes through, have declined so deep
Even with him for consort? I revolve

MS:§Roman numeral and period inserted above first line§   1| MS:form, gesture §crossed out and replaced above by§ bearing   2| MS:composure— §marginal note that ¶ begins§ "He   3| MS:Yes < > says— §between 2-4§   5| MS:soul! §exclamation mark over question mark§ Perhaps, §word and comma crossed out and dash inserted above§—has   7| MS:Exacted of me? You assent §last two words crossed out and replaced above by one word§ Silence and a §inserted on the line§ blush! §exclamation mark over question mark§ *1875:* He now exacts of me? A silent blush!   11| MS:—Hideously §dash in L margin§   15| MS:—Incorporate §dash in L margin§ < > serpentine— §dash erased§   16| MS:unmanliness— §dash erased§   17| MS:Beslime §additional s or d erased§ < > of hell, §altered to§ Hell,   18| MS:And, thus §crossed out and replaced above by§ so *1875:* And so   19| MS:The adversary §altered to§ Adversary   20| MS:will: but *1875:* will; but   21| MS:me that I *1875:* me as I   22| MS:—*You* §dash in L margin§   23| MS:Those §altered to§ The < > so low much §last two words crossed out and replaced above by§ deep

Much memory, pry into the looks and words
Of that day's walk beneath the College wall,
And nowhere can distinguish, in what gleams
Only pure marble through my dusky past,
A dubious cranny where such poison-seed
30 Might harbour, nourish what should yield to-day
This dread ingredient for the cup I drink.
Do not I recognize and honour truth
In seeming?—take your truth and for return,
Give you my truth, a no less precious gift?
35 You loved me: I believed you. I replied
—How could I other? *'I was not my own,'*
—No longer had the eyes to see, the ears
To hear, the mind to judge, since heart and soul
Now were another's. My own right in me,
40 For well or ill, consigned away—my face
Fronted the honest path, deflection whence
Had shamed me in the furtive backward look
At the late bargain—fit such chapman's phrase!—
As though—less hasty and more provident—
45 Waiting had brought advantage. Not for me
The chapman's chance! Yet while thus much was true,
I spared you—as I knew you then—one more
Concluding word which, truth no less, seemed best
Buried away for ever. Take it now
50 Its power to pain is past! Four years—that day—

25| MS:memory—pry *1875:* memory, pry   26| MS:College limes,
§crossed out and replaced above by§ wall,   28| MS:marble through
§over illegible word§   30| MS:should §next word illegibly crossed out and
replaced above by§ prove §crossed out and replaced by§ yield one day   *1875:* yield to-day
31| MS:Direst §inserted above first word crossed out, perhaps *Best*§ of §crossed out§
ingredients §altered to§ ingredient   *1875:* This dread ingredient   32| MS:Did not
1889a: Do not   33| MS:So seeming < > and in return   *1875:* In seeming < > and for
return,   34| MS:you back mine, no less a §last three words transposed to§ a no less
1875: you my truth, a   35| MS:me—I   *1875:* me: I   36| MS:other? I was not
my own—   *1875:* other? *'I was not my own,'*   37| MS:—No §dash in L margin§
39| MS:another's: my < > me   *1875:* another's. My < > me,   40| MS:ill consigned
away, my   *1875:* ill, consigned away—my   41| MS:deflexion *1875:* deflection
43| MS:fit would §crossed out and replaced above by§ the §crossed out and replaced
by§ such   45| MS:advantage: not < > me, *1875:* advantage. Not *1889a:* me
46| MS:chance! §exclamation mark apparently over dash§ yet §altered to§ Yet
49| MS:ever: take *1875:* ever. Take   50| MS:past! Two years *1875:* past! Four years

Those limes that make the College avenue!
I would that—friend and foe—by miracle,
I had, that moment, seen into the heart
Of either, as I now am taught to see!
55   I do believe I should have straight assumed
My proper function, and sustained a soul,
Nor aimed at being just sustained myself
By some man's soul—the weaker woman's-want!
So had I missed the momentary thrill
60   Of finding me in presence of a god,
But gained the god's own feeling when he gives
Such thrill to what turns life from death before.
'Gods many and Lords many,' says the Book:
You would have yielded up your soul to me
65   —Not to the false god who has burned its clay
In his own image. I had shed my love
Like Spring dew on the clod all flowery thence,
Not sent up a wild vapour to the sun
That drinks and then disperses. Both of us
70   Blameworthy,—I first meet my punishment—
And not so hard to bear. I breathe again!
Forth from those arms' enwinding leprosy
At last I struggle—uncontaminate:
Why must I leave *you* pressing to the breast
75   That's all one plague-spot? Did you love me once?
Then take love's last and best return! I think,
Womanliness means only motherhood;
All love begins and ends there,—roams enough,
But, having run the circle, rests at home.
80   Why is your expiation yet to make?

---

⁵²| MS:I §inserted in L margin§ Would that—my §crossed out§ friend— §dash over
comma§ my §crossed out and replaced above by§ and < > miracle   *1875:*I would < >
miracle,   ⁵³| MS:hearts   *1875:*heart   ⁵⁷| MS:—Not §dash in L margin§ aimed
*1889a:*Nor aimed   ⁶²| MS:turns flesh §crossed out and replaced above by§ life from
clay §crossed out and replaced above by§ death   ⁶³| MS:*many'*— §dash erased§ says
1875:many,' says   ⁶⁶| MS:image: I   *1875:*image. I   ⁶⁷| MS:Like May §crossed
out and replaced above by§ Spring < > clod that's §crossed out and replaced above by§ all
⁷¹| MS:again—   *1875:*again!   ⁷⁴| MS:you   *1875:you*   ⁷⁵| MS:That's
all §last two words inserted above§ One   *1875:*one   ⁷⁶| MS:take the §crossed
out and replaced above by§ love's < > best of love: §last two words and colon
crossed out and replaced above by one word and exclamation mark§ return!

Pull shame with your own hands from your own head
Now,—never wait the slow envelopment
Submitted to by unelastic age!
One fierce throe frees the sapling: flake on flake
85 Lull till they leave the oak snow-stupefied.
Your heart retains its vital warmth—or why
That blushing reassurance? Blush, young blood!
Break from beneath this icy premature
Captivity of wickedness—I warn
90 Back, in God's name! No fresh encroachment here!
This May breaks all to bud—no Winter now!
Friend, we are both forgiven! Sin no more!
I am past sin now, so shall you become!
Meanwhile I testify that, lying once,
95 My foe lied ever, most lied last of all.
He, waking, whispered to your sense asleep
The wicked counsel,—and assent might seem;
But, roused, your healthy indignation breaks
The idle dream-pact. You would die—not dare
100 Confirm your dream-resolve,—nay, find the word
That fits the deed to bear the light of day!
Say I have justly judged you! then farewell
To blushing—nay, it ends in smiles, not tears!
Why tears now? I have justly judged, thank God!"

105 He does blush boy-like, but the man speaks out,
—Makes the due effort to surmount himself.

"I don't know what he wrote—how should I? Nor

⁸¹| MS:hands on your *1875:* hands from your ⁸³| MS:age! §exclamation mark apparently over dash§ ⁸⁵| MS:snow-stupified. *1889a:* snow-stupefied.
⁸⁷| MS:reassurance: blush §colon and last word altered to§ reassurance? Blush
⁹⁰| MS:name: no §colon and last word altered to§ name! No ⁹¹| MS:no winter
1889a: no Winter ⁹¹⁻⁹²| MS:§marginal note that ¶ begins§ *1875:* §no ¶§
⁹²| MS:more,— *1875:* more! ⁹⁶| MS:to the sense *1875:* to your sense
⁹⁷| MS:seem: *1875:* seem; ⁹⁸| MS:roused, the healthy *1875:* roused,
your healthy ¹⁰²| MS:you—then *1875:* you! then ¹⁰³| MS:tears—
1875: tears! ¹⁰⁴⁻⁰⁵| MS:§marginal note that ¶ begins§ *1875:* §no¶§
1889a: §¶§ ¹⁰⁵| MS:He did §altered to§ does < > boy like < > spoke
§altered to§ speaks *1875:* boy-like ¹⁰⁶| MS:—Made §dash in L margin
and word altered to§ Makes ¹⁰⁶⁻¹⁰⁷| MS:§marginal note that ¶ begins§

116

How he could read my purpose which, it seems,
He chose to somehow write—mistakenly
110 Or else for mischief's sake. I scarce believe
My purpose put before you fair and plain
Would need annoy so much; but there's my luck—
From first to last I blunder. Still, one more
Turn at the target, try to speak my thought!
115 Since he could guess my purpose, won't you read
Right what he set down wrong? He said—let's think!
Ay, so!—he did begin by telling heaps
Of tales about you. Now, you see—suppose
Anyone told me—my own mother died
120 Before I knew her—told me—to his cost!—
Such tales about my own dead mother: why,
You would not wonder surely if I knew,
By nothing but my own heart's help, he lied,
Would you? No reason's wanted in the case.
125 So with you! In they burnt on me, his tales,
Much as when madhouse inmates crowd around,
Make captive any visitor and scream
All sorts of stories of their keeper—he's
Both dwarf and giant, vulture, wolf, dog, cat,
130 Serpent and scorpion, yet man all the same;
Sane people soon see through the gibberish!
I just made out, you somehow lived somewhere
A life of shame—I can't distinguish more—
Married or single—how, don't matter much:
135 Shame which himself had caused—that point was clear,
That fact confessed—that thing to hold and keep.
Oh, and he added some absurdity
—That you were here to make me—ha, ha, ha!—
Still love you, still of mind to die for you,
140 Ha, ha—as if that needed mighty pains!

110| MS:sake; I *1875:*sake. I   112| MS:much:—but *1875:*much; but
120| MS:cost! *1875:*cost!—   121| MS:mother—why, *1875:*mother:
why,   131| MS:Sanity soon sees through *1875:*Sane people soon see
through   132| MS:out—you *1875:*out, you   134| MS:much—
*1875:*much: 136| MS:confessed—that §over *a*§   138| MS:—That §dash
in L margin§ <> make you §crossed out and replaced above by§ me

117

Now, foolish as . . . but never mind myself
—What I am, what I am not, in the eye
Of the world, is what I never cared for much.
Fool then or no fool, not one single word
145 In the whole string of lies did I believe,
But this—this only—if I choke, who cares?—
I believe somehow in your purity
Perfect as ever! Else what use is God?
He is God, and work miracles He can!
150 Then, what shall I do? Quite as clear, my course!
They've got a thing they call their Labyrinth
I' the garden yonder: and my cousin played
A pretty trick once, led and lost me deep
Inside the briery maze of hedge round hedge;
155 And there might I be staying now, stock-still,
But that I laughing bade eyes follow nose
And so straight pushed my path through let and stop
And soon was out in the open, face all scratched,
But well behind my back the prison-bars
160 In sorry plight enough, I promise you!
So here: I won my way to truth through lies—
Said, as I saw light,—if her shame be shame
I'll rescue and redeem her,—shame's no shame?
Then, I'll avenge, protect—redeem myself
165 The stupidest of sinners! Here I stand!
Dear,—let me once dare call you so,—you said
Thus ought you to have done, four years ago,
Such things and such! Ay, dear, and what ought I?
You were revealed to me: where's gratitude,
170 Where's memory even, where the gain of you
Discernible in my low after-life
Of fancied consolation? why, no horse

141| MS:myself— *1875:*myself   142| MS:—What §dash in L margin§
143| MS:world is *1875:*world, is   146| MS:who minds?— *1889a:*who cares?—
149| MS:and he §altered to§ He can work miracles §last four words transposed to§ work
miracles He can!   151| MS:labyrinth §altered to§ Labyrinth   152| MS:yonder, and
*1875:*yonder: and   155| MS:stock-still *1875:*stock-still,   167| MS:done, two years
*1875:*done, four years   168| MS:what beside? *1875:*what ought I?   169| MS:You
once revealed to me,—where's *1875:*You were revealed to me: where's   170| MS:even,
what's the *1875:*even, where the   171| MS:in the low *1875:*in my low
172| MS:consolations? §question mark is alteration of colon§ *1875:*consolation

Once fed on corn, will, missing corn, go munch
Mere thistles like a donkey! I missed you,
175 And in your place found—him, made him my love,
Ay, did I,—by this token, that he taught
So much beast-nature that I meant . . . God knows
Whether I bow me to the dust enough! . . .
To marry—yes, my cousin here! I hope
180 That was a master-stroke! Take heart of hers,
And give her hand of mine with no more heart
Than now you see upon this brow I strike!
What atom of a heart do I retain
Not all yours? Dear, you know it! Easily
185 May she accord me pardon when I place
My brow beneath her foot, if foot so deign,
Since uttermost indignity is spared—
Mere marriage and no love! And all this time
Not one word to the purpose! Are you free?
190 Only wait! only let me serve—deserve
Where you appoint and how you see the good!
I have the will—perhaps the power—at least
Means that have power against the world. For time—
Take my whole life for your experiment!
195 If you are bound—in marriage, say—why, still,
Still, sure, there's something for a friend to do,
Outside? A mere well-wisher, understand!
I'll sit, my life long, at your gate, you know,
Swing it wide open to let you and him
200 Pass freely,—and you need not look, much less
Fling me a *'Thank you—are you there, old friend?'*
Don't say that even: I should drop like shot!
So I feel now at least: some day, who knows?
After no end of weeks and months and years
205 You might smile *'I believe you did your best!'*

177| MS:meant . . God *1875*:meant . . . God   178| MS:enough! . . *1875*:enough!
. . .   180| MS:hers *1875*:hers,   182| MS:upon the brow it strikes! *1875*:upon
this brow I strike!   185| MS:accord §apparently suffix (illegible) erased§
186| MS:The brow <> deign! *1875*:My brow <> deign,   190| MS:wait—only
1875:wait! only   199| MS:let you §over *him*§   200| MS:look—much *1875*:look,
much   202| MS:even—I *1875*:even: I   203| MS:least—some *1875*:least: some

And that shall make my heart leap—leap such leap
As lands the feet in Heaven to wait you there!
Ah, there's just one thing more! How pale you look!
Why? Are you angry? If there's, after all,
210   Worst come to worst—if still there somehow be
The shame—I said was no shame,—none, I swear!—
In that case, if my hand and what it holds,—
My name,—might be your safeguard now—at once—
Why, here's the hand—you have the heart! Of course—
215   No cheat, no binding you, because I'm bound,
To let me off probation by one day,
Week, month, year, lifetime! Prove as you propose!
Here's the hand with the name to take or leave!
That's all—and no great piece of news, I hope!"

220   "Give me the hand, then!" she cries hastily.
"Quick, now! I hear his footstep!"

                           Hand in hand
The couple face him as he enters, stops
Short, stands surprised a moment, laughs away
Surprise, resumes the much-experienced man.

225   "So, you accept him?"

                     "Till us death do part!"

"No longer? Come, that's right and rational!

206| MS:leap—leap so long §last two words crossed out and replaced above by two words§
such leap   207| MS:It §crossed out and replaced in L margin by§ As <> the legs in
1875: the feet in   208| MS:Wait once—there's §last three words crossed out and replaced
above by three words§ Ah, there's just   211| MS:shame,—no §altered to§ none
212| MS:case—say, my 1875: case, if my   215| MS:because so bound, 1875: because
I'm bound,   219| MS:all—a §altered to§ and §next word, perhaps *pretty*, crossed out
and replaced above by two words§ no great <> news, no doubt!" §last two words and
exclamation mark crossed out and replaced above by two words and exclamation mark§ I
hope!"   219-20| MS:§marginal note that ¶ begins§   220| MS:hand then <>
hastily 1875: hand, then <> hastily.   221| MS:footstep!" §marginal note that ¶
begins§ Hand in hand, 1875: hand   222| MS:enters—stops 1875: enters, stops
224-25| MS:§marginal note that ¶ begins§   225| MS:him?" §marginal note that ¶
begins§ "Till   225-26| MS:§marginal note that ¶ begins§ 1875: §no ¶§ 1889a:§¶§

I fancied there was power in common sense,
But did not know it worked thus promptly. Well—
At last each understands the other, then?
230 Each drops disguise, then? So, at supper-time
These masquerading people doff their gear,
Grand Turk his pompous turban, Quakeress
Her stiff-starched bib and tucker,—make-believe
That only bothers when, ball-business done,
235 Nature demands champagne and *mayonnaise.*
Just so has each of us sage three abjured
His and her moral pet particular
Pretension to superiority,
And, cheek by jowl, we henceforth munch and joke!
240 Go, happy pair, paternally dismissed
To live and die together—for a month,
Discretion can award no more! Depart
From whatsoe'er the calm sweet solitude
Selected—Paris not improbably—
245 At month's end, when the honeycomb's left wax,
—You, daughter, with a pocketful of gold
Enough to find your village boys and girls
In duffel cloaks and hobnailed shoes from May
To—what's the phrase?—Christmas-come-never-mas!
250 You, son and heir of mine, shall re-appear
Ere Spring-time, that's the ring-time, lose one leaf,
And—not without regretful smack of lip
The while you wipe it free of honey-smear—
Marry the cousin, play the magistrate,
255 Stand for the county, prove perfection's pink—
Master of hounds, gay-coated dine—nor die
Sooner than needs of gout, obesity,
And sons at Christ Church! As for me,—ah me,
I abdicate—retire on my success,

229| MS:other, eh? *1875:*other, then? 231| MS:Wise §over illegible erasure§ mas-
querading *1875:*These masquerading 236| MS:so, has < > us sage §over illegible
erasure§ *1875:*so has 238| MS: Pretention *1875:*Pretension 245| MS:honey-
comb's *1875:*honeycomb's 246| MS:—You §dash in L margin§ 248| MS:duffil
*1875:*duffel 250| MS:—You *1875:*You 256| MS:gay- §over illegible erasure§
258| MS:at Christ Church. As < > ah, me! *1875:*at Christ Church! As < > ah me,

²⁶⁰ Four years well occupied in teaching youth
      —My son and daughter the exemplary!
      Time for me to retire now, having placed
      Proud on their pedestal the pair: in turn,
      Let them do homage to their master! You,—
²⁶⁵ Well, your flushed cheek and flashing eye proclaim
      Sufficiently your gratitude: you paid
      The *honorarium*, the ten thousand pounds
      To purpose, did you not? I told you so!
      And you, but, bless me, why so pale—so faint
²⁷⁰ At influx of good fortune? Certainly,
      No matter how or why or whose the fault,
      I save your life—save it, nor less nor more!
      You blindly were resolved to welcome death
      In that black boor-and-bumpkin-haunted hole
²⁷⁵ Of his, the prig with all the preachments! *You*
      Installed as nurse and matron to the crones
      And wenches, while there lay a world outside
      Like Paris (which again I recommend)
      In company and guidance of—first, this,
²⁸⁰ Then—all in good time—some new friend as fit—
      What if I were to say, some fresh myself,
      As I once figured? Each dog has his day,
      And mine's at sunset: what should old dog do
      But eye young litters' frisky puppyhood?
²⁸⁵ Oh I shall watch this beauty and this youth
      Frisk it in brilliance! But don't fear! Discreet,
      I shall pretend to no more recognize

---

^{260|} MS:Two years *1875:* Four years   ^{261|} MS:—My §dash in L margin§
^{264|} MS:master—you, *1875:* master! You,—   ^{269|} MS:you,—but *1889a:* you, but
^{270|} MS:fortune? Certainly *1875:* fortune? Certainly,   ^{274|} MS:hole of his §last two
words crossed out§   ^{275|} MS:Of his, §last two words and comma inserted in L margin§
The §altered to§ the village §crossed out§   ^{276|} MS:Installed his §crossed out and re-
placed above by§ as   ^{278|} MS:Like Paris—which < > recommend— *1875:* Like Paris
(which < > recommend)   ^{279|} MS:this— *1875:* this,   ^{280|} MS:And §crossed out
and replaced above by§ Then   ^{281|} MS:say—some *1875:* say, some   ^{282|} MS:fig-
ured! Each < > has its §altered to§ his day— *1875:* figured? Each < > day,
^{284|} MS:litters frisk in puppyhood? *1875:* litters' frisky puppyhood?   ^{285|} MS:O
1889a: Oh   ^{286|} MS:brilliance—but §dash and last word altered to§ brilliance! But
^{287|} MS:shall no more pretend to recognize *1875:* shall pretend to no more recognize

My quondam pupils than the doctor nods
When certain old acquaintances may cross
His path in Park, or sit down prim beside
His plate at dinner-table: tip nor wink
Scares patients he has put, for reason good,
Under restriction,—maybe, talked sometimes
Of douche or horsewhip to,—for why? because
The gentleman would crazily declare
His best friend was—Iago! Ay, and worse—
The lady, all at once grown lunatic,
In suicidal monomania vowed,
To save her soul, she needs must starve herself!
They're cured now, both, and I tell nobody.
Why don't you speak? Nay, speechless, each of you
Can spare,—without unclasping plighted troth,—
At least one hand to shake! Left-hands will do—
Yours first, my daughter! Ah, it guards—it gripes
The precious Album fast—and prudently!
As well obliterate the record there
On page the last: allow me tear the leaf!
Pray, now! And afterward, to make amends,
What if all three of us contribute each
A line to that prelusive fragment,—help
The embarrassed bard who broke out to break down
Dumbfoundered at such unforeseen success?
'Hail, calm acclivity, salubrious spot'
You begin—*place aux dames!* I'll prompt you then!
'Here do I take the good the gods allot!'
Next you, Sir! What, still sulky? Sing, O Muse!
'Here does my lord in full discharge his shot!'

290

295

300

305

310

315

288| MS:doctors do *1875:* doctor nods   289| MS:acquaintance
comes across   *1875:*acquaintances may cross   290| MS:sits
1875: sit   291| MS:dinner-table—no, indeed §last two words crossed
out§ tip   *1875:*dinner-table: tip   292| MS:For patients *1875:*Scares
patients   298| MS:In §over perhaps *A*§ <> monomania vowed, §last
two words apparently alteration of *monomaniac vows*§   299| MS:she had
§apparently alteration of *has*§ to starve   *1875:*she needs must starve   303| MS:
shake! Left hands   *1875:* shake! Left-hands   304| MS:Yours then §crossed
out and replaced above by§ first   305| MS:album §altered to§ Album
314| MS:you, then!   *1875:*you then!   316| MS:sulky? Sing §over
illegible erasure§   317| MS:*my friend* §crossed out and replaced above by§ *lord*

Now for the crowning flourish! mine shall be . . .”

“Nothing to match your first effusion, mar
320   What was, is, shall remain your masterpiece!
Authorship has the alteration-itch!
No, I protest against erasure. Read,
My friend!” (she gasps out). “Read and quickly read
‘Before us death do part,’ what made you mine
325   And made me yours—the marriage-licence here!
Decide if he is like to mend the same!”

And so the lady, white to ghastliness,
Manages somehow to display the page
With left-hand only, while the right retains
330   The other hand, the young man’s,—dreaming-drunk
He, with this drench of stupefying stuff,
Eyes wide, mouth open,—half the idiot’s stare
And half the prophet’s insight,—holding tight,
All the same, by his one fact in the world—
335   The lady’s right-hand: he but seems to read—
Does not, for certain; yet, how understand
Unless he reads?

So, understand he does,
For certain. Slowly, word by word, *she* reads

---

³¹⁸| MS:be . .” *1889a:*be . . .”   ³¹⁸⁻¹⁹| MS:§marginal note that ¶ begins§
³¹⁹| MS:effusion, §apparently comma over partially erased exclamation mark§
That §crossed out and replaced above by§ mar   ³²⁰| MS:was, and §crossed
out and replaced above by§ is   ³²²| MS:erasure- §short dash rounded to full
stop§ read §altered to§ Read   ³²³| MS:My < > out) Read < > read §inserted
between 322-24§ *1875:*out.) “Read   *1889a:*out). “Read   ³²⁶| MS:Then say
§last two words crossed out and replaced above by§ Decide   ³²⁶⁻²⁷| MS:§marginal
note that ¶ begins§   ³³⁰| MS:man’s, dreaming-drunk   *1875:*man’s,—dreaming-drunk
³³¹| MS:He, §word and comma inserted in L margin§ With all §crossed out§ < >
stupifying   *1875:*with   *1889a:*stupefying   ³³⁵| MS:The other §crossed out
and replaced above by§ lady’s right hand   *1875:*right-hand   ³³⁶| MS:certain:
yet   *1875:*certain; yet   ³³⁷| MS:reads? §marginal note that ¶ begins§ and §crossed out
and replaced above by perhaps *Thus,* in turn crossed out and replaced by word and
comma§ So,   ³³⁸| MS:§below 338, last on MS page, are words illegibly crossed out§

Aloud that licence—or that warrant, say.

340   " *'One against two—and two that urge their odds*
To uttermost—I needs must try resource!
Madam, I laid me prostrate, bade you spurn
Body and soul: you spurned and safely spurned
So you had spared me the superfluous taunt
345   *"Prostration means no power to stand erect,*
Stand, trampling on who trampled—prostrate now!"
So, with my other fool-foe: I was fain
Let the boy touch me with the buttoned foil,
And him the infection gains, he too must needs
350   *Catch up the butcher's cleaver. Be it so!*
Since play turns earnest, here's my serious fence.
He loves you; he demands your love: both know
What love means in my language. Love him then!
Pursuant to a pact, love pays my debt:
355   *Therefore, deliver me from him, thereby*
Likewise delivering from me yourself!
For, hesitate—much more, refuse consent—
I tell the whole truth to your husband. Flat
Cards lie on table, in our gamester-phrase!
360   *Consent—you stop my mouth, the only way.'*

  "I did well, trusting instinct: knew your hand
Had never joined with his in fellowship
Over this pact of infamy. You known—
As he was known through every nerve of me.
365   Therefore I *'stopped his mouth the only way'*

339-40| MS:§marginal note that ¶ begins§   **340-60|** MS:§marginal note that lines are italicized§   **340|** MS:'One 1889a:"'One   **345|** MS:'Prostration <> to stand §altered to§ *start erect,* 1875:to stand erect, 1889a:"Prostration   **346|** MS:now!' 1889a:now!"   **352|** MS:you: he 1875:you; he   **353|** MS:him, then! §exclamation mark over comma§ 1875:him then!   **354|** MS:debt— 1875:debt: **355|** MS:him—thereby 1875:him, thereby   **356|** MS:yourself! §exclamation mark over dash§   **358|** MS:husband—that §dash and last word altered to§ *husband. Flat*   **359|** MS:table, in our §last two words over illegible erasures§   **360|** MS:way." 1875:way.'   **360-61|** MS:§marginal note that ¶ begins§   **361|** MS: I 1875:"I   **364|** MS:Still §crossed out in and replaced in pencil above by §As   **365|** MS:Likewise,— §word and comma-dash crossed out and replaced above— first in pencil, then in ink—by§ Therefore <> mouth' §apostrophe erased§

But *my* way! none was left for you, my friend—
The loyal—near, the loved one! No—no—no!
Threaten? Chastise? The coward would but quail.
Conquer who can, the cunning of the snake!
370 Stamp out his slimy strength from tail to head,
And still you leave vibration of the tongue.
His malice had redoubled—not on me
Who, myself, choose my own refining fire—
But on poor unsuspicious innocence;
375 And,—victim,—to turn executioner
Also—that feat effected, forky tongue
Had done indeed its office! Once snake's *'mouth'*
Thus *'open'*—how could mortal *'stop it'?"*

"So!"

A tiger-flash—yell, spring, and scream: halloo!
380 Death's out and on him, has and holds him—ugh!
But *ne trucidet coram populo*
Juvenis senem! Right the Horatian rule!

There, see how soon a quiet comes to pass!

367| MS:one! §exclamation mark over dash§   368| MS:Threaten? chastise? §apparently
last two question marks over colons§ the   *1875:* Threaten? Chastise? The
369| MS:snake! §exclamation mark over erased dash§   373| MS:choose §over perhaps
chose§   374| MS:poor unsuspecting §altered to§ unsuspicious innocence
1875: innocence;   375| MS:And §crossed out and replaced above by§ So
§erased and original word restored§ <> to turn §last two words over illegible
erasure§   376| MS:that too §inserted above§ effected   *1875:* that feat effected
377| MS:office!—once §dash erased and last word altered to§ Once <> *'mouth'*
1875:'mouth' *1889a:'mouth'*   378| MS:That §altered to§ Thus *'opens'* §altered
to§ *'open'*—how could mortal §last two words over words illegibly crossed
out§ *'stopped* §altered to§ *'stop it'?"* §marginal note that ¶ begins§ "Thus!"   *1875:it'?"*
§¶§ "So!"   379| MS:A tiger- §word and hyphen over word illegibly crossed out§
flash— tiger §crossed out and replaced above by§ yell, spring and <> halloo!
§exclamation mark over dash§   *1875:* spring, and   380–81| MS:out and §inserted above§
on him, death §crossed out and replaced above by two words§ has and holds him, death . . .
§last word and elipsis crossed out and replaced above by dash and word§ —ugh! / The white
eyes' uptwist—black the tongue protrudes!— §last line crossed out§ / But   *1875:* him—ugh!
382| MS:*Juvenis* <> rule! §between 381-83§   382–83| MS:§marginal note that ¶ begins§
§Following 383 four lines are crossed out illegibly, first in pencil, then in ink§

VIII

The youth is somehow by the lady's side.
His right-hand grasps her right-hand once again.
Both gaze on the dead body. Hers the word.

"And that was good but useless. Had I lived
5   The danger was to dread: but, dying now—
Himself would hardly become talkative,
Since talk no more means torture. Fools—what fools
These wicked men are! Had I borne four years,
Four years of weeks and months and days and nights,
10   Inured me to the consciousness of life
Coiled round by his life, with the tongue to ply,—
But that I bore about me, for prompt use
At urgent need, the thing that *'stops the mouth'*
And stays the venom? Since such need was now
15   Or never,—how should use not follow need?
Bear witness for me, I withdraw from life
By virtue of the licence—warrant, say,
That blackens yet this Album—white again,
Thanks still to my one friend who tears the page!
20   Now, let me write the line of supplement,

MS:§Roman numeral and period inserted above first line; marginal note that Part VIII
begins§   ²| MS:§first word illegibly crossed out§ His §inserted above§ <> grasps
§virgule inserted to separate last word from next word§ her right-hand once §inserted above§
³| MS:body §next word or words illegibly crossed out and replaced by three words§ Hers
the word.   ³⁻⁴| MS:§marginal note that ¶ begins§   ⁷| MS:torture. Fools—
§followed by two words crossed out, perhaps *my friend*, replaced above by two words§ what
fools   ⁸| MS:are! Could I bear two years, *1875:*are! Had I borne four years,
⁹| MS:Two years *1875:*Four years   ¹⁰| MS:Inure *1875:*Inured   ¹¹| MS:ply,—
§comma apparently over erased question mark§   ¹²| MS:me—for *1875:*me, for
¹³| MS:need—the *1875:*need, the   ¹⁴| MS:the snake or §last two words crossed out
followed by two words illegibly crossed out§ malice? since §last two words inserted above§
and §inserted above and then crossed out§ such §inserted above§ *1875:*the venom? Since
¹⁶| MS:Withdrawal from existence §last three words crossed out and replaced above by
four words and comma§ Bear witness for me, I withdraw from life §last two words
added§   ²⁰| MS:write my §crossed out and replaced above by§ the

127

As counselled by my foe there: *'each a line!'* "

And she does falteringly write to end.

"I die now through the villain who lies dead,
Righteously slain. He would have outraged me,
25 *So, my defender slew him. God protect*
The right! Where wrong lay, I bear witness now.
Let man believe me, whose last breath is spent
In blessing my defender from my soul!"

And so ends the Inn Album.

As she dies,
30 Begins outside a voice that sounds like song,
And is indeed half song though meant for speech
Muttered in time to motion—stir of heart
That unsubduably must bubble forth
To match the fawn-step as it mounts the stair.

35 "All's ended and all's over! Verdict found
'Not guilty'—prisoner forthwith set free,
Mid cheers the Court pretends to disregard!
Now Portia, now for Daniel, late severe,
At last appeased, benignant! *'This young man—*
40 *Hem—has the young man's foibles but no fault.*
He's virgin soil—a friend must cultivate.
I think no plant called 'love' grows wild—a friend
May introduce, and name the bloom, the fruit!'

21-23| MS:by the §crossed out and replaced above by§ my <> *line'!* §marginal
note that ¶ begins§ "I   1875:by <> line!' / And she does falteringly write to end. / 'I
1889a:line!' " <> / / "I   23-28| MS:§marginal note indicating italics§   25| MS:*So
my*   1875:*So, my*   26| MS:*right: where* §colon and last word altered to§ *right! Where*
28| MS:*In* §in margin§ *Blessing* §altered to§ *blessing my* §followed by word illegibly
crossed out§ <> *soul!'*   1889a:soul!' "   28-29| MS:§marginal note that ¶ begins§
29| MS:the Inn Album. §marginal note that ¶ begins§ As   30| MS:outside the §crossed
out and replaced above by§ a   31| MS:is half song indeed §last three words transposed
to§ indeed half song   34-35| MS:§marginal note that ¶ begins§   37| MS:disregard.
1875:disregard!   38| MS:Now, Portia, §next word illegibly crossed out and replaced
above by two words§ now, the Daniel   1875:Now Portia, now for Daniel   42-43| MS:I
<> plant like §crossed out and replaced above by§ called <> wild there §crossed out and

Here somebody dares wave a handkerchief—
45   She'll want to hide her face with presently!
Good-bye then! *'Cigno fedel, cigno fedel,*
Addio!' Now, was ever such mistake—
Ever such foolish ugly omen? Pshaw!
Wagner, beside! *'Amo te solo, te*
50   *Solo amai!'* That's worth fifty such!
But, mum, the grave face at the opened door!"

And so the good gay girl, with eyes and cheeks
Diamond and damask,—cheeks so white erewhile
Because of a vague fancy, idle fear
55   Chased on reflection!—pausing, taps discreet;
And then, to give herself a countenance,
Before she comes upon the pair inside,
Loud—the oft-quoted, long-laughed-over line—
" *'Hail, calm acclivity, salubrious spot!'*
60   Open the door!"

No: let the curtain fall!

---

replaced above by dash and word§ —a friend / May < > bloom, §comma added§ it bears.'
§last two words and full stop crossed out and replaced above by two words and exclamation
mark§ the fruit!' §Roman§   *1875:*§italics§   **44|** MS:(Here §parenthesis erased§
45| MS:She wants §last two words altered to§ She'll want to wipe §crossed out and replaced
above by§ hide her face §inserted above word illegibly crossed out§ < > presently!)
§parenthesis erased§   **46|** MS:Good bye, then *1875:*Good-bye then
47| MS:*Addio!'* Now, §last word and comma inserted above§ was there §crossed out§
48| MS:Ever < > Pshaw! §between 47-49§   **51-52|** MS:§marginal note that ¶ begins§
53-55| MS:damask,—cheeks so white erewhile / Because of a vague fancy, idle fear §dash and
last eleven words inserted between 52 and original 53 and in R margin§ / Chased on
reflection! §last three words and exclamation mark inserted below between first half of 53
and 56 with line drawn to connect with following three words, which originally formed the
last half of 53§ pausing, taps discreet; §semicolon over period; date and initials below 53§
56-59| MS:And < > countenance, / Before < > inside, / Loud < > line— / Hail, mild
§crossed out and replaced above by§ *calm* < > *spot!'* §four lines added after date of
completion recorded§ *1875:*" 'Hail   **60|** *1875:*§line added§

PACCHIAROTTO AND HOW HE WORKED IN DISTEMPER:
WITH OTHER POEMS

Edited by Ashby Bland Crowder

PACCHIAROTTO AND HOW HE WORKED IN DISTEMPER: WITH OTHER POEMS

PACCHIAROTTO AND HOW HE WORKED IN DISTEMPER: WITH OTHER POEMS

1876

PROLOGUE

I

O the old wall here! How I could pass
    Life in a long Midsummer day,
My feet confined to a plot of grass,
    My eyes from a wall not once away!

II

5   And lush and lithe do the creepers clothe
    Yon wall I watch, with a wealth of green:
Its bald red bricks draped, nothing loth,
    In lappets of tangle they laugh between.

III

Now, what is it makes pulsate the robe?
10   Why tremble the sprays? What life o'erbrims
The body,—the house, no eye can probe,—
    Divined as, beneath a robe, the limbs?

IV

And there again! But my heart may guess
    Who tripped behind; and she sang perhaps:
15   So, the old wall throbbed, and its life's excess
    Died out and away in the leafy wraps.

---

§MS in Balliol College Library, Oxford. Ed. 1876, 1889a; for B's 1876, see
Editorial Notes. In all poems, MS and 1876 count stanzas with arabic
numbers; roman numerals were introduced in 1889a.§ *PROLOGUE*
Title| MS:Dedication §crossed out and replaced by§ Prologue.   1| MS:wall
there! How *1876:*wall here! How   2| MS:long Midsummer Day,
*1876:*long Midsummer day,   14| MS:perhaps, *1876:*perhaps:
15| MS:So the *1876:*So, the   16| MS:wraps! *1889a:*wraps.

Wall upon wall are between us: life
    And song should away from heart to heart.
I—prison-bird, with a ruddy strife
20   At breast, and a lip whence storm-notes start—

VI

Hold on, hope hard in the subtle thing
    That's spirit: though cloistered fast, soar free;
Account as wood, brick, stone, this ring
    Of the rueful neighbours, and—forth to thee!

17| MS:us,—life   *1876:*us: life   18| MS:heart!   *1889a:*heart.   22| MS:spirit;
though   *1876:*spirit: though

OF PACCHIAROTTO, AND HOW HE WORKED IN DISTEMPER

I

Query: was ever a quainter
Crotchet than this of the painter
Giacomo Pacchiarotto
Who took "Reform" for his motto?

II

5   He, pupil of old Fungaio,
Is always confounded (heigho!)
With Pacchia, contemporaneous
No question, but how extraneous
In the grace of soul, the power
10   Of hand,—undoubted dower
Of Pacchia who decked (as *we* know,
My Kirkup!) San Bernardino,
Turning the small dark Oratory
To Siena's Art-laboratory,
15   As he made its straitness roomy
And glorified its gloomy,
With Bazzi and Beccafumi.

OF PACCHIAROTTO, AND HOW HE WORKED IN DISTEMPTER   Title| MS:Of
Pacchiarotto, and how he worked in distemper.   *1876:OF PACCHIAROTTO, AND HOW
HE WORKED IN DISTEMPER.*   B's *1876:OF* §crossed out§   *1889a:OF
PACCHIAROTTO* §At the beginning of Section 15 on MS, B repeated the number 14,
making all the remaining sections misnumbered as well§   2| MS:Scheme §crossed
out and replaced above by§ Crochet < > this scheme §crossed out§ < >
painter,   *1876:* painter   3| MS:Old §crossed out§ < > Pacchiarotto,
1876: Pacchiarotto   4| MS:took 'Reform' for   *1876:* took "Reform"
for   4-5| MS:§marginal note that ¶ begins; Arabic numeral inserted between
lines§   5| MS:He §crossed out, replaced above by word illegibly crossed
out, and then original reading restored§ < > of older §altered to§ old
6| MS:confounded—heigho!—   *1876:* confounded (heigho!)   7| MS:With
the §crossed out, replaced above by word illegibly crossed out, and then original
reading restored§ Pacchia,—contemporaneous   *1876:* With Pacchia, contemporaneous
8| MS:question,—but   *1876:* question, but   11| MS:of our §crossed out and replaced
above by§ the §crossed out and replaced by§ Pacchia who decked §crossed out,
replaced above by word illegibly crossed out, and then *decked* restored§

(Another heigho for Bazzi:
How people miscall him Razzi!)

III

²⁰ This Painter was of opinion
Our earth should be his dominion
Whose Art could correct to pattern
What Nature had slurred—the slattern!
And since, beneath the heavens,
²⁵ Things lay now at sixes and sevens,
Or, as he said, *sopra-sotto*—
Thought the painter Pacchiarotto
Things wanted reforming, therefore.
"Wanted it"—ay, but wherefore?
³⁰ When earth held one so ready
As he to step forth, stand steady
In the middle of God's creation
And prove to demonstration
What the dark is, what the light is,
³⁵ What the wrong is, what the right is,
What the ugly, what the beautiful,

---

^{18|}   MS:§parenthesis in L margin; first word illegibly crossed out and replaced
by§ Another §followed by word illegibly crossed out and replaced above
by four words illegibly crossed out and replaced by next two words§ heigho
for—Bazzi: §between 17 and 19§   *1876:*for Bazzi: ^{19|}   MS:§first word illegibly
crossed out§ How < > him—Razzi!)   *1876:*him Razzi!)   ^{19-20|}   MS:§marginal
note that ¶ begins; Arabic numeral inserted in R margin§   ^{20|}   MS:This
Painter §crossed out, replaced above by *other*, and then original reading restored§
had the §last two words crossed out and replaced above by two words§ was of
^{21|}   MS:dominion—   *1876:*dominion   ^{22|}   MS:His §crossed out and replaced above by§
Whose Art should §altered to§ could   ^{24|}   MS:since beneath < > heavens   *1876:*since,
beneath < > heavens,   ^{25|}   MS:Things lay now §crossed out§ at sixes and sevens
§transposed to§ at Things lay sixes and sevens §then transposed to§ at sixes Things lay and
sevens §then original order restored as well as crossed out word§   *1876:*sevens,
^{26|}   MS:Or, in his phrase, §last three words crossed out and replaced above by three words§ as
he said   ^{27|}   MS:Thought Giacomo §crossed out and replaced above by two words§ the
painter Pacchiarotto—   *1876:*Pacchiarotto   ^{28|}   MS:therefore: *1876:*therefore.
^{30|}   MS:When the §inserted above and then crossed out§   ^{33|}   MS:And show §crossed
out and replaced above by§ prove §next word illegibly crossed out and replaced above by
word illegibly crossed out§   ^{34|}   MS:What the §inserted above§ < > is, and §crossed
out§ what the §inserted above§   ^{35|}   MS:What the §inserted above§ < > is,
and §crossed out§ what the §inserted above§   ^{36|}   MS:What's §altered to§ What the
§inserted above§ ugly, and §crossed out§ what's §altered to§ what the §inserted above§

138

What the restive, what the dutiful,
In Mankind profuse around him?
Man, devil as now he found him,
40 Would presently soar up angel
At the summons of such evangel,
And owe—what would Man *not* owe
To the painter Pacchiarotto?
Ay, look to thy laurels, Giotto!

IV

45   But Man, he perceived, was stubborn,
Grew regular brute, once cub born;
And it struck him as expedient—
Ere he tried to make obedient
The wolf, fox, bear and monkey,
50 By piping advice in one key—
That his pipe should play a prelude
To something heaven-tinged not hell-hued,
Something not harsh but docile,
Man-liquid, not Man-fossil—
55 Not fact, in short, but fancy.
By a laudable necromancy
He would conjure up ghosts—a circle
Deprived of the means to work ill

37| MS:What's §altered to§ What the §inserted above§ restive, and §crossed out§
what's §altered to§ what the §inserted above§   38| MS:In man §altered to§ Man—in
§inserted above and then crossed out§ the marks around   *1876:* In Mankind profuse
around   40| MS:presently rise §crossed out and replaced above by§ soar
41| MS:the preaching §crossed out and replaced above by§ summons   42| MS:and,
angelic— §comma, word, and dash crossed out and replaced above by word and dash§ owe—
< > man §altered to§ Man   44-45| MS:§marginal note that ¶ begins; Arabic numeral
inserted between lines§   48-51| MS:obedient / By piping advice in one key / To the
§crossed out and replaced above by word and dash§ Man—wolf, fox, bear, and §crossed out§
monkey— / That   *1876:* obedient, / / The wolf, < > bear and monkey— / That
1889a: obedient / The < > monkey, / By < > key— / That   53| MS:Something still
§crossed out§   54| MS:Man-liquidity, §last three letters crossed out forming *liquid*§ not
man-fossil—   *1876:* not, Man-fossil—   55| MS:Not, §comma crossed out and replaced
above by dash, which was crossed out§   57| MS:He would bring in a spirit §last five
words crossed out and replaced above by five words§ might conjure up ghosts—a §then
might crossed out and *would* restored§   58| MS:Forms impotent §last two
words crossed out and replaced above by four words§ Deprived of the means

Should his music prove distasteful
60   And pearls to the swine go wasteful.
To be rent of swine—that *was* hard!
With fancy he ran no hazard:
Fact might knock him o'er the mazzard.

v

So, the painter Pacchiarotto
65   Constructed himself a grotto
In the quarter of Stalloreggi—
As authors of note allege ye.
And on each of the whitewashed sides of it
He painted—(none far and wide so fit
70   As he to perform in fresco)—
He painted nor cried *quiesco*
Till he peopled its every square foot
With Man—from the Beggar barefoot
To the Noble in cap and feather:
75   All sorts and conditions together.
The Soldier in breastplate and helmet
Stood frowningly—hail fellow well met—
By the Priest armed with bell, book and candle.
Nor did he omit to handle
80   The Fair Sex, our brave distemperer:
Not merely King, Clown, Pope, Emperor—
He diversified too his Hades

---

⁵⁹| MS:If §crossed out and replaced above by§ Should < > proved
§last letter crossed out forming *prove*§ distasteful,   *1889a:* distasteful
⁶⁰| MS:Should §crossed out and replaced above by§ And   ⁶¹| MS:To < > of the
§crossed out§ < > hard! §between 60-62§   ⁶³| MS:mazard.   *1889a:* mazzard.
⁶³⁻⁶⁴| MS: §marginal note that ¶ begins§   ⁶⁴| MS:Whereupon §crossed out and
replaced above by three words§ So the painter   *1876:* So, the   ⁷¹| MS:—Paint §dash
and word in L margin crossed out, restored, crossed out again and replaced above by§
He < > Painted §altered to§ painted   ⁷²| MS:peopled its §inserted above§
⁷³| MS:With Men   *1876:* With Man   ⁷⁵| MS:together—   *1876:* together.
⁷⁷| MS:Stood perforce there §last two words crossed out and replaced above by word
and dash§ frowningly,—hail < > met,—   *1876:* frowningly—hail < > met—
⁷⁸| MS:the Priest armed §inserted above§ with his §crossed out§ < > candle;   *1876:* candle.

Of all forms, pinched Labour and paid Ease,
With as mixed an assemblage of Ladies.

VI

85   Which work done, dry,—he rested him,
Cleaned pallet, washed brush, divested him
Of the apron that suits *frescanti*,
And, bonnet on ear stuck jaunty,
This hand upon hip well planted,
90   That, free to wave as it wanted,
He addressed in a choice oration
His folk of each name and nation,
Taught its duty to every station.
The Pope was declared an arrant
95   Impostor at once, I warrant.
The Emperor—truth might tax him
With ignorance of the maxim
"Shear sheep but nowise flay them!"
And the Vulgar that obey them,
100   The Ruled, well-matched with the Ruling,
They failed not of wholesome schooling
On their knavery and their fooling.

83| MS:Of all forms, if §crossed out§ < > Labour, §comma crossed out§ and §inserted
above§ < > Ease, §between 82-84§   84-85| MS: §marginal note that ¶ begins §
85| MS:Which— §dash erased§ work— §word and dash inserted above and then dash
crossed out§ done, and §crossed out§   86| MS:Cleaned brushes §crossed out and
replaced above by§ palate, washed hands §crossed out and replaced above by§ brush
89| MS:Left §crossed out and replaced above by§ This §crossed out and then restored in L
margin§   90| MS:Right §crossed out and replaced above by§ That §crossed out and
then restored in L margin§ —free < > as it §crossed out and replaced above by word illegibly
crossed out and then *it* restored§ *1876:*That, free   91| MS:a choice §crossed out and
replaced by§ long §crossed out and original reading restored§   92| MS:These §crossed
out and replaced by§ His < > nation, *1876:*nation *1889:*nation,   93| MS:On
the duty §altered to§ duties of every *1889a:*Taught its duty to every   95| MS:warrant:
*1876:*warrant.   97| MS:maxim— *1876:*maxim   98| MS:sheep and §crossed
out and replaced above by§ but < > them": *1876:*them!"   100| MS:The
§crossed out and then restored§ ruled §altered to§ Ruled ones §inserted
above and then crossed out§ well-matched *1876:*The Ruled, well-matched

141

As for Art—where's decorum? Pooh-poohed it is
By Poets that plague us with lewd ditties,
105 And Painters that pester with nudities!

VII

Now, your rater and debater
Is baulked by a mere spectator
Who simply stares and listens
Tongue-tied, while eye nor glistens
110 Nor brow grows hot and twitchy,
Nor mouth, for a combat itchy,
Quivers with some convincing
Reply—that sets him wincing?
Nay, rather—reply that furnishes
115 Your debater with just what burnishes
The crest of him, all one triumph,
As you see him rise, hear him cry "Humph!
Convinced am I? This confutes me?
Receive the rejoinder that suits me!

103-05| MS: §three lines not in MS§   102-06| MS: §marginal note that ¶ begins§
106| MS:And whereas your genuine debater   1876: Now, your rater and debater
107| MS:Were §crossed out and replaced above by§ Is < > spectator,   1876: spectator
108| MS:A blockhead §first two words crossed out§ who §altered to§ Who simply §inserted
above§ stared §altered to§ stares and listened §altered to§ listens   109| MS:Tongue-tied
< > glistened §altered to§ glistens   1889a: Tongue tied §emended to§ Tongue-tied §see
Editorial Notes§   110| MS:grows §altered to grew and then original reading restored§
< > twitchy   1876: twitchy,   111| MS:for the combat   1876: for a combat
112| MS: Had no trouble §last three words crossed out and replaced above by one word§
Quivers with that §crossed out and replaced above by§ the convincing   1876: with some
convincing   113| MS:Reply that §inserted above§ should §altered to§ shall soon
§crossed out§ set him wincing—   1876: Reply—that sets him wincing?   114| MS:Poor
man §last two words crossed out and replaced above by two words§ Vain boast! for §crossed
out and replaced above by§ not §then original reading restored§ replying §last three letters
crossed out forming reply§ but §inserted above§ furnishes   1876: Nay, rather—reply that
furnishes   115| MS:The §crossed out and replaced above by§ Our debater   1876: Your
debater   116| MS:His §crossed out and replaced above by§ The crest of him, §last two
words and comma inserted above word illegibly crossed out§   117| MS:As §inserted
in L margin§ You hear §crossed out and replaced above by§ see   1876: As you
118| MS:Convinced am I? §last three words and question mark crossed out, replaced
above by two illegible words and question mark, and then original three words and
question mark restored§ This man §crossed out§ confuted   1876: confutes   119| MS:I
make §last two words crossed out and replaced above by§ Receive

¹²⁰ Confutation of vassal for prince meet—
Wherein all the powers that convince meet,
And mash my opponent to mincemeat!"

VIII

So, off from his head flies the bonnet,
His hip loses hand planted on it,
¹²⁵ While t'other hand, frequent in gesture,
Slinks modestly back beneath vesture,
As,—hop, skip and jump,—he's along with
Those weak ones he late proved so strong with!
Pope, Emperor, lo, he's beside them,
¹³⁰ Friendly now, who late could not abide them,
King, Clown, Soldier, Priest, Noble, Burgess;
And his voice, that out-roared Boanerges,
How minikin-mildly it urges
In accents how gentled and gingered
¹³⁵ Its word in defence of the injured!
"O call him not culprit, this Pontiff!
Be hard on this Kaiser ye won't if
Ye take into con-si-der-ation
What dangers attend elevation!

---

¹²⁰| MS:Confutation of vassal for prince meet— §last six words and
dash crossed out and then restored§   ¹²²| MS:mincemeat." *1876:*mincemeat!"
¹²²⁻²³| MS: §marginal note that ¶ begins§   ¹²⁵| MS:t'other, §comma
crossed out; next word (perhaps *but*) crossed out and replaced above by word and comma§
hand, §crossed out and then restored§   ¹²⁶| MS:back to his §last two words crossed
out and replaced above by two words crossed out, the first of which is *beneath* and the
second of which was illegibly crossed out; *beneath* was then restored§   ¹²⁸| MS:late
proved §over illegible word§ <> with, *1876:*with!   ¹²⁹| MS:lo he's beside them,
§crossed out, replaced above by word illegibly crossed out, then *them* restored§ *1889a:*lo,
he's   ¹³⁰| MS:now—who <> abide them, §crossed out and replaced above by word
illegibly crossed out, then *them* restored§ *1876:*now, who   ¹³¹| MS:King, cobbler
§crossed out and replaced above by§ clown, soldier, priest, noble, burgess!
*1876:*King, Clown, Soldier, Priest, Noble, Burgess;   ¹³²| MS:that had
shamed §last two words crossed out and replaced above by§ out-roared
¹³⁴| MS:accents all sugared §last two words crossed out and replaced by two words§
how gentled and gingered— *1876:*gingered   ¹³⁶| MS:"O §quotation marks in
L margin§   ¹³⁷| MS:this Kaiser you §crossed out and replaced above by§ ye
¹³⁸| MS:You §crossed out and replaced above by§ Ye <> con-si-de-ration
*1889a:*con-si-der-ation   ¹³⁹| MS:What §first letter over illegible erasure§

140 The Priest—who expects him to descant
On duty with more zeal and less cant?
He preaches but rubbish he's reared in.
The Soldier, grown deaf (by the mere din
Of battle) to mercy, learned tippling
145 And what not of vice while a stripling.
The Lawyer—his lies are conventional.
And as for the Poor Sort—why mention all
Obstructions that leave barred and bolted
Access to the brains of each dolt-head?"

IX

150 He ended, you wager? Not half! A bet?
Precedence to males in the alphabet!
Still, disposed of Man's A, B, C, there's X,
Y, Z, want assistance,—the Fair Sex!
How much may be said in excuse of
155 Those vanities—males see no use of—
From silk shoe on heel to laced poll's-hood!
What's their frailty beside our own falsehood?
The boldest, most brazen of . . . trumpets,
How kind can they be to their dumb pets!
160 Of their charms—how are most frank, how few venal!
While as for those charges of Juvenal—
Quæ nemo dixisset in toto

140-41| MS:The Priest—who §over illegible erasures§ expects he §altered to§
him would §crossed out and replaced above by§ to descant / On < > cant? §two lines in R
margin§   142| MS:The Priest tells us stuff §last five words crossed out and replaced
above by four words§ He preaches but rubbish he §altered to§ he's was §crossed out§ < > in;
1876: in.   145| MS:stripling; *1876:* stripling.   146| MS:conventional;
1876: conventional.   149| MS:dolt-head? *1876:* dolt-head?"
149-50| MS: §marginal note that paragraph begins§   150| MS:He was §crossed out§
151| MS:alphabet,— *1876:* alphabet!   152| MS:But, §word and comma crossed out
and replaced above by word and comma§ Still, disposing of A.B.C., there's X. *1876:* Still,
disposed of Man's A.B.C. *1889a:* A,B,C, there's X,   153| MS:Y.Z. wants §next word,
perhaps *other*, crossed out§ *1876:* want *1889a:* Y,Z, want   154| MS:much might be
1876: much may be   156| MS:silk slipper §crossed out and replaced above by§ shoe < >
to lace-poll's-hood! *1876:* to laced poll's-hood!   157-60| MS:falsehood? / The < >
trumpets, / How < > pets! §158-59 in R margin§ Of < > are all frank < > venal! §160
between 157-61§ *1876:* are most frank   162| MS:*dixisset (in* *1876:dixisset in*

Nisi (œdepol) ore illoto—
He dismissed every charge with an *"Apage!"*

x

165 Then, cocking (in Scotch phrase) his cap a-gee,
Right hand disengaged from the doublet
—Like landlord, in house he had sub-let
Resuming of guardianship gestion,
To call tenants' conduct in question—
170 Hop, skip, jump, to inside from outside
Of chamber, he lords, ladies, louts eyed
With such transformation of visage
As fitted the censor of this age.
No longer an advocate tepid
175 Of frailty, but champion intrepid
Of strength, not of falsehood but verity,
He, one after one, with asperity
Stripped bare all the cant-clothed abuses,
Disposed of sophistic excuses,
180 Forced folly each shift to abandon,
And left vice with no leg to stand on.

164| MS:an *'Apage'. 1876:*an *'Apage!' 1889a:*an *"Apage!"* 164–65| MS:§marginal note that paragraph begins; Arabic numeral inserted between lines§ 165| MS:And §crossed out and replaced above by next word and comma§ Then, setting (in *1876:*Then, cocking (in 166| MS:He §crossed out; next word, perhaps *has*, crossed out§ right §altered to§ Right 167| MS:—Like §dash added in left margin§ landlord in house lately §last word crossed out and replaced above by two words§ he had sublet *1876:*landlord, in *1889a:*sub-let 168| MS:gestion *1876:*gestion, 170| MS:jump, from room's §last two words crossed out and replaced above by§ to < > outside— §dash crossed out§ 171| MS:Once again §last two words crossed out and replaced above by two words and comma§ Of chamber, < > ladies, and §crossed out§ 173| MS:fitted him— §last word and dash crossed out and replaced above by§ the Censor < > age: *1876:*censor < > age. 175| MS:frailty but *1889a:*frailty, but 176| MS:Of §in L margin§ Strength,—not *1876:*Of strength *1889a:*strength, not 177| MS:As one after one with *1876:*He, one after one, with 178–79| MS:He disposed §altered to§ Disposed of sophistic excuses, §last four words and comma transposed with next five words and comma§ Stripped bare all cant-covered §last half of word crossed out and replaced above by§ clothed abuses, *1876:*Stripped

So crushing the force he exerted,
That Man at his foot lay converted!

XI

    True—Man bred of paint-pot and mortar!
185 But why suppose folks of this sort are
More likely to hear and be tractable
Than folks all alive and, in fact, able
To testify promptly by action
Their ardour, and make satisfaction
190 For misdeeds *non verbis sed factis?*
"With folk all alive be my practice
Henceforward! O mortar, paint-pot O,
Farewell to ye!" cried Pacchiarotto,
"Let only occasion intérpose!"

XII

195   It did so: for, pat to the purpose
Through causes I need not examine,
There fell upon Siena a famine.
In vain did the magistrates busily
Seek succour, fetch grain out of Sicily,
200 Nay, throw mill and bakehouse wide open—
Such misery followed as no pen
Of mine shall depict ye. Faint, fainter
Waxed hope of relief: so, our painter,

182| MS:exerted! *1876:*exerted,   183| MS:That §crossed out and replaced above by§ So Man *1876:*That Man   183-84| MS: §marginal note that ¶ begins; Arabic numeral inserted in R margin§   184| MS:paint-pot §*pot* crossed out and replaced above by *brush*, which was crossed out and *pot* restored§ <> mortar: *1876:*mortar!   185| MS:of that sort *1876:*of this sort   189| MS:ardour, to §crossed out and replaced above by§ and   190| MS:For past §crossed out§   191| MS:folks *1889a:*folk   193| MS:cried Pacchiarotto *1876:*cried Pacchiarotto,   194-95| MS:§marginal note that paragraph begins§   195| MS:Accordingly §crossed out and replaced above by four words and comma§ It did so: for, <> purpose, *1876:*purpose   196| MS:examine *1876:*examine,   197| MS:There raged at §last two words crossed out and replaced above by two words§ fell upon   198| MS:bussily §altered to§ busily   199| MS:succour, bring §crossed out and replaced above by§ fetch   202| MS:Desires to preserve. §last three words and full stop crossed out and replaced above by five words and full stop§ Of mine shall depict ye. Faint, and §crossed out§   203| MS:so our *1876:*so, our

Emboldened by triumph of recency,
205 How could he do other with decency
Than rush in this strait to the rescue,
Play schoolmaster, point as with fescue
To each and all slips in Man's spelling
The law of the land?—slips now telling
210 With monstrous effect on the city,
Whose magistrates moved him to pity
As, bound to read law to the letter,
They minded their hornbook no better.

XIII

I ought to have told you, at starting,
215 How certain, who itched to be carting
Abuses away clean and thorough
From Siena, both province and borough,
Had formed themselves into a company
Whose swallow could bolt in a lump any
220 Obstruction of scruple, provoking
The nicer throat's coughing and choking:
Fit Club, by as fit a name dignified
Of "Freed Ones"—*"Bardotti"*—which signified
"Spare-Horses" that walk by the waggon
225 The team has to drudge for and drag on.
This notable club Pacchiarotto

204| MS:With triumph in §last three words crossed out and replaced above by three words§ Emboldened by triumph 206| MS:rescue— *1876:* rescue, 210| MS:With such sad effect < > city *1876:* With monstrous effect < > city, 213-14| MS:§marginal note that paragraph begins§ 215| MS:That §crossed out and replaced above by§ How certain who *1876:* certain, who 216-17| MS:§Illegible markings in L margin§ 217| MS:From Siena both *1876:* From Siena, both 219| MS:swallowed §last two letters crossed out forming *swallow*§ down §crossed out and replaced above by§ could 220| MS:Obstructions §last letter crossed out forming *Obstruction*§ 221| MS:throats §altered to§ throat's to §crossed out§ coughing nay, §word and comma crossed out and replaced above by§ and 222| MS:Which §crossed out and replaced above by§ Fit club §altered to§ Club < > fit a §inserted above§ name they §crossed out and replaced by word illegibly crossed out§ dignified— §dash crossed out§ 223| MS:Of §in L margin§ The §crossed out§ 224| MS:"Spare-Horses" which §crossed out and replaced above by§ that < > by that §crossed out and replaced above by§ the 225| MS:on: *1876:* on. 226| MS:This §crossed out and replaced above by§ Which *1876:* This

Had joined long since, paid scot and lot to,
As free and accepted "Bardotto."
The Bailiwick watched with no quiet eye
230 The outrage thus done to society,
And noted the advent especially
Of Pacchiarotto their fresh ally.

XIV

These Spare-Horses forthwith assembled:
Neighed words whereat citizens trembled
235 As oft as the chiefs, in the Square by
The Duomo, proposed a way whereby
The city were cured of disaster.
"Just substitute servant for master,
Make Poverty Wealth and Wealth Poverty,
240 Unloose Man from overt and covert tie,
And straight out of social confusion
True Order would spring!" Brave illusion—
Aims heavenly attained by means earthy!

XV

Off to these at full speed rushed our worthy,—
245 Brain practised and tongue no less tutored,
In argument's armour accoutred,—

228-32| MS:"Bardotto." / The < > eye / These outragers of society, / / < > ally. §insertion
note in L margin for last four lines inserted in R margin; marginal note that ¶ begins;
Arabic numeral inserted in R margin§   1876:eye / The outrage thus done to society,
1889a:Pacchiarotto §emended to§ Pacchiarotto §see Editorial Notes§   233| MS:This
§altered to§ These Company §crossed out and replaced above by two words§ Free Horses
1876:These Spare-Horses   234| MS:Spoke §crossed out and replaced above by§
Neighed—§dash crossed out§   235| MS:the Club §crossed out and replaced above by§
chiefs in   1876:chiefs, in   236| MS:Duomo proposed   1876:Duomo, proposed
237| MS:Their City < > disaster—   1876:The city < > disaster.   238| MS:"Just
§quotation marks in L margin§ substitute Servant for Master   1876:substitute servant for
master   241| MS:And §inserted above§ Straight < > of the §crossed out§   1876:And
straight   242| MS:illusion!—   1876:illusion—   243| MS:heavenly wrought out
§last two words crossed out and replaced above by§ attained   244| MS:So, §word
and comma crossed out§ off §altered to§ Off to these §last two words inserted above§
< > speed sets §last letter crossed out forming set§ our   1876:speed rushed our
245-46| MS:§illegible marking in L margin§   246| MS:arguments'   1876:argument's

Sprang forth, mounted rostrum and essayed
Proposals like those to which "Yes" said
So glibly each personage painted
250 O' the wall-side wherewith you're acquainted.
He harangued on the faults of the Bailiwick:
"Red soon were our State-candle's paly wick,
If wealth would become but interfluous,
Fill voids up with just the superfluous;
255 If ignorance gave way to knowledge
—Not pedantry picked up at college
From Doctors, Professors *et cætera*—
(*They say: 'kai ta loipa'*—like better a
Long Greek string of *kappas, taus, lambdas,*
260 Tacked on to the tail of each damned ass)—
No knowledge we want of this quality,
But knowledge indeed—practicality
Through insight's fine universality!
If you shout *'Bailiffs, out on ye all! Fie,*
265 *Thou Chief of our forces, Amalfi,*
Who shieldest the rogue and the clotpoll!'
If you pounce on and poke out, with what pole
I leave ye to fancy, our Siena's
Beast-litter of sloths and hyenas—"
270 (Whoever to scan this is ill able
Forgets the town's name's a dissyllable)
"If, this done, ye did—as ye might—place

247| MS:Stepped §last six letters crossed out and replaced by five letters
forming *Sprang*§ forth, mounted §crossed out and replaced above by two words§
rushed to rostrum *1876:*forth, mounted rostrum 249| MS:So lately §crossed out and
replaced above by§ glibly 250| MS:On the chamber §last two words crossed out and
replaced above by three words§ wall side where with which §crossed out§ *1876:*O' the
wall-side wherewith 251| MS:§line crossed out, at first to be replaced by 264-65, but
then original 251 restored with 264-65 being grouped with 266-273 and inserted between 263
and 274§ 252| MS:were the State-candle's *1876:*were our State-candle's
253| MS:become all- §word and hyphen crossed out and replaced above by§ but
254| MS:—Fill <> superfluous— *1876:*Fill <> superfluous; 257| MS:*cætera*
1876:cætera— 258| MS:say—"kai ta loipa" *1876:*say: 'kai ta loipa'
259| MS:Long §in L margin§ Greek appendage §crossed out and replaced above by§ string
260| MS:ass) *1876:*ass)— 261| MS:Not §last letter crossed out forming *No*§ <>
quality— §line inserted between 260-62§ *1876:*quality, 263| MS:universality—
*1876:*universality! 264-73| MS:Oh, Magistrates §last two words crossed out and replaced
above by four words and comma§ If you shout, Balliffs, out on ye all! Fie, / Thou Chief of

149

For once the right man in the right place,
If you listened to me . . ."

XVI

At which last "If"
275 There flew at his throat like a mastiff
One Spare-Horse—another and another!
Such outbreak of tumult and pother,
Horse-faces a-laughing and fleering,
Horse-voices a-mocking and jeering,
280 Horse-hands raised to collar the caitiff
Whose impudence ventured the late "If"—
That, had not fear sent Pacchiarotto
Off tramping, as fast as could trot toe,
Away from the scene of discomfiture—
285 Had he stood there stock-still in a dumb fit—sure
Am I he had paid in his person

---

our forces, Amalfi, / Who shieldest the faults of the Bailewick §last four words crossed out
and replaced below by three words§ rogue and clotpoll / If once §crossed out§ you would
§crossed out and replaced below by three words §pounce on and <> out with what pales
§last two words inserted below§ / <> fancy, our §inserted above§ <> / <> of sloths
§altered to§ Sloths <> hyenas / (Who ever <> / Forgets that the §followed by illegible
word, then last three words crossed out and replaced below by three words§ the town's
name's <> / If <> / <> right place, §word and comma inserted on slant below; last ten
lines inserted in R margin between 263-74§ *1876:* shout '*Baliffs* <> / / *clotpoll!*' / <>
out, with <> pole / / of sloths <> hyenas—" / (Whoever <> / / "If <> / /
274| MS:me". . . .   *1876:* me . . ."   274-75| MS:§marginal notes that ¶ begins§
276| MS:One §next word illegibly crossed out§ and §last word crossed out and replaced
above by two words and dash§ Free Horse—another, and another: *1876:* One
Spare-Horse—another and another!   277| MS:Such §beneath word illegibly crossed
out§ outcry §last three letters crossed out; hyphen and word inserted above§ -break and
§crossed out and replaced above by§ of <> pother   *1876:* pother,   278| MS:All-
§word and hyphen crossed out and replaced above by word and hyphen§
Horse-   279| MS:All §crossed out and replaced above by word and hypen§
Horse- <> jeering   *1876:* jeering,   280| MS:All §crossed out and replaced above by
word and hypen§ Horse-   281| MS:the late §crossed out, replaced above by word
illegibly crossed out, and then original reading restored§   282| MS:That had
1876: That, had   283| MS:Off scudding §crossed out and replaced above by§ tramping
as   *1876:* tramping, as   284| MS:of confusion §crossed out and replaced above by word
and dash§ discomfiture—   285| MS:Tis like §last two words crossed out and
replaced above by two words§ Am I §last two words crossed out§ like that for such a
prolusion §last six words crossed out and ten words inserted in R margin to
replace entire line§ Had <> fit,—sure   *1876:* fit—sure   286| MS:He
forthwith §last two words crossed out and replaced above by three words§ Am I he

150

Till his mother might fail to know her son,
Though she gazed on him never so wistful,
In the figure so tattered and tristful.
290 Each mouth full of curses, each fist full
Of cuffings—behold, Pacchiarotto,
The pass which thy project has got to,
Of trusting, nigh ashes still hot—tow!
(The paraphrase—which I much need—is
295 From Horace *"per ignes incedis."*)

XVII

Right and left did he dash helter-skelter
In agonized search of a shelter.
No purlieu so blocked and no alley
So blind as allowed him to rally
300 His spirits and see—nothing hampered
His steps if he trudged and not scampered
Up here and down there in a city
That's all ups and downs, more the pity
For folk who would outrun the constable.
305 At last he stopped short at the one stable
And sure place of refuge that's offered
Humanity. Lately was coffered

287| MS:Till his §crossed out, replaced above by perhaps *no,* and then original
reading restored§ mother failed §altered to§ fail to know §last three words crossed out and
replaced above by *might* and two or three words illegibly crossed out, then *failed to know*
restored§ *1876:* mother might fail to   288| MS:Did §crossed out and replaced in L
margin by§ Had she gazed §altered to§ gaze *1876:* Though she gazed   292| MS:The
end §crossed out and replaced above by two words§ pass which thy beginning §crossed out
and replaced above by§ mad §crossed out and replaced by§ project <> to! §exclamation
mark deleted and replaced by comma§   293| MS:Of §over *Or*§ bringing §crossed out
and replaced above by two words§ trusting, nigh—to ashes §over illegible word§ *1876:* nigh
ashes   294-95| MS:(The <> is / From Horace *"per* <> *incedis."*) §two lines added in
R margin, inserted between 293-96§ *1876:* From Horace *'per* <> *incedis.'*) *1889a:* From
Horace *"per* <> *incedis."*)   295-96| MS:§marginal note that ¶ begins; Arabic numeral
inserted in R margin§   296| MS:he rush helter-skelter *1876:* he dash helter-skelter
297| MS:shelter— *1876:* shelter.   300| MS:see that nought §last two words crossed out
and replaced above by dash and word§ —nothing §dash crossed out§ *1876:* see—nothing
301| MS:scampered— §dash crossed out§   303| MS:downs—more *1876:* downs, more
304| MS:folks <> constable— *1876:* constable. *1889a:* folk   305| MS:—Until
§dash in L margin crossed out§ he *1876:* At last he   307| MS:Humanity.
Lately had been §last two words crossed out and replaced above by§ was

151

A corpse in its sepulchre, situate
By St. John's Observance. "Habituate
310   Thyself to the strangest of bedfellows,
And, kicked by the live, kiss the dead fellows!"
So Misery counselled the craven.
At once he crept safely to haven
Through a hole left unbricked in the structure.
315   Ay, Misery, in have you tucked your
Poor client and left him conterminous
With—pah!—the thing fetid and verminous!
(I gladly would spare you the detail,
But History writes what I retail.)

XVIII

320   Two days did he groan in his domicile:
"Good Saints, set me free and I promise I'll
Abjure all ambition of preaching
Change, whether to minds touched by teaching
—The smooth folk of fancy, mere figments
325   Created by plaster and pigments,—
Or to minds that receive with such rudeness
Dissuasion from pride, greed and lewdness,
—The rough folk of fact, life's true specimens
Of mind—'*haud in posse sed esse mens*'

308| MS:its tomb §crossed out and replaced by§ sepulchre   309| MS:By Saint *1876:*By
St.   310| MS:Yourself §first four letters crossed out and replaced by *Thy* forming
Thyself§   312| MS:Did Misery counsel the craven: *1876:*So Misery counseled
the craven. *1889a:*counselled   318| MS:detail: *1876:*detail,   319| MS:writes
what §crossed out and replaced above by perhaps *and* and then original reading
restored§   319-20| MS:§marginal note that ¶ begins§   320| MS:domicile,
*1876:*domicile: 321| MS:"good §inserted above two words illegibly
crossed out, *good* crossed out and then restored with upper case§ < > me §followed
by perhaps *but* inserted above and then crossed out§   322| MS:Abjure the §crossed out
and replaced above by§ all   323| MS:As well to those §last four words crossed out and
replaced above by five words§ A §crossed out§ change §altered to§ Change—whether to
minds < > by my §crossed out§ *1876:*Change, whether   324| MS:fancy, the §crossed
out and replaced above by§ mere   326| MS:As those who §last three words
crossed out and replaced above by three words§ Or minds that *1876:*Or to minds
327| MS:Objections to pride, greed, and lewdness— *1876:*Dissuasion from pride, greed
and lewdness,   328| MS:The < > fact, the §crossed out and replaced above by§ life's
1876:—The   329| MS:mind: "*not* §crossed out and replaced above by§ *haud* < > *sed*
§over illegible erasure; illegible erasure above§ < > *mens*." *1876:*mind— '*haud* < > *mens*'

330　As it was, is, and shall be for ever
　　　Despite of my utmost endeavour.
　　　O live foes I thought to illumine,
　　　Henceforth lie untroubled your gloom in!
　　　I need my own light, every spark, as
335　I couch with this sole friend—a carcase!"

XIX

　　　Two days thus he maundered and rambled;
　　　Then, starved back to sanity, scrambled
　　　From out his receptacle loathsome.
　　　"A spectre!"—declared upon oath some
340　Who saw him emerge and (appalling
　　　To mention) his garments a-crawling
　　　With plagues far beyond the Egyptian.
　　　He gained, in a state past description,
　　　A convent of monks, the Observancy.

XX

345　Thus far is a fact: I reserve fancy
　　　For Fancy's more proper employment:
　　　And now she waves wing with enjoyment,
　　　To tell ye how preached the Superior

330| MS:is and <> forever　1876:for ever　1889a:is, and　332| MS:O minds—which
I <> illumine—　1876:O live foes I <> illumine,　333| MS:in,　1876:in!
335| MS:with my sole　1876:with this sole　335-36| MS:§marginal note that ¶
begins; Arabic numeral inserted between lines§　336| MS:rambled:　1876:rambled;
338| MS:loathsome—　1876:loathsome.　339| MS:spectre"—declared
1876:spectre!"—declared　340| MS:and—appalling　1876:and (appalling
341| MS:mention, §next word, perhaps *with*, crossed out and replaced below by§ his
1876:mention) his　342| MS:With horrors §crossed out and replaced above by two
words§ plagues far <> Egyptian,　1876:Egyptian.　343| MS:And §crossed out and
replaced above by§ To gain <> description,　1876:He gained <> description
1889a:description §emended to§ description, §see Editorial Notes§　344-45| MS:§marginal
note that ¶ begins§　345| MS:is mere §crossed out and replaced above by§ a §illegible
word above next word§ <> reserve §followed by illegible erasure§　347| MS:Let fancy
§last two words crossed out and replaced above by three words§ And now she wave §altered
to§ waves <> enjoyment.　1876:enjoyment,　348| MS:Importuning you §last two
words crossed out and replaced above by five words§ For fancy to tell ye §first two of these
five words crossed out§ to §altered to§ To §next word above word illegibly crossed out§

153

When somewhat our painter's exterior
350 Was sweetened. He needed (no mincing
The matter) much soaking and rincing,
Nay, rubbing with drugs odoriferous,
Till, rid of his garments pestiferous
And robed by the help of the Brotherhood
355 In odds and ends,—this gown and t'other hood,—
His empty inside first well-garnished,—
He delivered a tale round, unvarnished.

XXI

"Ah, Youth!" ran the Abbot's admonishment,
"Thine error scarce moves my astonishment.
360 For—why shall I shrink from asserting?—
Myself have had hopes of converting
The foolish to wisdom, till, sober,
My life found its May grow October.
I talked and I wrote, but, one morning,
365 Life's Autumn bore fruit in this warning:
'Let tongue rest, and quiet thy quill be!
Earth is earth and not heaven, and ne'er will be.'
Man's work is to labour and leaven—

350| MS:sweetened—he *1876:*sweetened. He   351| MS:rincing
*1876:*rincing,   352| MS:And §crossed out and replaced above by word and comma§
Nay,   353| MS:his garments §crossed out and replaced above by two words, the first of
which appears to be *tatter,* the second being illegible; these two words are replaced below
by§ garment *1876:* garments   357-58| MS:§marginal note that ¶ begins; Arabic
numeral inserted in R margin§   358| MS:"Ah, young man" §last word crossed out and
ster attached to *young* forming *youngster,* which is then crossed out and replaced above by
one word, comma, and quotation mark§ youth," so might §inserted above§ run the
admonishment *1876:*"Ah, Youth!" so < > admonishment, *1889a:*"Ah, Youth!" ran the
Abbot's admonishment,   359| MS:moves to §crossed out and replaced above by§ my
360| MS:My age §last two words crossed out and replaced above by word and dash§ For—
361| MS:Myself have §inserted above§ had such §crossed out§   362| MS:wisdom—
till sober *1876:* wisdom, till, sober   363| MS:grown §altered to§ grow
364| MS:wrote till, one *1876:*wrote, but, one   365| MS:The Autumn *1876:* Life's
Autumn   366| MS:Friend, tie up §followed by illegible word; last four words
crossed out and replaced above by quotation mark, four words, and dash§ "Let thy
§subsequently crossed out§ tongue rest,—and quiet §next word illegibly crossed out§ thy
§crossed out and then restored§ quill be! *1876:*'Let < > rest, and < > be!'
367| MS:Earth is earth and not heaven, and ne'er will be. *1876:Earth is earth and
not heaven, and ne'er will be.'*   368| MS:leaven *1876:* leaven—

As best he may—earth here with heaven;
370 'Tis work for work's sake that he's needing:
Let him work on and on as if speeding
Work's end, but not dream of succeeding!
Because if success were intended,
Why, heaven would begin ere earth ended.
375 A Spare-Horse? Be rather a thill-horse,
Or—what's the plain truth—just a mill-horse!
Earth's a mill where we grind and wear mufflers:
A whip awaits shirkers and shufflers
Who slacken their pace, sick of lugging
380 At what don't advance for their tugging.
Though round goes the mill, we must still post
On and on as if moving the mill-post.
So, grind away, mouth-wise and pen-wise,
Do all that we can to make men wise!
385 And if men prefer to be foolish,
Ourselves have proved horse-like not mulish:
Sent grist, a good sackful, to hopper,
And worked as the Master thought proper.
Tongue I wag, pen I ply, who am Abbot;

369| MS:may, earth <> heaven— *1876:* may—earth <> heaven;   370| MS:for the
§crossed out§ <> needing, *1876:* needing: 372| MS:The §crossed out§ work—
§altered to§ Work's §dash crossed out§ end, §word and comma inserted above§ <>
succeeding, *1876:* succeeding!   374| MS:Here §crossed out and replaced above by one
word and comma§ Why,   375-76| MS:A Free-horse <> thill-horse: / Or, §next word,
perhaps *rather,* crossed out and replaced above by§ what's <> truth,—just a mill-horse!
§two lines in R margin§ *1876:* A Spare-Horse <> / Or—what's <> truth—just
377| MS:We grind in a mill §last five words crossed out and replaced above by six words§
Earth's a mill where we grind   379| MS:pace sick *1876:* pace, sick
380| MS:tugging: *1876:* tugging.   382| MS:On and on §last three words inserted
above§ As if we were §last two words crossed out§ *1876:* on as   383| MS:away,
tongue-wise §first half of word crossed out and replaced above by *mouth-* forming
mouth-wise§   384| MS:wise *1876:* wise!   385| MS:to live §crossed out and replaced
above by§ be foolishly, §last two letters crossed out forming *foolish*§   386| MS:At least
we worked §last four words crossed out and replaced above by three words§ Ourselves have
proved <> mulishly: §last two letters crossed out forming *mulish:*§   387| MS:Have
§crossed out§ sent §altered to§ Sent <> a good §inserted above§   388| MS:proper:
1876: proper.   389| MS:ply—who <> Abbot: *1876:* ply, who <> Abbot;

390   Stick thou, Son, to daub-brush and dab-pot!
       But, soft! I scratch hard on the scab hot?
       Though cured of thy plague, there may linger
       A pimple I fray with rough finger?
       So soon could my homily transmute
395   Thy brass into gold? Why, the man's mute!"

                              XXII

       "Ay, Father, I'm mute with admiring
       How Nature's indulgence untiring
       Still bids us turn deaf ear to Reason's
       Best rhetoric—clutch at all seasons
400   And hold fast to what's proved untenable!
       Thy maxim is—Man's not amenable
       To argument: whereof by consequence—
       Thine arguments reach me: a non-sequence!
       Yet blush not discouraged, O Father!
405   I stand unconverted, the rather
       That nowise I need a conversion.
       No live man (I cap thy assertion)

---

³⁹⁰| MS:And §in L margin and crossed out§ Stick, you, son, §word
and comma inserted above§ to the §crossed out§ paint-brush and dab-pot!". . .
*1876:*Stick, thou, Son < > dab-pot! B's *1876:*Stick thou < > to daub-brush and
³⁹⁰⁻⁹¹| MS:§interlinear numeral denoting start of new section crossed out and space between
lines closed by R marginal note§   ³⁹¹| MS:Ah, Father, §last two words and commas
crossed out and replaced above by three words§ But where you §last two words crossed
out and replaced above by two words§ soft—I scratch softly §crossed out and replaced
above by§ of §crossed out and replaced by two words§ hard on < > hot! *1876:*soft! I < >
hot?   ³⁹²| MS:I'm healed §last two words crossed out and replaced above by two
words§ Though cured of my hives §last two words crossed out and replaced above by two
words§ your plague, but §crossed out§ there may §inserted above§ lingers §last letter crossed
out forming *linger*§ *1876:*of thy plague   ³⁹³| MS:A scar §followed by perhaps *which*§
you §last three words crossed out and replaced above by three words§ pimple yet, I §*yet* then
crossed out§ < > fingers— §last letter crossed out forming *finger*—§ *1876:*pimple I < >
finger?   ³⁹⁵| MS:Thy §crossed out and replaced above by§ Your brass *1876:*Thy brass
³⁹⁵⁻⁹⁶| MS:§marginal note that ¶ begins§   ³⁹⁶| MS:"Ay, Father I'm *1876:*"Ay, Father,
I'm   ³⁹⁹| MS:rhetoric—take at *1876:*rhetoric—clutch at   ⁴⁰⁰| MS:to pleasure
untenable. *1876:*to what's proved untenable!   ⁴⁰²| MS:whereof the §crossed out and
replaced above by§ by   ⁴⁰³| MS:me—a *1876:*me: a   ⁴⁰⁴| MS:Yet blush §inserted
above§ be not < > Father: *1876:*blush not < > Father!   ⁴⁰⁵| MS:stand
unconvinced §*inc* crossed out and replaced above by *ert* forming *unconverted*§ now §crossed
out§—the *1876:*unconverted, the   ⁴⁰⁶| MS:conversion: *1876:*conversion.
⁴⁰⁷| MS:man—I < > assertion— *1876:*man (I < > assertion)

By argument ever could take hold
Of me. 'Twas the dead thing, the clay-cold,
410 Which grinned *'Art thou so in a hurry*
That out of warm light thou must skurry
And join me down here in the dungeon
Because, above, one's Jack and one—John,
One's swift in the race, one—a hobbler,
415 *One's a crowned king, and one—a capped cobbler,*
Rich and poor, sage and fool, virtuous, vicious?
Why complain? Art thou so unsuspicious
That all's for an hour of essaying
Who's fit and who's unfit for playing
420 *His part in the after-construction*
—Heaven's Piece whereof Earth's the Induction?
Things rarely go smooth at Rehearsal.
Wait patient the change universal,
And act, and let act, in existence!
425 *For, as thou art clapped hence or hissed hence,*
Thou hast thy promotion or otherwise.
And why must wise thou have thy brother wise
Because in rehearsal thy cue be
To shine by the side of a booby?
430 *No polishing garnet to ruby!*

409| MS:me—'twas *1876:*me. 'Twas   410| MS:That grinned *1876:*Which grinned
410-45| MS:grinned "Art §double quotation mark altered to single quotation mark§
1876:§all words from single quotation mark on are in italics§   415| MS:crowned King
and *1876:crowned king 1889a:king,* and   416| MS:poor, fool and sage §last three
words transposed to§ sage and fool,—virtuous,—vicious,— §word inserted below *vicious* and
then illegibly crossed out§ *1876:fool, virtuous, vicious?*   417| MS:Whereof folks
complain—unsuspicious §line inserted between 416-18§ *1876:Why complain? Art thou so*
unsuspicious   418| MS:And §crossed out and replaced in L margin by§ That
420| MS:the After-production *1876:the after-production*   421| MS:—Heaven's true
Piece <> Induction. *1876:—Heaven's Piece <> Induction?*   422| MS:at Rehearsal:
1876:at Rehearsal.   423| MS:Look out for §last three words crossed out and replaced
above by two words§ Wait patient <> universal— *1876:universal,*   424| MS:in
Existence! *1876:in existence!*   425| MS:hence *1876:hence,*   426| MS:Depends thy
<> otherwise; *1876:Thou has thy <> otherwise.*   428| MS:If §crossed out; next word
illegibly crossed out and replaced above by§ now §crossed out§ whereas the rehearsal §last
three words crossed out and replaced above by two words§ Because in §*rehearsal* restored§
429| MS:To shine by the side of §last five words crossed out and replaced above by uncertain
number of words illegibly crossed out and then original five words restored§

157

All's well that ends well—through Art's magic.
Some end, whether comic or tragic,
The Artist has purposed, be certain!
Explained at the fall of the curtain—
435 *In showing thy wisdom at odds with*
That folly: he tries men and gods with
No problem for weak wits to solve meant,
But one worth such Author's evolvement.
So, back nor disturb play's production
440 *By giving thy brother instruction*
To throw up his fool's-part allotted!
Lest haply thyself prove besotted
When stript, for thy pains, of that costume
Of sage, which has bred the imposthume
445 *I prick to relieve thee of,—Vanity!'*

XXIII

"So, Father, behold me in sanity!
I'm back to the palette and mahlstick:
And as for Man—let each and all stick
To what was prescribed them at starting!
450 Once planted as fools—no departing
From folly one inch, *sæculorum*
In sæcula! Pass me the jorum,

431| MS:magic: *1876:magic.* *1889a:magic* §emended to§ *magic.* §see Editorial Notes§
432| MS:Such §crossed out and replaced above by§ Some < > tragic *1876:tragic,*
433| MS:The Artist intended §crossed out and replaced above by two words§ has
purposed < > certain— *1876:certain!* 436| MS:he treats §crossed out and replaced
above by§ tries 437| MS:meant— *1876:meant,* 438| MS:one—worth such
§crossed out and replaced above by *the* and then original restored§ *1876:one worth*
439| MS:disturb his §crossed out and replaced above by§ play's 441| MS:He §crossed
out and replaced in L margin by§ To < > up the fool's-part allotted— *1876:up his*
fool's-part allotted! 443| MS:stript for the §altered to§ thy pains of *1876:stript,*
for < > pains, of 444| MS:Of Sage *1876:Of sage* 445| MS:of Vanity."
§double quotation mark changed to single quotation mark§ *1876:of,—Vanity!'*
445-46| MS:§marginal note that ¶ begins§ 446| MS:sanity. *1876:* sanity!
447| MS:the paint brush and mahlstick *1876:* paint-brush < > mahlstick: *1889a:* the
palette and 448| MS:for mankind— §crossed out and replaced above by§ men—
let them §crossed out and replaced above by two words§ each and *1876:* for Man
449| MS:prescribed each §crossed out and replaced above by§ them < > starting:
1876: starting! *1889a:* starting §emended to§ starting! §see Editorial Notes§

158

And push me the platter—my stomach
Retains, through its fasting, still some ache—
455   And then, with your kind *Benedicite,*
Good-bye!"

XXIV

I have told with simplicity
My tale, dropped those harsh analytics,
And tried to content you, my critics,
Who greeted my early uprising!
460   I knew you through all the disguising,
Droll dogs, as I jumped up, cried "Heyday!
This Monday is—what else but May-day?
And these in the drabs, blues and yellows,
Are surely the privileged fellows.
465   So, saltbox and bones, tongs and bellows,"
(I threw up the window) "your pleasure?"

XXV

Then he who directed the measure—
An old friend—put leg forward nimbly,
"We critics as sweeps out your chimbly!

---

^{456|} MS:Good-bye!" §marginal note that ¶ begins§ I have told §crossed out and replaced
above by word illegibly crossed out and then *told* restored§   ^{458|} MS:to repay
§crossed out and replaced above by§ content   ^{459|} MS:uprising: *1876:* uprising!
^{460|} MS:disguising— *1876:* disguising,   ^{461|} MS:You §crossed out§ droll §altered
to§ Droll < > as first §crossed out§ up I jumped §last three words transposed to§ I
jumped up—cried §inserted above§ "Hey day! *1876:* up, cried "Heyday *1889a:* cried
"Heyday!   ^{462|} *1876:* but May-day *1889a:* but May-day?   ^{463|} MS:And §crossed
out and replaced above by word illegibly crossed out and then *And* restored§ who play
§inserted below followed by word illegibly crossed out; *play* crossed out§ < > the reds, blues
< > yellows— *1876:* the drabs, blues < > yellows. *1889a:* yellows,   ^{464|} MS:fellows!
1876: fellows *1889a:* fellows.   ^{465|} MS:Ah, saltbox < > tongs— §dash crossed out§ < >
bellows—" §between 464-66§ *1876:* So, saltbox < > bellows!" *1889a:* bellows,"
^{466|} MS:window) "Your pleasure?" *1876:* pleasure?' *1889a:* window) "your pleasure?"
^{466-67|} MS:§marginal note that ¶ begins§   ^{467|} MS:measure *1876:* measure—
^{468|} MS:—An < > puts < > nimbly *1876:* An < > put < > nimbly,   ^{469|} MS:"With
§crossed out and replaced above by§ 'Tis we, sir, as §over perhaps *all*§ cleans
§crossed out and replaced above by§ sweeps *1876:* "We critics as

159

470   Much soot to remove from your flue, sir!
Who spares coal in kitchen an't you, sir!
And neighbours complain it's no joke, sir,
—You ought to consume your own smoke, sir!"

XXVI

      Ah, rogues, but my housemaid suspects you—
475   Is confident oft she detects you
In bringing more filth into my house
Than ever you found there! I'm pious
However: 'twas God made you dingy
And me—with no need to be stingy
480   Of soap, when 'tis sixpence the packet.
So, dance away, boys, dust my jacket,
Bang drum and blow fife—ay, and rattle
Your brushes, for that's half the battle!
Don't trample the grass,—hocus-pocus
485   With grime my Spring snowdrop and crocus,—
And, what with your rattling and tinkling,
Who knows but you give me an inkling
How music sounds, thanks to the jangle

---

⁴⁷⁰⁻⁷³| MS:Much <> flue, Sir, / <> you, Sir, / <> joke, Sir, / <> smoke, Sir!" §four lines in R margin, inserted between 469-74§ *1876:*flue sir! / <> you, sir! / <> joke, sir, / <> smoke, sir!" *1889a:*flue, sir!   ⁴⁷³⁻⁷⁴| MS:§marginal note that section begins§ ⁴⁷⁴| MS:§no ¶ indentation§ "Ah, rogue, *1876:*§¶ indentation§ Ah, rogues, ⁴⁷⁵| MS:confident that §crossed out and replaced above by§ oft <> you §partly over illegible erasure§   ⁴⁷⁷| MS:there! §perhaps exclamation mark over colon§ ⁴⁷⁸| MS:However;—twas §inserted above§ God makes §altered to§ made you both §crossed out§ *1876:*However: 'twas   ⁴⁷⁹| MS:And clean: such I make myself §last five words crossed out; next word illegibly crossed out and these six words replaced above by seven words§ me—with no need to be stingy   ⁴⁸⁰| MS:With §crossed out and replaced above by§ Of soap's §last letter and apostrophe crossed out forming *soap*§ at a shilling §last three words crossed out and replaced above by comma and three words§ , when tis sixpence <> packet. *1876:*'tis <> packet.   ⁴⁸¹| MS:dust your §crossed out and replaced above by§ each §crossed out and replaced by§ the jacket, *1876:*dust my jacket,   ⁴⁸³| MS:brushes—for <> battle— §first letter probably over illegible erasure§ *1876:*brushes, for <> battle!   ⁴⁸⁴| MS:(Don't <> the beds, §word and comma crossed out and replaced above by word and comma-dash§ grass,— *1876:*Don't ⁴⁸⁵| MS:my fresh §crossed out and replaced above by§ Spring snow-drop <> crocus!) *1876:*crocus,— *1889a:*snowdrop   ⁴⁸⁶| MS:And so with <> tinkling *1876:*And, what <> tinkling,   ⁴⁸⁸| MS:What music may be— §last two words and dash crossed out and replaced above by three words§ is, thanks to the true §crossed out§ *1876:*How music sounds, thanks

Of regular drum and triangle?
490 Whereby, tap-tap, chink-chink, 'tis proven
I break rule as bad as Beethoven.
"That chord now—a groan or a grunt is't?
Schumann's self was no worse contrapuntist.
No ear! or if ear, so tough-gristled—
495 He thought that he sung while he whistled!"

XXVII

So, this time I whistle, not sing at all,
My story, the largess I fling at all
And every the rough there whose *aubade*
Did its best to amuse me,—nor *so* bad!
500 Take my thanks, pick up largess, and scamper
Off free, ere your mirth gets a damper!
You've Monday, your one day, your fun-day,
While mine is a year that's all Sunday.
I've seen you, times—who knows how many?—
505 Dance in here, strike up, play the zany,
Make mouths at the tenant, hoot warning

489| MS:triangle *1876:* triangle? 490| MS:Where by tap, tap, tap, tap, §last two
words and comma crossed out and replaced above by word and comma§ chink-chink,
1876: Whereby, tap-tap 491| MS:I know of no more than §last five words crossed out
and replaced above by five words§ break rule as bad as 492–93| MS:"That <> is't? /
Schumann's <> contrapuntist. §two lines in R margin, inserted between 491-94§
494| MS:ear,—of §crossed out§ <> eared, §last two letters crossed out forming *ear*, which is
crossed out and replaced above by§ so *1876:* ear! or 495| MS:sung—while he §over
I§ *1876:* sung while 496| MS:§no ¶ indentation§ *1876:* §¶ indentation§
496| MS:time I've §apostrophe and last two letters crossed out forming I§ whistled §last
letter crossed out forming *whistle*§ <> sung §altered to§ sing <> all; §semi-colon altered
to comma-dash§ *1876:* all, 497| MS:The story,—The <> I've §apostrophe and
last two letters crossed out forming I§ flung §altered to§ fling <> all §perhaps followed
by a full stop§ *1876:* My story, the <> all 498| MS:aubade *1876:* *aubade*
499| MS:amuse— §dash crossed out§ me— §word and dash inserted above§ nor was §crossed
out§ *1876:* me,—nor 501| MS:free—ere <> damper: *1876:* free, ere <> damper!
502| MS:You §apostrophe and two letters inserted above forming *You've*§ have but your
May day—this Monday: §last seven words and colon crossed out and replaced above by six
words and full stop§ Monday, your one day, your fun-day. *1876:* fun-day, 505| MS:in
and §crossed out and replaced above by word and comma§ here, <> zany *1876:* zany,
506| MS:the Master—hoot *1876:* the Tenant, hoot *1889a:* the tenant

You'll find him decamped next May-morning;
Then scuttle away, glad to 'scape hence
With—kicks? no, but laughter and ha'pence!
510 Mine's freehold, by grace of the grand Lord
Who lets out the ground here,—my landlord:
To him I pay quit-rent—devotion;
Nor hence shall I budge, I've a notion,
Nay, here shall my whistling and singing
515 Set all his street's echoes a-ringing
Long after the last of your number
Has ceased my front-court to encumber
While, treading down rose and ranunculus,
You *Tommy-make-room-for-your-Uncle* us!
520 Troop, all of you—man or homunculus,
Quick march! for Xanthippe, my housemaid,
If once on your pates she a souse made
With what, pan or pot, bowl or *skoramis*
First comes to her hand—things were more amiss!
525 I would not for worlds be your place in—
Recipient of slops from the basin!
You, Jack-in-the-Green, leaf-and-twiggishness
Won't save a dry thread on your priggishness!
While as for Quilp-Hop-o'-my-thumb there,
530 Banjo-Byron that twangs the strum-strum there—
He'll think, as the pickle he curses,

507| MS:find me decamped <> May-morning—   *1876:*find him
decamped <> May-morning;   508| MS:away—glad   *1876:*away, glad
509| MS:no,—but   *1876:*no, but   510| MS:Mine's §over illegible erasure§
512| MS:devotion   *1876:*devotion;   517| MS:encumber,   *1876:*encumber
518-20| MS:While <> ranunculus / You— §dash over two-dot ellipsis§
Tommy-make-room-for-your-Uncle <> / §first word illegibly crossed out§ all <>
homunculus, §three lines between 518-22, in R margin§   *1876:*ranunculus, / You
Tommy-make-room-for-your-Uncle <> / Troop, all   521| MS:march, for
Xantippe <> housemaid   *1876:*march! for Xanthippe <> housemaid,
523| MS:what, in the way of utensil §last five words crossed out and replaced above by six
words§ pan or pot, bowl or—skoramis   *1876:*or *skoramis*   524| MS:hand . . Pacchia's
pencil §last two words crossed out and replaced by four words§ things were more amiss!
*1876:*hand—things   526| MS:basin—   *1876:*basin!   527| MS:My
Jack-in-the-Green   *1876:*You, Jack-in-the-Green   528| MS:save from the pickle your
*1876:*save a dry thread on your   529| MS:for you, §word and comma crossed out and
replaced above by§ my Hop-o'-my-thumb   *1876:*for Quilp-Hop-o'-my-thumb
530| MS:Banjo-Byron §first half of word is above illegible erasure§

I've discharged on his pate his own verses!
"Dwarfs are saucy," says Dickens: so, sauced in
Your own sauce, . . .[1]

XXVIII

535   But, back to my Knight of the Pencil,
Dismissed to his fresco and stencil!
Whose story—begun with a chuckle,
And throughout timed by raps of the knuckle,—
To small enough purpose were studied
540   If it ends with crown cracked or nose bloodied.
Come, critics,—not shake hands, excuse me!
But—say have you grudged to amuse me
This once in the forty-and-over

[1] No, please! For
      "Who would be satirical
      On a thing so very small?"—PRINTER'S DEVIL.

532| MS:I've §next three or four words illegibly crossed out and replaced above by word illegibly crossed out and replaced by§ discharged §followed by three words inserted above§ on his pate his own §last two words crossed out and replaced by§ with §crossed out and followed by word illegibly crossed out, *his own* then being restored§ verses— *1876:* verses!
533-34| MS:As if they should touch §last two words crossed out and replaced above by probably one word illegibly crossed out§ my §crossed out and replaced above by§ an utensil! §exclamation mark crossed out§ / Of mine—do thy slops such immense ill! §no footnoot in MS§ *1876:* "Dwarfs are saucy," says Dickens: so sauced in / Your own sauce, . . .* §note appears at bottom of page§ B's *1876:* §*Dickens* underlined, X in R margin designating footnote, and the following note at bottom of page§ Nay, Homer $\theta\acute{\alpha}\rho\sigma\sigma$ (αol:$\theta\acute{\epsilon}\rho\sigma\sigma$) inde $\theta\epsilon\zeta\sigma\acute{\iota}\tau\eta s$. §An explanation of this curious combination of languages follows: αol is clearly B's abbreviation for *Aeolic*. $\theta\epsilon\rho\sigma\sigma$ is Aeolic for the Greek noun $\theta\acute{\alpha}\rho\sigma\sigma$, which means *courage*, but does sometimes have the connotation of audacity (or sauciness!). The Latin adverb *inde* means "hence" or "from which (is derived)," and the proper name $\theta\epsilon\rho\sigma\acute{\iota}\tau\eta s$ means "the bold one" and is clearly a derivative of the Aeolic/Greek cited previously.§ *1889a:* sauce, . . .[1]
535| MS:§no ¶ indentation§ <> the Pencil,—§dash crossed out§ *1876:* §¶ indentation§   536| MS:My hero of §last three words crossed out§ Dismissed <> stencil— §between 536-38§ *1876:* stencil!   538| MS:And ended to a §last four words crossed out and replaced above by three words§ And timed throughout §last two words transposed to§ throughout timed raps <> knuckled, §last letter crossed out forming *knuckle*§ *1876:* timed by raps <> knuckle,—   540| MS:Did it end <> bloodied! *1876:* If it ends <> bloodied.   541| MS:Come back and . . not *1876:* Come, critics,—not
542| MS:But say *1876:* But—say   543| MS:forty-and over *1876:* forty-and-over

Long years since you trampled my clover
545 And scared from my house-eaves each sparrow
I never once harmed by that arrow
Of song, *karterotaton belos,*
(Which Pindar declares the true *melos*)
I was forging and filing and finishing,
550 And no whit my labours diminishing
Because, though high up in a chamber
Where none of your kidney may clamber
Your hullabaloo would approach me?
Was it "grammar" wherein you would "coach" me—
555 You,—pacing in even that paddock
Of language allotted you *ad hoc,*
With a clog at your fetlocks,—you—scorners
Of me free of all its four corners?
Was it "clearness of words which convey thought?"
560 Ay, if words never needed enswathe aught
But ignorance, impudence, envy
And malice—what word-swathe would then vie
With yours for a clearness crystalline?
But had you to put in one small line
565 Some thought big and bouncing—as noddle

545| MS:house eaves *1876:* house-eaves   546| MS:That §crossed
out and replaced above by§ I never was shot §last two words crossed out and
replaced above by three words§ have I harmed §*I* crossed out§ *1876:* never once harmed
547| MS:*belos*— *1876:belos,*   548| MS:Which < > *melos,* *1876:* (Which < >
melos)   550| MS:And §in L margin§ No *1876:* And no   551| MS:Because, since
high *1876:* Because, though high   552| MS:You §over illegible erasure§ were not
§last three words crossed out and replaced above by three words§ Where none of
553| MS:Your hullabalooing §last three letters crossed out forming *hullabaloo*§ would §next
word illegibly crossed out and replaced above by§ approach me;— *1876:* me?
554| MS:grammar you offered to teach me— §last four words crossed out and replaced above
by five words§ wherein you would "coach" me— *1876:* "grammar"   555| MS:You
§crossed out and replaced above by§ Who—even in that bit of the paddock
1876: You,—pacing in even that paddock   556| MS:Of §over *The*§ < > *hoc* *1876:hoc,*
557| MS:Pace back and forward, proud §last four words crossed out and replaced above by
five words§ still to and fro, forsooth, scorners *1876:* With a clog at your
fetlocks,—you—scorners   558| MS:Of those who explore §last two words crossed out
and replaced above by three words§ free of all *1876:* Of me free   560| MS:Ay—if
1876: Ay, if   563| MS:for revealment is §last two words crossed out and
replaced above by three words§ a clearness crystalline?   565| MS:Some §over
illegible erasure§ < > bouncing—no noddle *1876:* bouncing—as noddle

Of goose, born to cackle and waddle
And bite at man's heel as goose-wont is,
Never felt plague its puny *os frontis*—
You'd know, as you hissed, spat and sputtered,
570   Clear cackle is easily uttered!

XXIX

Lo, I've laughed out my laugh on this mirth-day!
Beside, at week's end, dawns my birth-day,
That *hebdome, hieron emar*—
(More things in a day than you deem are!)
575   —*Tei gar Apollona chrusaora*
Egeinato Leto. So, gray or ray
Betide me, six days hence, I'm vexed here
By no sweep, that's certain, till next year!
"Vexed?"—roused from what else were insipid ease!
580   Leave snoring a-bed to Pheidippides!
We'll up and work! won't we, Euripides?

566| MS:goose born *1876:*goose, born   568| MS:Ever felt crush §crossed out and replaced above by§ plague *1876:*Never felt   569| MS:He'd know as he hissed *1876:*You'd know, as you hissed   570| MS:Clear quack-quack is *1876:*Clear "quack-quack" is B's *1876:*Clear cackle is   571| MS:§no ¶ indentation§ *1876:*§¶ indentation§   572| MS:Besides <> end, is my *1876:*Beside <> end, dawns my   574| MS:—(More *1876:*(More   576| MS:*Egeinato Leto:* so *1876:Egeinato Leto.* So   578| MS:year! / §Below at R§ L.D.I.E. Apr. 15. '76. May 1, '76. §crossed out§   579-81| *1876:*§lines added§

AT THE "MERMAID"

The figure that thou here seest . . . Tut!
Was it for gentle Shakespeare put?
        B. JONSON. (*Adapted.*)

I

I—"Next Poet?" No, my hearties,
    I nor am nor fain would be!
Choose your chiefs and pick your parties,
    Not one soul revolt to me!
5   I, forsooth, sow song-sedition?
        I, a schism in verse provoke?
    I, blown up by bard's ambition,
        Burst—your bubble-king? You joke.

II

Come, be grave! The sherris mantling
10   Still about each mouth, mayhap,
Breeds you insight—just a scantling—
        Brings me truth out—just a scrap.
Look and tell me! Written, spoken,
        Here's my life-long work: and where
15 —Where's your warrant or my token
        I'm the dead king's son and heir?

III

Here's my work: does work discover—
    What was rest from work—my life?
Did I live man's hater, lover?
20   Leave the world at peace, at strife?

AT THE "MERMAID"   Epigraph| MS:It was §last two words crossed out and
replaced in left margin by two words§ *Was* it <> put. B. Jonson. (Adapted.)   *1876:* Was
<> put? / B. Jonson. (*Adapted.*)   1| MS:I—'next Poet'? No   *1876:* I—"Next Poet"?
No   3| MS:and smell their §last two words crossed out and replaced above by
two words§ pick your   9| MS:grave! the   *1876:* grave! The   12| MS:truth
thence §crossed out and replaced above by§ out   15| MS:—Where's §dash
inserted in left margin§   17| MS:discover   *1889a:* discover—

Call earth ugliness or beauty?
  See things there in large or small?
Use to pay its Lord my duty?
  Use to own a lord at all?

IV

25 Blank of such a record, truly
  Here's the work I hand, this scroll,
Yours to take or leave; as duly,
  Mine remains the unproffered soul.
So much, no whit more, my debtors—
30 How should one like me lay claim
To that largess elders, betters
  Sell you cheap their souls for—fame?

V

Which of you did I enable
  Once to slip inside my breast,
35 There to catalogue and label
  What I like least, what love best,
Hope and fear, believe and doubt of,
  Seek and shun, respect—deride?
Who has right to make a rout of
40 Rarities he found inside?

VI

Rarities or, as he'd rather,
  Rubbish such as stocks his own:
Need and greed (O strange) the Father
  Fashioned not for him alone!

25| MS:truly, *1889:* truly   27| MS:leave: as *1876:* leave; as   29| MS:debtors, *1876:* debtors—   33| MS:you have §crossed out and replaced above by§ did I enabled §last letter crossed out forming *enable*§   34| MS:Sly §crossed out and replaced above by§ Once < > breast *1889a:* breast,   35| MS:There he §crossed out and replaced above by§ to catalogued §last letter crossed out forming *catalogue*§ and labeled §last two letters crossed out forming *label*§   36| MS:liked §last letter crossed out forming *like*§   40| MS:finds *1876:* found   43| MS:strange!) the *1876:* strange) the   44| MS:alone. *1876:* alone!

45 Whence—the comfort set a-strutting,
　　　Whence—the outcry "Haste, behold!
Bard's breast open wide, past shutting,
　　　Shows what brass we took for gold!"

VII

Friends, I doubt not he'd display you
50　　　Brass—myself call orichalc,—
Furnish much amusement; pray you
　　　Therefore, be content I baulk
Him and you, and bar my portal!
　　　Here's my work outside: opine
55 What's inside me mean and mortal!
　　　Take your pleasure, leave me mine!

VIII

Which is—not to buy your laurel
　　　As last king did, nothing loth.
Tale adorned and pointed moral
60　　　Gained him praise and pity both.
Out rushed sighs and groans by dozens,
　　　Forth by scores oaths, curses flew:
Proving you were cater-cousins,
　　　Kith and kindred, king and you!

IX

65 Whereas do I ne'er so little
　　　(Thanks to sherris) leave ajar
Bosom's gate—no jot nor tittle
　　　Grow we nearer than we are.
Sinning, sorrowing, despairing,
70　　　Body-ruined, spirit-wrecked,—

46| MS:outcry 'Haste *1876:* outcry "Haste   48| MS:gold!' *1876:* gold!"
50| MS:oricalch— *1876:* oreichalch,— B's *1876:* oreichalch,— §e and second *h*
marked out forming *orichalc*§   53| MS:Both alike and *1876:* Him and you, and
58| MS:As your King *1876:* As last king   62| MS:scores what §crossed out and
replaced above by word and comma§ oaths, <> flew— *1876:* flew:

Should I give my woes an airing,—
    Where's one plague that claims respect?

X

Have you found your life distasteful?
    My life did, and does, smack sweet.
75 Was your youth of pleasure wasteful?
    Mine I saved and hold complete.
Do your joys with age diminish?
    When mine fail me, I'll complain.
Must in death your daylight finish?
80   My sun sets to rise again.

XI

What, like you, he proved—your Pilgrim—
    This our world a wilderness,
Earth still grey and heaven still grim,
    Not a hand there his might press,
85 Not a heart his own might throb to,
    Men all rogues and women—say,
Dolls which boys' heads duck and bob to,
    Grown folk drop or throw away?

XII

My experience being other,
90   How should I contribute verse
Worthy of your king and brother?
    Balaam-like I bless, not curse.
I find earth not grey but rosy,
    Heaven not grim but fair of hue.
95 Do I stoop? I pluck a posy.
    Do I stand and stare? All's blue.

71| MS:Now I *1876:*Should I   72| MS:plague to claim *1876:*plague that claims
74| MS:did and does smack *1889a:*did, and does, smack   80| MS:My sut sets
*1876:*My sun sets   81| MS:What, he proved like you—your pilgrim— *1876:*What,
like you, he proved—your Pilgrim—   83| MS:Still grey earth *1876:*Earth still
gray *1889a:*grey   87| MS:boy's *1876:*boys'   93| MS:grey *1876:*gray
*1889:*grey   94| MS:hue, *1876:*hue.   95| MS:posy: *1876:*posy.

XIII

Doubtless I am pushed and shoved by
    Rogues and fools enough: the more
Good luck mine, I love, am loved by
100   Some few honest to the core.
Scan the near high, scout the far low!
    "But the low come close:" what then?
Simpletons? My match is Marlowe;
    Sciolists? My mate is Ben.

XIV

105 Womankind—"the cat-like nature,
    False and fickle, vain and weak"—
What of this sad nomenclature
    Suits my tongue, if I must speak?
Does the sex invite, repulse so,
110   Tempt, betray, by fits and starts?
So becalm but to convulse so,
    Decking heads and breaking hearts?

XV

Well may you blaspheme at fortune!
    I "threw Venus" (Ben, expound!)
115 Never did I need importune
    Her, of all the Olympian round.
Blessings on my benefactress!
    Cursings suit—for aught I know—
Those who twitched her by the back tress,
120   Tugged and thought to turn her—so!

99| MS:Good §inserted in left margin§ Luck §altered to§ luck is §crossed out§
100| MS:Many §crossed out and replaced above by two words§ Some few
102| MS:'But <> close': what   *1876:*"But <> close:" what
105| MS:Womankind—'the catlike   *1876:*Womankind—"the cat-like
106| MS:weak'—   *1876:*weak"—   107| MS:Naught §crossed out and
replaced above by§ What <> this your §crossed out and replaced above
by§ sad   110| MS:starts *1876:*starts?   114| MS:I 'threw Venus'
(Ben *1876:*I "threw Venus" (Ben   118| MS:suit,—for <>
know,— *1876:*suit— for <> know—   120| MS:*so!* *1876:*so!

XVI

Therefore, since no leg to stand on
    Thus I'm left with,—joy or grief
Be the issue,—I abandon
    Hope or care you name me Chief!
125   Chief and king and Lord's anointed,
    I?—who never once have wished
Death before the day appointed:
    Lived and liked, not poohed and pished!

XVII

"Ah, but so I shall not enter,
130   Scroll in hand, the common heart—
Stopped at surface: since at centre
    Song should reach *Welt-schmerz*, world-smart!"
"Enter in the heart?" Its shelly
    Cuirass guard mine, fore and aft!
135   Such song "enters in the belly
    And is cast out in the draught."

XVIII

Back then to our sherris-brewage!
    "Kingship" quotha? I shall wait—
Waive the present time: some new age . . .
140   But let fools anticipate!
Meanwhile greet me—"friend, good fellow,
    Gentle Will," my merry men!
As for making Envy yellow
    With "Next Poet"—(Manners, Ben!)

124| MS:me Chief: *1876:*me Chief!   125| MS:and King <> lord's Anointed,
*1876:*and king <> Lord's anointed,   129| MS:'Ah   *1889a:*"Ah   132| MS:reach
Welt-schmerz, World-smart! *1876:*reach *Welt-schmerz,* world-smart!"   133| MS:'Enter
<> heart?' A shelley *1876:*"Enter <> heart?" Its shelly   134| MS:guards §last letter
crossed out forming *guard*§ it §crossed out and replaced above by word and comma§ mine,
135| MS:song 'enters *1876:*song "enters   136| MS:draught.' *1876:*draught."
138| MS:As for §last two words crossed out§ 'kingship'— §altered to§ 'Kingship'—quotha?
§word and question mark inserted above§ *1876:*"Kingship" quotha   140| MS:But I
won't §last two words crossed out and replaced above by two words§ let fools anticipate.
*1876:*anticipate!   141| MS:me—'friend *1876:*me—"friend   142| MS:Gentle Will',
my *1876:*Gentle Will," my   144| MS:With 'Next Poet'—(Manners *1876:*With "Next
Poet"—(Manners   MS:§At lower R§ L.D.I.E. Jan 15. '76. RB. §crossed out§

171

HOUSE

I

Shall I sonnet-sing you about myself?
    Do I live in a house you would like to see?
Is it scant of gear, has it store of pelf?
    "Unlock my heart with a sonnet-key?"

II

5   Invite the world, as my betters have done?
    "Take notice: this building remains on view,
Its suites of reception every one,
    Its private apartment and bedroom too;

III

"For a ticket, apply to the Publisher."
10   No: thanking the public, I must decline.
A peep through my window, if folk prefer;
    But, please you, no foot over threshold of mine!

IV

I have mixed with a crowd and heard free talk
    In a foreign land where an earthquake chanced:
15   And a house stood gaping, nought to baulk
    Man's eye wherever he gazed or glanced.

V

The whole of the frontage shaven sheer,
    The inside gaped: exposed to day,
Right and wrong and common and queer,
20   Bare, as the palm of your hand, it lay.

HOUSE ⁴| MS:Unlock < > sonnet-key? *1876:*"Unlock < > sonnet-key?"
1889a: sonnet-key? §emended to§ sonnet-key?" §see Editorial Notes§ ⁵| MS:done,
1876: done? ⁶| MS:—"Take §dash in L margin§ *1876:*"Take ⁷| MS:suites
§crossed out and re-written above§ ⁸| MS:too: *1876:* too; ⁹| MS:For
1876:"For ¹¹| MS:folks prefer: *1876:* prefer; *1889a:* folk ¹⁴| MS:chanced,
1876: chanced *1889a:* chanced: ¹⁶| MS:wherever it gazed *1876:* wherever he
gazed ¹⁸| MS:There lay §crossed out and replaced above by§ gaped the inside
§last three words transposed to§ the inside gaped *1876:* The inside

VI

The owner? Oh, he had been crushed, no doubt!
    "Odd tables and chairs for a man of wealth!
What a parcel of musty old books about!
    He smoked,—no wonder he lost his health!

VII

25   "I doubt if he bathed before he dressed.
        A brasier?—the pagan, he burned perfumes!
    You see it is proved, what the neighbours guessed:
        His wife and himself had separate rooms."

VIII

    Friends, the goodman of the house at least
30   Kept house to himself till an earthquake came:
    'Tis the fall of its frontage permits you feast
        On the inside arrangement you praise or blame.

IX

    Outside should suffice for evidence:
        And whoso desires to penetrate
35   Deeper, must dive by the spirit-sense—
        No optics like yours, at any rate!

X

    "Hoity toity! A street to explore,
        Your house the exception! *'With this same key
    Shakespeare unlocked his heart,'* once more!"
40   Did Shakespeare? If so, the less Shakespeare he!

¹⁹| MS:Its §crossed out§ right §altered to§ Right   ²¹| MS:owner? O he
*1876:*owner? Oh, he   ²⁵| MS:dressed; *1876:*dressed.   ²⁶| MS:brasier,—the
<> perfumes; *1876:*brasier?—the <>perfumes!   ²⁷| MS:guessed—
*1876:*guessed: ³⁰| MS:Kept all §crossed out and replaced above by§ house
³⁵| MS:Deeper—must *1876:*Deeper, must   ³⁷| MS:toity! A house §crossed out
and replaced above by§ street   ³⁸| MS:And §crossed out§ yours §altered to§
Your house §inserted above§ <> With this same §inserted above§ key *1876:*exception! *'With
this same key*   ³⁹| MS:Shakespeare unlocked his heart, once *1876:Shakespeare
unlocked his heart,'* once   MS:§At lower R§ Feb. 1. '74. §crossed out§

I

So, friend, your shop was all your house!
    Its front, astonishing the street,
Invited view from man and mouse
    To what diversity of treat
5   Behind its glass—the single sheet!

II

What gimcracks, genuine Japanese:
    Gape-jaw and goggle-eye, the frog;
Dragons, owls, monkeys, beetles, geese;
    Some crush-nosed human-hearted dog:
10   Queer names, too, such a catalogue!

III

I thought "And he who owns the wealth
    Which blocks the window's vastitude,
—Ah, could I peep at him by stealth
    Behind his ware, pass shop, intrude
15   On house itself, what scenes were viewed!

IV

"If wide and showy thus the shop,
    What must the habitation prove?
The true house with no name a-top—
    The mansion, distant one remove,
20   Once get him off his traffic-groove!

SHOP ³| MS:mouse, *1876:* mouse   ⁶⁻¹⁰| MS:What <> genuine Japanese! / <> Frog; / <> geese— / <> dog— / <> catalogue §lines 6-10 added in R margin§ *1876:* genuine Japanese: / <> frog; / <> geese; / <> dog: / <> catalogue!   ¹²| MS:That §crossed out and replaced above by§ Which ¹³| MS:—Ah, §dash in R margin§ could one peep *1876:* could I peep ¹⁷| MS:prove, *1876:* prove?   ²⁰| MS:traffic-grove? *1876:* traffic-grove!

"Pictures he likes, or books perhaps;
 And as for buying most and best,
Commend me to these City chaps!
 Or else he's social, takes his rest
25 On Sundays, with a Lord for guest.

VI

"Some suburb-palace, parked about
 And gated grandly, built last year:
The four-mile walk to keep off gout;
 Or big seat sold by bankrupt peer:
30 But then he takes the rail, that's clear.

VII

"Or, stop! I wager, taste selects
 Some out o' the way, some all-unknown
Retreat: the neighbourhood suspects
 Little that he who rambles lone
35 Makes Rothschild tremble on his throne!"

VIII

Nowise! Nor Mayfair residence
 Fit to receive and entertain,—
Nor Hampstead villa's kind defence
 From noise and crowd, from dust and drain,—
40 Nor country-box was soul's domain!

21| MS:Pictures *1876:* "Pictures 23| MS:those §altered to§ these merchant §crossed out and replaced above by§ city *1889a:* these City 25| MS:Some *1876:* "Some 28| MS:walk that §crossed out and replaced above by§ to keeps §last letter crossed out forming *keep*§ 31| MS:And yet, §last two words and comma crossed out and replaced above by two words and exclamation mark§ Or, stop! *1876:* "Or 32| MS:way, and §crossed out and replaced above by§ some 34| MS:who walks §crossed out and replaced above by§ rambles alone§ first letter crossed out forming *lone*§ 35| MS:throne. *1876:* throne!" 36-40| MS:§lines added on verso§ domain. *1876:* domain!

IX

Nowise! At back of all that spread
　　Of merchandize, woe's me, I find
A hole i' the wall where, heels by head,
　　The owner couched, his ware behind,
45　　　—In cupboard suited to his mind.

X

For why? He saw no use of life
　　But, while he drove a roaring trade,
To chuckle "Customers are rife!"
　　To chafe "So much hard cash outlaid
50　　　Yet zero in my profits made!

XI

"This novelty costs pains, but—takes?
　　Cumbers my counter! Stock no more!
This article, no such great shakes,
　　Fizzes like wildfire? Underscore
55　　　The cheap thing—thousands to the fore!"

XII

'Twas lodging best to live most nigh
　　(Cramp, coffinlike as crib might be)
Receipt of Custom; ear and eye
　　Wanted no outworld: "Hear and see
60　　　The bustle in the shop!" quoth he.

---

⁴²| MS:merchandize, contrived §crossed out and replaced above by two words
and comma§ woe's me, I　　⁴⁵| MS:—In §over perhaps a§ lodging
§crossed out and replaced above by§ cupboard　　⁴⁶| MS:no good §crossed out
and replaced above by§ joy §crossed out and replaced above by§ use of §over in§
⁴⁸| MS:Now chuckling "Customers　1876: To chuckle "Customers　　⁴⁹| MS:Now
chafing "Much good §crossed out and replaced above by§ hard <> outlaid,　1876: To chafe
"So much <> outlaid　　⁵⁰| MS:Yet stand still §last two words crossed out and replaced
above by§ zero in the §crossed out and replaced above by §my profits-made!"　1876: profits
made!　　⁵¹| MS:pains: but, takes?　1876: pains, but—takes?　　⁵²| MS:No, says §last
two words crossed out and replaced above by§ Cumbers my leger §crossed out and replaced
above by§ counter: stock　1876: counter! Stock　　⁵⁴| MS:Goes off §last two words
crossed out and replaced above by§ Fizzes <> wild fire: underscore　1876: fire?
Underscore　1889a: wildfire　　⁵⁵| MS:fore!"　1876: fore!'　1899a: fore!"

My fancy of a merchant-prince
    Was different. Through his wares we groped
Our darkling way to—not to mince
    The matter—no black den where moped
65   The master if we interloped!

XIV

Shop was shop only: household-stuff?
    What did he want with comforts there?
"Walls, ceiling, floor, stay blank and rough,
    So goods on sale show rich and rare!
70   *'Sell and scud home'* be shop's affair!"

XV

What might he deal in? Gems, suppose!
    Since somehow business must be done
At cost of trouble,—see, he throws
    You choice of jewels, everyone,
75   Good, better, best, star, moon and sun!

---

⁶²| MS:Was §crossed out and replaced above by§ How different, §comma altered to exclamation mark§ I supposed §last two words crossed out and replaced above by three words§ Through the door §last two words crossed out and replaced above by two words§ his wares   *1876:*Was different. Through   ⁶³| MS:to . . not   *1876:*to—not
⁶⁴| MS:matter . . dingy §crossed out and replaced above by two words§ some black §*some* crossed out and replaced above by *no*§   *1876:*matter—no   ⁶⁵| MS:master when he §last two words crossed out and replaced above by two words§ if we   ⁶⁶| MS:This den §last two words crossed out and replaced above by§ For §crossed out and next word added above§ Shop <> shop only, §word and comma inserted above§ and fine §last word crossed out and replaced above by§ plain enough;   *1876:*Shop <> only: household-stuff?
⁶⁷| MS:with gimcracks there?   *1876:*with comforts there?   ⁶⁸| MS:Walls <> floor, how §crossed out and replaced above by§ be <> rough!   *1876:*"Walls <> floor, stay <> rough,   ⁶⁹| MS:The §first word crossed out and replaced above by word and comma§ But, §word and comma crossed out and replaced by§ And §crossed out and replaced by word in L margin§ So <> sale, how §comma and last word crossed out and replaced above by two words§ the show §*the* crossed out§   ⁷⁰| MS:"Sell and get done"—this §altered to§ the main §crossed out and replaced above by§ shop's affair.   *1876:*'Sell *and scud home,'* be shop's affair!"   *1889a:home'* be   ⁷¹| MS:What did §crossed out and replaced above by§ might   ⁷²| MS:done,   *1876:*done
⁷⁴| MS:everyone   *1876:*everyone.   *1889a:*everyone,   ⁷⁵| MS:sun.   *1876:*sun!

XVI

Which lies within your power of purse?
    This ruby that would tip aright
Solomon's sceptre? Oh, your nurse
    Wants simply coral, the delight
80   Of teething baby,—stuff to bite!

XVII

Howe'er your choice fell, straight you took
    Your purchase, prompt your money rang
On counter,—scarce the man forsook
    His study of the "Times," just swang
85   Till-ward his hand that stopped the clang,—

XVIII

Then off made buyer with a prize,
    Then seller to his "Times" returned
And so did day wear, wear, till eyes
    Brightened apace, for rest was earned:
90   He locked door long ere candle burned.

XIX

And whither went he? Ask himself,
    Not me! To change of scene, I think.
Once sold the ware and pursed the pelf,
    Chaffer was scarce his meat and drink,
95   Nor all his music—money-chink.

82| MS:your pieces rang   *1876:*your money rang   85| MS:Till-wards   *1876:*Till-ward
86| MS:Then, off < > with the §crossed out and replaced above by§ a   *1876:*Then off
87| MS:While §crossed out and replaced above by§ And §crossed out and replaced by§
Then < > returned, *1889a:*returned   88| MS:wear, on §crossed out and replaced
above by§ wear   94| MS:Shop-talk §crossed out and replaced above by§ Chaffer

XX

Because a man has shop to mind
    In time and place, since flesh must live,
Needs spirit lack all life behind,
    All stray thoughts, fancies fugitive,
100   All loves except what trade can give?

XXI

I want to know a butcher paints,
    A baker rhymes for his pursuit,
Candlestick-maker much acquaints
    His soul with song, or, haply mute,
105   Blows out his brains upon the flute!

XXII

But—shop each day and all day long!
    Friend, your good angel slept, your star
Suffered eclipse, fate did you wrong!
    From where these sorts of treasures are,
110   There should our hearts be—Christ, how far!

96| MS:Because the man had   *1876:* Because a man has   98| MS:Lacked §crossed out
and replaced above by§ Must §crossed out and replaced by§ Needs spirit, then, §word and
two commas crossed out and replaced above by§ lack < > behind? §question mark crossed
out and replaced by comma§   99| MS:All §over *No*§ < > fugitive? §question mark
crossed out and replaced by comma§   100| MS:All §over *No*§   102| MS:A Baker,
with §crossed out§ verse for   *1876:* A baker rhymes for   103| MS:Candlestickmaker that
acquaints   *1876:* Candlestick-maker much acquaints   105| MS:flute.   *1876:* flute!
106| MS:But shop all §crossed out and replaced above by§ each   *1876:* But—shop
109| MS:where this sort < > are   *1876:* where these sorts < > are,   110| MS:should
your heart   *1876:* should our hearts   MS:§At lower R§ L.D.I.E. Feb. 11 '71. §crossed out§

I

Over the ball of it,
    Peering and prying,
How I see all of it,
    Life there, outlying!
5 Roughness and smoothness,
    Shine and defilement,
Grace and uncouthness:
    One reconcilement.

II

Orbed as appointed,
10   Sister with brother
Joins, ne'er disjointed
    One from the other.
All's lend-and-borrow;
    Good, see, wants evil,
15 Joy demands sorrow,
    Angel weds devil!

III

"Which things must—*why* be?"
    Vain our endeavour!
So shall things aye be
20   As they were ever.
"Such things should *so* be!"
    Sage our desistence!
Rough-smooth let globe be,
    Mixed—man's existence!

PISGAH-SIGHTS I 16| MS:devil. *1876:*devil! 22| MS:Sage §first two letters over illegible erasure§

25   Man—wise and foolish,
          Lover and scorner,
      Docile and mulish—
          Keep each his corner!
      Honey yet gall of it!
30   There's the life lying,
      And I see all of it,
          Only, I'm dying!

29| MS: Honey yet §over *and*§ <> it—   *1876:*it!   30| MS:lying   *1876:*lying,
MS: §At lower R§ L.D.I.E. Dec. 28. '75. §crossed out§

I

Could I but live again,
　　Twice my life over,
Would I once strive again?
　　Would not I cover
5　Quietly all of it—
　　Greed and ambition—
So, from the pall of it,
　　Pass to fruition?

II

"Soft!" I'd say, "Soul mine!
10　　Three-score and ten years,
Let the blind mole mine
　　Digging out deniers!
Let the dazed hawk soar,
　　Claim the sun's rights too!
15 Turf 'tis thy walk's o'er,
　　Foliage thy flight's to."

III

Only a learner,
　　Quick one or slow one,
Just a discerner,
20　　I would teach no one.
I am earth's native:
　　No rearranging it!
I be creative,
　　Chopping and changing it?

PISGAH-SIGHTS II　*Title*|　MS: Pisgah Sights. §first letter over lowercase§ 2.
9|　MS:say "Soul mine,—　*1876:*say, "Soul mine!　　12|　MS:deniers:　*1876:*deniers!
14|　MS:too:　*1876:*too!　　16|　MS:to!"　*1876:*to."　　21|　MS:native,—　*1876:*native:

25   March, men, my fellows!
      Those who, above me,
  (Distance so mellows)
      Fancy you love me:
  Those who, below me,
30   (Distance makes great so)
  Free to forego me,
      Fancy you hate so!

V

  Praising, reviling,
      Worst head and best head,
35   Past me defiling,
      Never arrested,
  Wanters, abounders,
      March, in gay mixture,
  Men, my surrounders!
40   I am the fixture.

VI

  So shall I fear thee,
      Mightiness yonder!
  Mock-sun—more near thee,
      What is to wonder?
45   So shall I love thee,
      Down in the dark,—lest
  Glowworm I prove thee,
      Star that now sparklest!

28| MS:Fancy they love *1876:*Fancy you love   32| MS:Fancy they hate *1876:*Fancy
you hate   38| MS:March in *1876:*March, in   41| MS:thee; *1876:*thee,
45| MS:thee— *1876:*thee,   46| MS:dark, lest *1876:*dark,—lest   MS: §At lower R§
L.D.I.E. Feb. 19. '76 §crossed out§

I

Here's my case. Of old I used to love him,
    This same unseen friend, before I knew:
Dream there was none like him, none above him,—
    Wake to hope and trust my dream was true.

II

5   Loved I not his letters full of beauty?
    Not his actions famous far and wide?
Absent, he would know I vowed him duty;
    Present, he would find me at his side.

III

Pleasant fancy! for I had but letters,
10   Only knew of actions by hearsay:
He himself was busied with my betters;
    What of that? My turn must come some day.

IV

"Some day" proving—no day! Here's the puzzle.
    Passed and passed my turn is. Why complain?
15   He's so busied! If I could but muzzle
    People's foolish mouths that give me pain!

V

"Letters?" (hear them!) "You a judge of writing?
    Ask the experts!—How they shake the head
O'er these characters, your friend's inditing—
20   Call them forgery from A to Z!

FEARS AND SCRUPLES   1| MS:case: of < > him,   *1876:* case. Of
1889a: him §emended to§ him, §see Editorial Notes§   6| MS:actions
bruited §crossed out and replaced above by§ famous   7| MS:duty,
1889a: duty;   10| MS:hearsay—   *1876:* hearsay: 13| MS:puzzle!   *1876:* puzzle.
14| MS:is! Why   *1876:* is. Why   18| MS:experts! How   *1889a:* experts!—How
20| MS:from A. to Z!   *1876:* from A. to Z.!   *1889a:* from A to Z!

"Actions? Where's your certain proof" (they bother)
    "He, of all you find so great and good,
He, he only, claims this, that, the other
    Action—claimed by men, a multitude?"

VII

25 I can simply wish I might refute you,
        Wish my friend would,—by a word, a wink,—
    Bid me stop that foolish mouth,—you brute you!
        He keeps absent,—why, I cannot think.

    Never mind! Though foolishness may flout me,
30   One thing's sure enough: 'tis neither frost,
    No, nor fire, shall freeze or burn from out me
        Thanks for truth—though falsehood, gained—though lost.

    All my days, I'll go the softlier, sadlier,
        For that dream's sake! How forget the thrill
35 Through and through me as I thought "The gladlier
        Lives my friend because I love him still!"

    Ah, but there's a menace someone utters!
        "What and if your friend at home play tricks?
    Peep at hide-and-seek behind the shutters?
40   Mean your eyes should pierce through solid bricks?

22| MS:That, of *1876:*"He, of   23| MS:only did *1876:*only, claims
31| MS:freeze or §inserted above§ burn, §comma crossed out and next word illegibly crossed
out§   32| MS:truth so gained and falsehood lost. *1876:*truth—though falsehood,
gained—though lost.   39| MS:Play §first word crossed out and replaced by§ Peep
40| MS:Want your eyes to pierce *1876:*Mean your eyes should pierce

"What and if he, frowning, wake you, dreamy?
 Lay on you the blame that bricks—conceal?
Say *'At least I saw who did not see me,*
 Does see now, and presently shall feel'?"

45 "Why, that makes your friend a monster!" say you:
 "Had his house no window? At first nod,
Would you not have hailed him?" Hush, I pray you!
 What if this friend happen to be—God?

41| MS:"What <> he frowning wake you dreamy? *1876:*'What <> he, frowning,
wake you, dreamy *1889a:*"What <> dreamy?   42| MS:bricks conceal?
*1876:*bricks—conceal?   43| MS:Say *'I plainly* §crossed out§ *saw at least* §last two words
inserted above§ *who* *1876:*Say *'At least I saw who*   44| MS:*now and* <> *feel?'"*
1876:now, and *1889a:feel'?"*   45| MS:"Why, he *1876:*"Why, that   46| MS:Had
<> windows: §colon altered to question mark§ where, §crossed out§ at first §inserted above§
1876:"Had <> window? At   47| MS:You'd §crossed out and replaced above by three
words§ Would you not have known and §last two words crossed out§   48| MS:For
§first word crossed out and replaced by two words§ What if this same §crossed out§
<> happens §last letter crossed out forming *happen*§ B's *1876:*What if §first
two words crossed out and then restored§ this §followed by word inserted
above and then illegibly erased and crossed out§ <> happen §*s* added and then
deleted§ <> God? §question mark crossed out, full stop added, then deleted
and question mark restored§ MS: §At lower R§ Feb. 26. '76. L.D.I.E. §crossed out§

NATURAL MAGIC

I

All I can say is—I saw it!
The room was as bare as your hand.
I locked in the swarth little lady,—I swear,
From the head to the foot of her—well, quite as bare!
5   "No Nautch shall cheat me," said I, "taking my stand
At this bolt which I draw!" And this bolt—I withdraw it,
And there laughs the lady, not bare, but embowered
With—who knows what verdure, o'erfruited, o'erflowered?
    Impossible! Only—I saw it!

II

10   All I can sing is—I feel it!
This life was as blank as that room;
I let you pass in here. Precaution, indeed?
Walls, ceiling and floor,—not a chance for a weed!
Wide opens the entrance: where's cold now, where's gloom?
15 No May to sow seed here, no June to reveal it,
Behold you enshrined in these blooms of your bringing,
These fruits of your bearing—nay, birds of your winging!
    A fairy-tale! Only—I feel it!

NATURAL MAGIC   MS: §All lines are not flush left, being indented in varying degrees§
2| MS:hand; 1876:hand.   3| MS:swear 1876:swear,   4| MS:bare. 1876:bare!
5| MS:me" said 1876:me," said   6| MS:bolt, I 1876:bolt—I   7| MS:laughs
§last letter over *ed*, which is mostly rubbed out§ my lady <> bare but 1876:laughs the lady
<> bare, but   8| MS:o'erflowered! 1876:o'erflowered?   11| MS:My life
1876:This life   12| MS:you play tricks §last two words crossed out and replaced above
by two words§ pass in there. Precaution 1876:in here. Precaution   13| MS:floor, not
1876:floor,—not   14| MS:entrance—where's 1876:entrance: where's   15| MS:No
April §crossed out and replaced above by§ May <> seed there, no 1876:seed here, no
16| MS:Behold the §crossed out and replaced above by§ you <> those §altered to§ these
<> bringing 1876:bringing,   17| MS:Those §altered to§ These

187

I

Flower—I never fancied, jewel—I profess you!
    Bright I see and soft I feel the outside of a flower.
Save but glow inside and—jewel, I should guess you,
    Dim to sight and rough to touch: the glory is the dower.

II

5   You, forsooth, a flower? Nay, my love, a jewel—
    Jewel at no mercy of a moment in your prime!
Time may fray the flower-face: kind be time or cruel,
    Jewel, from each facet, flash your laugh at time!

MAGICAL NATURE ¹| MS:you; *1876:*you!   ²| MS:of the flower: *1876:*of a flower.   ³| MS:but glory §crossed out and replaced above by§ gift inside, §comma crossed out§ and— §word and dash inserted above§ *1876:*but glow inside
⁵| MS:jewel! *1876:*jewel—   ⁶| MS:in its prime; *1876:*in your prime!
⁷| MS:flower-face §hyphen over illegible erasure, perhaps *s*§   MS: §Next to l.6§ March 4. '76

BIFURCATION

We were two lovers; let me lie by her,
My tomb beside her tomb. On hers inscribe—
"I loved him; but my reason bade prefer
Duty to love, reject the tempter's bribe

5   Of rose and lily when each path diverged,
And either I must pace to life's far end
As love should lead me, or, as duty urged,
Plod the worn causeway arm-in-arm with friend.
So, truth turned falsehood: *'How I loathe a flower,*

10   *How prize the pavement!'* still caressed his ear—
The deafish friend's—through life's day, hour by hour,
As he laughed (coughing) *'Ay, it would appear!'*
But deep within my heart of hearts there hid
Ever the confidence, amends for all,

15   That heaven repairs what wrong earth's journey did,
When love from life-long exile comes at call.
Duty and love, one broadway, were the best—
Who doubts? But one or other was to choose.
I chose the darkling half, and wait the rest

20   In that new world where light and darkness fuse."

Inscribe on mine—"I loved her: love's track lay
O'er sand and pebble, as all travellers know.
Duty led through a smiling country, gay
With greensward where the rose and lily blow.

25   *'Our roads are diverse: farewell, love!'* said she;
''Tis duty I abide by: homely sward

BIFURCATION MS:§arabic number 1, crossed out§   1| MS:lovers: let *1876:*lovers;
let   3| MS:'I <> him: but *1876:*"I <> him; but   8| MS:arm in arm
*1889a:*arm-in-arm   9| MS:falsehood: 'How I loathe a flower, *1876:*falsehood: *'How I
loathe a flower,*   10| MS:How prize the pavement!' still *1876:How prize the
pavement!'* still   12| MS:Till he <> 'Ay, it would appear!' *1876:*As he <> *'Ay, it
would appear!'*   14| MS:Meanwhile the *1876:*Ever the   20-21| MS:fuse.'/
§Arabic numeral indicating section 2 is crossed out; spacial division retained§ Inscribe <>
mine—'I *1876:*fuse."/Inscribe <> mine—"I   25| MS:"Our roads are diverse:
farewell, love!" said she *1876:'Our* <> *love!'* said she: *1889a:*she;   26| MS:"Tis duty
I descend on §last two words crossed out and replaced by three words§ abide by, for
§crossed out§— homely sward *1876:*§italics§ *''Tis* <> *by: homely*

And not the rock-rough picturesque for me!
Above, where both roads join, I wait reward.
Be you as constant to the path whereon
30   *I leave you planted!'* But man needs must move,
Keep moving—whither, when the star is gone
Whereby he steps secure nor strays from love?
No stone but I was tripped by, stumbling-block
But brought me to confusion. Where I fell,
35   There I lay flat, if moss disguised the rock,
Thence, if flint pierced, I rose and cried *'All's well!*
Duty be mine to tread in that high sphere
Where love from duty ne'er disparts, I trust,
And two halves make that whole, whereof—since here
40   *One must suffice a man—why, this one must!' "*

Inscribe each tomb thus: then, some sage acquaint
The simple—which holds sinner, which holds saint!

²⁷| MS:§not underlined§ *1876:*§italics§   ²⁸| MS:§not underlined§ roads meet, expect
§last two words crossed out and replaced above by three words§ join, I wait *1876:*§italics§
²⁹| MS:§not underlined§ Prove §crossed out and replaced above by§ Be you but §crossed out
and replaced above by§ as *1876:*§italics§   ³⁰| MS: I leave you planted." But *1876:I*
<> *planted.'* But   ³¹| MS:whither? when *1876:*whither, when   ³³| MS:but I
have §crossed out and replaced above by§ was tripped at §last word crossed out and replaced
above by§ by   ³⁴| MS:confusion: where *1876:*confusion. Where   ³⁶| MS:Thence,
§over either *When* or *Whence*§ if §inserted above§ <> pierced, up §crossed out§ <>
cried "All's well! *1876:*cried *'All's well!*   ³⁷⁻³⁸| MS:§not underlined§
1876:§italics§   ³⁹| MS:But two halves make that whole, whereof, since here
1876:And two <> *whereof—since here*   ⁴⁰| MS:§not underlined§
must!" *1876:*§italics§ *must!' "*   ⁴⁰⁻⁴¹| MS:§Arabic numeral indicating
section 3 is crossed out, spacial division retained§   ⁴²| MS:simple—which
was §crossed out and replaced above by§ holds sinner here, §crossed out§
which holds §inserted above§   MS: §At lower R§ Nov. 29, '75. §crossed out§

Still you stand, still you listen, still you smile!
Still melts your moonbeam through me, white awhile,
Softening, sweetening, till sweet and soft
Increase so round this heart of mine, that oft
5   I could believe your moonbeam-smile has past
The pallid limit, lies, transformed at last
To sunlight and salvation—warms the soul
It sweetens, softens! Would you pass that goal,
Gain love's birth at the limit's happier verge,
10   And, where an iridescence lurks, but urge
The hesitating pallor on to prime
Of dawn!—true blood-streaked, sun-warmth, action-time,
By heart-pulse ripened to a ruddy glow
Of gold above my clay—I scarce should know
15   From gold's self, thus suffused! For gold means love.
What means the sad slow silver smile above
My clay but pity, pardon?—at the best,
But acquiescence that I take my rest,
Contented to be clay, while in your heaven
20   The sun reserves love for the Spirit-Seven
Companioning God's throne they lamp before,
—Leaves earth a mute waste only wandered o'er
By that pale soft sweet disempassioned moon
Which smiles me slow forgiveness! Such the boon
25   I beg? Nay, dear, submit to this—just this
Supreme endeavour! As my lips now kiss
Your feet, my arms convulse your shrouding robe,

NUMPHOLEPTOS   Title| MS:Νυμϑόληπτος §crossed out and replaced by§
Numpholeptos.   ¹| MS:smile: *1876:*smile!   ⁵| MS:I half believe
*1876:*I could believe   ⁶| MS:The pallor-limit and, transformed < > last,
*1876:*The pallid limit   *1889a:*limit, lies, transformed < > last   ⁷| MS:Lies,
sunlight < > salvation, warms   *1876:*salvation—warms   *1889a:*To sunlight
⁸| MS:softens. Would   *1876:*softens! Would   ¹²| MS:dawn, true
blood-streaked sun-warmth   *1876:*dawn!—true blood-streaked,
sun-warmth   ¹³| MS:Your heart-pulse < > to one ruddy   *1876:*By
heart-pulse < > to a ruddy   ¹⁷| MS:pity—pardon—at   *1876:*pity,
pardon?—at   ¹⁸| MS:Cold acquiescence   *1876:*But acquiescence
²⁰| MS:reserves life for   *1876:*reserves love for   ²²| MS:And leaves a
1876:—Leaves earth a   ²⁴| MS:me just §crossed out and replaced above by§
slow forgiveness. Such, the   *1876:*forgiveness! Such   *1889a:*forgiveness! Such the

My eyes, acquainted with the dust, dare probe
Your eyes above for—what, if born, would blind
30 Mine with redundant bliss, as flash may find
The inert nerve, sting awake the palsied limb,
Bid with life's ecstasy sense overbrim
And suck back death in the resurging joy—
Love, the love whole and sole without alloy!

35 Vainly! The promise withers! I employ
Lips, arms, eyes, pray the prayer which finds the word,
Make the appeal which must be felt, not heard,
And none the more is changed your calm regard:
Rather, its sweet and soft grow harsh and hard—
40 Forbearance, then repulsion, then disdain.
Avert the rest! I rise, see!—make, again
Once more, the old departure for some track
Untried yet through a world which brings me back
Ever thus fruitlessly to find your feet,
45 To fix your eyes, to pray the soft and sweet
Which smile there—take from his new pilgrimage
Your outcast, once your inmate, and assuage
With love—not placid pardon now—his thirst
For a mere drop from out the ocean erst
50 He drank at! Well, the quest shall be renewed.
Fear nothing! Though I linger, unembued
With any drop, my lips thus close. I go!
So did I leave you, I have found you so,
And doubtlessly, if fated to return,
55 So shall my pleading persevere and earn

Pardon—not love—in that same smile, I learn,
And lose the meaning of, to learn once more,
Vainly!

What fairy track do I explore?
What magic hall return to, like the gem
60   Centuply-angled o'er a diadem?
You dwell there, hearted; from your midmost home
Rays forth—through that fantastic world I roam
Ever—from centre to circumference,
Shaft upon coloured shaft: this crimsons thence,
65   That purples out its precinct through the waste.
Surely I had your sanction when I faced,
Fared forth upon that untried yellow ray
Whence I retrack my steps? They end to-day
Where they began—before your feet, beneath
70   Your eyes, your smile: the blade is shut in sheath,
Fire quenched in flint; irradiation, late
Triumphant through the distance, finds its fate,
Merged in your blank pure soul, alike the source
And tomb of that prismatic glow: divorce
75   Absolute, all-conclusive! Forth I fared,
Treading the lambent flamelet: little cared
If now its flickering took the topaz tint,
If now my dull-caked path gave sulphury hint
Of subterranean rage—no stay nor stint

56| MS:love in   B's *1876:* love—in §dash inserted in R margin§   58| MS:Vainly! What
magic §crossed out and replaced above by§ fairy track do I explore, §last six words and
punctuation crossed out and rewritten below to create ¶; question mark replaces comma§
59| MS:to, made §inserted above§ like the §crossed out§ gem   *1876:* to, like the gem
62| MS:forth, through   *1876:* forth—through   63| MS:Ever, from   *1876:* Ever—from
67| MS:yellow waste §crossed out and replace by§ ray   68| MS:steps? which §crossed
out and replaced above by§ They   69| MS:began, before   *1889a:* began—before
70| MS:smile: The §crossed out and replaced above by§ and   *1876:* smile: the
71| MS:flint, irradiation   *1876:* flint; irradiation   74| MS:of such prismatic   *1876:* of
that prismatic   76| MS:True to your birth, the §last five words crossed out and replaced
above by three words§ Treading the lambent   77| MS:tint   *1876:* tint,   78| MS:And
now dull-caked my §transposed to§ my dull-caked path §road inserted above and crossed
out§ < > hint §followed by hole scraped in paper§   *1876:* If now   79| MS:rage §fire
inserted above and crossed out; illegible word inserted below and crossed out§

To yellow, since you sanctioned that I bathe,
      Burnish me, soul and body, swim and swathe
      In yellow license. Here I reek suffused
      With crocus, saffron, orange, as I used
      With scarlet, purple, every dye o' the bow
85   Born of the storm-cloud. As before, you show
      Scarce recognition, no approval, some
      Mistrust, more wonder at a man become
      Monstrous in garb, nay,—flesh disguised as well,
      Through his adventure. Whatsoe'er befell,
90   I followed, whereso'er it wound, that vein
      You authorized should leave your whiteness, stain
      Earth's sombre stretch beyond your midmost place
      Of vantage,—trode that tint whereof the trace
      On garb and flesh repel you! Yes, I plead
95   Your own permission—your command, indeed,
      That who would worthily retain the love
      Must share the knowledge shrined those eyes above,
      Go boldly on adventure, break through bounds
      O' the quintessential whiteness that surrounds
100   Your feet, obtain experience of each tinge
      That bickers forth to broaden out, impinge
      Plainer his foot its pathway all distinct

80| MS:since §first letter over illegible erasure§ <> bathe 1876:bathe,
83| MS:With saffron, orange, crocus §transposed to§ crocus, saffron, orange
84| MS:With scarlet §over illegible erasure§   85| MS:the cloud. And, as before
1876:the storm-cloud. As before   88| MS:garb, nay §crossed out and replaced above by
word illegibly erased§ flesh <> well! §exclamation mark crossed out and replaced by dash
and comma: well—,§ 1876:nay—flesh <> well,   89| MS:Through his §last two words
crossed out and then restored; word[s] illegibly crossed out above§ adventured, §last letter
crossed out forming adventure§ whatsoe'er 1876:adventure. Whatsoe'er   90| MS:To
follow, wheresoe'er 1876:I followed, whereso'er   91| MS:leave your §crossed out,
replaced above by§ the §crossed out and your restored§ whiteness,—stain 1876:whiteness,
stain   92| MS:The §first word crossed out and replaced above by§ Earth's <> beyond
that §crossed out, replaced above by§ your §crossed out and that restored§ midmost
1876:beyond your midmost   93| MS:vantage,—with §crossed out and replaced above
by perhaps§ troad that §followed by illegible word above§ 1876:trode
94| MS:you—though I 1876:you! Yes, I   95| MS:command indeed, 1876:command,
indeed,   96| MS:retain the §formed by crossing out last two letters of their§ love,
1876:love   99| MS:of that essential whiteness which surrounds 1876:O' the
quintessential whiteness that surrounds   101| MS:That flutters §crossed out and
replaced above by§ bickers   102| MS:Plainer my soul its §last two words crossed out
and replaced above by two words§ foot a pathway 1876:Plainer his foot its pathway

From every other. Ah, the wonder, linked
With fear, as exploration manifests
105 What agency it was first tipped the crests
Of unnamed wildflower, soon protruding grew
Portentous mid the sands, as when his hue
Betrays him and the burrowing snake gleams through;
Till, last . . . but why parade more shame and pain?
110 Are not the proofs upon me? Here again
I pass into your presence, I receive
Your smile of pity, pardon, and I leave . . .
No, not this last of times I leave you, mute,
Submitted to my penance, so my foot
115 May yet again adventure, tread, from source
To issue, one more ray of rays which course
Each other, at your bidding, from the sphere
Silver and sweet, their birthplace, down that drear
Dark of the world,—you promise shall return
120 Your pilgrim jewelled as with drops o' the urn
The rainbow paints from, and no smatch at all
Of ghastliness at edge of some cloud-pall
Heaven cowers before, as earth awaits the fall
O' the bolt and flash of doom. Who trusts your word

103| MS:other,—yellow wonder 1876:other. Ah, the wonder   106–08| MS:§brace in R
margin marking triplet is crossed out§   106| MS:protruded §altered to§ protruding
through §crossed out and replaced by§ grew   107| MS:Portentous mid §first two words
inserted above, *mid* perhaps over in§ The §altered to§ the <> when the §crossed out and
replaced above by§ his   108| MS:Betrays §over illegible erasure§ <> snake shines
§crossed out and replaced above by§ gleams through: 1876:through;   109| MS:Till,
§over *And*§ last . . but <> parade the §crossed out and replaced above by§ more
1889a:last . . . but   112| MS:Your smile of §last two words inserted above§
113| MS:No, Lady, §above word illegibly scratched out over which B had tried
unsuccessfully to insert *Lady*§ not this time I 1876:No, not this last of times I
115| MS:May finally §last two words crossed out and replaced above by three words,
the first of which is illegibly crossed out and replaced above by *May* and next two
words§ once again <> tread from 1876:May yet again <> tread, from
116| MS:issue some untried ray—such as course 1876:issue, one more ray
of rays which course   118| MS:sweet, your birthplace 1876:sweet,
their birthplace   119| MS:world, they promise 1876:world,—you
promise   120| MS:Your §crossed out and replaced above by *Their*,
which is crossed out and *Your* restored§   121–23| MS:§brace in R margin
marking triplet is crossed out§   122| MS:of the storm's §last
two words crossed out and replaced above by two words§ some cloud-pall,
1876:cloud-pall   123| MS:before as 1876:before, as   124| MS:trusts
their §crossed out and replaced above by§ your word, 1876:word

195

¹²⁵ Tries the adventure: and returns—absurd
As frightful—in that sulphur-steeped disguise
Mocking the priestly cloth-of-gold, sole prize
The arch-heretic was wont to bear away
Until he reached the burning. No, I say:
¹³⁰ No fresh adventure! No more seeking love
At end of toil, and finding, calm above
My passion, the old statuesque regard,
The sad petrific smile!

                    O you—less hard
And hateful than mistaken and obtuse
¹³⁵ Unreason of a she-intelligence!
You very woman with the pert pretence
To match the male achievement! Like enough!
Ay, you were easy victors, did the rough
Straightway efface itself to smooth, the gruff
¹⁴⁰ Grind down and grow a whisper,—did man's truth
Subdue, for sake of chivalry and ruth,
Its rapier-edge to suit the bulrush-spear
Womanly falsehood fights with! O that ear
All fact pricks rudely, that thrice-superfine
¹⁴⁵ Feminity of sense, with right divine
To waive all process, take result stain-free
From out the very muck wherein . . .

                              Ah me!

---

^{125|} MS:adventure and *1876:* adventure: and   ^{126|} MS:disguise, *1876:* disguise
^{129|} MS:say, *1876:* say: ^{130|} MS:No more §crossed out and replaced above by§ fresh
adventure:! to §crossed out§ no *1876:* adventure! No   ^{131|} MS:toil and finding, still
§crossed out and replaced above by§ calm *1876:* toil, and   ^{132|} MS:The §first word
crossed out and replaced above by four words§ My passion, the old < > regard, §comma
perhaps over exclamation mark§ the slow sad glance §comma and last four words crossed
out§ *1876:* regard,   ^{133|} MS:The sad §inserted above§ smile! O you less *1876:* smile!
§¶§ O you—less   ^{139|} MS:Ever efface < > smooth, the §crossed out and replaced above
by *and* and then restored§ *1876:* Straightway efface   ^{140|} MS:whisper,—did §over
as§   ^{141|} MS:Subdued §last letter crossed out forming *Subdue*§   ^{144|} MS:Fact
pricks so rudely, that all §crossed out and replaced above by§ thrice superfine
1876: All fact pricks rudely, that thrice-superfine   ^{145|} MS:sense with *1876:* sense,
with   ^{147|} MS:wherein . . Ah *1876:* wherein . . . §¶§ Ah

The true slave's querulous outbreak! All the rest
Be resignation! Forth at your behest
150 I fare. Who knows but this—the crimson-quest—
May deepen to a sunrise, not decay
To that cold sad sweet smile?—which I obey.

¹⁴⁸| MS:outbreak: all *1876:*outbreak! All ¹⁴⁹| Is resignation: forth *1876:*Be
resignation! Forth ¹⁵⁰| MS:fare: who *1876:*fare. Who ¹⁵²| MS:smile—which
*1876:*smile?—which MS: §At lower R§ L.D.I.E. Apr. 25. '76. §crossed out§

APPEARANCES

I

And so you found that poor room dull,
    Dark, hardly to your taste, my dear?
Its features seemed unbeautiful:
    But this I know—'twas there, not here,
5   You plighted troth to me, the word
Which—ask that poor room how it heard!

II

And this rich room obtains your praise
    Unqualified,—so bright, so fair,
So all whereat perfection stays?
10   Ay, but remember—here, not there,
The other word was spoken! Ask
This rich room how you dropped the mask!

APPEARANCES ³| MS:seemed §last two letters crossed out forming *seem,* then
original reading restored§ unbeautiful, *1876:* unbeautiful: ⁵| MS:The §first word
crossed out and replaced above by§ You < > me—the *1876:* me, the   ⁶| MS:how
I heard! *1876:* how it heard *1889a:* heard §emended to§ heard! §see Editorial
Notes§   ⁸| MS:Unqualified,—all §crossed out and replaced above by§
so bright and fair, *1876:* bright, so fair,   ⁹| MS:The point whereat
1876: So all whereat   ¹⁰| MS:there *1876:* there,   ¹¹| MS:spoken—ask
1876: spoken!—Ask B's *1876:* spoken!—Ask §first letter marked in R margin
as lower case and then upper case restored§ *1889a:* spoken! Ask   ¹²| MS:how
he §crossed out and replaced above by§ you < > mask! *1889a:* mask §emended
to§ mask! §see Editorial Notes§ MS: §At lower R§ L.D.I.E. Apr. 6' '76. §crossed out§

ST. MARTIN'S SUMMER

I

No protesting, dearest!
　　Hardly kisses even!
　　　　Don't we both know how it ends?
How the greenest leaf turns serest,
5　　Bluest outbreak—blankest heaven,
　　　　Lovers—friends?

II

You would build a mansion,
　　I would weave a bower
　　　　—Want the heart for enterprise.
10　Walls admit of no expansion:
　　　　Trellis-work may haply flower
　　　　　　Twice the size.

III

What makes glad Life's Winter?
　　New buds, old blooms after.
15　　　　Sad the sighing "How suspect
Beams would ere mid-Autumn splinter,
　　Rooftree scarce support a rafter,
　　　　Walls lie wrecked?"

ST. MARTIN'S SUMMER　¹|　MS:dearest,—　*1876:*dearest!　　　³|　MS:ends—
*1876:*ends　*1889a:*ends?　　　⁹|　MS:—Wanting §last three letters crossed out forming
Want§ the §inserted above§　　　¹³|　MS:glad the §crossed out and replaced above by§
Life's　　　¹⁵|　MS:Spare our §last two words crossed out and replaced above by two
words§ Sad the　　　¹⁶|　MS:Ere mid-Autumn beams would splinter,　*1876:*Beams
would ere mid-Autumn splinter,　　　¹⁸|　MS:wrecked?　*1876:*wrecked?"

You are young, my princess!
20   I am hardly older:
            Yet—I steal a glance behind.
Dare I tell you what convinces
      Timid me that you, if bolder,
            Bold—are blind?

25   Where we plan our dwelling
            Glooms a graveyard surely!
                  Headstone, footstone moss may drape,—
Name, date, violets hide from spelling,—
            But, though corpses rot obscurely,
30   Ghosts escape.

Ghosts! O breathing Beauty,
      Give my frank word pardon!
            What if I—somehow, somewhere—
Pledged my soul to endless duty
35   Many a time and oft? Be hard on
                  Love—laid there?

20| MS:Am §first word crossed out§ I so much §last two words crossed out and
replaced above by two words§ am hardly older?   *1876:* older: 21| MS:behind—
1876: behind!   *1889a:* behind.   26| MS:Is a   *1876:* Glooms a
27| MS:Tombstones §first five and last letters crossed out and *Head* inserted above
forming§ Headstone, these which §last two words crossed out and replaced above by
three words§ footstone moss may violets drape;   *1876:* may drape,—   28| MS:Name,
and §crossed out§ date mosses §crossed out and replaced above by§ violets hides §last
letter crossed out forming *hide*§ <> spelling;   *1876:* date, violets <>
spelling,—   32| MS:Give the §crossed out and replaced above by§ my

Nay, blame grief that's fickle,
    Time that proves a traitor,
        Chance, change, all that purpose warps,—
40 Death who spares to thrust the sickle
    Laid Love low, through flowers which later
        Shroud the corpse!

VIII

And you, my winsome lady,
    Whisper with like frankness!
45   Lies nothing buried long ago?
Are yon—which shimmer mid the shady
    Where moss and violet run to rankness—
        Tombs or no?

IX

Who taxes you with murder?
50   My hands are clean—or nearly!
        Love being mortal needs must pass.
Repentance? Nothing were absurder.
    Enough: we felt Love's loss severely;
        Though now—alas!

39| MS:§line is flush left§ change, and §crossed out§   *1876:*§line indented according to stanza pattern§   40| MS:Blame §first word crossed out§   41| MS:That laid   *1876:*Laid   45| MS:Was §first word crossed out and replaced above by§ Lies < >
ago   *1876:*ago?   46| MS:yon,—which < > shady,   *1876:*yon—which < >
shady   47| MS:rankness,—   *1876:*rankness—   49| MS:Who §first word crossed out and replaced above by *I,* crossed out and *Who* restored§ taxes §last two letters crossed out forming *tax* and then original reading restored§ you with §followed by illegible word or part of word inserted above§   53| MS:severely: *1876:*severely;

55 Love's corpse lies quiet therefore,
       Only Love's ghost plays truant,
          And warns us have in wholesome awe
       Durable mansionry; that's wherefore
          I weave but trellis-work, pursuant
60   —Life, to law.

xi

       The solid, not the fragile,
          Tempts rain and hail and thunder.
             If bower stand firm at Autumn's close,
       Beyond my hope,—why, boughs were agile;
65   If bower fall flat, we scarce need wonder
                Wreathing—rose!

xii

       So, truce to the protesting,
          So, muffled be the kisses!
             For, would we but avow the truth,
70   Sober is genuine joy. No jesting!
          Ask else Penelope, Ulysses—
             Old in youth!

---

⁵⁸| MS:§mark in L margin indicating alignment of line§   ⁶⁰| MS:—Life
to *1876:*—Life, to   ⁶²| MS:rain, and §inserted above§ hail, snow
§crossed out§ and thunder; *1876:* rain and hail and thunder.   ⁶⁴| MS:§mark in
L margin indicating alignment of line§ agile: *1876:* agile;   ⁶⁵| MS:If flat bower fall, I
§crossed out and replaced above by two words§ why, who need §altered to§ needs scarce
§crossed out§ wonder *1876:* If bower fall flat, we scarce need wonder   ⁶⁶| MS:rose?
1876: rose!   ⁶⁷| MS:So, spare me the pro §last five words started on line needed for
stanza number; therefore crossed out and *12.* inserted; line restarted next line down§
So, spare me §last two words crossed out and replaced above by two words§ truce to
⁶⁸| MS:And §first word crossed out and replaced above by word and comma§ So, muffles
§altered to§ muffled up §crossed out and replaced above by§ be   ⁷⁰| MS:Sad joy's
the §last three words crossed out and replaced above by two words§ Sober is

For why should ghosts feel angered?
 Let all their interference
75   Be faint march-music in the air!
"Up! Join the rear of us the vanguard!
 Up, lovers, dead to all appearance,
  Laggard pair!"

XIV

The while you clasp me closer,
80 The while I press you deeper,
  As safe we chuckle,—under breath,
Yet all the slyer, the jocoser,—
 "So, life can boast its day, like leap-year,
  Stolen from death!"

XV

85 Ah me—the sudden terror!
 Hence quick—avaunt, avoid me,
  You cheat, the ghostly flesh-disguised!
Nay, all the ghosts in one! Strange error!
 So, 'twas Death's self that clipped and coyed me,
90   Loved—and lied!

76| MS:"March §first word crossed out and replaced above by§ "Up   79| MS:me
closelier, *1876:*me closer,   80| MS:you deeplier, *1876:*you deeper,
81| MS:breath,— §dash crossed out§   82| MS:the slilier, the jocoselier,— *1876:*the
slyer, the jocoser,—   83| MS:"Our life <> day—like leap-year— *1876:*"So, life <>
day, like leap-year,   84| MS:Cribbed §first word crossed out and replaced above by§
Stolen   86| MS:Quick hence §transposed to§ Hence quick   89| MS:death's
§altered to§ Death's <> that kissed §crossed out and replaced above by§ clipped

XVI

Ay, dead loves are the potent!
    Like any cloud they used you,
        Mere semblance you, but substance they!
    Build we no mansion, weave we no tent!
95   Mere flesh—their spirit interfused you!
        Hence, I say!

XVII

All theirs, none yours the glamour!
    Theirs each low word that won me,
        Soft look that found me Love's, and left
100 What else but you—the tears and clamour
    That's all your very own! Undone me—
        Ghost-bereft!

91| MS:So §first word crossed out and replaced above by§ Ay   94| MS:Build you no mansion, I weave no   *1876:* Build we no mansion, weave we no   97-102| MS:§stanza 17 is on verso of MS p. 52§   99| MS:me theirs §crossed out and replaced above by§ Love's—and   *1876:* Love's, and   MS:§At lower R§ L.D.I.E. March 27. '76. §crossed out§

HERVÉ RIEL

I

On the sea and at the Hogue, sixteen hundred ninety-two,
   Did the English fight the French,—woe to France!
And, the thirty-first of May, helter-skelter through the blue,
Like a crowd of frightened porpoises a shoal of sharks pursue,
5   Came crowding ship on ship to Saint-Malo on the Rance,
   With the English fleet in view.

II

'Twas the squadron that escaped, with the victor in full chase;
   First and foremost of the drove, in his great ship, Damfreville;
     Close on him fled, great and small,
10   Twenty-two good ships in all;
And they signalled to the place
"Help the winners of a race!
   Get us guidance, give us harbour, take us quick—or, quicker still,
   Here's the English can and will!"

HERVÉ RIEL § original MS in Pierpont Morgan Library; subsequent MS with
additional revisions in Balliol College. Quotation marks repeated at the beginning of
each line of a passage on PMMS are not recorded as variants.§ *Title*| PMMS:
Hervé Riel. By Robert Browning. BMS:Hervé Riel *1876:HERVE RIEL*
§emended to§ *HERVÉ* §see Editorial Notes§   1| PMMS:the Hogue, Sixteen
<> ninety-two, BMS:the Hogue, sixteen <> ninety two, *1876:*ninety-two,
2| PMMS:the English fight §part of word over illegible letters§   3| PMMS:helter
skelter thro' BMS:helter-skelter *1889a:*through   5| PMMS:to St Malo BMS:to St.
Malo *1889a:*to Saint-Malo   7| PMMS:victors §last letter crossed out§
8| PMMS:ship, Damfreville: BMS:ship, Damfreville;   9| PMMS:§line not
indented§ BMS:§line indented§   10| PMMS:§line not indented§ all, BMS:§line
indented§ all;   11| PMMS:place, BMS:place   12| PMMS:of the
§crossed out and replaced above by§ a   13| PMMS:§line indented§ Get
§over *Give*§ us guides §altered to§ guidance, give §over *get*§ <> quick, or
quicker still BMS:§line not indented§ quick—or, quicker still, *1876:*§line
indented§   14| PMMS:the English can and §last two words crossed out and
replaced by two words§ fleet that §last two words crossed out and *can and* restored§

III

15   Then the pilots of the place put out brisk and leapt on board;
        "Why, what hope or chance have ships like these to pass?"
        laughed they:
    "Rocks to starboard, rocks to port, all the passage scarred and scored,—
    Shall the 'Formidable' here, with her twelve and eighty guns,
        Think to make the river-mouth by the single narrow way,
20   Trust to enter—where 'tis ticklish for a craft of twenty tons,
        And with flow at full beside?
        Now, 'tis slackest ebb of tide.
    Reach the mooring? Rather say,
    While rock stands or water runs,
25   Not a ship will leave the bay!"

IV

    Then was called a council straight.
    Brief and bitter the debate:
    "Here's the English at our heels; would you have them take in tow
    All that's left us of the fleet, linked together stern and bow,
30   For a prize to Plymouth Sound?
    Better run the ships aground!"
        (Ended Damfreville his speech).
    "Not a minute more to wait!

---

¹⁵| PMMS:board: BMS:board;   ¹⁶⁻¹⁸| PMMS:§line 16 indented§ "Why, §crossed out and restored§ what §quotation marks added before last word, first letter made upper case, then quotation marks crossed out§ <> pass?"—laughed they: / "Shall the Formidable here, with <> guns,   BMS:§line 16 not indented§ "Why, what <> pass?" laughed they: / "Rocks <> scored,—/ Shall the *'Formidable'* here with <> guns   *1876:*§line 16 indented§/ <> scored, *1889a:*scored,—/ <> 'Formidable' <> guns,   ¹⁹| PMMS:to reach §crossed out and replaced above by§ make <> way? BMS:way,   ²⁰| PMMS:Shall she §last two words crossed out and replaced above by two words§ Trust to enter where <> tons? §question mark crossed out and replaced by comma§ *1889a:*enter—where   ²¹| PMMS:And §inserted above§ With the §crossed out§ BMS:And with   ²²| PMMS:'tis deadest §crossed out and replaced above by§ slackest <> tide: BMS:tide.   ²³| PMMS:§line not indented§ *1876:* §line indented§   ²⁴| PMMS:§line indented§ stands and §crossed out and replaced above by§ or BMS:§line not indented§   ²⁵| PMMS:§line indented§ *1889a:* §line indented§   ²⁶| PMMS:Then they §crossed out and replaced above by§ was <> straight; BMS:straight.   ²⁸| PMMS:heels, would BMS:heels; would   ³⁰| PMMS:to Plymouth sound §altered to§ Sound   ³¹| PMMS:aground! BMS:aground!"   ³²⁻³³| PMMS:"Not <> wait! / (Ended <> speech) §lines transposed to§ (Ended <> speech) / "Not <> wait! BMS:speech.) *1876:*speech).

Let the Captains all and each
Shove ashore, then blow up, burn the vessels on the beach!
France must undergo her fate.

V

Give the word!" But no such word
Was ever spoke or heard;
For up stood, for out stepped, for in struck amid all these
—A Captain? A Lieutenant? A Mate—first, second, third?
No such man of mark, and meet
With his betters to compete!
But a simple Breton sailor pressed by Tourville for the fleet,
A poor coasting-pilot he, Hervé Riel the Croisickese.

VI

And "What mockery or malice have we here?" cries Hervé Riel:
"Are you mad, you Malouins? Are you cowards, fools, or rogues?
Talk to me of rocks and shoals, me who took the soundings, tell
On my fingers every bank, every shallow, every swell
'Twixt the offing here and Grève where the river disembogues?
Are you bought by English gold? Is it love the lying's for?

34| PMMS:Bid §first word crossed out and replaced above by§ Let
35| PMMS:ashore, then §inserted above§ <> vessel §altered to§ vessels §followed by word inserted above and illegibly crossed out§ upon §altered to§ on BMS:a-shore *1876:* ashore 36| PMMS:fate!" BMS:fate.
38| PMMS:spoke not §altered to§ or heard. BMS:heard; 39| PMMS:§line not indented§ up there §crossed out§ stood, for §inserted above§ out there §crossed out§ stepped, for §inserted above§ in there §crossed out§ BMS:§line indented§ out-stepped *1876:* out stepped 40| PMMS:§first word illegibly crossed out, perhaps *Would*§ a Captain, nor §crossed out and replaced above by§ a Lieutenant, a Mate first <> third, BMS:—A Captain? A Lieutenant? A Mate,—first <> third? *1876:* —A Captain? A Lieutenant? A Mate—first 41| PMMS:—Not §altered to§ —No a §crossed out and replaced above by§ such <> mark and BMS:No <> mark, and 42| PMMS:compete, §comma altered to exclamation mark§ 43| PMMS:simple Breton §inserted above§
44| PMMS:A mere §crossed out and replaced above by§ poor <> he,—Hervé BMS:he, Hervé 45| PMMS:cried BMS:cries 46| PMMS:"Are BMS:Are *1876:* "Are
47| PMMS:of Malo harbour, me BMS:of rocks and shoals, me 49| PMMS:'Twixt the offing §last two words inserted above§ <> and the §crossed out§ <> where your §crossed out and replaced above by§ the 50| PMMS:you feed §crossed out and replaced above by§ bought <> English §word inserted above and illegibly crossed out§ gold? What §crossed out and replaced above by§ Then §next two words illegibly crossed out and replaced above by four words§ Is it love the BMS:gold? Is

Morn and eve, night and day,
Have I piloted your bay,
Entered free and anchored fast at the foot of Solidor.
Burn the fleet and ruin France? That were worse than fifty Hogues!
55   Sirs, they know I speak the truth! Sirs, believe me there's a way!
Only let me lead the line,
Have the biggest ship to steer,
Get this 'Formidable' clear,
Make the others follow mine,
60   And I lead them, most and least, by a passage I know well,
Right to Solidor past Grève,
And there lay them safe and sound;
And if one ship misbehave,—
—Keel so much as grate the ground,
65   Why, I've nothing but my life,—here's my head!" cries Hervé Riel.

VII

Not a minute more to wait.
"Steer us in, then, small and great!

51| PMMS:and eve §over illegible word§   52| PMMS:Have I entered port from §last
three words crossed out and replaced above by two words§ piloted your   53| PMMS:Ay,
and anchored vessel §last four words crossed out and replaced above by two words§ Entered
free §followed by word illegibly crossed out; *and anchored* then restored§ < > of
Solidor! BMS:of Solidor.   55| PMMS:§line not indented§ believe me §crossed out and
then restored§ there's §next word inserted below, illegibly crossed out, and replaced by two
words§ a way! BMS:§line indented§   56| PMMS:§line indented§ BMS:§line not
indented§   57| PMMS:Let me steer §last three words crossed out§ Have
58| PMMS:The guide ship here, §last four words and comma crossed out and replaced to
the right by four words and comma§ Get the Formidable clear, BMS:Get this Formidable
clear, *1876:* this *'Formidable'* clear, *1889a:* this 'Formidable' clear,   60| PMMS:lead
them §crossed out and replaced above by§ you, most < > by the way §last two words crossed
out and replaced above by two words§ a passage I know so §crossed out§ BMS:lead them,
most   61| PMMS:Up §crossed out and replaced above by§ Right < > Solidor
thro' §crossed out and replaced above by§ past   62| PMMS:§line not indented
additionally§ lay them §crossed out and then restored§ < > sound, BMS:§line indented
additonally§ sound;   63| PMMS:one helm §crossed out and replaced above by word
illegibly crossed out and replaced by§ ship misbehave— BMS: misbehave,
1889a: misbehave,—   64| PMMS:§line not indented additionally§ So that one
§last three words crossed out and dash inserted above§ —keel so much as §last three
words inserted above§ < > ground,— BMS:§line indented additionally§ —Keel
< > ground,   65| PMMS:cried §altered to§ cries   66| PMMS:wait! BMS:wait.

Take the helm, lead the line, save the squadron!" cried its chief.
Captains, give the sailor place!
70   He is Admiral, in brief.
Still the north-wind, by God's grace!
See the noble fellow's face
As the big ship, with a bound,
Clears the entry like a hound,
75 Keeps the passage, as its inch of way were the wide sea's profound!
    See, safe thro' shoal and rock,
    How they follow in a flock,
Not a ship that misbehaves, not a keel that grates the ground,
    Not a spar that comes to grief!
80 The peril, see, is past.
All are harboured to the last,
And just as Hervé Riel hollas "Anchor!"—sure as fate,
Up the English come,—too late!

68| PMMS:§line not indented§ squadron!" cried its Chief. BMS:§line
indented§ *1876:* squadron! cried its chief. *1889a:* squadron!" cried
69| PMMS:§line indented§ Hervé Riel is at his §last five words crossed out and
replaced above by indeterminate number of words illegibly crossed out and replaced
by four words§ Captains, give the sailor place! §exclamation mark over comma§
BMS:§line not indented§   70| PMMS:§line not indented§ BMS:§line indented§
71| PMMS:There is a §last three words crossed out and replaced above by word illegibly
crossed out and replaced in L margin by§ Still the §inserted above§ north wind < > grace!
BMS: north-wind < > grace. *1876:* grace! *1889a:* grace §emended to§ grace! §see
Editorial Notes§   72| PMMS:§line indented§ noble fellows §*Bretons* inserted above
as possible alternative but crossed out; *fellows* retained§ BMS:§line not indented§ fellow's
73| PMMS:ship with a bound BMS:ship, with a bound,   74| PMMS:Clears §crossed
out and replaced above by *Takes* and then *Clears* restored§ the barrier §crossed out and
replaced above by§ entry   75| PMMS:passage as < > inch of width §last two words
crossed out and replaced above by two words§ wide way §last two words crossed out and
replaced above by§ way < > the whole §crossed out and replaced above by§ wide BMS:inch
of way *1889a:* passage, as   76| PMMS:thro < > rock BMS:thro' < > rock,
77| PMMS:How §inserted to L§ They have §crossed out§ followed §last two letters
crossed out forming *follow*§ BMS:How they   78| PMMS:Not a helm that BMS:Not
a ship that   79| PMMS:grief— BMS:grief!   80| PMMS:And §crossed out
and replaced above by word illegibly crossed out; *And* restored and then restoration
cancelled§ the §altered to§ The < > past, *1889a:* past.   81| PMMS:All are
§crossed out and replaced above by word illegibly crossed out and then *are*
restored§   82| PMMS:as Hervé Riel §next word illegibly crossed out and
replaced above by§ hollas them §crossed out§ "Anchor!." like a §last two words
crossed out and replaced above by two words§ sure as BMS:Anchor!"—sure
83| PMMS:come, too late! BMS:late. *1876:* late! *1889a:* come,—too

So, the storm subsides to calm:
85   They see the green trees wave
        On the heights o'erlooking Grève.
Hearts that bled are stanched with balm.
"Just our rapture to enhance,
        Let the English rake the bay,
90   Gnash their teeth and glare askance
        As they cannonade away!
'Neath rampired Solidor pleasant riding on the Rance!"
How hope succeeds despair on each Captain's countenance!
Out burst all with one accord,
95   "This is Paradise for Hell!
        Let France, let France's King
        Thank the man that did the thing!"
What a shout, and all one word,
        "Hervé Riel!"

84| PMMS:So the §over perhaps a§ storm subsides §over illegible word§ < >
calm; BMS:So, the < > calm: 85| PMMS:When §first word crossed out§
they §altered to§ They   86| PMMS:heights that took our §last three words crossed
out and replaced above by three words§ which top the §last three words crossed out and
replaced below by two words§ oer looking §next word inserted above and illegibly crossed
out§ Grève, BMS:o'erlooking Grève: 1876:o'erlooking Grève.   87| PMMS:balm:
BMS:balm.   88| PMMS:§line indented§ BMS:§line not indented§
89| PMMS:§line not indented§ BMS:§line indented§   90| PMMS:§line not indented§
and look §crossed out and replaced above by§ glare BMS:§line indented, and the
following note in R Margin: *Print this line further back—§ 1876:*§line not indented§
91| PMMS:While §crossed out and replaced above by§ As BMS:§line not indented but
following note in R margin: *put forward.*§   92| PMMS:'Neath the wall of §last three
words crossed out and replaced above by§ rampired < > Rance! BMS:Rance!"
93| PMMS:How the hope < > countenance, BMS:How hope < > countenance!
94| PMMS:§line indented§ As §in L margin and crossed out§ Out broke §crossed out and
replaced above by§ burst all §crossed out and then restored§ < > accord, §following line
inserted to R and crossed out: *no way a tongue that all the same,*§ BMS:§line not indented§
accord 1876:accord,   95| PMMS:§line not indented; originally second half of l. 97;
line drawn to indicate position between 94 and 96§ gave us §last two words crossed out and
replaced above by two words§ This is < > Hell!" BMS:§line indented§ "This < > Hell!
96| PMMS:§between 94 and 97; first word blotted illegibly§ France, let the §crossed out
and replaced below by§ France's king BMS: let France's King   97| PMMS:§line
not indented§ "Thank §perhaps over illegible word§ < > thing, BMS:§line
indented§ thing!" 1876:Thank   98| PMMS:§line indented§ 'Twas §crossed
out and replaced above by§ What a shout, no word that names §last two words
crossed out and three words inserted above, after *shout*§ and all one §no
inadvertently retained§ word, §comma added§ BMS:§line not indented§ one word,
99| PMMS:"Hervé Riel!" BMS:"Hervé Riel," 1876:"Hervé Riel!"

As he stepped in front once more,
  Not a symptom of surprise
  In the frank blue Breton eyes,
Just the same man as before.

       IX

Then said Damfreville, "My friend,
105 I must speak out at the end,
  Though I find the speaking hard.
Praise is deeper than the lips:
You have saved the King his ships,
  You must name your own reward.
110 'Faith, our sun was near eclipse!
Demand whate'er you will,
France remains your debtor still.
Ask to heart's content and have! or my name's not Damfreville."

       X

Then a beam of fun outbroke
115 On the bearded mouth that spoke,
As the honest heart laughed through
Those frank eyes of Breton blue:
"Since I needs must say my say,

104| PMMS:said Damfreville, "My   BMS:said Damfreville "My   *1876:*said
Damfreville, "My   105| PMMS:One §crossed out and replaced above by§ We
§crossed out and replaced to R by§ I   106| PMMS:§line not indented§ Though I
§crossed out and replaced above by *we* and then *I* restored§ < > the speech §altered to§
speaking hard: BMS:§line indented§ hard.   108-09| PMMS:You < > reward, / You
< > ships: §transposed to§ You < > the king < > ships: / "You < > reward §last line not
indented§ BMS:the King < > ships, / < > reward. §last line indented§
110-11| PMMS:Make §crossed out§ demand §altered to§ Demand, what'er < > will! /
'Faith < > was near §crossed out and replaced above by *nigh* and then *near* restored§
eclipse! §transposed to§ 'Faith < > eclipse! / Demand < > will! BMS:Demand whate're
< > will,   112| PMMS:We shall be §last three words crossed out and replaced by two
words§ France remains < > debtors §altered to§ debtor   113| PMMS:have!—or
*1876:*have! or   114| PMMS:Then §crossed out and replaced above by illegible word
and then restored§ < > of laughter §crossed out and replaced above by two words§ fun out
broke BMS:outbroke   115| PMMS:bearded §over perhaps *beard* of§ face
§crossed out and replaced above by§ mouth < > spoke— BMS:spoke,   116| PMMS:As
§over perhaps *And*§ < > laughes §over perhaps *looks*§ BMS:laughed
117| PMMS:blue,— BMS:blue: 118| PMMS:my say,— BMS:my say,

Since on board the duty's done,

120 And from Malo Roads to Croisic Point, what is it but a run?—
Since 'tis ask and have, I may—
Since the others go ashore—
Come! A good whole holiday!
Leave to go and see my wife, whom I call the Belle Aurore!"

125 That he asked and that he got,—nothing more.

XI

Name and deed alike are lost:
Not a pillar nor a post
In his Croisic keeps alive the feat as it befell;
Not a head in white and black

130 On a single fishing-smack,
In memory of the man but for whom had gone to wrack
All that France saved from the fight whence England bore the bell.
Go to Paris: rank on rank
Search the heroes flung pell-mell

<hr />

119| PMMS:Since §over perhaps *Here*§ <> done BMS:done,   120| PMMS:to
Croisic Point, §over *Port*§ an easy §last two words crossed out, followed by word
illegibly crossed out, and replaced above by five words§ what is it but a BMS:to
Croisic Port §last two letters crossed out and replaced above by *int* forming
Point§   121| PMMS:(Since §parenthesis crossed out§ <> may—)
§parenthesis crossed out§   122| PMMS:§line not indented§ Since §over
When§ <> a-shore, §first letter over *on*§ BMS:§line indented§ ashore—
123| PMMS:Come,—a <> holiday, BMS:Come! A <> holiday!   124| PMMS:§line
not indented§ the Belle Aurore! BMS:§line begins flush L with *Le*; these letters were erased
and line indented§ the Belle Aurore!"   125| PMMS:§line not indented§ asked & that
<> got and §blotted out and replaced above by dash§ —nothing BMS:asked and that <>
got, and §crossed out and replaced above by dash§ —nothing *1876:*§line indented§
126| PMMS:lost; BMS:lost: 127| PMMS:pillar, §comma crossed out§ not §altered to§
nor   128| PMMS:§line not indented§ keeps no alive §inserted above§ fame §lightly
crossed out§ the thing as <> befell: BMS:§line marked for indention; note in R margin:
*Print more forw*d§ keeps alive the thing §crossed out and replaced above by§ feat as <>
befell: *1876:*befell;   130| PMMS:fishing-smack BMS:fishing-smack,
131| PMMS:To the §last two words crossed out and replaced above by§ In <> man but
§crossed out and replaced above by word illegibly crossed out§ for BMS:man but for
132| PMMS:§line not indented§ What §crossed out and replaced above by two words§ All
that <> whence the §crossed out§ English §altered to§ England §word inserted above and
illegibly crossed out§ <> bell: BMS:§line indented§ bell.   133| PMMS:As for
§last two words crossed out and replaced above by two words§ Go to Paris, rank
BMS:Paris; rank *1876:*Paris: rank   134| PMMS:§line not indented§ heroes, flung
BMS:§line marked for indention; note in R margin: *put forw*d§ heroes flung

¹³⁵ On the Louvre, face and flank!
　　　You shall look long enough ere you come to Hervé Riel.
　　　So, for better and for worse,
　　　Hervé Riel, accept my verse!
　　　In my verse, Hervé Riel, do thou once more
¹⁴⁰ Save the squadron, honour France, love thy wife the Belle Aurore!

---

^{135|}　PMMS:the Louvre face <> flank:　BMS:the Louvre, face <> flank;　*1876:* flank!
^{136|}　PMMS:§line not indented§ You §crossed out and replaced by word illegibly crossed
and *You* restored§ shall look §lightly crossed out and replaced above by word illegibly
crossed out§ there §inserted above and crossed out§ long <> you §two or three words
inserted above and illegibly marked out§　BMS:§line indented§ shall look long
^{137|}　PMMS:better or for　BMS:better and for　　　^{138|}　PMMS:verse—　BMS:verse!
^{139|}　PMMS:In my verse, §last three words and comma crossed out and then restored§
Give the world one hero §last five words crossed out and replaced above by six
words§ Hervé Riel whoever reads my verse §last six words crossed out and replaced
by five words§ Hervé Riel, do thou once more,　BMS:more　　　^{140|}　PMMS:squadron,
§next word illegibly crossed out and replaced above by§ honour　B's *1876:* honour France,
§slanted line perhaps indicating dash inserted§ love <> wife §perhaps comma
inserted but immediately followed by what looks like the mirror image of a comma§
the　*1889a:* honour France, love <> wife the　PMMS:§At lower L§ Croisic, / Sept. 30. '67
BMS:§At lower L§ Croisic, Sept. 30. '67 §At lower R§ Robert Browning.

A FORGIVENESS

I am indeed the personage you know.
As for my wife,—what happened long ago,—
You have a right to question me, as I
Am bound to answer.

                ("Son, a fit reply!"
5   The monk half spoke, half ground through his clenched teeth,
At the confession-grate I knelt beneath.)

Thus then all happened, Father! Power and place
I had as still I have. I ran life's race,
With the whole world to see, as only strains
10   His strength some athlete whose prodigious gains
Of good appal him: happy to excess,—
Work freely done should balance happiness
Fully enjoyed; and, since beneath my roof
Housed she who made home heaven, in heaven's behoof
15   I went forth every day, and all day long
Worked for the world. Look, how the labourer's song
Cheers him! Thus sang my soul, at each sharp throe
Of labouring flesh and blood—"She loves me so!"

One day, perhaps such song so knit the nerve
20   That work grew play and vanished. "I deserve
Haply my heaven an hour before the time!"
I laughed, as silverly the clockhouse-chime
Surprised me passing through the postern-gate
—Not the main entry where the menials wait

A FORGIVENESS Title| MS: §begins with word illegibly crossed out§ Spanisch!
§followed to the R by§ (Egmont) *1876:A FORGIVENESS.*   ¹| MS:know;
1876: know.   ⁴| MS:answer. §¶§ "Son B's *1876:* answer. §¶§ ("Son
§parenthesis inserted§   ⁵| MS:spoke, half spat §crossed out and replaced above
by§ ground me through his teeth *1876:* ground through his clenched teeth,
⁶| MS:beneath. B's *1876:* beneath.) §parenthesis inserted§   ⁸| MS:race
1876: race,   ¹¹| MS:excess, *1876:* excess,—   ¹²| MS:Work §over illegible
erasure§ <> done must §crossed out and replaced above by§ should
¹⁷| MS:soul at *1876:* soul, at   ²¹| MS:heaven this §crossed out and
replaced above by§ an <> time,' *1876:* time!"   ²⁴| MS:—Not §dash in L margin§

214

25 And wonder why the world's affairs allow
The master sudden leisure. That was how
I took the private garden-way for once.

Forth from the alcove, I saw start, ensconce
Himself behind the porphyry vase, a man.

30 My fancies in the natural order ran:
"A spy,—perhaps a foe in ambuscade,—
A thief,—more like, a sweetheart of some maid
Who pitched on the alcove for tryst perhaps."
"Stand there!" I bid.

Whereat my man but wraps
35 His face the closelier with uplifted arm
Whereon the cloak lies, strikes in blind alarm
This and that pedestal as,—stretch and stoop,—
Now in, now out of sight, he thrids the group
Of statues, marble god and goddess ranged
40 Each side the pathway, till the gate's exchanged
For safety: one step thence, the street, you know!

Thus far I followed with my gaze. Then, slow,
Near on admiringly, I breathed again,
And—back to that last fancy of the train—
45 "A danger risked for hope of just a word
With—which of all my nest may be the bird
This poacher covets for her plumage, pray?
Carmen? Juana? Carmen seems too gay
For such adventure, while Juana's grave
50 —Would scorn the folly. I applaud the knave!
He had the eye, could single from my brood

---

²⁶| MS:leisure; that *1876:* leisure. That ²⁷| MS:took for once the
private garden-way. §transposed to§ took the private garden-way for once.
²⁸| MS:see *1876:* saw ³⁴| MS:there!" I cry. §marginal note that ¶
begins§ Whereat *1876:* there!" I bid. §¶§ Whereat ³⁶| MS:lay
1876: lies ³⁹| MS:statues, marble §inserted above§ God and Goddess
1876: marble god and goddess ⁴¹⁻⁴²| MS:§marginal note that ¶
begins§ ⁴⁵| MS:'All §last two letters crossed out forming *A*§ *1876:* "A

His proper fledgeling!"

As I turned, there stood
In face of me, my wife stone-still stone-white.
Whether one bound had brought her,—at first sight
55 Of what she judged the encounter, sure to be
Next moment, of the venturous man and me,—
Brought her to clutch and keep me from my prey:
Whether impelled because her death no day
Could come so absolutely opportune
60 As now at joy's height, like a year in June
Stayed at the fall of its first ripened rose:
Or whether hungry for my hate—who knows?—
Eager to end an irksome lie, and taste
Our tingling true relation, hate embraced
65 By hate one naked moment:—anyhow
There stone-still stone-white stood my wife, but now
The woman who made heaven within my house.
Ay, she who faced me was my very spouse
As well as love—you are to recollect!

70 "Stay!" she said. "Keep at least one soul unspecked
With crime, that's spotless hitherto—your own!
Kill me who court the blessing, who alone
Was, am, and shall be guilty, first to last!
The man lay helpless in the toils I cast
75 About him, helpless as the statue there
Against that strangling bell-flower's bondage: tear
Away and tread to dust the parasite,
But do the passive marble no despite!
I love him as I hate you. Kill me! Strike
80 At one blow both infinitudes alike
Out of existence—hate and love! Whence love?
That's safe inside my heart, nor will remove

52| MS:fledgeling!' §marginal note that ¶ begins§ As   1876:fledgeling!"§¶§ As
65| MS:moment: anyhow   1876:moment:—anyhow   66| MS:wife—but   1876:wife,
but   73| MS:am and <> guilty first   1876:guilty, first   1889a:am, and
79| MS:you: strike me—strike   1876:you. Kill me! Strike   81| MS:love. Whence
1876:love! Whence   82| MS:nor shall §crossed out and replaced above by§ will

216

For any searching of your steel, I think.
Whence hate? The secret lay on lip, at brink
85   Of speech, in one fierce tremble to escape,
At every form wherein your love took shape,
At each new provocation of your kiss.
Kill me!"

We went in.

Next day after this,
I felt as if the speech might come. I spoke—
90   Easily, after all.

"The lifted cloak
Was screen sufficient: I concern myself
Hardly with laying hands on who for pelf—
Whate'er the ignoble kind—may prowl and brave
Cuffing and kicking proper to a knave
95   Detected by my household's vigilance.
Enough of such! As for my love-romance—
I, like our good Hidalgo, rub my eyes
And wake and wonder how the film could rise
Which changed for me a barber's basin straight
100 Into—Mambrino's helm? I hesitate
Nowise to say—God's sacramental cup!
Why should I blame the brass which, burnished up,
Will blaze, to all but me, as good as gold?
To me—a warning I was overbold
105 In judging metals. The Hidalgo waked
Only to die, if I remember,—staked
His life upon the basin's worth, and lost:
While I confess torpidity at most

85| MS:one next §crossed out and replaced above by§ fierce <> escape
*1876:*escape,   86| MS:§between 85-87§   88| MS:me!" §¶§ We <>
in. §marginal note that ¶ begins§ Next <> this   *1876:*me! §¶§ We <> §¶§ <> this,
B's *1876:*me!" §quotation mark inserted§   89| MS:the words §crossed out and replaced
above by§ speech   90| MS:all. §marginal note that ¶ begins§ "The
99| MS:bason   B's *1876:*bason §o crossed out and i inserted in R margin forming *basin*§
105| MS:In §inserted in L margin§ judging of §crossed out§   107| MS:bason's
B's *1876:*bason's §o crossed out and i inserted in R margin forming *basin's*§

In here and there a limb; but, lame and halt,
110 Still should I work on, still repair my fault
Ere I took rest in death,—no fear at all!
Now, work—no word before the curtain fall!"

The "curtain"? That of death on life, I meant:
My "word," permissible in death's event,
115 Would be—truth, soul to soul; for, otherwise,
Day by day, three years long, there had to rise
And, night by night, to fall upon our stage—
Ours, doomed to public play by heritage—
Another curtain, when the world, perforce
120 Our critical assembly, in due course
Came and went, witnessing, gave praise or blame
To art-mimetic. It had spoiled the game
If, suffered to set foot behind our scene,
The world had witnessed how stage-king and queen,
125 Gallant and lady, but a minute since
Enarming each the other, would evince
No sign of recognition as they took
His way and her way to whatever nook
Waited them in the darkness either side
130 Of that bright stage where lately groom and bride
Had fired the audience to a frenzy-fit
Of sympathetic rapture—every whit
Earned as the curtain fell on her and me,

109| MS:limb: but 1876:limb; but   112| MS:And now §first two words crossed out
and replaced above by two words and dash§ Now, work—<> words <> fall." 1876:word
<> fall."   113| MS:The curtain? That 1876:The "curtain?" That 1889a:The
"curtain"? That   114| MS:And words permissible in that §crossed out and replaced
above by§ such event 1876:My "word" permissible in death's event, 1889a:"word,"
permissible   115| MS:Were—truth from soul 1876:Would be—truth, soul
118| MS:§between 117-19§ We public players §last three letters crossed out§ doomed to
§transposed to§ We doomed to public play 1876:Ours, doomed   119| MS:A §six
letters added below forming Another§ curtain, truly, §crossed out§
121| MS:witnessing, for §crossed out and replaced above by§ gave   122| MS:Our
§crossed out and replaced above by§ To art-mimetic. This had spoiled their §last two letters
crossed out forming the§ 1876:art-mimetic. It had   123| MS:behind the §crossed out
and replaced above by§ our   124| MS:witnessed when stage-king 1876:witnessed how
stage-king   125| MS:Galant 1876:Gallant   130| MS:bride §first letter over
illegible erasure§   133| MS:As well-bestowed as §last three words crossed out and
replaced above by five words§ Earned as the curtain fell on my wife §last two words crossed

—Actors. Three whole years, nothing was to see
135   But calm and concord; where a speech was due
There came the speech: when smiles were wanted too
Smiles were as ready. In a place like mine,
Where foreign and domestic cares combine,
There's audience every day and all day long;
140   But finally the last of the whole throng
Who linger lets one see his back. For her—
Why, liberty and liking: I aver,
Liking and liberty! For me—I breathed,
Let my face rest from every wrinkle wreathed
145   Smile-like about the mouth, unlearned my task
Of personation till next day bade mask,
And quietly betook me from that world
To the real world, not pageant: there unfurled
In work, its wings, my soul, the fretted power.
150   Three years I worked, each minute of each hour
Not claimed by acting:—work I may dispense
With talk about, since work in evidence,
Perhaps in history; who knows or cares?

After three years, this way, all unawares,
155   Our acting ended. She and I, at close
Of a loud night-feast, led, between two rows
Of bending male and female loyalty,
Our lord the king down staircase, while, held high
At arm's length did the twisted tapers' flare
160   Herald his passage from our palace, where
Such visiting left glory evermore.

out and replaced above by§ her   134| MS:Actors   1876:—Actors
135| MS:concord: where   1889a:concord; where   136| MS:speech: when < > were
wanting too   1876:speech; when < > were wanted too   1889a:speech: when
139| MS:long: 1876:long;   141| MS:That §crossed out and replaced above by§ Who
145| MS:Smile-like around the §inserted above§ mouth, and eye §last two words crossed
out§   1876:Smile-like about the   148| MS:the world—real not pageant—there
1876:the real world, not pageant: there   149| MS:In work, my soul, Its §altered to§ its
wings §transposed to§ its wings, In work, my soul §transposed to§ In work, its wings, my
soul   151| MS:acting: work   1876:acting:—work   152| MS:work's   1876:work
153| MS:history—who   1876:history; who   158| MS:the King   1876:the king
159| MS:tapers   1876:tapers'   160| MS:palace where   1889a:palace, where

Again the ascent in public, till at door
As we two stood by the saloon—now blank
And disencumbered of its guests—there sank
165   A whisper in my ear, so low and yet
So unmistakable!

                    "I half forget
The chamber you repair to, and I want
Occasion for one short word—if you grant
That grace—within a certain room you called
170   Our 'Study,' for you wrote there while I scrawled
Some paper full of faces for my sport.
That room I can remember. Just one short
Word with you there, for the remembrance' sake!"

"Follow me thither!" I replied.

                              We break
175   The gloom a little, as with guiding lamp
I lead the way, leave warmth and cheer, by damp
Blind disused serpentining ways afar
From where the habitable chambers are,—
Ascend, descend stairs tunnelled through the stone,—
180   Always in silence,—till I reach the lone
Chamber sepulchred for my very own
Out of the palace-quarry. When a boy,
Here was my fortress, stronghold from annoy,
Proof-positive of ownership; in youth
185   I garnered up my gleanings here—uncouth
But precious relics of vain hopes, vain fears;

163| MS:stood of §crossed out and replaced above by§ by   166| MS:unmistakable!
§marginal note that ¶ begins§ "I   168| MS:for a §crossed out and replaced above by
two words§ one short < > you will §crossed out§   170| MS:Your §first letter erased and
o reshaped forming *Our*§ 'study   *1876:* Our 'Study   *1889a:* Our 'Study   171| MS:faces
done for sport: *1876:* faces for my sport.   172| MS:room I well §crossed out and
replaced above by§ can   173| MS:there for old §crossed out and replaced above by§ the
< > sake?"   *1876:* there, for < > sake!"   175| MS:little as   *1876:* little, as
176| MS:way from warmth < > cheer through damp   *1876:* way, leave warmth < > cheer, by
damp   182| MS:boy   *1876:* boy,   184| MS:Proof positive   *1876:* Proof-positive

Finally, this became in after years
My closet of entrenchment to withstand
Invasion of the foe on every hand—
190   The multifarious herd in bower and hall,
State-room,—rooms whatsoe'er the style, which call
On masters to be mindful that, before
Men, they must look like men and something more.
Here,—when our lord the king's bestowment ceased
195   To deck me on the day that, golden-fleeced,
I touched ambition's height,—'twas here, released
From glory (always symbolled by a chain!)
No sooner was I privileged to gain
My secret domicile than glad I flung
200   That last toy on the table—gazed where hung
On hook my father's gift, the arquebuss—
And asked myself "Shall I envisage thus
The new prize and the old prize, when I reach
Another year's experience?—own that each
205   Equalled advantage—sportsman's—statesman's tool?
That brought me down an eagle, this—a fool!"

Into which room on entry, I set down
The lamp, and turning saw whose rustled gown
Had told me my wife followed, pace for pace.
210   Each of us looked the other in the face.
She spoke. "Since I could die now . . ."

                              (To explain
Why that first struck me, know—not once again
Since the adventure at the porphyry's edge
Three years before, which sundered like a wedge

187| MS:Finally this   1876:Finally, this   195| MS:on that §crossed out and replaced
above by§ a day when, golden-fleeced,   1876:on the day that, golden-fleeced,
197| MS:symboled   1889a:symbolled   204| MS:experience,—own   1876:experience?
—own   205| MS:tool—   1876:tool?   206| MS:That §last two letters
over illegible erasure§ brought §first two letters over illegible erasure§ < > fool?"
1876:fool!"   207| MS:Into which §crossed out and replaced above by perhaps this,
which is erased§ room   1876:Into which room   209| MS:followed pace
1876:followed, pace   211| MS:now" . . .   1876:now . . ."   212| MS:that now
struck   1876:that first struck   214| MS:before, dissevered §crossed out and replaced

215   Her soul from mine,—though daily, smile to smile,
     We stood before the public,—all the while
     Not once had I distinguished, in that face
     I paid observance to, the faintest trace
     Of feature more than requisite for eyes
220   To do their duty by and recognize:
     So did I force mine to obey my will
     And pry no further. There exists such skill,—
     Those know who need it. What physician shrinks
     From needful contact with a corpse? He drinks
225   No plague so long as thirst for knowledge—not
     An idler impulse—prompts inquiry. What,
     And will you disbelieve in power to bid
     Our spirit back to bounds, as though we chid
     A child from scrutiny that's just and right
230   In manhood? Sense, not soul, accomplished sight,
     Reported daily she it was—not how
     Nor why a change had come to cheek and brow.)

     "Since I could die now of the truth concealed,
     Yet dare not, must not die—so seems revealed
235   The Virgin's mind to me—for death means peace,
     Wherein no lawful part have I, whose lease
     Of life and punishment the truth avowed
     May haply lengthen,—let me push the shroud
     Away, that steals to muffle ere is just
240   My penance-fire in snow! I dare—I must
     Live, by avowal of the truth—this truth—
     I loved you! Thanks for the fresh serpent's tooth
     That, by a prompt new pang more exquisite

---

above by two words§ which sundered §comma probably added after *before* at time of
this change§   217| MS:that §last two letters over perhaps *er*§
225| MS:knowledge,—not   *1889a:* knowledge—not   226| MS:impulse,—prompts < >
What, §erasure over comma suggesting exclamation mark§   *1889a:* impulse—prompts
230| MS:manhood? Eyes §crossed out and replaced above by§ Sense   234| MS:die—so
1876: die,—so   *1889a:* die—so   235| MS:me,—for   *1889a:* me—for
236| MS:—Wherein §dash erased§ what §crossed out and replaced above by§ no
240| MS:snow. I   *1876:* snow! I   242| MS:you! Thanked §last two letters
crossed out and replaced above by *s* forming *Thanks*§ be §crossed out and
replaced above by§ for   243| MS:by this prompt   *1876:* by a prompt

Than all preceding torture, proves me right!
245   I loved you yet I lost you! May I go
Burn to the ashes, now my shame you know?"

I think there never was such—how express?—
Horror coquetting with voluptuousness,
As in those arms of Eastern workmanship—
250   Yataghan, kandjar, things that rend and rip,
Gash rough, slash smooth, help hate so many ways,
Yet ever keep a beauty that betrays
Love still at work with the artificer
Throughout his quaint devising. Why prefer,
255   Except for love's sake, that a blade should writhe
And bicker like a flame?—now play the scythe
As if some broad neck tempted,—now contract
And needle off into a fineness lacked
For just that puncture which the heart demands?
260   Then, such adornment! Wherefore need our hands
Enclose not ivory alone, nor gold
Roughened for use, but jewels? Nay, behold!
Fancy my favourite—which I seem to grasp
While I describe the luxury. No asp
265   Is diapered more delicate round throat
Than this below the handle! These denote
—These mazy lines meandering, to end
Only in flesh they open—what intend
They else but water-purlings—pale contrast
270   With the life-crimson where they blend at last?

246| MS:ashes now   *1876:*ashes, now   246-47| MS: §¶§   *1889a:* §no ¶,
emended to restore ¶; see Editorial Notes§   248| MS:voluptuousness
*1876:*voluptuousness,   252| MS:ever with §crossed out and replaced
above by§ keep   253| MS:Love gay §crossed out and replaced above by§
still   254| devising: why *1876:*devising. Why   255| MS:writhe §first four
letters over illegible erasure§   256| MS:flame? Now *1876:*flame?—now
261| MS:not simple §crossed out§ ivory, and §comma and last word crossed out
and replaced above by two words§ alone, nor   263| MS:This was §last two
words crossed out and replaced above by§ Fancy <> favorite *1889a:*favourite
265| MS:Was §crossed out and replaced above by§ Is   266| MS:Than
here below *1876:*Than this below   267| MS:meandering to
*1876:*meandering, to   269| MS:but harmless purlings *1876:*but water-purlings

And mark the handle's dim pellucid green,
Carved, the hard jadestone, as you pinch a bean,
Into a sort of parrot-bird! He pecks
A grape-bunch; his two eyes are ruby-specks
275 Pure from the mine: seen this way,—glassy blank,
But turn them,—lo the inmost fire, that shrank
From sparkling, sends a red dart right to aim!
Why did I choose such toys? Perhaps the game
Of peaceful men is warlike, just as men
280 War-wearied get amusement from that pen
And paper we grow sick of—statesfolk tired
Of merely (when such measures are required)
Dealing out doom to people by three words,
A signature and seal: we play with swords
285 Suggestive of quick process. That is how
I came to like the toys described you now,
Store of which glittered on the walls and strewed
The table, even, while my wife pursued
Her purpose to its ending. "Now you know
290 This shame, my three years' torture, let me go,
Burn to the very ashes! You—I lost,
Yet you—I loved!"

The thing I pity most
In men is—action prompted by surprise
Of anger: men? nay, bulls—whose onset lies
295 At instance of the firework and the goad!

271| MS:And note the handle, §comma crossed out and word altered to§ handle's
1876:And mark the   272| MS:bean 1876:bean,   273| MS:parrot-bird. He
1876:parrot-bird! He   274| MS:grape-bunch,—his 1876:grape-bunch; his
276| MS:low §last letter crossed out forming lo§   277| MS:sends the §crossed out and
replaced above by§ a < > aim. 1876:aim!   278| MS:choose such §inserted above§
281| MS:statesfolk §last four letters over perhaps men§   282| MS:merely, when < >
required, 1876:merely (when < > required)   283| MS:out death §crossed out and
replaced above by§ doom   286| MS:now— 1876:now,   289| MS:to this §crossed
out and replaced above by§ its ending—"Now 1876:ending. "Now   291| MS:ashes:
you 1876:ashes! You   292| MS:And §crossed out and replaced above by§ Yet < >
loved!" §¶§ What I despise the §last four words crossed out and replaced above by four
words§ The thing I pity   294| MS:men? §question mark inserted§ like §crossed
out and word and comma inserted above§ nay, bulls,—their §crossed out and
replaced above by§ whose 1876:bulls—whose   295| MS:goad: 1876:goad!

Once the foe prostrate,—trampling once bestowed,—
Prompt follows placability, regret,
Atonement. Trust me, blood-warmth never yet
Betokened strong will! As no leap of pulse
300 Pricked me, that first time, so did none convulse
My veins at this occasion for resolve.
Had that devolved which did not then devolve
Upon me, I had done—what now to do
Was quietly apparent.

               "Tell me who
305 The man was, crouching by the porphyry vase!"

"No, never! All was folly in his case,
All guilt in mine. I tempted, he complied."

"And yet you loved me?"

                   "Loved you. Double-dyed
In folly and in guilt, I thought you gave
310 Your heart and soul away from me to slave
At statecraft. Since my right in you seemed lost,
I stung myself to teach you, to your cost,
What you rejected could be prized beyond
Life, heaven, by the first fool I threw a fond

---

²⁹⁶| MS:§between 295-97§ Victim is §last two words crossed out and replaced
in L margin by three words§ Once the foe <> trampling well bestowed,—
1876: trampling once bestowed,—   ²⁹⁷| MS:Then §crossed out and replaced
in L margin by§ Prompt   ²⁹⁸| MS:Atonement! Trust *1876:* Atonement. Trust
²⁹⁹| MS:will. As *1876:* will! As   ³⁰⁰| MS:Pryed §first three letters crossed out and
replaced above by *Prick* forming *Pricked*§   ³⁰³| MS:done what *1876:* done—what
³⁰⁵| MS:was—crouching *1876:* was, crouching   ³⁰⁶| MS:"No," she said §last
quotation mark crossed out and last two words crossed out and replaced above by§ never.
"All §quotation mark crossed out§ *1876:* never! All   ³⁰⁸| MS:—"And §dash in L
margin and word inserted above§ Yet you §inserted above§ <> me?" §¶§ "For I §last two
words crossed out§ loved §altered to§ Loved *1876:* "And yet   ³¹²| MS:you to your
cost *1876:* you, to your cost,   ³¹³| MS:rejected would §altered to§ could

315   Look on, a fatal word to."

                                        "And you still
        Love me? Do I conjecture well or ill?"

        "Conjecture—well or ill! I had three years
        To spend in learning you."

                                        "We both are peers
        In knowledge, therefore: since three years are spent
320   Ere thus much of yourself *I* learn—who went
        Back to the house, that day, and brought my mind
        To bear upon your action, uncombined
        Motive from motive, till the dross, deprived
        Of every purer particle, survived
325   At last in native simple hideousness,
        Utter contemptibility, nor less
        Nor more. Contemptibility—exempt
        How could I, from its proper due—contempt?
        I have too much despised you to divert
330   My life from its set course by help or hurt
        Of your all-despicable life—perturb
        The calm, I work in, by—men's mouths to curb,
        Which at such news were clamorous enough—
        Men's eyes to shut before my broidered stuff
335   With the huge hole there, my emblazoned wall

315| MS:to." §¶§ "But §crossed out and replaced above by§ And   316| MS:Loved §last
letter crossed out forming *Love*§ and do love me §last four words crossed out and replaced
above by word and question mark§ me?   319| MS:therefore, since < > years I §crossed
out and replaced above by§ are *1876:*therefore: since   320| MS:yourself was §crossed
out and replaced above by§ I learnt §last letter crossed out forming *learn*§ —I §dash and
word crossed out and replaced above by dash and word§ —who *1876:*Yourself *I*
322| MS:action, uncombined B's *1876:*action, §comma crossed out and colon inserted in
R margin§ uncombined *1889a:*action, uncombined   327| MS:more: contemptibility
*1876:*more. Contemptibility   328| MS:could I from its punishment §crossed out and
replaced above by two words§ proper due *1876:*could I, from   331| MS:Of the
all-despicable: I perturb *1876:*Of your all-despicable life—perturb   332| MS:calm I
< > in by some §crossed out and replaced above by§ mens < > curb *1876:*in, by—men's
< > curb, *1889a:*calm, I   333| MS:That §crossed out and replaced above by§ Which

226

Blank where a scutcheon hung,—by, worse than all,
Each day's procession, my paraded life
Robbed and impoverished through the wanting wife
—Now that my life (which means—my work) was grown
340 Riches indeed! Once, just this worth alone
Seemed work to have, that profit gained thereby
Of good and praise would—how rewardingly!—
Fall at your feet,—a crown I hoped to cast
Before your love, my love should crown at last.
345 No love remaining to cast crown before,
My love stopped work now: but contempt the more
Impelled me task as ever head and hand,
Because the very fiends weave ropes of sand
Rather than taste pure hell in idleness.
350 Therefore I kept my memory down by stress
Of daily work I had no mind to stay
For the world's wonder at the wife away.
Oh, it was easy all of it, believe,
For I despised you! But your words retrieve
355 Importantly the past. No hate assumed
The mask of love at any time! There gloomed
A moment when love took hate's semblance, urged

336| MS:hung once, my rich life §last three words crossed out and replaced below by§ public
§crossed out and replaced above by dash, three words, and comma§ —worse than all,
*1876:*hung,—by, worse   337| MS:§between 336-38§   338| MS:wife? *1876:*wife
339| MS:—Now §dash in L margin§ <> life, which <> work, was *1876:*life (which <>
work) was   340| MS:indeed! For just §over illegible erasure, perhaps a dash§
*1876:*indeed! Once, just   341| MS:Had work once that fruits I §last two words crossed
out and replaced above by§ profit <> thereby, *1876:*Seemed work to have, that profit <>
thereby   342| MS:All §crossed out and replaced above by§ Of good, all §crossed out and
replaced above by§ and *1876:*good and   343| MS:feet §over *foot*§   344| MS:love,
which §inserted above and then crossed out§ my own §crossed out§ love should §inserted
above§ crowned §last two letters crossed out forming *crown*§   345| MS:love remained
to *1876:*love remaining to   346| MS:And love stopped working, but *1876:*My love
stopped work now: but   347| MS:Urged §crossed out and replaced above by§ Impelled
me to §crossed out§   349| MS:taste their §crossed out and replaced above by§ pure
<> idleness; *1876:*idleness.   350| MS:my memory § perhaps alteration of
memories§   352| MS:When §crossed out and replaced above by§ For <> wondered
§last two letters crossed out forming *wonder*§   354| MS:you! §¶ indicators erased§
But   356| MS:time? There *1876:*time! There B's *1876:*The §crossed
out§ mask <> gloomed §followed by word illegibly rubbed out§
*1889a:*The mask   357| MS:semblance—urged *1876:*semblance, urged

By causes you declare; but love's self-purged
Away a fancied wrong I did both loves
360 —Yours and my own: by no hate's help, it proves,
Purgation was attempted. Then, you rise
High by how many a grade! I did despise—
I do but hate you. Let hate's punishment
Replace contempt's! First step to which ascent—
365 Write down your own words I re-utter you!
'I loved my husband and I hated—who
He was, I took up as my first chance, mere
Mud-ball to fling and make love foul with!' Here
Lies paper!"

"Would my blood for ink suffice!"

370 "It may: this minion from a land of spice,
Silk, feather—every bird of jewelled breast—
This poignard's beauty, ne'er so lightly prest
Above your heart there . . ."

"Thus?"

"It flows, I see.
Dip there the point and write!"

"Dictate to me!
375 Nay, I remember."

And she wrote the words.
I read them. Then—"Since love, in you, affords

358| MS:declare: but *1876:* declare; but   360| MS:—Yours §dash in L margin§ <>
own—by *1876:* own: by   361| MS:attempted? §question mark over colon§ then
§altered to *Then§ 1876:* attempted. Then   363| MS:Now, do *1876:* I do
365| MS:you. *1876:* you!   366–68| MS:§not underlined§ with.' Here
1876: §italics§ *with!'* Here   369| MS:paper!" §¶§ "Would but §crossed out and
replaced above by§ my   373| MS:there . ." §¶§ "Thus *1889a:* there . . ."
§¶§ "Thus   374| MS:me!" §quotation mark erased§   375| MS:remember!"
§bar of exclamation mark erased forming a period; marginal note that ¶
begins§ And   376| MS:love in you affords *1876:* love, in you, affords

License for hate, in me, to quench (I say)
Contempt—why, hate itself has passed away
In vengeance—foreign to contempt. Depart
380 Peacefully to that death which Eastern art
Imbued this weapon with, if tales be true!
Love will succeed to hate. I pardon you—
Dead in our chamber!"

                                    True as truth the tale.
She died ere morning; then, I saw how pale
385 Her cheek was ere it wore day's paint-disguise,
And what a hollow darkened 'neath her eyes,
Now that I used my own. She sleeps, as erst
Beloved, in this your church: ay, yours!

                                             Immersed
In thought so deeply, Father? Sad, perhaps?
390 For whose sake, hers or mine or his who wraps
—Still plain I seem to see!—about his head
The idle cloak,—about his heart (instead
Of cuirass) some fond hope he may elude
My vengeance in the cloister's solitude?
395 Hardly, I think! As little helped his brow
The cloak then, Father—as your grate helps now!

377| MS:hate in me to quench—I say— _1876:_ hate, in me, to quench (I say)
378| MS:itself should §perhaps over illegible word§ pass §last two letters over
illegible erasure§ _1876:_ itself has passed   380| MS:to your §crossed out and
replaced above by§ that   381| MS:tales are §crossed out and replaced above by§ be true.
_1876:_ true!   382| MS:Love shall §over perhaps _has_§ succeeded §last two letters crossed
out forming _succeed_§ to §inserted above§ hate: I   _1876:_ Love will succeed <> hate. I
383| MS:in your chamber!" §¶§ <> tale: _1876:_ in our chamber!" §¶§ <> tale.
384| MS:morning; and §crossed out and replaced above by word and comma§ then, I
386| MS:eyes _1876:_ eyes,   387| MS:Had I once used _1876:_ Now that I used
388| MS:yours! §no ¶§ Immersed _1876:_ yours! §¶§ Immersed   391| MS:—Still
§probably over _Hold_§   392| MS:The coward §crossed out and replaced above by§ idle
cloak, about <> heart—instead   _1876:_ cloak,—about <> heart (instead
393| MS:cuirass—some _1876:_ cuirass) some   395| MS:think—as
_1876:_ think! As   396| MS:grate does §crossed out and replaced above
by§ helps   MS: §At lower R§ L.D.I.E. Feb. 5. '76. §crossed out§

CENCIAJA

Ogni cencio vuol entrare in bucato.—Italian Proverb.

    May I print, Shelley, how it came to pass
    That when your Beatrice seemed—by lapse
    Of many a long month since her sentence fell—
    Assured of pardon for the parricide,—
5   By intercession of staunch friends, or, say,
    By certain pricks of conscience in the Pope
    Conniver at Francesco Cenci's guilt,—
    Suddenly all things changed and Clement grew
    "Stern," as you state, "nor to be moved nor bent,
10   But said these three words coldly *'She must die;'*
    Subjoining *'Pardon? Paolo Santa Croce*
    Murdered his mother also yestereve,
    And he is fled: she shall not flee at least!'"
    —So, to the letter, sentence was fulfilled?
15   Shelley, may I condense verbosity
    That lies before me, into some few words
    Of English, and illustrate your superb
    Achievement by a rescued anecdote,
    No great things, only new and true beside?
20   As if some mere familiar of a house
    Should venture to accost the group at gaze
    Before its Titian, famed the wide world through,
    And supplement such pictured masterpiece
    By whisper "Searching in the archives here,
25   I found the reason of the Lady's fate,
    And how by accident it came to pass
    She wears the halo and displays the palm:
    Who, haply, else had never suffered—no,

Nor graced our gallery, by consequence."
30   Who loved the work would like the little news:
Who lauds your poem lends an ear to me
Relating how the penalty was paid
By one Marchese dell' Oriolo, called
Onofrio Santa Croce otherwise,
35   For his complicity in matricide
With Paolo his own brother,—he whose crime
And flight induced "those three words—She must die."
Thus I unroll you then the manuscript.

"God's justice"—(of the multiplicity
40   Of such communications extant still,
Recording, each, injustice done by God
In person of his Vicar-upon-earth,
Scarce one but leads off to the self-same tune)—
"God's justice, tardy though it prove perchance,
45   Rests never on the track until it reach
Delinquency. In proof I cite the case
Of Paolo Santa Croce."

Many times
The youngster,—having been importunate
That Marchesine Costanza, who remained
50   His widowed mother, should supplant the heir
Her elder son, and substitute himself
In sole possession of her faculty,—
And meeting just as often with rebuff,—
Blinded by so exorbitant a lust
55   Of gold, the youngster straightway tasked his wits,
Casting about to kill the lady—thus.

He first, to cover his iniquity,

31| MS:your play may lend an   1876:your poem lends an   32| MS:Relating
how the   1876:Relating who the   B's 1876:Relating who §letters transposed
forming how§   38-39| MS:§no ¶§   1876:§¶§   41| MS:done to §crossed
out and replaced above by§ by   42| MS:his Vicar upon earth,   1876:his
Vicar-upon-earth,   44| MS:God's   1876:"God's   47| MS:§no
¶§ Many   1876:§¶§ Many   55| MS:youngster straighty tasked
1876:youngster straightway tasked   56-57| MS:§no ¶§   1876:§¶§

Writes to Onofrio Santa Croce, then
Authoritative lord, acquainting him
60 Their mother was contamination—wrought
Like hell-fire in the beauty of their House
By dissoluteness and abandonment
Of soul and body to impure delight.
Moreover, since she suffered from disease,
65 Those symptoms which her death made manifest
Hydroptic, he affirmed were fruits of sin
About to bring confusion and disgrace
Upon the ancient lineage and high fame
O' the family, when published. Duty bound,
70 He asked his brother—what a son should do?

      Which when Marchese dell' Oriolo heard
By letter, being absent at his land
Oriolo, he made answer, this, no more:
"It must behove a son,—things haply so,—
75 To act as honour prompts a cavalier
And son, perform his duty to all three,
Mother and brothers"—here advice broke off.

      By which advice informed and fortified,
As he professed himself—since bound by birth
80 To hear God's voice in primogeniture—
Paolo, who kept his mother company
In her domain Subiaco, straightway dared
His whole enormity of enterprise
And, falling on her, stabbed the lady dead;
85 Whose death demonstrated her innocence,
And happened,—by the way,—since Jesus Christ
Died to save man, just sixteen hundred years.
Costanza was of aspect beautiful

70-71| MS:§no ¶§ *1876:*§¶§   73| MS:more. *1876:*more B's *1876:*
more: §colon inserted in R margin§   76| MS:And, son <> three
*1876:*And son <> three,   77-78| MS:§no ¶§ <> fortified *1876:*§¶§
B's *1876:*fortified, §comma inserted in R margin§   79| MS:himself—the
bound *1889a:*himself—since bound   84| MS:dead— *1876:*dead;
87| MS:Died §crossed out and replaced above by§ Came to *1876:*Died to

Exceedingly, and seemed, although in age
90 Sixty about, to far surpass her peers
The coëtaneous dames, in youth and grace.

Done the misdeed, its author takes to flight,
Foiling thereby the justice of the world:
Not God's however,—God, be sure, knows well
95 The way to clutch a culprit. Witness here!
The present sinner, when he least expects,
Snug-cornered somewhere i' the Basilicate,
Stumbles upon his death by violence.
A man of blood assaults a man of blood
100 And slays him somehow. This was afterward:
Enough, he promptly met with his deserts,
And, ending thus, permits we end with him,
And push forthwith to this important point—
His matricide fell out, of all the days,
105 Precisely when the law-procedure closed
Respecting Count Francesco Cenci's death
Chargeable on his daughter, sons and wife.
"Thus patricide was matched with matricide,"
A poet not inelegantly rhymed:
110 Nay, fratricide—those Princes Massimi!—
Which so disturbed the spirit of the Pope
That all the likelihood Rome entertained
Of Beatrice's pardon vanished straight,

89| MS:age,— 1876:age   90| MS:about,—to 1876:about, to
91-92| MS:dames in <> §no ¶§ 1876:dames, in <> §¶§   95| MS:here— 1876:here!
98| MS:violence, 1876:violence.   99| MS:assaults the man 1889a:assaults a man
100| MS:somehow: this <> afterward— 1876:somehow. This <> afterward:
101| MS:he met <> deserts, you see, 1876:he promptly met <> deserts,   103| MS:And
come §crossed out and replaced above by§ push   104| MS:His §over perhaps The§
107| MS:wife 1876:wife.   108| MS:"So §crossed out and replaced above by§ When
patricide with matricide was matched" §transposed to§ was matched with matricide
1876:"Thus patricide <> matricide,"   109| MS:inelegantly sang §crossed out§
rhymed— 1876:rhymed: 111| MS:And §crossed out and replaced above by§ Which

And she endured the piteous death.

                                         Now see
115   The sequel—what effect commandment had
     For strict inquiry into this last case,
     When Cardinal Aldobrandini (great
     His efficacy—nephew to the Pope)
     Was bidden crush—ay, though his very hand
120   Got soil i' the act—crime spawning everywhere!
     Because, when all endeavour had been used
     To catch the aforesaid Paolo, all in vain—
     "Make perquisition" quoth our Eminence,
     "Throughout his now deserted domicile!
125   Ransack the palace, roof and floor, to find
     If haply any scrap of writing, hid
     In nook or corner, may convict—who knows?—
     Brother Onofrio of intelligence
     With brother Paolo, as in brotherhood
130   Is but too likely: crime spawns everywhere."

     And, every cranny searched accordingly,
     There comes to light—O lynx-eyed Cardinal!—
     Onofrio's unconsidered writing-scrap,
     The letter in reply to Paolo's prayer,
135   The word of counsel that—things proving so,
     Paolo should act the proper knightly part,
     And do as was incumbent on a son,

114-15| MS:death. §no ¶§ Now comes *1876:* death. §¶§ Now see *1889a:* §no
space between ¶s; emended to provide spacing; see Editorial Notes§   116| MS:enquiry
1876: inquiry   117| MS:When Cardinal Aldobrandini—great *1876:* When Cardinal
Aldobrandini (great   118| MS:the Pope! *1876:* the Pope!) *1889a:* the Pope)
119| MS:Saw need to crush *1876:* Was bidden crush   120| MS:Caught soil <>
everywhere. *1876:* Got soil <> everywhere!   121| MS:Therefore when *1876:* Because,
when   123| MS:our Eminence *1876:* our Eminence,   124| MS:Throughout <>
domicile— *1876:* "Throughout <> domicile!   126| MS:any correspondence §crossed
out and replaced above by three words§ scrap of writing   127| MS:corner may <>
knows? *1876:* corner, may <> knows?—   129| MS:With Brother <> brotherhood
§first letter over illegible erasure§ *1876:* With brother   130| MS:likely—crime <>
everywhere!" *1876:* likely: crime *1889a:* everywhere."   130-31| MS:§no ¶¶§ *1876:* §¶§

A brother—and a man of birth, be sure!

Whereat immediately the officers
140 Proceeded to arrest Onofrio—found
At foot-ball, child's play, unaware of harm,
Safe with his friends, the Orsini, at their seat
Monte Giordano; as he left the house
He came upon the watch in wait for him
145 Set by the Barigel,—was caught and caged.

News of which capture being, that same hour,
Conveyed to Rome, forthwith our Eminence
Commands Taverna, Governor and Judge,
To have the process in especial care,
150 Be, first to last, not only president
In person, but inquisitor as well,
Nor trust the by-work to a substitute:
Bids him not, squeamish, keep the bench, but scrub
The floor of Justice, so to speak,—go try
155 His best in prison with the criminal:
Promising, as reward for by-work done
Fairly on all-fours, that, success obtained
And crime avowed, or such connivency
With crime as should procure a decent death—
160 Himself will humbly beg—which means, procure—
The Hat and Purple from his relative
The Pope, and so repay a diligence
Which, meritorious in the Cenci-case,

138-39| MS:§no ¶§ *1876:*§¶§ *1889a:*§no space between ¶s; emended
to provide ¶ spacing; see Editorial Notes§   143| MS:Monte Giordano: as
*1876:*Monte Giordano; as   145-46| MS:§no ¶§ *1876:*§¶§   150| MS:Be
president—not only first to last *1876:*Be, first to last, not only
president   151| MS:well *1876:*well,   152| MS:bye-work
*1889a:*by-work   153| MS:Bade him not squeamish keep < >
bench but *1876:*Bids him not, squeamish, keep < > bench, but
154| MS:speak, go *1876:*speak,—go   155| MS:criminal,—
*1876:*criminal; *1889a:*criminal: 156| MS:Promising this reward < > bye-
work *1876:*Promising, as reward *1889a:*by-work   158| MS:crime
confessed §crossed out and replaced above by§ avowed, so much of sympathy
§last two words crossed out and replaced above by§ connivency *1876:*avowed,
or such connivency   160| MS:Himself engaged to beg < >
means procure *1876:*Himself will humbly beg < > means, procure—
163| MS:Notable in < > Cenci-trial too, *1876:*Which, meritorious in < > Cenci-case,

Mounts plainly here to Purple and the Hat.

165   Whereupon did my lord the Governor
So masterfully exercise the task
Enjoined him, that he, day by day, and week
By week, and month by month, from first to last
Toiled for the prize: now, punctual at his place,
170 Played Judge, and now, assiduous at his post,
Inquisitor—pressed cushion and scoured plank,
Early and late. Noon's fervour and night's chill,
Nought moved whom morn would, purpling, make amends!
So that observers laughed as, many a day,
175 He left home, in July when day is flame,
Posted to Tordinona-prison, plunged
Into a vault where daylong night is ice,
There passed his eight hours on a stretch, content,
Examining Onofrio: all the stress
180 Of all examination steadily
Converging into one pin-point,—he pushed
Tentative now of head and now of heart.
As when the nuthatch taps and tries the nut
This side and that side till the kernel sound,—
185 So did he press the sole and single point
—What was the very meaning of the phrase
'Do as beseems an honoured cavalier'?

Which one persistent question-torture,—plied

164| MS:But here . . Enough! The Purple <> the Hat! *1876:*Mounts
plainly here to Purple *1889a:*the Hat.   164-65| MS:§no ¶§ *1876:*§¶§
169| There was §last two words crossed out and replaced above by§ Deserved the prize, now
*1876:*prize: now *1889a:*Toiled for the   170| MS:The Judge <> now assiduous <>
post *1876:*Played Judge <> now, assiduous <> post,   171| MS:The Inquisitor <>
plank *1876:*Inquisitor <> plank,   172| MS:late, noon's fervor *1876:*late. Noon's
*1889a:*fervour   173| MS:moved him—morn would purpling make *1876:*moved whom
morn would, purpling, make   174| MS:a time, §crossed out and replaced above by§
day,   176| MS:to Tordinona- §the letters *on* over illegible erasure§
181| MS:pin-point he *1876:*pin-point,—he   182| MS:heart,— *1876:*heart.
184| MS:sounds,— *1876:*sound,—   186| MS:"What *1876:*—What
187-88| MS:*Do what beseems* <> *honored cavalier?'* / §no ¶§ / Which *1876:*'Do <>
cavalier?' / §¶§ / Which B's *1876:*'Do what §crossed out and replaced in R margin by§ *as
beseems 1889a:*honoured cavalier'? §no space between ¶s, though indentation indicating ¶

Day by day, week by week, and month by month,
190　Morn, noon and night,—fatigued away a mind
Grown imbecile by darkness, solitude,
And one vivacious memory gnawing there
As when a corpse is coffined with a snake:
—Fatigued Onofrio into what might seem
195　Admission that perchance his judgment groped
So blindly, feeling for an issue—aught
With semblance of an issue from the toils
Cast of a sudden round feet late so free,
He possibly might have envisaged, scarce
200　Recoiled from—even were the issue death
—Even her death whose life was death and worse!
Always provided that the charge of crime,
Each jot and tittle of the charge were true.
In such a sense, belike, he might advise
205　His brother to expurgate crime with . . . well,
With blood, if blood must follow on *'the course
Taken as might beseem a cavalier.'*

　　Whereupon process ended, and report
Was made without a minute of delay
210　To Clement who, because of those two crimes
O' the Massimi and Cenci flagrant late,
Must needs impatiently desire result.

　　Result obtained, he bade the Governor
Summon the Congregation and despatch.

remains; emended to provide ¶ spacing; see Editorial Notes§　　189| MS:month
1876:month,　　192| MS:And a vivacious　1876:And one vivacious
194| MS:Fatigued　1876:—Fatigued　　197| MS:issue—from　1876:issue from
199| MS:That possibly he might envisage　1876:He possibly might have envisaged
200| MS:Recoil　1876:Recoiled　　201| MS:worse:　1876:worse!
205| MS:with . . well,　1889a:with . . . well,　　206| MS:"the course　1876:'the
course　　207-08| MS:§not underlined§ cavalier."　§no ¶§ < > ended and　1876:§italics§
cavalier.'　§¶§ < > ended, and　　210| MS:those misdeeds　1876:those two crimes
212| MS:result.　1889a:result §emended to§ result. §see Editorial Notes§
212-13| MS:§no ¶§　1876:§¶§　1889a:§no space between ¶s, though indentation
indicating ¶ remains; emended to provide ¶ spacing; see Editorial Notes§

215 Summons made, sentence passed accordingly
—Death by beheading. When his death-decree
Was intimated to Onofrio, all
Man could do—that did he to save himself.
'Twas much, the having gained for his defence
220 The Advocate o' the Poor, with natural help
Of many noble friendly persons fain
To disengage a man of family,
So young too, from his grim entanglement:
But Cardinal Aldobrandini ruled
225 There must be no diversion of the law.
Justice is justice, and the magistrate
Bears not the sword in vain. Who sins must die.

So, the Marchese had his head cut off,
With Rome to see, a concourse infinite,
230 In Place Saint Angelo beside the Bridge:
Where, demonstrating magnanimity
Adequate to his birth and breed,—poor boy!—
He made the people the accustomed speech,
Exhorted them to true faith, honest works,
235 And special good behaviour as regards
A parent of no matter what the sex,
Bidding each son take warning from himself.
Truly, it was considered in the boy
Stark staring lunacy, no less, to snap
240 So plain a bait, be hooked and hauled ashore

215| MS:Call was made *1876:*Summons made   217| MS:to Onofrio; all   *1876:*to
Onofrio, all   218| MS:himself— *1876:*himself.   219| MS:Beside the   *1876:*'Twas
much, the   222| MS:family; *1876:*family,   223| MS:from such grim
entanglement: *1876:*from his grim entanglement. *1889a:*entanglement:
225| MS:law: *1876:*law.   227-28| MS:§no ¶§ *1876:*§¶§   228-31| MS:So the <>
off / In Place Saint Angelo beside the Bridge / With Rome to see, a concourse infinite,
/ He demonstrating magnanimity §first two letters over illegible erasure§
*1876:*So, the <> / <> Bridge, / <> infinite; / Where, demonstrating
B's *1876:*Where, demonstrating magnanimity §two words transposed to§ magnanimity
demonstrating *1889a:*off, / With <> infinite, / In <> Bridge: / Where,
demonstrating magnanimity   232| MS:boy! *1876:*boy!—
233| MS:speech *1876:*speech,   234| MS:Exhorted all §crossed
out and replaced above by§ them   235| MS:And specially behaviour
*1876:*And special good behaviour   236| MS:sex *1876:*sex,
237| MS:Bidding sons take fair warning *1876:*Bidding each son take warning

By such an angler as the Cardinal!
Why make confession of his privity
To Paolo's enterprise? Mere sealing lips—
Or, better, saying "When I counselled him
245   *'To do as might beseem a cavalier,'*
What could I mean but *'Hide our parent's shame*
As Christian ought, by aid of Holy Church!
Bury it in a convent—ay, beneath
Enough dotation to prevent its ghost
250   *From troubling earth!' "* Mere saying thus,—'tis plain,
Not only were his life the recompense,
But he had manifestly proved himself
True Christian, and in lieu of punishment
Got praise of all men. So the populace.

255   Anyhow, when the Pope made promise good
(That of Aldobrandini, near and dear)
And gave Taverna, who had toiled so much,
A Cardinal's equipment, some such word
As this from mouth to ear went saucily:
260   "Taverna's cap is dyed in what he drew
From Santa Croce's veins!" So joked the world.

        I add: Onofrio left one child behind,
A daughter named Valeria, dowered with grace
Abundantly of soul and body, doomed
265   To life the shorter for her father's fate.

---

²⁴¹| MS:the Cardinal; *1876:* the Cardinal!   ²⁴³| MS:enterprise—when
sealing lips *1876:* enterprise? Mere sealing lips—   ²⁴⁴| MS:saying—"When
I counseled *1876:* saying "When I counselled   ²⁴⁵| MS:*cavalier'* *1876:cavalier,'*
²⁴⁶⁻⁵⁰| MS:§not underlined§ *1876:* §italics§   ²⁵⁰| MS: earth!' Mere
1876:earth!'" Mere   ²⁵⁴| MS:Had praise < > men! §exclamation mark
probably over colon§ so *1876:* Been praised of < > men!—So *1889a:* Got
praise of < > men. So   ²⁵⁴⁻⁵⁵| MS:§no ¶§ *1876:* §¶§   ²⁵⁶| MS:§(Aldobrandini's,
nephew near *1876:* (That of Aldobrandini, near   ²⁵⁷| MS:And made §crossed
out and replaced above by§ gave   ²⁵⁸| MS:A §slightly in L margin§
< > equipment some *1876:* equipment, some   ²⁵⁹| MS:this went saucily
from mouth to ear *1876:* this from mouth to ear went saucily: ²⁶⁰| MS:"Taverna's
cap §inserted above§   ²⁶¹⁻⁶²| MS:veins." So < > §no ¶§ *1876:* veins!" So < > §¶§
1889a: §no space between ¶s, though indentation indicating ¶ remains; emended to
provide ¶ spacing; see Editorial Notes§   ²⁶⁵| MS:fate *1876:* fate.

By death of her, the Marquisate returned
To that Orsini House from whence it came:
Oriolo having passed as donative
To Santa Croce from their ancestors.

270   And no word more? By all means! Would you know
The authoritative answer, when folk urged
"What made Aldobrandini, hound-like staunch,
Hunt out of life a harmless simpleton?"
The answer was—"Hatred implacable,
275 By reason they were rivals in their love."
The Cardinal's desire was to a dame
Whose favour was Onofrio's. Pricked with pride,
The simpleton must ostentatiously
Display a ring, the Cardinal's love-gift,
280 Given to Onofrio as the lady's gage;
Which ring on finger, as he put forth hand
To draw a tapestry, the Cardinal
Saw and knew, gift and owner, old and young;
Whereon a fury entered him—the fire
285 He quenched with what could quench fire only—blood.
Nay, more: "there want not who affirm to boot,
The unwise boy, a certain festal eve,
Feigned ignorance of who the wight might be
That pressed too closely on him with a crowd.

268| MS:her the   1876:her, the   269-70| MS:§no ¶§ 1876:§¶§   270| MS:means,
this word more— 1876:means! Would you know   271| MS:Authoritative answer
when folks 1876:The authoritative answer, when 1889a:folk   272| MS:"Why §last
letter crossed out and replaced above by two letters, at, forming What§ did §crossed out
and replaced above by§ made Aldobrandini prosecute 1876:made Aldobrandini, hound-like
staunch,   273| MS:His hunting out <> life a simpleton?" 1876:Hunt out <> life a
harmless simpleton?"   274| MS:implacable 1876:implacable,   275| MS:love.
1876:love."   277| MS:was Onofrio's: pricked 1876:was Onofrio's. Pricked
279| MS:a love-gift ring, the Cardinal's §transposed to§ a ring, the Cardinal's love-gift
1876:love-gift,   280| MS:gage: 1876:gage;   281| MS:Ring upon finger <> puts
1876:Which ring on finger <> put   282| MS:tapestry, lo the 1876:tapestry, the
283| MS:Sees and knows gift <> and new 1876:Saw and knew, gift <> and
young;   284| MS:enters 1876:entered   285| MS:quench it only, blood
1876:quench fire only—blood.   286| MS:more, there <> boot 1876:more:
"there <> boot,   288| MS:who might be the wight 1876:who the wight
might be   289| MS:Who pressed <> crowd 1876:That pressed <>
crowd,   B's 1876:crowd, §comma crossed out and replaced by full stop§

He struck the Cardinal a blow: and then,
To put a face upon the incident,
Dared next day, smug as ever, go pay court
I' the Cardinal's antechamber. Mark and mend,
Ye youth, by this example how may greed
295 Vainglorious operate in worldly souls!"

So ends the chronicler, beginning with
"God's justice, tardy though it prove perchance,
Rests never till it reach delinquency."
Ay, or how otherwise had come to pass
300 That Victor rules, this present year, in Rome?

290| MS:And struck   B's *1876:* And §first word crossed out and replaced by §He
struck   294| MS:how much greed   *1876:* how may greed   295| MS:operates < >
souls!   *1876:* operate < > souls!'   *1889a:* souls!"   295-96| MS:§no ¶§   *1876:* §¶§
296| MS:So far the   *1876:* So ends the   300| MS:rules the roost this year in
1876: rules, this present year, in   MS:§At lower R§ L.D.I.E. Apr. 28 '76. §crossed out§

241

FILIPPO BALDINUCCI ON THE PRIVILEGE OF BURIAL

A REMINISCENCE OF A.D. 1676

I

"No, boy, we must not"—so began
    My Uncle (he's with God long since)
A-petting me, the good old man!
    "We must not"—and he seemed to wince,
5 And lost that laugh whereto had grown
    His chuckle at my piece of news,
How cleverly I aimed my stone—
    "I fear we must not pelt the Jews!

II

"When I was young indeed,—ah, faith
10 Was young and strong in Florence too!
We Christians never dreamed of scathe
    Because we cursed or kicked the crew.
But now—well, well! The olive-crops
    Weighed double then, and Arno's pranks
15 Would always spare religious shops
    Whenever he o'erflowed his banks!

III

"I'll tell you"—and his eye regained
    Its twinkle—"tell you something choice!
Something may help you keep unstained

---

*FILIPPO BALDINUCCI ON THE PRIVILEGE OF BURIAL Title and
Epigraph*| MS:Filippo Baldinucci on the law §crossed out and replaced above
by§ Privilege of Burial. / A Reminiscence of A. D. 1676. §Note to printer in R
margin§ Print this poem *the last but one* in the volume—i.e., immediately before
"Cowslip Wine".   5| MS:And lost §inserted above§ that broad §crossed out§
B's *1876:* And lost §last letter crossed out and replaced by *e* in L margin forming *lose;*
then original reading restored§   6| MS:news,— §dash crossed out§   8| MS:the
Jews!" §quotation mark crossed out§   9| MS:young in Florence §last two words
crossed out and replaced above by word and comma-dash§ indeed,—ah   10| MS:too;
§semi-colon crossed out and replaced by exclamation mark§   13| MS:now—Well
1876: now—well   17| MS:I'll *1876:* "I'll   18| MS:choice *1876:* choice!

Your honest zeal to stop the voice
Of unbelief with stone-throw—spite
        Of laws, which modern fools enact,
That we must suffer Jews in sight
        Go wholly unmolested! Fact!

IV

25   "There was, then, in my youth, and yet
        Is, by our San Frediano, just
Below the Blessed Olivet,
        A wayside ground wherein they thrust
Their dead,—these Jews,—the more our shame!
30   Except that, so they will but die,
Christians perchance incur no blame
        In giving hogs a hoist to stye.

V

"There, anyhow, Jews stow away
        Their dead; and,—such their insolence,—
35   Slink at odd times to sing and pray
        As Christians do—all make-pretence!—
Which wickedness they perpetrate
        Because they think no Christians see.
They reckoned here, at any rate,
40   Without their host: ha, ha, he, he!

VI

"For, what should join their plot of ground
        But a good Farmer's Christian field?
The Jews had hedged their corner round
        With bramble-bush to keep concealed
45   Their doings: for the public road

26| MS:by Gate §crossed out§ San Friano §*ed* inserted above forming *Frediano*§
28| MS:A plot of §last two words crossed out and replaced above by§ wayside
29| MS:shame! *1876:* shame *1889a:* shame!   31| MS:We may perchance
1889a: Christians perchance   34| MS:dead: and *1876:* dead; and
38| MS:see: *1876:* see.   41| MS:their burial §crossed out and replaced
above by two words§ plot of   45| MS:doings—for *1876:* doings: for

Ran betwixt this their ground and that
The Farmer's, where he ploughed and sowed,
Grew corn for barn and grapes for vat.

VII

"So, properly to guard his store
50   And gall the unbelievers too,
He builds a shrine and, what is more,
Procures a painter whom I knew,
One Buti (he's with God) to paint
A holy picture there—no less
55 Than Virgin Mary free from taint
Borne to the sky by angels: yes!

VIII

"Which shrine he fixed,—who says him nay?—
A-facing with its picture-side
Not, as you'd think, the public way,
60   But just where sought these hounds to hide
Their carrion from that very truth
Of Mary's triumph: not a hound
Could act his mummeries uncouth
But Mary shamed the pack all round!

IX

65 "Now, if it was amusing, judge!
—To see the company arrive,
Each Jew intent to end his trudge
And take his pleasure (though alive)
With all his Jewish kith and kin
70   Below ground, have his venom out,
Sharpen his wits for next day's sin,
Curse Christians, and so home, no doubt!

46| MS:Ran §alteration of perhaps *Runs*§ <> their yard §crossed out and
replaced above by§ ground   47| MS:The Farmer's, acre §crossed out and
replaced above by two words§ where he   48| MS:grapes for a §crossed out§
52| MS:Hires §crossed out and replaced above by§ Procures a painter that I knew
1876: painter whom I knew,   59| MS:way— *1876:* way,   63| MS:Could
henceforth §crossed out and replaced above by two words§ act his

"Whereas, each phyz upturned beholds
      Mary, I warrant, soaring brave!
75 And in a trice, beneath the folds
      Of filthy garb which gowns each knave,
Down drops it—there to hide grimace,
      Contortion of the mouth and nose
At finding Mary in the place
80   They'd keep for Pilate, I suppose!

XI

"At last, they will not brook—not they!—
      Longer such outrage on their tribe:
So, in some hole and corner, lay
      Their heads together—how to bribe
85 The meritorious Farmer's self
      To straight undo his work, restore
Their chance to meet and muse on pelf—
      Pretending sorrow, as before!

XII

"Forthwith, a posse, if you please,
90   Of Rabbi This and Rabbi That
Almost go down upon their knees
      To get him lay the picture flat.
The spokesman, eighty years of age,
      Grey as a badger, with a goat's
95 Not only beard but bleat, 'gins wage
      War with our Mary. Thus he dotes:—

73| MS:each snout upturned   1876:each phyz upturned   78| MS:Contorsion
1889a:Contortion   82| MS:tribe, 1876:tribe: 87| MS:meet and <> pelf
1876:meet, and <> pelf— 1889a:meet and   89| MS:"Forthwith a 1876:"Forthwith,
a   91| MS:almost §altered to§ Almost   95| MS:—Not 1889a:Not

" 'Friends, grant a grace! How Hebrews toil
  Through life in Florence—why relate
To those who lay the burden, spoil
100 Our paths of peace? We bear our fate.
But when with life the long toil ends,
  Why must you—the expression craves
Pardon, but truth compels me, friends!—
  Why must you plague us in our graves?

XIV

105 " 'Thoughtlessly plague, I would believe!
  For how can you—the lords of ease
By nurture, birthright—e'en conceive
  Our luxury to lie with trees
And turf,—the cricket and the bird
110 Left for our last companionship:
No harsh deed, no unkindly word,
  No frowning brow nor scornful lip!

XV

" 'Death's luxury, we now rehearse
  While, living, through your streets we fare
115 And take your hatred: nothing worse
  Have we, once dead and safe, to bear!
So we refresh our souls, fulfil
  Our works, our daily tasks; and thus
Gather you grain—earth's harvest—still
120 The wheat for you, the straw for us.

98| MS:*in Florence,* §comma crossed out and replaced by dash§   101| MS:*ends*
1876:ends,   105| MS:*believe: 1876:believe!*   106| MS:§not underlined§
1876:§italics§   112| MS:*brow and* §crossed out and replaced above by§
nor   113| MS:*"Ours—for, while living, we rehearse 1876:"* 'Death's luxury,
we now rehearse   114| MS:*Dying, as through 1876:While, living,*
through   115| MS:*hatred:"* §quotation mark rubbed out§ *nothing*
worse 1876:nothing worse   117| MS:*Thus we 1876:So we*

" ' 'What flouting in a face, what harm,
    In just a lady borne from bier
By boys' heads, wings for leg and arm?'
    You question. Friends, the harm is here—
125 *That just when our last sigh is heaved,*
    And we would fain thank God and you
For labour done and peace achieved,
    Back comes the Past in full review!

XVII

" *'At sight of just that simple flag,*
130   *Starts the foe-feeling serpent-like*
From slumber. Leave it lulled, nor drag—
    Though fangless—forth, what needs must strike
When stricken sore, though stroke be vain
    Against the mailed oppressor! Give
135 *Play to our fancy that we gain*
    Life's rights when once we cease to live!

" *'Thus much to courtesy, to kind,*
    To conscience! Now to Florence folk!
There's core beneath this apple-rind,
140   *Beneath this white-of-egg there's yolk!*
Beneath this prayer to courtesy,
    Kind, conscience—there's a sum to pouch!
How many ducats down will buy
    Our shame's removal, sirs? Avouch!

121-23| MS:"'What flouting in a face, what harm / In just a lady borne aloft / By boys' heads, wings, for leg and arm?' 1876:"'What flouting in a face, what harm, / In just a lady borne aloft / By boys' heads, wings for leg and arm?' B's 1876:borne aloft §crossed out and replaced by two words§ from bier 124| MS:Y §letter crossed out; line re-begins with proper indention§ 126| MS:And §over Then§ 129| MS:flag 1876:flag, 135| MS:to a fancy 1876:to our fancy

XIX

145   " 'Removal, not destruction, sirs!
      Just turn your picture! Let it front
The public path! Or memory errs,
      Or that same public path is wont
To witness many a chance befall
150   Of lust, theft, bloodshed—sins enough,
Wherein our Hebrew part is small.
      Convert yourselves!'—he cut up rough.

XX

"Look you, how soon a service paid
      Religion yields the servant fruit!
155 A prompt reply our Farmer made
      So following: 'Sirs, to grant your suit
Involves much danger! How? Transpose
      Our Lady? Stop the chastisement,
All for your good, herself bestows?
160   What wonder if I grudge consent?

XXI

   " '—Yet grant it: since, what cash I take
      Is so much saved from wicked use.
We know you! And, for Mary's sake,
      A hundred ducats shall induce
165 Concession to your prayer. One day
      Suffices: Master Buti's brush
Turns Mary round the other way,
      And deluges your side with slush.

146| MS:*picture:* §colon altered to exclamation mark§   152| MS:*yourselves!'*
§single quotation mark over double quotation mark§ —he §probably
alteration of He§   156| MS:following: '*Sirs,* §single quotation mark
over double quotation mark§   158| MS:*Our Lady? Stop Your* §crossed
out and replaced above by§ *the*   159| MS:*good, which she* §last two words
crossed out and replaced above by§ *herself*   162| MS:*Is removed*
§crossed out and replaced above by three words§ *so much saved* <> *use—*   *1876:use.*

XXII

" 'Down with the ducats therefore!' Dump,
170   Dump, dump it falls, each counted piece,
Hard gold. Then out of door they stump,
      These dogs, each brisk as with new lease
Of life, I warrant,—glad he'll die
      Henceforward just as he may choose,
175 Be buried and in clover lie!
      Well said Esaias—'stiff-necked Jews!'

XXIII

"Off posts without a minute's loss
      Our Farmer, once the cash in poke,
And summons Buti—ere its gloss
180   Have time to fade from off the joke—
To chop and change his work, undo
      The done side, make the side, now blank,
Recipient of our Lady—who,
      Displaced thus, had these dogs to thank!

XXIV

185 "Now, boy, you're hardly to instruct
      In technicalities of Art!
My nephew's childhood sure has sucked
      Along with mother's-milk some part
Of painter's-practice—learned, at least,
190   How expeditiously is plied
A work in fresco—never ceased
      When once begun—a day, each side.

169| MS:*therefore!"* §double quotation mark altered to single quotation mark§   171| MS:stump *1876:*stump,   172| MS:each glad §crossed out and replaced above by§ brisk   173| MS:warrant,—that §crossed out and replaced above by§ glad   176| MS:said Esaias—*'stiff-necked Jews!'* §single quotation mark over double quotation mark§   178| MS:poke, *1889a:*poke §emended to§ poke, §see Editorial Notes§   179| MS:ere the §crossed out and replaced by§ its   180| MS:joke,— §comma crossed out§   186| MS:of Art: *1876:*of Art!   187| MS:My grandson's childhood *1876:*My nephew's childhood

XXV

"So, Buti—(he's with God)—begins:
    First covers up the shrine all round
195 With hoarding; then, as like as twins,
    Paints, t'other side the burial-ground,
New Mary, every point the same;
    Next, sluices over, as agreed,
The old; and last—but, spoil the game
200   By telling you? Not I, indeed!

XXVI

"Well, ere the week was half at end,
    Out came the object of this zeal,
This fine alacrity to spend
    Hard money for mere dead men's weal!
205 How think you? That old spokesman Jew
    Was High Priest, and he had a wife
As old, and she was dying too,
    And wished to end in peace her life!

XXVII

"And he must humour dying whims,
210   And soothe her with the idle hope
They'd say their prayers and sing their hymns
    As if her husband were the Pope!
And she did die—believing just
    This privilege was purchased! Dead

195| MS:hoarding: then *1876:* hoarding; then 197| MS:New §over illegible word; the new reading is crossed out and written above more clearly§ < > same: *1876:* same; 198| MS:Then §crossed out and replaced above by§ Next 199| MS:old, §comma crossed out and replaced by colon§ and then §crossed out and replaced above by§ last *1876:* old; and 201| MS:"Now, ere < > week had §crossed out and replaced above by§ was well at *1876:* "Well, ere < > was half at 202| MS:the §next word illegibly crossed out§ 206| MS:Was then §crossed out§ < > and he §inserted above§ 207| MS:As §over perhaps *has*§ old, as he, §last two words and comma crossed out§ and she was §last two words inserted above§ 209| MS:whims *1876:* whims, 211| MS:They'd §followed by *pra,* presumably the first three letters of *pray,* which are crossed out and replaced above by§ say < > and Sing *1876:* and sing 214| MS:privileged §last letter crossed out forming *privilege*§

215   In comfort through her foolish trust!
       '*Stiff-necked ones,*' well Esaias said!

XXVIII

    "So, Sabbath morning, out of gate
       And on to way, what sees our arch
    Good Farmer? Why, they hoist their freight—
220   The corpse—on shoulder, and so, march!
    '*Now for it, Buti!*' In the nick
      Of time 'tis pully-hauly, hence
    With hoarding! O'er the wayside quick
      There's Mary plain in evidence!

XXIX

225   "And here's the convoy halting: right!
      O they are bent on howling psalms
    And growling prayers, when opposite!
      And yet they glance, for all their qualms,
    Approve that promptitude of his,
230   The Farmer's—duly at his post
    To take due thanks from every phyz,
      Sour smirk—nay, surly smile almost!

XXX

    "Then earthward drops each brow again;
      The solemn task's resumed; they reach
235   Their holy field—the unholy train:

---

216 | MS:"*Stiff-necked*" §last quotation mark crossed out and next word
and following quotation mark probably inserted§ *Ones*" well   *1876:*'*Stiff-necked
ones,*' well   218| MS:arch §unclearly written, crossed out and re-written above§
220| MS:The corpse— §last two words and dash inserted above§ On shoulder,
§comma over dash§ and quick §crossed out and replaced above by word and dash§
so—march! *1876:*corpse—on <> so, march!   221| MS:"Now for it, Buti!" In
1876:'*Now for it, Buti!*' In   225| MS:"And there's §first letter crossed out forming
here's§   227| MS:prayers, to heart's delight §last three words crossed out§
<> opposite: *1876:*opposite!   228| MS:they glanced §last letter crossed out forming
glance§   229| MS:Approved §last letter crossed out forming *Approve*§ of §crossed
out§   231| MS:take its §crossed out and replaced above by§ due <> phyz—
*1876:*phyz,   233| MS:again: *1876:*again;   234| MS:resumed: they
*1876:*resumed; they   235| MS:Their Holy Field *1876:*Their holy field

Enter its precinct, all and each,
Wrapt somehow in their godless rites;
Till, rites at end, up-waking, lo
They lift their faces! What delights
240   The mourners as they turn to go?

XXXI

"Ha, ha, he, he! On just the side
They drew their purse-strings to make quit
Of Mary,—Christ the Crucified
Fronted them now—these biters bit!
245 Never was such a hiss and snort,
Such screwing nose and shooting lip!
Their purchase—honey in report—
Proved gall and verjuice at first sip!

XXXII

"Out they break, on they bustle, where,
250   A-top of wall, the Farmer waits
With Buti: never fun so rare!
The Farmer has the best: he rates
The rascal, as the old High Priest
Takes on himself to sermonize—
255 Nay, sneer 'We Jews supposed, at least,
Theft was a crime in Christian eyes!'

236| MS:There §crossed out and replaced above by§ Enter <> each, §comma inserted after what appears to be a semi-colon is crossed out§   237| MS:Wrapt wholly in then §last letter crossed out forming *the*§ godless rites   *1876:*Wrapt somehow in their godless rites;   239| MS:Their lift   *1876:*They lift   241| MS:"Ha ha, he he *1876:*"Ha, ha, he, he   242| MS:purse strings   *1876:*purse-strings   244| MS:now! The biters   *1876:*now—these biters   246| MS:Such screws §last letter crossed out forming *screw*§ of nose and shoots §last letter crossed out forming *shoot*§ of lip! *1876:*Such screwing nose and shooting lip!   249| MS:bustle: where, §altered to§ there,   *1876:*bustle, where,   253| MS: Them roundly, as   *1876:*The rascal, as   255| MS:To sneer *"We* §double quotation mark altered to single quotation mark§   *1876:*Nay, sneer   256| MS:*eyes!"* §quotation mark altered from double to single§ *1889a:eyes!* §emended to§ *eyes!'* §see Editorial Notes§

" *'Theft?'* cries the Farmer. *'Eat your words!*
  Show me what constitutes a breach
Of faith in aught was said or heard!
260   *I promised you in plainest speech*
I'd take the thing you count disgrace
  And put it here—and here 'tis put!
Did you suppose I'd leave the place
  Blank, therefore, just your rage to glut?

265 " *'I guess you dared not stipulate*
  For such a damned impertinence!
So, quick, my greybeard, out of gate
  And in at Ghetto! Haste you hence!
As long as I have house and land,
270   *To spite you irreligious chaps*
Here shall the Crucifixion stand—
  Unless you down with cash, perhaps!'

"So snickered he and Buti both.
  The Jews said nothing, interchanged
275 A glance or two, renewed their oath
  To keep ears stopped and hearts estranged
From grace, for all our Church can do;
  Then off they scuttle: sullen jog
Homewards, against our Church to brew
280   Fresh mischief in their synagogue.

257| MS:" "*Theft?*" §double quotation marks immediately before
and after *Theft* are altered to single quotation marks§ cries < > Farmer,
"*Eat* §double quotation mark altered to single quotation mark§   264| MS:*Blank*
therefore 1889a:Blank, therefore   267| MS:*quick my masters* §crossed out and
replaced above by§ *greybeard 1876:quick, my*   273| MS:he: §colon crossed out§
< > Buti joined §crossed out and replaced above by word and period§ both.
277| MS:grace for all the §crossed out and replaced above by§ our < > do: *1876:*grace,
for < > do; 278| MS:scuttle; sullen *1876:*scuttle: sullen 279| MS:against
the Church *1876:*against our Church 280| MS:Some §crossed out and
replaced in L margin by§ Fresh < > their Synagogue. *1876:*their synagogue.

XXXVI

"But next day—see what happened, boy!
    See why I bid you have a care
How you pelt Jews! The knaves employ
    Such methods of revenge, forbear
285 No outrage on our faith, when free
    To wreak their malice! Here they took
So base a method—plague o' me
    If I record it in my Book!

XXXVII

"For, next day, while the Farmer sat
290   Laughing with Buti, in his shop,
At their successful joke,—rat-tat,—
    Door opens, and they're like to drop
Down to the floor as in there stalks
    A six-feet-high herculean-built
295 Young he-Jew with a beard that baulks
    Description. *'Help ere blood be spilt!'*

XXXVIII

—"Screamed Buti: for he recognized
    Whom but the son, no less nor more,
Of that High Priest his work surprised
300   So pleasantly the day before!
Son of the mother, then, whereof
    The bier he lent a shoulder to,
And made the moans about, dared scoff
    At sober Christian grief—the Jew!

282| MS:That's why *1876:*See why 285| MS:faith when *1876:*faith, when
287| MS:plague of §crossed out and replaced above by§ o' 289| MS:"Listen
§crossed out and replaced above by word and comma§ For, Next day, while
§inserted above§ *1876:*"For, next 290| MS:Laughing, §comma crossed out§
293| MS:Down in a fit, §last three words crossed out and replaced above by three
words§ to the floor, as *1876:*floor as 296| MS:Description. *"Help <>*
spilt!"— §dash crossed out§ *1876:*Description. *'Help <> spilt!* *1889a:spilt!'*
297| MS:"—Howls §crossed out and replaced above by§ Screamed *1876:*—"Screamed
303| MS:about which §over illegible word§ scoff *1876:*about, dared scoff

254

XXXIX

305   " '*Sirs, I salute you! Never rise!*
        No apprehension!' (Buti, white
  And trembling like a tub of size,
      Had tried to smuggle out of sight
  The picture's self—the thing in oils,
310   You know, from which a fresco's dashed
  Which courage speeds while caution spoils)
     '*Stay and be praised, sir, unabashed!*

XL

  " '*Praised,—ay, and paid too: for I come*
     To buy that very work of yours.
315   *My poor abode, which boasts—well, some*
     Few specimens of Art, secures
  Haply, a masterpiece indeed
     If I should find my humble means
  Suffice the outlay. So, proceed!
320   *Propose—ere prudence intervenes!*'

XLI

  "On Buti, cowering like a child,
     These words descended from aloft,
  In tone so ominously mild,
     With smile terrifically soft
325   To that degree—could Buti dare
     (Poor fellow) use his brains, think twice?
  He asked, thus taken unaware,
     No more than just the proper price!

305| MS:" "*Sirs* §double quotation mark closest to *Sirs* altered to single quotation mark§
306| MS:*apprehension!*" §double quotation mark altered to single quotation mark§ < >
white, *1876:* white   308| MS:Was fain to   *1876:* Had tried to   310| MS:dashed—
1876: dashed   312| MS:"*Stay* §double quotation mark altered to single quotation mark§
314| MS:*very piece* §crossed out and replaced above by§ *work*   316| MS:*of art* §altered
to§ *Art*   318| MS:*Provided that* §last two words crossed out and replaced below by four
words§ *If I should prove* §crossed out and replaced by§ *find*   319| MS:*outlay: so*
1876: outlay. So   323| MS:mild *1876:* mild,   325| MS:dare, *1876:* dare
326| MS:Poor fellow, use *1876:* (Poor fellow) use   328| MS:the proper
§crossed out, replaced above by *picture's*, and then *proper* restored§

XLII

" 'Done!' cries the monster. 'I disburse
330   Forthwith your moderate demand.
      Count on my custom—if no worse
      Your future work be, understand,
      Than this I carry off! No aid!
      My arm, sir, lacks nor bone nor thews:
335   The burden's easy, and we're made,
      Easy or hard, to bear—we Jews!'

XLIII

"Crossing himself at such escape,
      Buti by turns the money eyes
And, timidly, the stalwart shape
340   Now moving doorwards; but, more wise,
The Farmer,—who, though dumb, this while
      Had watched advantage,—straight conceived
A reason for that tone and smile
      So mild and soft! The Jew—believed!

XLIV

345   "Mary in triumph borne to deck
      A Hebrew household! Pictured where
No one was used to bend the neck
      In praise or bow the knee in prayer!

329| MS:" "*Done!*" §double quotation marks immediately before and after *Done* are altered
to single quotation marks§ < > "*I* §double quotation mark altered to single quotation
mark§   332| MS:*understand!*— §exclamation mark and dash crossed out and replaced
by comma§   334| MS:*arm,* §perhaps an *s,* either meant to be attached to last word or to
be first letter of next word, erased§ *Sir 1876:arm, sir*   336| MS:*we Jews!"* §double
quotation mark altered to single quotation mark§   340| MS:doorwards: with his
prize §last three words crossed out and replaced by§ but, more wise, *1876:*doorwards;
but   341| MS:But §first word crossed out§ the §altered to§ The good §crossed out§ < >
who, though dumb, §last two words and commas inserted above§   342| MS:watched
in silence §last two words crossed out and replaced above by two words, which
were illegibly crossed out and replaced below by word and comma-dash§
advantage,—   344| MS:soft! The Jew §over *man*§   347| MS:to bend §over
illegible word§   348| MS:prayer! §exclamation mark over question mark§

Borne to that domicile by whom?
350   The son of the High Priest! Through what?
An insult done his mother's tomb!
          Saul changed to Paul—the case came pat!

XLV

" 'Stay, dog-Jew . . . gentle sir, that is!
          Resolve me! Can it be, she crowned,—
355 Mary, by miracle,—Oh bliss!—
          My present to your burial ground?
Certain, a ray of light has burst
          Your veil of darkness! Had you else,
Only for Mary's sake, unpursed
360   So much hard money? Tell—oh, tell's!'

XLVI

"Round—like a serpent that we took
          For worm and trod on—turns his bulk
About the Jew. First dreadful look
          Sends Buti in a trice to skulk
365 Out of sight somewhere, safe—alack!
          But our good Farmer faith made bold:
And firm (with Florence at his back)
          He stood, while gruff the gutturals rolled—

351| MS:An outrage §crossed out and replaced above by§ insult
353| MS:dog-Jew . . gentle Sir   1876:gentle sir   1889a:dog-Jew . . . gentle
354| MS:crowns   1876:crowns,—   B's 1876:crowns,— §last letter crossed out and
replaced by ed forming crowned,—§   355| MS:miracle,—the bliss!—
1876:miracle,—Oh bliss!—   356| MS:My service §crossed out and replaced below
by§ present < > burial-ground?   1889a:burial ground?   357| B's 1876:light has
burst §last two words crossed out, replaced by dispersed, and then has burst
restored§   358| MS:else   1876:else,   359| MS:sake disbursed   1876:sake,
disbursed   B's 1876:sake, dispursed §first three letters crossed out and replaced in R margin
by unp forming unpursed§   360| MS:tell's!" §double quotation mark altered to
single quotation mark§   361| MS:"Round,—like   1876:"Round—like
362| MS:on,—turns   1876:on—turns   368| MS:rolled:—   1876:rolled—

" 'Ay, sir, a miracle was worked,
370   By quite another power, I trow,
 Than ever yet in canvas lurked,
   Or you would scarcely face me now!
 A certain impulse did suggest
   A certain grasp with this right-hand,
375 Which probably had put to rest
   Our quarrel,—thus your throat once spanned!

XLVIII

" 'But I remembered me, subdued
   That impulse, and you face me still!
 And soon a philosophic mood
380   Succeeding (hear it, if you will!)
 Has altogether changed my views
   Concerning Art. Blind prejudice!
 Well may you Christians tax us Jews
   With scrupulosity too nice!

XLIX

385 " 'For, don't I see,—let's issue join!—
   Whenever I'm allowed pollute
 (I—and my little bag of coin)
   Some Christian palace of repute,—
 Don't I see stuck up everywhere
390   Abundant proof that cultured taste
 Has Beauty for its only care,
   And upon Truth no thought to waste?

369| MS:" 'Ay, Sir <> worked 1876:" 'Ay, sir <> worked, 374| MS:right-hand
1876:right-hand, 376| MS:All controversy, understand! §last word and
exclamation mark crossed out and replaced above by dash, three words, and exclamation
mark§ —throat once spanned! 1876:Our quarrell,—thus your throat
378| MS:My impulse 1876:That impulse 380| MS:Succeeding §last three
letters over ed§ 382| MS:Concerning Art: blind 1876:Concerning Art.
Blind 385| MS:join!,— 1876:join!— 387| MS:I <> coin—
1876:(I <> coin) 389–92| MS: §not underlined§ 1876: §italics§

L

" ' 'Jew, since it must be, take in pledge
    Of payment' *—so a Cardinal*
395 *Has sighed to me as if a wedge*
    Entered his heart— 'this best of all
My treasures!' *Leda, Ganymede*
    Or Antiope: swan, eagle, ape,
(Or what's the beast of what's the breed)
400   *And Jupiter in every shape!*

LI

" *'Whereat if I presume to ask*
'But, Eminence, though Titian's whisk
Of brush have well performed its task,
    How comes it these false godships frisk
405 In presence of—what yonder frame
    Pretends to image? Surely, odd
It seems, you let confront The Name
    Each beast the heathen called his god!'

LII

" *'Benignant smiles me pity straight*
410   *The Cardinal. '* 'Tis Truth, we prize!

393| MS:§Line for italics crossed out, and *common type* written in R margin;
the following note on verso of MS p. 99 connected to this line by asterisk§
To the Printer. I propose to avoid ambiguity by introducing an inverted comma to the
left and right '/'/' to indicate, as here, that a second speaker quotes from a
third speaker: with a change of type in each case—thus
    First Speaker "—common type"
quoting Second "/'Italic'/"
who quotes a Third "/'/' common type '/'/"/
394| MS:*Of payment* §italics removed§   396| MS:*heart, 'this bed of all* §italics removed
from last four words; *common type* in R margin§   *1876:*heart 'this   *1889a:*heart— 'this
397| MS:*My treasures!'* §italics removed; exclamation mark over dash§   398| MS:*Or
Antiope!* §exclamation mark crossed out and replaced by colon§ *Swan <> ape* §Italic in R
margin§   *1876:Or Antiope: swan <> ape,*   401| MS:"'*Whereat, if*   *1876:*"'*Whereat if*
406| MS:*odd—* §dash crossed out§   407| MS:confront '*The Name*' §quotation marks
and italics crossed out for last two words§   408| MS:the Heathen <> god!" §double
quotation mark altered to single quotation mark§   *1876:* the heathen   410| MS:*The
Cardinal. "Tis Art we prize—* §italic underlining crossed out for last four words, and
common type in R margin§   *1876:The Cardinal. '* 'Tis Truth, we prize!

259

Art's the sole question in debate!
　　These subjects are so many lies.
We treat them with a proper scorn
　　When we turn lies—called gods forsooth—
415 To lies' fit use, now Christ is born.
　　Drawing and colouring are Truth.

LIII

" ' 'Think you I honour lies so much
　　As scruple to parade the charms
Of Leda—Titian, every touch—
420 　Because the thing within her arms
Means Jupiter who had the praise
　　And prayer of a benighted world?
He would have mine too, if, in days
　　Of light, I kept the canvas furled!'

LIV

425 " 'So ending, with some easy gibe.
　　What power has logic! I, at once,
Acknowledged error in our tribe
　　So squeamish that, when friends ensconce
A pretty picture in its niche
430 　To do us honour, deck our graves,
We fret and fume and have an itch
　　To strangle folk—ungrateful knaves!

411-16| MS:§italic underlining crossed out§   411| MS:Art; the sole subject §last word
crossed out and replaced above by§ question in debate: 1876:Art's the <> debate!
414| MS:lies—then gods—to truth §dash and last two words crossed out§   1876:lies—called
gods   415| MS:born. 1876:born.   416| MS:and colouring §second letter over two
illegible letters§ are truth. 1876:are Truth.   417-24| MS:§marginal note to printer
indicates that underlining for italics is to be disregarded§   417| MS:you I'd honor
1876:you I honor 1889a:honour   423| MS:mine, §comma crossed
out§   424| MS:light I <> canvass furled!' ' 1876:light, I <> canvas
furled!'   425-40| MS:§marginal note that all lines are in italics§
425| MS:"'The ending §last three letters crossed out and replaced above
by ed forming ended§ 1876:"'So ending   427| MS:tribe, 1876:tribe
431| MS:—We <> fume,—nay, have 1876:We <> fume and have

LV

" 'No, sir! Be sure that—what's its style,
Your picture?—shall possess ungrudged
435   A place among my rank and file
Of Ledas and what not—be judged
Just as a picture! and (because
I fear me much I scarce have bought
A Titian) Master Buti's flaws
440   Found there, will have the laugh flaws ought!'

LVI

"So, with a scowl, it darkens door—
This bulk—no longer! Buti makes
Prompt glad re-entry; there's a score
Of oaths, as the good Farmer wakes
445   From what must needs have been a trance,
Or he had struck (he swears) to ground
The bold bad mouth that dared advance
Such doctrine the reverse of sound!

LVII

"Was magic here? Most like! For, since,
450   Somehow our city's faith grows still
More and more lukewarm, and our Prince
Or loses heart or wants the will
To check increase of cold. 'Tis 'Live
And let live! Languidly repress

433| MS:" 'No, Sir <> style   1876:" 'No, sir <> style,   434| MS:*The* §crossed out and replaced in L margin by§ *Your*   436| MS:*not!—* §exclamation mark crossed out§
437| MS:*picture, and—because*   1876:*picture! and (because*   439| MS:*A Titian—Master*
1876:*A Titian) Master*   440| MS:*have the* §over illegible word§ <> *ought!"*
§double quotation mark crossed out and replaced above by single quotation mark§
441| MS:scowl, he darkens   1876:scowl, it darkens   442| MS:This bulk— §last two
words and dash inserted above§ No longer. Buti makes §first letter over illegible erasure§
1876:bulk—no longer! Buti   446| MS:struck (he §parenthesis over comma-dash§
swears) §first letter over illegible erasure; parenthesis over comma-dash§   451| MS:and
its §crossed out and replaced above by§ our   454| MS:*live!* §quotation mark crossed out§

The Dissident! In short,—contrive
        Christians must bear with Jews: no less!'

LVIII

"The end seems, any Israelite
        Wants any picture,—pishes, poohs,
Purchases, hangs it full in sight
In any chamber he may choose!
In Christ's crown, one more thorn we rue!
        In Mary's bosom, one more sword!
No, boy, you must not pelt a Jew!
        O Lord, how long? How long, O Lord?"

MS:*The Heretic.* §word and full stop crossed out and replaced above by
word and exclamation mark§ *Dissident! In*   457| MS:The end is— §word and dash
crossed out and replaced above by word and dash§ seems—any   *1876:* "The <> seems, any
458| MS:Eyes §crossed out and replaced above by§ Wants   461| MS:In Christs'
crown—one <> thorn to rue!   *1876:* In Christ's crown, one <> thorn we rue!
462| MS:bosom—one   *1876:* bosom, one   464| MS:long, O Lord?
1876: long, O Lord?"   MS:§At lower R§ L.D.I.E. May 19. '76. §crossed out§

EPILOGUE

μεστοὶ . . .

οἱ δ' ἀμφορῆς ο'ίνου μέλανος ἀνθοσμίου.

I

"The poets pour us wine—"
　　Said the dearest poet I ever knew,
Dearest and greatest and best to me.
You clamour athirst for poetry—
5　We pour. "But when shall a vintage be"—
　　You cry—"strong grape, squeezed gold from screw,
Yet sweet juice, flavoured flowery-fine?
That were indeed the wine!"

II

One pours your cup—stark strength,
10　　Meat for a man; and you eye the pulp
Strained, turbid still, from the viscous blood
Of the snaky bough: and you grumble "Good!
For it swells resolve, breeds hardihood;
　　Despatch it, then, in a single gulp!"
15　So, down, with a wry face, goes at length
The liquor: stuff for strength.

III

One pours your cup—sheer sweet,
　　The fragrant fumes of a year condensed:
Suspicion of all that's ripe or rathe,
20　From the bud on branch to the grass in swathe.
"We suck mere milk of the seasons," saith
　　A curl of each nostril—"dew, dispensed

EPILOGUE Title | MS:Cowslip wine §last two words crossed out and replaced
by one word and full stop§ Epilogue. §last line of each stanza indented in MS and 1876;
1889a aligns each last line flush left§　　¹| MS: §underlined§ *The <> Wine—*
1876: §Roman§ "The <> wine—"　　⁷| MS:flavored　*1889a:* flavoured
¹³| MS:hardihood:　*1876:* hardihood;　　¹⁴| MS:it then　*1876:* it, then
¹⁸| MS:year §followed by hole rubbed in paper perhaps to remove a comma§
condensed,　*1876:* condensed:　　²¹| MS:seasons" saith　*1876:* seasons," saith

Nowise for nerving man to feat:
Boys sip such honeyed sweet!"

IV

25   And thus who wants wine strong,
        Waves each sweet smell of the year away;
    Who likes to swoon as the sweets suffuse
    His brain with a mixture of beams and dews
    Turned syrupy drink—rough strength eschews:
30   "What though in our veins your wine-stock stay?
    The lack of the bloom does our palate wrong.
    Give us wine sweet, not strong!"

V

    Yet wine is—some affirm—
        Prime wine is found in the world somewhere,
35   Of potable strength with sweet to match.
    You double your heart its dose, yet catch—
    As the draught descends—a violet-smatch,
        Softness—however it came there,
    Through drops expressed by the fire and worm:
40   Strong sweet wine—some affirm.

VI

    Body and bouquet both?
        'Tis easy to ticket a bottle so;
    But what was the case in the cask, my friends?
    Cask? Nay, the vat—where the maker mends
45   His strong with his sweet (you suppose) and blends
        His rough with his smooth, till none can know

25| MS:thus, who <> strong   *1876:* thus who <>strong,   29| MS:syropy
1876: syrupy   30| MS:your vine-stock stay? *1876:* your wine-stock stay?
34| MS:There is prime wine in <> somewhere—   *1876:* Prime wine there is in <>
somewhere, *1889a:* wine is found in   35| MS:strength that's sweet *1876:* strength
with sweet   36| MS:§line indented§ We double our heart   *1876:* §line flush L§ You
double your heart   37-39| MS:violet-smatch, / Though <> worm—   *1876:* worm:
1889a: violet-smatch, / Softness—however it came there, / Through   42| MS:so
1876: so;   44| MS:The §first word crossed out§ cask §altered to§ Cask? Nay,
§word and comma inserted above§   45| MS:sweet—you suppose—and
1876: sweet (you suppose) and   46| MS:smooth till *1876:* smooth, till

How it comes you may tipple, nothing loth,
Body and bouquet both.

VII

"You" being just—the world.
50   No poets—who turn, themselves, the winch
Of the press; no critics—I'll even say,
(Being flustered and easy of faith to-day)
Who for love of the work have learned the way
        Till themselves produce home-made, at a pinch:
55 No! You are the world, and wine ne'er purled
Except to please the world!

VIII

"For, oh the common heart!
        And, ah the irremissible sin
Of poets who please themselves, not us!
60 Strong wine yet sweet wine pouring thus,
How please still—Pindar and Æschylus!—
        Drink—dipt into by the bearded chin
Alike and the bloomy lip—no part
Denied the common heart!

IX

65 "And might we get such grace,
        And did you moderns but stock our vault
With the true half-brandy half-attar-gul,
How would seniors indulge at a hearty pull
While juniors tossed off their thimbleful!
70   Our Shakespeare and Milton escaped your fault,
So, they reign supreme o'er the weaker race
That wants the ancient grace!"

---

⁵¹| MS:press: no *1876:* press; no   ⁵²⁻⁵³| MS:Who < > way / (I am flustered < > faith,
to-day) *1876:* (I < > to-day) / Who < > way *1889a:* (Being flustered < > faith to-day)
⁵⁵| MS:the many §crossed out and replaced above by two words§ world, and—wine
1876: and wine   ⁶¹| MS:They §crossed out and replaced above by§ How
⁶⁹| MS:thimble-full! *1876:* thimblefull!   ⁷⁰| MS:escaped such fault, *1876:* escaped
your fault,   ⁷¹| MS:So they *1876:* So, they   ⁷²| MS:want *1889a:* wants

265

X

If I paid myself with words
    (As the French say well) I were dupe indeed!
75 I were found in belief that you quaffed and bowsed
At your Shakespeare the whole day long, caroused
In your Milton pottle-deep nor drowsed
    A moment of night—toped on, took heed
Of nothing like modern cream-and-curds.
80 Pay me with deeds, not words!

XI

For—see your cellarage!
    There are forty barrels with Shakespeare's brand.
Some five or six are abroach: the rest
Stand spigoted, fauceted. Try and test
85 What yourselves call best of the very best!
    How comes it that still untouched they stand?
Why don't you try tap, advance a stage
With the rest in cellarage?

XII

For—see your cellarage!
90   There are four big butts of Milton's brew.
How comes it you make old drips and drops
Do duty, and there devotion stops?
Leave such an abyss of malt and hops
    Embellied in butts which bungs still glue?
95 You hate your bard! A fig for your rage!
Free him from cellarage!

78| MS:§line flush L§ One §crossed out and replaced above by§ A < > toped wine §crossed out and replaced by§ on *1889a:* §line indented§   79| MS:like our weak §last two words crossed out and replaced above by two words§ modern poor §last word crossed out§ cream-and-curds! *1889a:* cream-and-curds.   86| MS:§line flush L§ Why is it < > still unbroached they *1876* still untouched they *1889a:* §line indented§ How comes it
87| MS:tap and advance *1876:* tap, advance   92-96| MS:stops? / You < > rage! §line not indented§ / Leave < > hops / Embellied < > glue? §line indented; last three lines transposed to§ Leave < > hops / Embellied < > glue? / You < > rage! / Free §line indented§ *1876:* Embellied < > §line not indented§ / You < > §line indented§ / Free < > §line indented farther to R than 95§ *1889a:* Embellied < > §line indented§ / You < > §line

XIII

'Tis said I brew stiff drink,
But the deuce a flavour of grape is there.
Hardly a May-go-down, 'tis just
100 A sort of a gruff Go-down-it-must—
No Merry-go-down, no gracious gust
Commingles the racy with Springtide's rare!
"What wonder," say you, "that we cough, and blink
At Autumn's heady drink?"

XIV

105 Is it a fancy, friends?
Mighty and mellow are never mixed,
Though mighty and mellow be born at once.
Sweet for the future,—strong for the nonce!
Stuff you should stow away, ensconce
110 In the deep and dark, to be found fast-fixed
At the century's close: such time strength spends
A-sweetening for my friends!

XV

And then—why, what you quaff
With a smack of lip and a cluck of tongue,
115 Is leakage and leavings—just what haps
From the tun some learned taster taps
With a promise "Prepare your watery chaps!
Here's properest wine for old and young!
Dispute its perfection—you make us laugh!
120 Have faith, give thanks, but—quaff!"

---

not indented§ / Free < > §line not indented§   97| MS:drink 1876:drink,
98| MS:a gust §crossed out and replaced above by§ flavor of the §crossed out§ 1889a:flavour
102| MS:Commingling §last three letters crossed out and replaced by *es* forming
commingles§ < > with May, the rare, 1876:rare! 1889a:with Springtide's rare!
103| MS:What wonder, say you, we cough and 1876:"What wonder," say you "we cough,
and 1889a:you §emended to§ you, §see Editorial Notes§ "that we   104| MS:October's
heady drink? 1876:drink?" 1889a:At Autumn's heady   108| MS:nonce:
1876:nonce!   110| MS:dark—to 1876:dark, to   111| MS:close—such
1876:close: such   114| MS:tongue 1876:tongue,   116| MS:learned
taps taster §transposed to§ taster taps   117| MS:chaps!" §quotation mark erased§

XVI

Leakage, I say, or—worse—
    Leavings suffice pot-valiant souls.
Somebody, brimful, long ago,
Frothed flagon he drained to the dregs; and lo,
125 Down whisker and beard what an overflow!
    Lick spilth that has trickled from classic jowls,
Sup the single scene, sip the only verse—
Old wine, not new and worse!

XVII

I grant you: worse by much!
130   Renounce that new where you never gained
One glow at heart, one gleam at head,
And stick to the warrant of age instead!
No dwarf's-lap! Fatten, by giants fed!
    You fatten, with oceans of drink undrained?
135 *You* feed—who would choke did a cobweb smutch
The Age you love so much?

XVIII

A mine's beneath a moor:
    Acres of moor roof fathoms of mine
Which diamonds dot where you please to dig;
140 Yet who plies spade for the bright and big?
Your product is—truffles, you hunt with a pig!
    Since bright-and-big, when a man would dine,
Suits badly: and therefore the Koh-i-noor
May sleep in mine 'neath moor!

121| MS:or, worse, *1876:*or worse, *1889a:*or—worse— 125| MS:what an
§inserted above§ 131| MS:head *1876:*head, 132| MS:instead—
*1876:*instead! 135| MS:choke at §crossed out and replaced by§
did a cobweb-smutch §hyphen erased§ 136| MS:In §first word
crossed out§ the §altered to§ The 137| MS:moor, *1876:*moor:
139| MS:dot if §crossed out and replaced above by§ where <> dig:
*1876:*dig; 141| MS:truffles you <> pig— *1876:*truffles,
you <> pig! 142| MS:bright and big *1876:*bright-and-big

268

XIX

145 Wine, pulse in might from me!
　　　It may never emerge in must from vat,
　　Never fill cask nor furnish can,
　　Never end sweet, which strong began—
　　God's gift to gladden the heart of man;
150 　　But spirit's at proof, I promise that!
　　No sparing of juice spoils what should be
　　Fit brewage—mine for me.

XX

　　Man's thoughts and loves and hates!
　　　Earth is my vineyard, these grew there:
155 From grape of the ground, I made or marred
　　My vintage; easy the task or hard,
　　Who set it—his praise be my reward!
　　　Earth's yield! Who yearn for the Dark Blue Sea's,
　　Let them "lay, pray, bray"—the addle-pates!
160 Mine be Man's thoughts, loves, hates!

XXI

　　But someone says "Good Sir!"
　　　('Tis a worthy versed in what concerns
　　The making such labour turn out well)
　　"You don't suppose that the nosegay-smell
165 Needs always come from the grape? Each bell
　　　At your foot, each bud that your culture spurns,
　　The very cowslip would act like myrrh
　　On the stiffest brew—good Sir!

148| MS:sweet which *1876:*sweet, which　　149| MS:man: *1876:*man;
154| MS:there— *1876:*there:　　155| MS:ground I *1876:*ground, I
156| MS:vintage: easy *1876:*vintage; easy　　158| MS:yearn §followed
by erasure§ <> the Dark Blue Sea's *1889a:*the Dark Blue Sea's,　　162| MS:a
rustic §crossed out and replaced above by§ worthy　　164| MS:You
1876:"You　　166| MS:that your Worship §crossed out and replaced above
by§ Honour spurns, *1876:*your Honor *1889a:*your culture spurns,

269

XXII

"Cowslips, abundant birth
170   O'er meadow and hillside, vineyard too,
—Like a schoolboy's scrawlings in and out
Distasteful lesson-book—all about
Greece and Rome, victory and rout—
    Love-verses instead of such vain ado!
175 So, fancies frolic it o'er the earth
Where thoughts have rightlier birth.

XXIII

"Nay, thoughtlings they themselves:
    Loves, hates—in little and less and least!
Thoughts? *'What is a man beside a mount!'*
180 Loves? *'Absent—poor lovers the minutes count!'*
Hates? *'Fie—Pope's letters to Martha Blount!'*
    These furnish a wine for a children's-feast:
Insipid to man, they suit the elves
Like thoughts, loves, hates themselves."

XXIV

185 And, friends, beyond dispute
    I too have the cowslips dewy and dear.
Punctual as Springtide forth peep they:
I leave them to make my meadow gay.
But I ought to pluck and impound them, eh?
190   Not let them alone, but deftly shear

169| MS:Cowslips—abundant *1876:*"Cowslips, abundant   170| MS:hillside—vineward
*1876:*hillside, vineyard   171| MS:Like *1876:*—Like   175| MS:So
fancies *1876:*So, fancies   177| MS:Nay themselves— *1876:*"Nay themselves:
179| MS:Thoughts? "What is a man beside a mount!" *1876:*Thoughts? *'What* <>
mount!'   180| MS:Loves? "Absent—how §crossed out and replaced above by§ poor
lovers the minutes count!" *1876:*Loves? *'Absent* <> *count!'* *1889a:count!* §emended
to§ *count!'* §see Editorial Notes§   181| MS:Hates? "Fie—Pope's letters to
Martha Blount!" *1876:*Hates? *'Fie* <> *Blount!'* *1889a:to Martha Blount!*
§emended to§ *Blount!'* §see Editorial Notes§   182| MS:children's
feast: *1876:*children's-feast: 184| MS:themselves. *1876:*themselves."
187| MS:they— *1876:*they: 188| MS:make the §crossed out and
replaced above by§ my   190| MS:alone but *1876:*alone, but

And shred and reduce to—what may suit
Children, beyond dispute?

XXV

And, here's May-month, all bloom,
　　All bounty: what if I sacrifice?
195　If I out with shears and shear, nor stop
Shearing till prostrate, lo, the crop?
And will you prefer it to ginger-pop
　　When I've made you wine of the memories
Which leave as bare as a churchyard tomb
200　My meadow, late all bloom?

XXVI

Nay, what ingratitude
　　Should I hesitate to amuse the wits
That have pulled so long at my flask, nor grudged
The headache that paid their pains, nor budged
205　From bunghole before they sighed and judged
　　"Too rough for our taste, to-day, befits
The racy and right when the years conclude!"
Out on ingratitude!

XXVII

Grateful or ingrate—none,
210　　No cowslip of all my fairy crew
Shall help to concoct what makes you wink
And goes to your head till you think you think!
I like them alive: the printer's ink
　　Would sensibly tell on the perfume too.

192| MS:Children—beyond dispute! *1876:* Children, beyond dispute?　　193|　MS:And
here's < > bloom　*1876:* And, here's < > bloom,　　196|　MS:till I §crossed out§ prostrate,
lo, §word inserted above; comma inserted on the line§　　199|　MS:churchyard-tomb
1876: churchyard tomb　　200|　MS:meadow—late　*1876:* meadow, late
201|　MS:§line indented§ For—what　*1876:* §line flush L§ Nay, what　　202|　MS:§line
flush L§ If §crossed out and replaced above by§ Should　*1876:* §line indented§
203|　MS:flask,—nor　*1876:* flask, nor　　207|　MS:conclude."　*1876:* conclude!"
209|　MS:ingrate,—none—　*1876:* ingrate—none,　　211|　MS:wink
1876: wink, *1889a:* wink　　212|　MS:think! *1876:* think *1889a:* think!

215   I may use up my nettles, ere I've done;
      But of cowslips—friends get none!

XXVIII

      Don't nettles make a broth
          Wholesome for blood grown lazy and thick?
      Maws out of sorts make mouths out of taste.
220   My Thirty-four Port—no need to waste
      On a tongue that's fur and a palate—paste!
          A magnum for friends who are sound! The sick—
      I'll posset and cosset them, nothing loth,
      Henceforward with nettle-broth!

215| MS:done, *1876:*done;   216| MS:cowslips friends <> none.
*1876:*cowslips—friends <> none!   219| MS:taste: *1876:*taste.   220| MS:My
Twenty-two Port is not §last two words crossed out and replaced above by dash
and two words§ —no need   *1876:*My Thirty-four Port   222| MS:Keep some §last two
words crossed out and replaced above by two words§ A magnum for the §crossed out§ <>
sound; not §crossed out and replaced above by§ the sick   *1876:*sound! the sick—   *1889a:*
sound! The   224| MS:Henceforward §first part of word inserted to L and last four
letters below§ With the best of §last three words crossed out§ nettle-broth.   *1876:*
Henceforward with nettle-broth!   MS:§At lower R§ L.D.I.E. Apr. 24. '76. §crossed out§

272

THE INN ALBUM

Emendations to the Text

The following emendations have been made to the 1889a text:

Section 1.

1.174: The MS-1875 apostrophe preceding *Wish* (for "I wish") was erroneously set in 1889a at the end of the line as if it were a quotation mark. The MS-1875 reading is restored.
1.175: A comma necessary to set off appositive is omitted in 1889a; the MS-1875 reading is restored.

Section 2

1.13: B's alteration of the MS reading *and* to *with* in 1875 required the alteration of *mix* to *mixes,* which B failed to do. The grammatically correct MS reading is restored.
1.514: The single quotation mark for the quotation within the quotation is misplaced in 1875-1889a, and the exclamatory remark interrupting the quoted question has been given an inappropriate question mark in 1875-1889a. The MS reading has been restored in each case.

Section 3

1.13: The 1889a compositors failed to convert the 1875 single quotation mark after *stranger* to the required double mark; the double quotation mark is supplied.
1.155: The 1889a omits the comma required after the phrase modifying *Who.* The MS-1875 reading is restored.
1.248: The single quotation mark, required to close the quotation beginning on 1.244, is missing in 1889a; the MS-1875 reading is restored.

Section 5

1.316: The exclamation mark required by the interjection *Whew* is omitted in 1889a. The MS and 1875 punctuation is restored.
1.339: Both 1875 and 1889a have a single quotation mark to close a passage that opens with a double quotation mark. The MS punctuation is restored.

Section 6

1.138: The comma at the end of this line, necessary to separate phrases in a series, is missing in 1889a. The MS-1875 reading is restored.

In *The Inn Album* B indicated divisions in discourse by line spacing rather than by indentation. During the printing history of the poem, these divisions were occasionally lost when they were placed at the bottoms or tops of pages. I have restored all of B's paragraphs, specifically in the following instances:

2.17-18, 89-90
3.18-19, 252-53
4.66-67, 238-39, 458-59
5.339-40.

Texts

The manuscript of *The Inn Album* is in Balliol College Library, Oxford, and is bound with *Red Cotton Night-Cap Country* (1873) in brown morocco. The front cover is stamped in gold with the B family coat of arms. The poems together are labeled Balliol MS.388.

The Inn Album was written on 20" x 8" lined paper. Apparently B used folio sheets and wrote on only one side of each page; this fact would account for the appearance of the original numberings on every other page (except for the last numbering which is for only one page). The 51½ folio sheets were renumbered with blue pencil when the manuscript was bound, each page being given a number.

Centered on the title page of the manuscript are the words "The Inn Album / by Robert Browning," with penciled lines indicating that "The" should be centered above "Inn Album" and "by" above "Robert Browning," and at the bottom of the page is written "Smith E and Co." in a lighter ink that has now turned pink. At a slant to the title appears in pencil: "Prf Thurs. morn." This does not seem to be in B's hand. The over 3,000 lines of irregular blank verse which follow were divided into eight unequal parts after the poem was completed, for the thick black Roman numerals that designate the divisions are squeezed between lines of the manuscript. These divisions are, however, natural; for they in every instance indicate either a change in scene or the appearance (or exit) of a character. Beside the title at the top of page one (where the title contains a hyphen between "Inn" and "Album") is written in brackets preceded by an asterisk: "Print the parts on half-pages," which is the author's indication that each section of the poem was to begin mid-way on the printed page. Then, preceding the dates of composition he added the abbreviation that is written at the end of all of his manuscripts in the Balliol Collection: "L.D.I.E."—his expression of relief and thanks that his poem is completed: *"Laus Deo in excelsis."* Next the poet signed the MS with "RB." On the reverse of this last sheet, he wrote the publisher's address. "George Smith Esq. / 15. Waterloo Place, / London.

On 19 November 1875, the first edition of *The Inn Album* was published by Smith, Elder, & Co. The 211 pages plus title pages of the octavo volume were bound in boards of green cloth, and 2,000 copies at seven shillings were printed. A full bibliographical description of the 1875 edition is given in Leslie Nathan Broughton, Clark Sutherland Northup, Robert Pearsall, *Robert Browning: A Bibliography, 1830-1950* (Ithaca, New York, 1953), 18-19. In 1876, the poem was published in the United States by James R. Osgood and Co., a Boston publisher, and sold for about $2.00. B did not participate in the preparation of this first American edition. Finally, before B died in 1889, he had overseen the collected edition of his complete works, published by Smith. Elder & Co. in sixteen octavo volumes. *The Inn Album,* along with *Red Cotton Night-Cap Country,* is in volume twelve. The 311 pages plus title pages and "Contents" are, like the other volumes, bound in brown cloth boards (see Broughton *et al.,* 36).

Composition

The manuscript reveals that B wrote *The Inn Album* in what Griffin and Minchin say was the poet's general manner of composition: "very fast indeed, and [shrinking] from the labor of revision" (300). On the final page B indicates that he began the poem on 1 June 1875 and finished it on 1 August 1875. In spite of the haste with which he wrote, averaging about a page a day, he did not "protest against erasure"; in fact, "Authorship ha[d] the alteration-itch!" (7.321). For there are several hundred substantive alterations on the manuscript, including over a hundred lines added, plus punctuation, spelling, capitalization and paragraphing revisions. Most of the lines added were squeezed between existing lines, although several were inserted in the right margin and sometimes were run vertically down the right. B sometimes added two lines at once by placing them side by side, with a virgule to separate them, between two existing lines. This sort of addition is noted in the variant listings with the editorial comment §two lines on one line§. Word changes and insertions were also generally done between the lines, some on the line; but those alterations affecting the head of a line were most often made in the left margin. Words were generally deleted by a single cancellation line, either straight or wavy, and in these cases the poet's first choice can be made out easily. Sometimes, however, he used vertical lines, and a few times he rubbed a word out, and the new reading was written over. The discarding of entire lines was, except in one instance, done with close-together vertical lines as well as with a thick horizontal mark, making them undecipherable.

Some of these changes were made as the poet wrote, others at a later time. Those made during the process of the initial writing of the poem are sometimes easily detectable as such, for the discarded word is marked out *on* the line and replaced by the substitute *on* the line to the side. Most of the MS changes, however, were made later, either while the poet was still writing the poem or after it was finished. The use of a darker ink for nearly half of the later revisions suggests that there might have been two occasions for these revisions. Likewise, some of the alterations were done with a very thick pen-mark and some with a very thin pen-mark; however, no guesses can be made as to their chronology, for it is possible that B could have used the side of the point of his thick correction-pen to write smaller in confined areas on the MS.

Concentrated current revision occurs in only a few places. DeVane notes that the blotting and crossing at the end of Section 7, the description of the Younger Man's murder of the Elder Man, indicates considerable rewriting (*Hbk.*, 389), and B also had difficulties in deciding how to conclude the last section of the poem, the final six lines not being added until sometime after the 1 August completion date. There were other more minor yet significant points that obstructed the generally smooth flow of writing. In these instances clusters of four or five lines have been added—and there is one instance of 22 word changes on one MS page.

Although the second leaf of p. 7 shows only three very minor changes, there is reason to suppose that this part of the poem, where the Elder Man explains why the Younger Man compliments him too much and why he did feel obliged to help the youth learn to live, caused B a great deal of trouble. For it is the only second leaf of a folio that is numbered (it is numbered 7½), which suggests that it is fair copy. There would have been no reason for B to have numbered the second leaf of the folio (which he did in no other instance) had it not been detached for some reason, and to make a passage obscured by extensive correction clear for the printer seems the most likely explanation.

Viewing the MS of *The Inn Album* as a whole, the several hundred substantive changes and new readings are fairly evenly distributed throughout the poem. Section 1, it seems, was written with greatest ease, though it had relatively more lines inserted (21 in all). Section 2 shows an increase in frequency of revisions but a slight decrease in inter-lining verses. Correction or revision occurred most often from Section 3 through Section 6, which contain all of the tense verbal conflicts of the poem. When the Elder Woman and the Younger Man meet with mutual respect in Section 7, the frequency of all changes goes back to the relative infrequency of Section 2; actually, 7 contains substantial revision only at the start and at the troublesome conclusion mentioned earlier. Furthermore, the instance of lines added here is less frequent than at any point in the poem. Because of the difficulties with the poem's finish and the shortness of Section 8 (only 62 lines), it ranks highest in percentage of manuscript emendation.

For a fuller discussion of the manuscript and other revisions of *The Inn Album*, see "Stages in the Composition of *The Inn Album*," in Ashby Bland Crowder, *Poets and Critics, Their Means and Meanings* (1993), 98-137, first published in *Browning Institute Studies*, 5 (1977), 37-74.

Sources and Influences

The main source for *The Inn Album* is a story that B said "he had heard . . . told thirty odd years ago of Lord de Ros." DeVane identifies the man as Henry William, 19th Baron de Ros, but more probably B had in mind the 22nd Baron de Ros, who was born in 1793 and who died on 29 March 1839 (Griffin and Minchin, 257; *Hbk.*, 386; *Burke's Genealogical and Heraldic History of the Peerage, Baronetage, and Knightage*, 104th ed. [1967], 734; *The Academy*, 9 [22 January 1876], 74-5). There are no detailed contemporary accounts of the story that "made a great sensation in London," the fullest being Frederick J. Furnivall's in *Notes and Queries:*

> The original story was . . . too repulsive to be adhered to in all its details, of, first, the gambling lord producing the portrait of the lady he had seduced and abandoned, and offering his expected dupe, but real beater, an introduction to the lady, as a bribe to induce him to wait for payment of the money he had won; secondly, the eager

acceptance of the bribe by the young gambler, and the suicide of the lady from horror of the base proposal of her old seducer.

(No. 117, 5th Series [25 March 1876], 244-45)

The Elder Man of B's poem attempts to pay his gambling debt to the green young man who has unexpectedly beaten him at cards by trading the sexual favors of the Elder Woman, whom he had earlier seduced and whom he thinks he still controls; she also is a suicide.

About this polished member of London society there is much in the famous *Greville Memoirs, A Journal of the Reigns of King George IV and King William IV by the late Charles C.F. Greville, Esq. Clerk of the Council to those Sovereigns,* which was published in three volumes in 1874. Although the story upon which *The Inn Album* is based does not appear in the *Memoirs,* the character of the worldly lord of fashionable society who lives by his wits, mainly as a swindler of green young men, is presented; for example:

> I went to see [The Earl of] Glengall's [Richard Butler] play [*The Follies of Fashion*] again. . . . Henry de Ros, Glengall, and I went together. I was very much amused (but did not venture to show it) at the point in one of the scenes between Lureall and Sir S. Foster: the latter said, "Let me tell you, sir, that a country gentleman residing on his estate is as valuable a member of society as a man of fashion in London who lives by plundering those who have more money and less wit than himself;" when de Ros turned to Glengall and said, "Richard, there appears to me to be a great deal of twaddle in this play; besides, you throw over the good cause."

In addition to fleecing young men, Greville's friend also plays tutor to the undeveloped abilities of youth, a feature significant in the Elder Man-Younger Man relationship in B's poem (See *Memoirs* 1.250, 128-29, 172; 2.362).

It is possible that when B looked at the Greville *Memoirs* he was reminded of de Ros's being accused of cheating at cards while playing at Graham's Club in July of 1836. The incident was publicized in the newspapers when de Ros attempted to save his reputation by suing his accuser for libel. The main evidence used against de Ros in the libel trial centered on *"sauter la coupe"* ("changing the the turn-up card"), which B's Younger Man alludes to in 5.275 (*The Times,* 11 February 1837, 2-4; 13 February 1837, 2-3; 14 February 1837, 5).

There were also a number of literary characters influenced by the life of Henry de Ros, or at least his type. It is probable that B had been attracted to the character of Henry de Ros as early as 1830 when the novel *Paul Clifford* was published, for B had admired Bulwer-Lytton's plays and novels. Also Browning could have seen an adaptation of this novel when it was produced at John Philip Kemble's Covent Garden in

1835. At any rate, "the insinuating Henry Finish," a minor character in *Paul Clifford*, is a frequenter of Fish Lane, "where there was a club celebrated among men who live by their wits. . . ." Finish is an excellent master "for initiating a man into knowledge of the world" where "debts of honour are not paid now as they used to be," a possible reminder to B of the scandal alluded to by Furnivall. (DeVane, *Hbk.*, 387; Griffin and Minchin, 105; *Paul Clifford* [1830], 61, 77, 120).

Sir Mulberry Hawk, in Dickens's *Nicholas Nickleby* (1838-39), seems an even more striking literary reflection of Lord Henry de Ros, and Hawk's relationship with Frederick Verisopht is very close to that between the male characters in *The Inn Album*. Dickens's nobleman is a notorious "trainer of young noblemen and gentlemen"; he is mainly interested in cheating "his pupil in every possible way," the most common being that of facilitating "the passage of coin (pretty frequent and speedy . . .) from the pockets of Lord Frederick Verisopht to those of Sir Mulberry Hawk." Hawk's outraging of Kate Nickleby—first by making physical advances (chap. 19) and then by making her "the subject of course and insolent wages"—as well as his general disregard for an innocent young woman's virtue also reflects de Ros and suggests B's lord. (See *Nicholas Nickleby* [London: Oxford UP, 1950], 657, 660, 334, 414.)

It is just possible, too, that B found a more recent novel, Trollope's *Framley Parsonage* (1861), a model for the character of his Elder Man, for he and EBB considered Trollope "first rate as a novelist" and "Framley Parsonage [as] perfect." There appear to be some significant similarities between this novel and *The Inn Album*. Trollope's Duke of Omnium as well as Sowerby, both wicked corruptors of youth, conceivably suggest B's elder roué. Sowerby is the better candidate, however. For as Sowerby struggles in the midst of his financial ruin, Trollope's narrator assesses the fallen man's character in a way that seems in keeping with B's presentation of his Elder Man. Neither Trollope's nor B's *roué* gets his second chance, and so, faced with absolute ruin, Sowerby seems to turn bad as does B's lord: "what further possibility was there now that he should care for Robarts, or any other human being; he that was to be swept at once into the dung-heap?" Trollope, however, provides for the same possibility for recovery that B was to present: "There was yet within him the means of repentance, could a *locus penitentiae* have been supplied to him." And since Trollope included many allusions to current affairs in his novel in order to give "the impression that the characters of the novel inhabited the same world and read the same newspapers as he did," it is likely that Trollope's approach had some influence on B's including so many topical references in his poem (Landis and Freeman, 248; *Framley Parsonage,* eds. David Skilton and Peter Miles [Harmondsworth:Penguin, 1984], 333, 519, 13). B's numerous topical allusions will be pointed out in the annotations.

Seeing de Ros's name in the Greville *Memoirs* and having a familiarity with *Paul Clifford, Nicholas Nickleby,* and *Framley Parsonage* surely helped the poet's recollection of the real-life scandal of the late 1830's, but there was also a current event to remind him of that story. The famous saga of the "Tichborne Claimant" (the trials began in May, 1871, and ended in February 1874) was still a very frequent subject in the news and conversation in 1875. Because B had, since before the writing of *The Ring and the Book* (1868-69), been fascinated by court trials and stories related to them, it is not surprising that he took an enthusiastic interest in the Tichborne Trials. During the trial, B "breakfasted with the Attorney-General [John D. Coleridge] and accompanied him to the Court . . ." while he was in the midst of his twenty-six-day address to the jury, in which he reviewed every assertion made by the Claimant. Then about the second trial, Domett records in his *Diary* for 3 February 1874 that B had dined with the Chief Justice, Sir Alexander Cockburn, "a fortnight since"; and had been "present during the whole of his summing-up on the Tichborne case." The judge's summing-up lasted a month, and he reviewed in detail the entire case. William Allingham and Carlyle had agreed, upon the publication of *Red Cotton Night-Cap Country* (which has to do with a trial involving the claim upon a fortune), that B's next poem would be based upon the case of the Tichborne Claimant. This prophecy was not quite accurate, yet the poet did draw upon certain details from the Tichborne Trials. The use of these details in his dramatic poem might to some degree have been suggested by a play based upon the Tichborne Trials that was produced in Paris about six weeks before *The Inn Album* was begun, *L'Affaire Coverley.* B might have read about it in *The Times* for 21 April 1875 (5). Nevertheless, in addition to supplying details for *The Inn Album,* the seduction scandal that came out during the Tichborne Trials could have reminded B of the de Ros scandal and thus contributed to his treatment of sexual relationships (see DeVane, *Hbk.,* 385-86, 389-90; DeVane and Knickerbocker, 207; Hartley Coleridge, *Life and Correspondence of John Duke Lord Coleridge, Lord Chief Justice of England* [1904], 2. 1825; Domett, 116-17; Douglas Woodruff, *The Tichborne Claimant: A Victorian Mystery* [New York, 1957], 358-59; *William Allingham: A Diary,* ed. H. Allingham and D. Radford [London, 1907], 225).

The case concerns a man claiming to be Sir Roger Tichborne, who

Illustrated London News, 31 Jan. 1874

The Tichborne Trial, attended by Browning, supplied details for *The Inn Album*.

returned to England in 1866 in answer to the wide advertising of the mother of Sir Roger after her son had been presumed lost at sea. When she, who had accepted the claimant as her son, died, he demanded his inheritance, was forced to bring suit against those he said were his relatives, and was defeated in a trial that lasted 103 days. Following this defeat, he was charged with two counts of perjury, tried for 188 days, found guilty and sent to prison for fourteen years. During these trials the early life of the claimant was brought to light in detail, and his alleged seduction of his cousin and the consequent situation are remarkably similar to what occurs in *The Inn Album.*

Considering B's interest in and knowledge of the Tichborne case, it is reasonable to suppose that he took an interest in the wealth of books and pamphlets published during and after the trial, many of which expounded particular points of view regarding the authenticity of the man's claim. One of these in particular, the *Tichborne Romance: Its Matter-of-Fact and Moral* (1872), may have aided in directing the details of the trial towards the poet's growing conception of the nature and position of the lord.

At any rate, the story of love, seduction, outrage, and gambling, which came out in the Tichborne Trial, might well have played a significant role in starting the poet's mind to working on the society scandal of the 1830's. To be sure, B had the trials in mind as he composed the poem, because in the manuscript version he had first used the name *Kenealy* instead of *Tennyson* in 2.37, Edward Vaughan Kenealy being the defense attorney in the perjury trial of the Tichborne Claimant.

B might also have had in mind a play by Fanny Kemble, *An English Tragedy,* which was written in 1837 but not published until 1863. Although there are variations in plot and emphasis, this play contains largely the story presented in *The Inn Album,* for it was based upon the same ugly scandal about Lord de Ros: Kemble remarks that "An anecdote of real life, which I heard my father relate, suggested to me the Third Scene of the Third Act of the following play. . . ." Charles Kemble had heard the story of de Ros's villainy at Lady Blessington's; he told his daughter when he came home, and she jotted down the third act of the play while the story was fresh in her mind. In this scene, a married woman, who has been made a wretch by the lord who lured her into committing adultery, is told by him (since they are no longer lovers) that he is still a suitor to her but for another's benefit. If the woman refuses to follow his instructions, he threatens not only to tell her husband of her indiscretions but to make him a laughingstock by publishing the sordid affair. The woman succumbs to these threats. What happens in Sections 5 and 6 of *The Inn Album* is very close to that same story (*Plays by F. A. Kemble* [1863], 2; Margaret Armstrong, *Fanny Kemble: A Passionate Victorian* [New York, 1938], 200).

Probably B owes something to having read *An English Tragedy*, and he may even owe his initial knowledge of the de Ros scandal to circumstances related to Miss Kemble's play. DeVane suggests that it was in 1838, when Fanny Kemble sent the manuscript of her play to Charles Macready, that B first heard the story of Lord de Ros (DeVane, *Hbk.*, 387). B had yet another chance to hear the de Ros story when he and EBB spent time with Fanny Kemble in Rome in 1853 (Loeta Driver, *Fanny Kemble* [Chapel Hill, 1933], 170; *Letters from Owen Meredith to Robert and Elizabeth Barrett Browning*, eds. Aurelia Brooks Harlan and J. Lee Harlan, Jr. [Waco, Texas, 1936], 59).

Reception

Although B had some supporters in 1875, most of the critics agreed that he was not the poet he used to be, and their reviews consisted almost entirely of complaints. *The Inn Album* was judged to be immoral, distasteful, its subject as well as its characters inappropriate, and its poetry not poetry at all.

Most of the reviewers scored B for the objectionable subject of the poem, and the religious papers, from the Anglo-Catholic *Guardian* to the dissenting *British Quarterly Review* were particularly strong in their condemnation. *The Guardian* saw it as "an advanced specimen of criminal literature" (1 Dec. 1875, [Supplement], 1537), with its nonconformist counterpart observing that the story was nothing but "an imitation of a very bad sensational paragraph in the 'Police News'" without an accompanying "moralizing element"; therefore, the poem was termed "retrograde and perverted" (63 [Jan. 1876], 236).

Some of the secular reviews were not far behind those with a religious slant in condemning B's poem. *John Bull,* whose reputation as a literary paper was high, opined that B's "poetic fire" must have burnt "with a lurid glow" for it to produce such a "repulsive poem"; and the reviewer regretted that "so much talent should have been employed on so unsatisfactory a subject" (60 [27 Nov. 1875], 813). Richard Holt Hutton, editor of *The Spectator,* said, "it is . . . impossible to say that we find anything really admirable in this repulsive . . . story" (48 [11 Dec. 1875], 1555). There were other objections: for example, John Addington Symonds complained of the poem's "improbabilities of plot" and "paradoxical circumstances that outrage the realities of life" (*The Academy*, 27 Nov. 1875, 344).

It is surprising to note, then, that *The Saturday Review* not only found the subject of *The Inn Album* acceptable but devoted considerable attention to praising B's handling of it; for its part B had "never chosen a more dramatic . . . subject," and here "more than anywhere else" he had "displayed" the "essentially dramatic power of concentration which he possesse[d] in a marked degree" (40 [4 Dec. 1875], 716). A notably strong defender among the reviewers, however, was *The Athenaeum,* one of the first periodicals to carry a notice of the poem; it actually predicted many of the protests and prepared a partial defense: "Once admit that such subjects are to be handled at all, and who is there but Mr. Browning to handle them?" (27 Nov. 1875, 702).

Though there was some effort on the part of a few reviewers to praise B's "analytic examination of character and motive" (for example *The Examiner* [11 Dec. 1875, 1389]), others found an indecent aspect to the characterization in the poem. The *BQR* lamented that the poem contains no character like Pompilia who could have given *The Inn Album* a moral unity. The resulting moral ambiguity means for this critic that the poem must be "visious in conception" (238). Hutton complained with an air of solemn severity about particular distasteful utterances of individual characters: the Elder Woman describes "her husband, the poor Evangelical clergyman, in a style of harsh contempt which strikes us as singularly undignified and treacherous. . ." (*Spectator,* 1556).

As to the poetry in general, the critics were displeased. Mostly they trotted out the comments that had become the fashion to use as regards the style of anything B wrote. The most common comment on his style in the 1870's was that "he thinks so much more of his substance than the form of what he says. . ." (See Litzinger and Smalley, *Browning: The Critical Heritage* [London, 1970], 376). And B playfully alludes to this common response when he makes the elder lord of the poem react to the verse he had read in the Album by remarking,

> That bard's a Browning; he neglects the form:
> But ah, the sense, ye gods, the weighty sense!
>
> (1.17-18)

Several reviewers responded to the poet's allusion to himself. A. C. Bradley, who was in 1875 a fellow at Balliol College, allowed that it was true negligence that was responsible for lines "even less poetical than . . . ordinary conversation." This critic, offering a list of illustrations, complained of the poetry's abrupt, peculiar, and "wearisomely alliterative" features (*Macmillan's Magazine,* 33 [Feb. 1876], 199). In another comment on B's allusion to himself, *The Guardian* held that

> It would be possible to maintain a still stronger thesis, and bring evidence to prove that Mr. Browning, instead of neglecting mere form, does it positive violence. The blank verse of the poem is often of the most extraordinary description. Lines occur in abundance that have little resemblance to metre except on the possession of ten syllables, and need absolute violence on the part of the reader to force them into rhythmical conformity.
>
> (1538)

And the young Robert Louis Stevenson felt that B's "ragged, renegade versification" was "a thing infinitely more easy to write than anything like careful prose" (*Vanity Fair*, 11 Dec. 1875, 332). Although the other reviewers were largely in agreement with these three, they also quoted a few "graceful passages . . . that relieve the general ruggedness" (see, for example, *John Bull*, 813 and *The Graphic*, 12 [4 Dec. 1875], 543). While *The Saturday Review* complained, it acknowledged the poem's intrinsic power:

> He may think his powerful thought is better conveyed in the "springless and uncushioned vehicles" which he is apt to choose for it than in some more gracious fashion. If so, we venture to conceive that he is wrong, and that his works will live, not in any way by reason of the gnarled form which snatches rather than attracts attention, but by the strong imagination and thought which overcome their uncouth clothing.
>
> (716)

Thus the reviewer agreed with the jocular judgment contained in the Album of *The Inn Album* itself.

There were others who objected to the obscurity of B's poetry. Symonds found that "there are qualities in Mr. Browning's style which render the reading of his poetry a strain upon the mental faculties, and it is, perhaps, imprudent to expect that twice in one year the public will care to undergo the labour necessary for arriving at the gist of what their poet has to tell them" (543). *The Guardian* complained that the characters often speak in riddles and that "What they have to say they put into so indirect a shape, that the attention of the reader is divided between matter and manner" (1538).

Thus by and large, reviews of the poem were not favorable.

Section 1

12] *we burn daylight*   We burn candles in the daytime, or we waste the daylight. *Cf. Romeo and Juliet* 1.4.43 and Thomas Kyd, *The Spanish Tragedy*, 3.12.30.
14-15] 'If a fellow . . . well here   Ryals has argued that the doggerel hints at the meaning that the album will acquire: it contains the "facts"

that B fashioned his art from, much as *The Old Yellow Book* contained the basis for The *Ring and the Book*. In the case of the inn's album, however, the facts get written in as the poem proceeds, and the oft-repeated *"Hail, calm acclivity"* line increases with ironic significance as the action takes place (130).

17-18] *That bard's a Browning . . . weighty sense* B jokes about what is commonly said of his poetry, as he does in "Of Pacchiarotto," Section 26. He also refers to himself in "A Light Woman," "Development," "A Round Robin," "Rawdon Brown," and extensively elsewhere in the *Pacchiarotto* volume.

23] Ecarté "A game of cards for two persons, in playing which the cards from 2 to 6 are excluded" (*OED*).

Blind Hookey "This is the ordinary tavern rooking game, and consists simply in risking a stake upon it, which is won or lost by the dealer according as his own card is higher or lower than that of the player" (George Frederick Pardon, *Hoyle's Games Modernized* [London, 1863], 172).

27] *Shabby-genteel* Dickens's *Martin Chuzzlewit* (1843-44) speaks of this as a popular term of the day (Ch. 4), made so perhaps by Thackeray's "A Shabby Genteel Story" in *Frazer's Magazine* in 1840 and by Dickens's own "Shabby-Genteel People" in *Sketches by Boz* (1836-37).

31] *coign of vantage* Cf. *Macbeth*, 1.6.7.

34] *sprig-pattern-papered wall* Perhaps a design by Christopher Dresser, who was well-known during the last half of the 19th century for his wall-papers with regularized plant arrangements (Ray Watkinson, *William Morris as Designer* [New York: Reinhold, 1967], 48). But the reference might be to a design by William Morris, for in 1872 he designed a series of naturalistic wallpapers with intricate sprig patterns, including "Vine," "Willow," and "Apple."

35-36] *Complaint to sky . . . creature corresponds* The first reproduction is *The Stag at Bay* (1846) by Sir Edwin Landseer (1802-73); the corresponding painting is probably a reproduction of his *A Distinguished Member of the Humane Society* (1838), which is described by James A. Mason as a painting "representing a grand Newfoundland sitting at ease on the seaward end of a pier. It is high tide and the water in its gentle swell laps the iron ring to which boats are moored. The darkening sky flecked with a few gulls indicates that dirty weather may be expected, when, should the occasion arise, the noble animal will do his duty." After 1823 Landseer's style became larger but lost the quality of "elaborate draughtsmanship." Although fashionable, he "enjoyed a greater degree of popularity than technical judgment justified" and is thus appropriate in the country inn which no longer pleases good taste (see 11.29-30 above; *Sir Edwin Landseer* [London, 1902], 92; *Encyclopædia Britannica*, 1910 ed.).

37] *They face the Huguenot . . . World* *The Huguenot* (1852) by John Everett Millais (1829-96) and *The Light of the World* (1853) by Holman Hunt (1827-1910) face Landseer's works. Both paintings were extremely popular in their day, *The Huguenot*'s popularity owing in part to its anti-Catholic implications. *The Light of the World* was probably the most widely known religious painting of the Victorian Period, its popularity being enhanced by the phenomenal sales of the engravings by W. H. Simmons and W. Ridgway—and additional unauthorized photographic reproductions. Carlyle was prompted to criticize it uncompromisingly: "You call that thing, I ween, a picture of Jesus Christ" (*The Pre-Raphaelites* [London: The Tate Gallery and Penguin, 1984], 119); H. W. Shrewsbury, *Brothers in Art* [London, 1920], 113).

38-39] *Grim o'er the mirror . . . ferox glares* Described is a mounted and inglassed salmon, such as is often found over bars in English country public houses.

50-63] *He leans into . . . civilized existence* These lines contain a description of English country scenery, which is only rarely found in B's poetry. See 3.60-69n.

For the description in 11.50-55 B might have had in mind Gerard de Lairesse's *The Art of Painting* (Book 5, *Of Lights and Shades*, Ch. 17); the poet read many times the second English edition of 1778. On *The Morning* Lairesse writes: "This light, at breaking out, gives uncommon sweetness when the objects shine in the water; as also a certain freshness mixed with vapours, which bind the parts of things so well together, as entirely to please the eye of the knowing" (180). Cf. the morning description in *Parleying with Gerard de Lairesse*, 9.210-18 (W. C. DeVane, *Browning's Parleyings, The Autobiography of a Mind*, 2nd ed. [New York: Russell and Russell, 1964], 215, 222). See 1. 77n.

65] *Place* "a manor-house; a country-house with its surroundings" (*OED*).

72] *Guillim* John Guillim, *A Display of Heraldrie* (1610), contains descriptions of coats and blazons of knights and baronets.

74] *but who plan* but those who plan. Such elliptical expression is especially characteristic of *The Inn Album*; see, for example, 2.206 and 5.1.

77] *Corot* Jean Baptiste Camille Corot (1796-1875) was a French landscape painter who died on 22 February 1875. According to *The Examiner*, 29 May 1875, M. Deschamps' gallery at 168 Bond Street exhibited paintings by Millet and Corot after their deaths (612). Corot's work depicts scenes such as that described by B in 11.50-63; the painter sought to give "an impression of serenity . . . in his pure and placid ponds, in the mists which float over their surfaces . . ." (see 11.51-53). His *Ville d'Array* (c. 1835-38) is of a small village with its rooftops seen from a "calm acclivity" and is surrounded by much natural scenery. This painting is similar to what the poet describes in 11.55-58. And the painter attempted to present "joyousness, freshness, and grace," which is what the poet does in his description. B might, in addition to Lairesse (see 11.50-55n), have had the French artist in mind when he wrote these lines. It is interesting that one of B's few descriptions of English land-scape seems to have been suggested to him, in part, by a French painter (see *Masters in Art* [Boston, 1901], 2.29).

106] *crowfoot* "One of the small wrinkles formed by age or anxiety round the outer corner of the eye" (*OED*).

108] *Colenso* John William Colenso (1814-83), Bishop of Natal from 1853, aroused controversy with *The Pentateuch and Book of Joshua Critically Examined* (published in seven parts from 1862 to 1879), in which he demonstrated that it was impossible that Moses wrote all of the books traditionally attributed to him. Colenso was accused of heresy.

120] Apollinaris Short for *Apollinaris Natural Mineral Water,* which was advertised throughout the spring and summer of 1875 in *The Times.*

132-34] *(Three-two fives)* . . . in mild content In a letter of 7 June 1887, B answers questions about *The Inn Album* from the Rev. J. D. Williams; B says, " 'Two fives, &c' are the expeditious way of adding up, *half to one's self*—the important business being to arrive at the *Total*—which is told out plainly (Collins, 46).

139] *Simpkin* A simpleton. "Simkin," an alternate spelling, also means "a silly fellow" (see John S. Farmer and W. E. Henley, eds., *Slang and Its Analogues* [n.p., 1903]; Joseph Wright, *The English Dialect Dictionary* [London, 1904]; J. O. Halliwell, *A Dictionary of Archaic and Provincial Words,* 7th ed. [London, 1924]).

143] *snob* Here used simply to mean "a commoner."

158] *entoil* "to entrap, ensnare" (archaic). Last *OED* citation of this usage is to this line.

160] *shuttle-work* Going first one way and then the other, like a shuttle, which is what the Elder Man does (see 11.162-202) in first suggesting that the Younger Man accompany him to Paris and then that he accompany the Younger Man to the country inn.

163] Opera The Théâtre de l'Opéra was completed in 1874, and it opened "with joyful ceremony" ("Opening of the Paris Opera House," *The Examiner,* 9 January 1875, 41-42).

164] Salon An annual art show held in Paris for living artists.

China-sale "Chinamania," a Victorian neologism, suggests the enormous interest in the collecting of fine porcelain during the period and was the subject of many articles in the periodicals. The seriousness of the interest in china-collecting is indicated by Mrs. Bury Palliser's *The China Collector's Pocket Companion* (London, 1874), advertised in *The Examiner* during April, 1875.

165] *Chantilly* Scene of the French Jockey Club's annual races. Watkins notes from *The Graphic*, 29 May 1875, that the "Paris Derby" had been held on 23 May 1875.

175] *A Man of much newspaper-paragraph* See *Sources*, above, and 5.275n.

189] *crow-nest nook* "Crow's-nest" is a term used in society from about the middle of the 19th century meaning "small bedroom for bachelors high up in country houses, and on a level with the tree-tops" (Partridge).

194] *Pisgah* The mountain ridge east of Jordan from which Moses saw the Promised Land (Deuteronomy 34:1). The allusion proves to be ironic; for, as Moses soon died after his Pisgah-view, so will the Elder Man in this poem.

205] snack Snap, bite (*OED*, sense 1), and with the aim of having his "share" (sense 3a).

238] poke "A pocket worn on the person" (according to *OED*, obsolete or archaic). See 2.414.

240] doit A small, obsolete Dutch coin worth half an English farthing; hence it is used to signify a small or trifling sum (*OED*).

277, 279] *snob* See 1.143n.

281-85] *Clap wings . . . courtyard-paling* An allusion to the fable of the jackdaw and the peacocks; see *"Le Geai paré des plumes du Paon"* (Fable 9), in *Œuvres Complètes de La Fontaine* (Paris, 1865), 81.

295] *Dalmatia* On the east bank of the Adriatic Sea, this wild mountainous region was continuously a crownland of Austria from 1815, after Napoleon's fall, until 1918. On 15 May 1875 *The Illustrated London News* carried a story on the Emperor of Austria visiting Dalmatia, and *Rambles in Istria, Dalmatia, and Montenegro* by R. H. R. was published early in 1875. Dalmatia was part of what used to be Yugoslavia.

302] *Ruskin* John Ruskin (1819-1900) spent many years studying how he could best give away the large fortune that he had inherited from his father, most of which did go for philanthropic purposes. He also tried to get other wealthy men to contribute portions of their yearly income to the alleviation of misery; see, for example, his *Political Economy of Art* (a Manchester Lecture given in 1859 and later published

Illustrated London News, 15 May 1875

The Emperor of Austria's tour in Dalmatia.

under the title *A Joy Forever,* in *The Works of John Ruskin,* eds., E. T. Cook and Alexander Wedderburn [London, 1903-12], 16:102-03).

305] *Timon* Cf. Shakespeare's *Timon of Athens.* Like Ruskin, Timon gave away vast sums of money, but when misfortune overtook him he got only ingratitude; thus he became a misanthrope and isolated himself.

311] front Forehead from the Latin *frons* (*OED* sense la).

314] haught "High in one's own estimation; bearing oneself loftily; haughty." Last citation in *OED* for this archaic form is this line. See 1.321n.

316] stone "The stone of 14 lb. is the common unit used in stating the weight of a man . . ." (*OED*).

318] Rothschild Probably a reference to Nathan Mayer Rothschild (1840-1915), of the London house of the banking family that controlled finance in Europe. B's uncles Reuben and William were associated with Rothschilds' bank in Paris.

321] hight Called or named (*OED,* sense 4). This archaism, like the obsolete "haught" above, is used jocosely and ironically. Its inappropriateness lends humor to the imaginative description. Last two citations in *OED* are 1807-08, Washington Irving, *Salmagunde,* and 1845, Thomas Hood, "A Recipe—for Civilization"; both authors are noted for their use of archaic language. See 4.601n; 5.329n.

325] giving science . . . asteroid After the fifth asteroid was discovered by an amateur astronomer in 1845, the rate of discovery rapidly increased. In 1874 R. A. Proctor wrote: "Not a year passes without the recognition of two or three and sometimes ten or twelve of those bodies termed asteroids, which travel between the orbits of Mars and Jupiter." Astronomers contested to compile the longest list of asteroid discoveries. The latest discovery as of the completion of B's poem was in January 1875 (*The Expanse of Heaven,* 2nd edn. [London, 1874], 114; *The Astronomical Register,* 13 [1876], 75).

326] *Brief* In brief.

327] *Alfred's* The Alfred was a London club (1808-55) somewhat like the Athenæum Club of which B was a member. The Alfred was mainly for men of letters and travellers, but was called by one of its members "the asylum of doting Tories and drivelling quidnuncs." See Ralph Neville, *London Clubs: Their History and Treasures* [London, 1911], 283.

Istria A peninsula in the Adriatic Sea to the northwest of Dalmatia (see 1.295n).

snob See 1.143n.

333] *Polo*   The first recorded polo match in England took place on Hounslow Heath in 1871; the game was brought back from India.

   Tent-pegging   On 26 May 1875, *The World* carried a long article on a newly adopted sport in England: "Next Saturday at Hurlingham will witness the formal introduction into England of a novel diversion [Tent-pegging], which as a manly exercise will soon be acclimatised, and take its place in the foremost rank of fashionable amusements." And this article describes the Indian cavalry sport: "A wooden tent-peg, similar to those ordinarily used in Indian camps, is driven firmly into the ground, and the object of the horseman is to draw this with the point of his lance as he passes at full speed" ("Tent-Pegging," 17).

   Hurlingham   The Hurlingham Club provided for its members "a ground for Pigeon Shooting, Polo, etc., surrounded with such accessories and so situated as to render it an agreeable country resort. . . ." The Hurlingham Polo Association was founded in 1874 (*Hurlingham Club*, [London: privately printed, 1891], 3).

   Rink   There was a great deal in the papers throughout 1875 about the establishment of asphalt roller-skating rinks in London and its suburbs. See, for example, "What the World Says," *The World*, 16 June 1875, 16; at the end of the year, John Bull reprinted an article from *The Globe* on "Rinko-Mania," 11 December 1875, 855.

338] *look*   Seem the same as.

340] *kite*   A toy kite is the image for the Place used to suggest the life of ease which the Younger Man will acquire upon marrying his cousin.

348-49] *Hid somewhere . . . on* 'Balance'   The Younger Man is referring to his passbook.

353] *Galopin*   According to *The Times*, 14 July 1875, this race horse won the Derby at Epsom (and £4,950) on 28 May 1875; he sold for 8,000 guineas several years later.

   that Gainsborough   A painting by Thomas Gainsborough (1727-88), usually considered a painter of portraits for the wealthy.

357] *Dalmatia*   See 1.295n and 2.99, 558.

362-63] *So endeth . . . lesson*   The Younger Man mocks his own hortatory tone with this liturgical phrase from *The Book of Common Prayer*.

366] *down-train*   Train going away from London (sense 1c; earliest *OED* citation is 1851, official *Catalogue of the Great Exhibition*).

369] *farthing*   A quarter of an old penny—practically nothing.

377] *clearing out*   A 19th-century slang term, "clear out" means "to rid of cash, to 'clean out'" (*OED*, sense 26b). See 1.378n.

378] *cleaned [out]*   A 19th-century gambling slang term used by Dickens meaning "deprived of cash, rooked" (*OED*, sense 4b).

Illustrated London News, 12 June 1875

Tent-pegging was one of the "fashionable amusements" available at the Hurlingham Club in 1875.

Illustrated London News Supplement, 5 June 1875

Galopin, winner of the Derby on 28 May 1875.

379] *set . . . flush again* Filled the empty gaming trough with a plentiful supply of money. "Kennel" is used in a different sense in 6.21.
383-88] *but those . . . in the 'World'* An allusion to the Garrick Club quarrel precipitated by Edmund Yates' description of Thackeray's private conversation at the club in *Town Talk,* June 1858. The 'World,' founded in 1874 by Edmund Yates and Henry Labonchere, was celebrated for its daring criticisms. Mrs. FitzGerald sent it to B whenever he and Sarianna went to Europe on holiday. (See Hesketh Pearson, *Dickens, His Character, Comedy, and Career* [London: Methuen, 1949], 269-72; *Learned Lady,* 13).
393] *Correggio's . . . Leda* The Italian painter Antonio Allegri called "Correggio" (c. 1489-1534) is included in Vasari's *Lives of the Painters.* Correggio painted a nude figure of Leda for the Duke of Mantua. In 1648 the Swedes stole the Leda from Italy; however, Queen Christina of Sweden returned the painting to Rome, and it became the property of the Duke of Bracciano and the Regent Orleans. Condemning the Leda as indecent, Louis d'Orleans, son of the regent, cut the head from the canvas. The head was repainted by Jacob Schlesinger (1792-1855). It is probably this lost head of Leda to which the Younger Man in the poem is referring.
397-98] *Silk purse . . . sow-ear-born* A reference to the English proverb that says, "You cannot make a silk purse of a sow's ear."
Roughs To make rough.
412] *pitched and tossed* The 19th-century term "pitch and toss" means "play at the game pitch-and-toss." According to *OED,* "Each player pitches a coin at a mark: the one whose coin lies nearest to the mark then tosses all the coins and keeps those that turn up 'head'; the one whose coin lay next in order does the same with the remaining ones, and so on till all the coins are disposed of." Played by boys and common people; cf. Dickens, *A Christmas Carol* ("Stave Three").
413] *As* Elliptical for "as if."
Scotch-pebble An obsolete term for "An agate or other gem found as a pebble in streams, especially in Scotland" (*OED*).
417-19] *Yet here I stand . . . my outside's blank* The Younger Man compares himself to a faultily cut or unpolished diamond. A "brilliant" is "a diamond of the finest cut and brilliancy" (*OED*).
433] *uprise* "Ascent to power or dignity; rise to wealth or importance" (*OED,* sense 3a).
439] *coupons* A term first used in 19th century (first citation in *OED* is 1822): "One of a set of certificates attached to a bond running for a term of years, to be detached and presented as successive payments of interest become due to the holder. . . ."

443] *wind-egg* B alludes to Aristophanes, *The Birds*, 1.695: The neuter noun ωον means "egg" and is modified by the adjective υπηνεμιον, which means "windy" or "carried aloft on the wind" but also carries the connotation of "empty" or "full of nothing but air."

447] *or . . . or* Used in the sense of "either . . . or" (poetic). See 2.209, 303.

447-48] The Elder Man clears the way to pay his debt with something other than money, which he does attempt to do in Section 6.

451] *trap* 19th-century colloquial term for a small carriage on springs; a gig (*OED*).

Section 2

13] *The road's . . . mix* When for the first edition B had revised the line to read "The road's end with the sky's beginning mix," *The Saturday Review*, 30 (4 December 1875) 716, commented on this "strange disregard of grammatical rule." Domett writes: B "confessed to a slip in grammar noticed by the *Saturday Review*. . . ." Domett records that B said he disliked " 'end and' together, so struck out 'and', put 'with', forgetting to alter 'mix' to 'mixes' " (*Diary*, 162). But cf. 4.229 below where B leaves "end and." It is conceivable that when revising this poem B deliberately left the subject-verb disagreement in order to spite his *Saturday Review* critic, who had gone on to exaggerate the significance of a single error: "That he [B] should cast off all restrictions of grammar is intolerable" (716).

25] *done for* Lost for good, forgotten (colloquial).

29] *Unlimited Loo* A card game played for a pool made up of stakes and forfeits. *Encyclopœdia Britannica* (1883 ed.) says, "At *Unlimited Loo* each player looed has to put in the amount there was in the pool. But it is generally agreed to *limit* the loo, so that it shall not exceed a certain fixed sum." *The Examiner*, 13 March 1875, lists "unlimited loo" as an extravagance of wealthy Oxford students ("Oxford Commemoration," 296).

37] *Gladstone, Carlyle, the Laureate* With the names of the statesman William E. Gladstone (1809-98) and the writer Thomas Carlyle (1795-1881), Kenealy's name had appeared in B's MS instead of the allusion to Tennyson (1809-92), who had become Poet Laureate in 1850. Edward Vaughan Kenealy (1819-80) defended the person claiming to be Sir Roger Charles Doughty Tichborne in the perjury trial, which began 22 April 1873 and ended 28 February 1874. During 1875 Kenealy often spoke to excited crowds about the injustice of the outcome of the trial, and he was elected to the House of Commons in that year (See *Sources,* above).

39-40] *by right . . . head for* I.e., you ought to have the things I lack the ability to appreciate, because you *can* appreciate them.

49] *teeth on edge* Cf. *Ezekiel* 18:2

61] Rule Britannia Composed by Thomas Augustine Arne (1710-78) for *Alfred* (1740), a masque by James Thomson (1700-48) and David Mallet (1705?-65).

63] *Appendaged* "Furnished with, or having, an appendage." *OED* cites this line, there being but one other citation (in 1854).

78] *stuff* "capacity for achievement" (*OED*, sense 3b).

81] *Dizzy* A common nickname for Benjamin Disraeli (1804-81). He was a member of Parliament, leader of the opposition in Commons, three times Chancellor of the Exchequer and twice Prime Minister (1868, 1874-80). These things were accomplished in spite of early difficulties and setbacks. The speaker is perhaps implying that if Disraeli can be a success, then the Elder Man has no excuse for being a failure.

81-86] *Come,—what . . .* who tripped you The conversation that begins here is reminiscent of one in Thomas Hardy's *A Pair of Blues Eyes* (1873) that takes place between the elder man who is the master (Knight) and the younger man who is his pupil (Stephen) concerning failure in love and life; for example, "I lost the woman I was going to marry; you have not married as you intended. We might have compared notes" (Ch. 37).

85] Who . . . woman? The French saying, *cherchez la femme,* is generally attributed to Joseph Fouche (1789-1820), French statesman and organizer of the police, but its origin is uncertain.

97] *grizzling* Grey-hair rendering (*OED*); widely used in 19th century.

98-100] *Then . . . creature* I.e., does that mean the hurt that caused your suffering came from a woman as did mine? See 1.227-31.

99] *Dalmatia* See 1.295n and 1.357; 2.558.

131] *plaguy* Colloquial meaning "confounded" (*OED*, sense 2b).

146] *Mister* Sufficiently-Instructed The point of this sarcasm is that the Elder Man has not "sufficiently polished" the "snob," for the Younger Man remains impolite and boorish, as was just evidenced in 11.140-45 where he blunders into an insult.

164-67] *I plucked . . . into my button-hole* As peonies and poppies are usually red or scarlet and big-blossomed, showy flowers, the implication is that the women "plucked" by the Elder Man were often blowzy and certainly not virgins.

169] *Ess* A reference to the trade name of a perfume, Ess Bouquet.

Psidium A perfume made from the pomegranate flower, which was "the fashion for the season of 1875," much advertised in *The Times* (see, for example, 1 April 1875, 15).

179-80] *Nay, her fault . . . just perfection* B puts into the Elder Man's mouth his own doctrine of imperfection; cf. "Old Pictures in Florence," 11.129-44; *Pippa Passes,* 4.36-37. And see 4.449-50n.

188] *struck on heap* Paralyzed, prostrated mentally (sense 5e; last citation in *OED* of this obsolete and colloquial usage is 1875, Benjamin Jowett, *Plato,* 2nd ed.).

189] *cockney* Edward FitzGerald, in using "cockney" to describe B, defined the word to Tennyson as follows (and it appears to be the sense in which the word is here used): "the affected and overstrained style 'of Londoners on subjects with which neither their Birth nor Breeding (both rather plebian) has made them familiar' " (Maisie Ward, *Robert Browning and his World* [New York: Holt, Rinehart and Winston, 1969], 2.239).

192] *prig* One who pretends to be virtuous (See *OED,* sense 6a). For this word used in a different sense, see 7.275n.

203] *Leporello-list* In Mozart's *Don Giovanni* the licentious nobleman's servant Leporello keeps a list, which is quite long, of Don Giovanni's sexual conquests (see Act 1, Aria 11). This opera was performed in London twelve times during the 1875 season (James Mason, *The Annual Summary: A Complete Chronicle of Events at Home and Abroad* [London, 1877], 129, 130). Its successful *debut* was proclaimed in *The Examiner* on 24 April 1875 (474).

209] *or . . . or* See 1.447n.

225-26] *her- the world . . . / To see* Cf. "A Face": "All heaven, meanwhile, condensed into one eye / Which fears to lose the wonder, should it wink" (11.21-22).

230] *'a head reposed'* The French phrase is *la téte reposée.*

238] *to read* "To occupy oneself seriously with reading, esp. with a view to examination; to study (sense 15c; earliest citation in *OED* is 1826, Disraeli, *Vivian Grey*).

Long Vacation Summer vacation, during which some study was expected.

290] *past* Beyond the ability or power of.

292] *Turned nun* As a consequence of the Oxford Movement, the Church of England revived religious orders for women.

303] *or . . . or* See 1.447n.

339] *shaveling* "A contemptuous epithet for a tonsured ecclesiastic" (*OED*).

340-42] *His Magdalen's . . . says* Cf. Alexander Pope, *Epistles to Several Persons*, 2.11-12: "Let then the Fair one beautifully cry, / In Magdalen's loose hair and lifted eye. . . ." This letter "To a Lady" indicates that the only consistent thing about women is their inconsistency, and the Elder Man uses the Pope allusion to indicate what he sees to be the fickleness of the Elder Woman. Nevertheless, the prayerful pose in which Pope depicts Mary Magdalen is the one painted by most 17th-century artists. Mark 16:9 tells that Mary was changed into a devout follower of Christ when he cast seven tormenting devils from her. As such a character the Elder Woman must perceive herself; see Section 4. To the Rev. Williams, B writes of this allusion: "the careless fellow was made purposely unsure in his quotations" (Collins, 46).

346] *Orton* Arthur Orton, in February 1874, as the false claimant, had been convicted on a charge of perjury at the Tichborne Trial. "Dartmoor and its Prison: The Convict Orton," *The Examiner*, 24 July 1875, 825-27, says that Orton has the "dream that a Kenealyte House of Commons [see 2.37n] will one day set him at liberty." The Tichborne claimant's supporters did in 1879 persuade him to stand for Parliament as a means of obtaining his release from prison, but he changed his mind (see Geddes MacGregor, *The Tichborne Imposter*, [New York: J. B. Lippincott, 1957], 282-83); perhaps B had heard talk of this attempt before 1879, when it became widely known. In Augustine Birrell's edition of B's works, "Orton" is identified as the Tichborne claimant (437).

I cannot explain why B used the name "Finsbury." The General Election in February 1874 was the first in which the secret ballot was used, but the *Islington Gazette* does not indicate any unusual circumstances in the election.

350-54] *That with her . . . never lift now* This image is of the woman bringing about the motivating steam that would enable the engine of the man to accomplish some of the things of which his mind is capable, such as heading a governmental department or writing a book (See 1.423-24); it concludes on 1.360: the steam returns to ice when she leaves him. Joseph E. Duncan, "The Intellectual Kinship of John Donne and Robert Browning," *Studies in Philology*, 50 (January 1953), 96, cites this image as an example of B's giving "a new mechanical twist" to the Renaissance convention of the metaphysical conceit.

359] *string* "brace, give vigour or tone to (the nerves . . . the mind, its ideas . . .)" (*OED*, sense 3a).

372] *The list . . . train* B to the Rev. Williams: "The missed Train, shall be a little-patronized one, connected with the Duke's place mainly" (Collins, 46).

373] *swart* In the general sense the word means *black,* but, as the missed train is the black sign that signals the Elder Man's dreadful fate, *swart* carries also the figurative sense of "baleful, malignant," which apparently fell out of use in the 17th and 18th centuries but appears again in the mid-19th century.

381] *Bestow* Archaic for "put up."

390] *I'll work well the Duke* In trying to persuade the aunt to allow the Elder Man to visit the Place, the Younger Man will play up the fact that his friend's brother is a Duke and that the man is postponing a visit there in order to pay his respects to the aunt.

393-94] *shake the dust . . . from your shoes* Cf. Mark 6:11: "And whosoever shall not receive you, nor hear you, when ye depart thence, shake off the dust under your feet for a testimony against them." See also Matthew 10:14.

414] *poke* See 1.238n

429-430] *Am I born . . . may be Pope* See Cervantes, *Don Quixote,* Part 2. Ch. 47.

438] *Westminster* Parliament.

445] *wonder of a woman* These are the very words used by the Elder Man in describing unknowingly the same woman (see 2.174).

446] *Commemoration-week* "At Oxford, an annual celebration, held in the Act or Trinity Term, in memory of the Founders and Benefactors of the University, in whose honour a Latin Oration is delivered" (*OED*).

In 1875 there was a deal of controversy about Commemoration-week. It was first announced that there would be a curtailment of college balls and parties, but in the end Oxford experienced, according to *The Examiner,* "the usual burst of balls, concerts, lunches, dinners, intensi-fied by the presence and participation of Princes and Princesses . . ." ("Commemoration," 12 June 1875, 659; also see 659 and "Oxford Com-memoration," *The Examiner,* 13 March 1875, 295-96).

484] *Apollo Ball* Held by Apollo University Lodge of Freemasons during Commemoration-week; in 1875 it was held at Christ Church.

485-86] *pours her wine . . . wound* "[A Samaritan] went to him, and bound up his wounds, pouring in oil and wine . . ." (Luke 10:34).

503] *if by "won" . . . "sold"* The whisperer seems to be referring to something similar to the scandal over Lord de Ros's attempt to sell the love of a lady he had won in order to relieve himself of a gambling debt. The similar event in *The Inn Album* does not occur until Sec-tion 6.

558] *Dalmatia* See 1.295n and 1.357; 2.99.

558-59] *drew me . . . Badger-like* *Draw,* in this colloquial sense, was apparently first used in the 19th century (Thackeray in 1860): "To rouse (a person) to action . . .; to induce to come forth . . . (*OED,* sense 47). From "drawing a badger"; *draw* in this sense means "to drag or force (a badger or fox) from his hole."

572] *still to make* As yet to be disclosed.

584] *flaunt the blazon* The Elder Man displays very ostentatiously a replica of his coat of arms.

596] *conceit* Imagine, fancy (*OED,* sense 2b). See 3.82n and 6.27n.

612] *cut* Colloquial for "move quickly; run."

Section 3

2] *resource* Capability in meeting difficulties (sense 5; earliest citation in *OED* is 1853).

3] *left-hand* In the sense of ill-omened, sinister, as "left-hand" is used in Kyd's *The Spanish Tragedy* (cf. 3.12.60-63). See 7.303n.

7] *Barry's building* Sir Charles Barry (1795-1860), after designing the classical plan for the Houses of Parliament in 1836, developed a more spectacular style. He designed numerous large and expensive country houses in the Italian Renaissance style combined with belvederes, which provided an element of the picturesque, but he also, because of his clients' demands, designed houses in the Castle style with towers and pinnacles. For all of these houses he laid out formal gardens. The Younger Man is walking towards his aunt's country-house and through her gardens, both of which were probably planned by Barry. (See Roger Dixon and Stefan Muthesius, *Victorian Architecture* [London: Thames and Hudson, 1978], 34, 38.)

19] *him* The Younger Man who was supposed to have arrived on the train to be met by the Younger Woman.

46-47] *dread Arctic expedition* See 4.287n; the Younger Woman is speaking ironically here.

60-69] *On the great elm-tree . . . help* Stopford Brooke in *Poetry of Robert Browning* [London, 1902], 108, says this description is "the third, and only the third, reference to English scenery in the multitude of Browning verses." The other two he mentions are in *Pauline* and "Oh, to Be in England." He overlooks 11.50-63 above.

76] *tent* Cf. *Sordello,* 6.380: "Of pure loquacious pearl, the soft tree-tent."

82] *conceit* "A fanciful notion; a fancy, a whim" (*OED,* sense 7a). See 2.596n and 6.27n.

98] *Fear sinks to freezing* Fear immobilizes.

144] *pink* "The most perfect condition or degree of something; the height, extreme" (*OED,* sense 2b). See 7.255.

161-62]   Ach, mein Gott / Sagen Sie "easy"?   Oh, my God! / Do you say "easy"?

164]   Raff   Joseph Joachim Raff (1822-82), a Swiss composer and orchestral conductor, was very successful and highly recognized during his lifetime; he taught piano and wrote plano pieces. *The Athenæum,* 17 April 1875, called Raff "one of the most representative musicians of the period"; *The Examiner,* 8 May 1875, reports that Raff's piano concerto in C minor, Op. 185, was performed in the Crystal Palace; and *The Guardian,* 28 July 1875, commenting on the premiere English performance of "Inn Walde," judged it "the event of the season, as far as the Philharmonic Society is concerned" (see Watkins, 13).

165]   Czerny   Karl Czerny (1791-1857), an Austrian pianist, wrote nearly 1,000 compositions. Few of them possess high merit, and none is the production of genius. He, too, taught pianoforte and wrote books of exercises elementary and advanced, the most famous being *Etudes de la velocité.* His exercises had a wider circulation than any other works of their class.

166-67]   *Am I to roll . . . month*   As her piano instructor advised the Younger Woman to "roll up" Raff and practice at the elementary exercises of Czerny, she now asks the Elder Woman if she ought to put aside the cousin because of the uncertainty she feels concerning him and his proposal of marriage and "exercise" in preparation for real life by reading novels of Anthony Trollope. The girl might be alluding to the contemporary joke that Trollope enjoyed a loving intimacy with his young heroines; thus her suggestion might be that she would set aside her cousin and take up a safe "relationship" with the novelist.

178]   *joyance*   The state of showing joy.

231]   *dispenses*   Exempts, excuses (*OED,* sense 6b).

281]   *ferny feet*   Of the elm tree (see 1.256 above)

Section 4

24]   *silly-sooth*   Cf. *Twelfth Night* 2.4.47.

47]   *perdue*   Hidden away (*OED,* sense 3b).

48]   *damnified*   Caused the loss of, brought to destruction or ruin (sense 3); last citation of this obsolete term in *OED* is 1693.

77]   *Babies*   Pupils of the eyes, from *OED,* sense 3 (obsolete): "the small image[s] of oneself reflected in the pupil[s] of another's eye[s]. . . ."

85]   *Greek . . . body*   See 2.174-79.

90-93]   *Value . . . back of*   Perhaps this is a hint of the Elder Man's attempt in VI to "vend" the beautiful body of the Elder Woman as a payment for his £10,000 gambling debt. The lord suggests an awareness that the beauty before him is no longer for him to enjoy for itself.

96] *nullity* Nonentity (sense 5c; only one citation of this sense in *OED* (1657) before B used it in 1846, *Letters*).

110] *fulsome* Full and plump, overgrown in a bad sense (*OED*, sense 2a, obsolete).

110-20] *Or, fattened . . . heiress in a grin* These lines contain the Elder Man's bitter ironic fancy that the Elder Woman has grown steadily more beautiful as a result of his defeats: he asks, how much more beautiful did your hair become when you brought on my ruin by somehow causing me to contest the county-seat in Parliament with my brother's (the Duke) own nominee? And did your lips become a richer red when I behaved in such a way as to lose my heiress?

140] holy cambric Mention of the "cambric" (very fine linen) handkerchief is part of the lord's utterly false picture of the Elder Woman's marriage, which he thinks is to a luxurious clergyman, like Thackeray's Mr. Honeyman in *The Newcomes* (1853-55), who always carries a cambric handkerchief.

144] *flamboyant* Flaming.

146-47] 'Love's flame . . . fiercelier thence The Elder Man is cynically imagining the clergyman's saying that his love was made more intense by her revelation.

160] in petto In the breast, in the heart; therefore, secretly, not revealed.

163] *sunk* Left out of consideration (sense 25e; first citation of this sense in *OED* is 1860).

164-65] *And so my lawless . . . with a rush* I.e., My wicked passion for you destroyed our love only to enable you and your clergyman-suitor to come together even more eagerly.

166] surely . . . sucked me dry Cf. 4.110-20n.

189] *spoiled* Violated might be implied.

214] *broke in bloom* Blossomed. *OED* gives only one citation (1325) of this idiom prior to the 19th century when Darwin apparently revived it (1868). See 7.91.

228] *Prince of the Power of the Air* Cf. Ephesians 2:2-3.

229] *end and* See 2.13n.

230] *"Good!" he smiles, "true Lord Byron* The Elder Man teases the Elder Woman for the Byron-like expression of her unhappiness. B's implicit attack on Byron comes as the disrepute into which that poet had fallen after his death was on the wane, for there was in the 1870's "an extraordinary increase in [Byron's] posthumous renown. . . ."

However, Alfred Austin's praise of Byron and attack upon B in *The Poetry of the Period* "seems to have produced the curious result of turning Browning, who had . . . been in earlier life an admirer of Byron, against him." Perhaps Austin's active support of the Byron Memorial Fund in 1875 served as a bellows to keep B's anger going. This attack upon Byron was inserted into *The Inn Album* after the rest of the passage was completed. In the following year B assaults both Byron and Austin in *Pacchiarotto;* cf. also *Fifine at the Fair* (1872), 67; 6.61n below. In *La Saisaz* (1872), however, B makes amends for these remarks against Byron (see 1.556; "What the World Says," *The World,* 21 July 1875, 15; Samuel C. Chew, *Byron in England* [London: John Murray, 1924], 264, 285; DeVane, *Hbk.,* 423).

237]   *Bloodstone*   A precious stone spotted or streaked with red. In former times, it was believed to have had the power to stop bleeding when worn as an amulet (*OED*).

238]   *Your Ritualists . . . for spouse*   The Elder Man is jeering at the Ritualists' imitation of the Roman Church's insistence on clerical celibacy. (Those involved in the Ritualist Movement intended to copy the services and ritual of the medieval church but also imitated Roman Catholic practices of more recent date (Elliott-Binns, *Religion in the Victorian Era,* 2nd ed. [London: Lutterworth Press], 1964, 230, 231; and see 226-42). See 6.111n.

254-56]   *The one rule . . . laboured—tame*   Cf. John Stuart Mill, *On Liberty* (London, 1859): "According to [the Calvinistic theory], the one great offence of man is Self-will. All the good of which humanity is capable, is comprised in Obedience. You have no choice; thus you must do, and no otherwise: 'whatever is not a duty, is a sin.' Human nature being radically corrupt, there is no redemption for any one until human nature is killed within him. . . . In some such insidious form there is at present a strong tendency to this narrow theory of life, and to the pinched and hidebound type of human character which it patronises. Many persons, no doubt, sincerely think that human beings thus cramped and dwarfed, are as their Maker designed them to be . . ." (111-12).

257]   *mill-track blinked on from above*   This curious image of one blindly following the rote of duty perhaps owes something to *Samson Agonistes.* Samson, whose strength was "Put to the labor of a Beast" (1.37) at the mill, believed God to be presiding over the grim labor. See 2.225-26n.

267]   *himself   OED* cites only Tennyson, *Aylmer's Field* (1864) as using this archaism in the 19th century. See 7.135; 8.6.

277] *burthen* Johnson says under *burden:* "By den, *Sax.* and therefore properly written *burthen*" (*Dictionary*).

283] *hides talent in a napkin* Cf. Luke 19:20.

287] *Arctic voyagers* "The Arctic Expedition of 1875, the organization and prospects of which had occupied a great deal of the public attention," set out on 29 May to plant the British flag on the earth's apex. Another expedition left England on 26 June to follow the same course. Between 1 January and 30 June 1875 there were forty-six articles in *The Times* on the Arctic Expedition (e.g., 31 May 1875, 10).(*The Annual Register: A Review of Public Events at Home and Abroad, for the Year 1875*, Part 1 [London, 1875], 69, 73). See 3.46-47.

310] *Brief* See 1.326n.

317] *Bistre* OED quotes *Chamber's Cyclopœdia of English Literature* (1727-51): "among painters . . . a colour made of chimney-soot boiled, and afterwards diluted with water."

341-42] *No new books . . . these divert* To the Puritan "the soul was nothing but moral. Intellect and the artistic sense did not touch it. . . ." Thus, the Puritan was not concerned with beauty or artistic richness. And, according to John Calvin, man's imagination is distempered; therefore, the Christian should scorn the products of man's imagination. This Puritan characteristic lingered in the Evangelical and Dissenting churches (Andrew Macphail, *Essays in Puritanism* [London, 1905], 31-32; *A Compend of the Institutes of the Christian Religion*, ed., H. T. Kerr [Philadelphia, 1939,] 18).

415] *Bach and Brahms* Johann Sebastian Bach (1685-1750): ironically, many of his compositions are of a sacred character. The choice of Johannes Brahms (1833-97) as one of the composers whose music the Elder Woman is no longer allowed to play is particularly significant since in *Parleying with Charles Avison* Brahms represents "part of man's continuing efforts to express the infinite through the finite" (Roma King, *The Focusing Artifice* [Athens, Ohio: Ohio University Press, 1968], 266). She has been prevented from doing this by her husband's notion that products of the imagination are frivolous works of the devil (see 11.341-42n), and that one's allegiance should remain "True to the mill-track blinked on from above" (1.257 above).

449-50] *Better have failed . . . low aim succeed* This idea is often observed in B's poetry. For example, see "Old Pictures in Florence," "Rabbi Ben Ezra," but especially "Andrea del Sarto": "Ah, but a man's reach should exceed his grasp, / Or what's a heaven for?" (11.97-98).

471] *Judas-like . . . Field* Cf. Matthew 27:3-7.

Illustrated London News, 22 May 1875

The Arctic Expedition of 1875: the *Discovery* and the *Alert*.

478] *Love once . . . love always*   Cf. "A Lover's Quarrel," which is an expression of the belief that real love cannot be destroyed.

483] *Obeah-man*   One practicing a form of witchcraft or magic found in Africa, and formerly also in the West Indies (*OED*).

523] *faith moves mountains*   Cf. Matthew 21:21 and Mark 11:23.

544] *All's well that ends well*   This may not merely be the use of a cliché but a deliberate allusion to Shakespeare's play (5.1.25) and the estrangement of Bertram and Helena: see 11.545-46n.

545-46] *"Had you no . . . spoil the play*   In *All's Well That Ends Well* Helena was ready to accept Bertram even after he had wronged her; she did not reject him as he had, for a time, rejected her. B's character is asking his lady not to reverse the plot Shakespeare had worked out with a happy ending, for such would "spoil the play."

577] *strike work*   Cease working (sense 24b); original to the 19th century.

578] *hand forget its cunning*   Cf. Psalms 137:5

579] *savage*   Hostile (*OED*, sense 10), a 19th-century colloquialism.

585] *trial-test*   Cf. "The Statue and the Bust," esp. 11.227-28; and *Parleying with Bernard de Mandeville*, 11.36-37.

601] *witless*   Unwittingly (*OED*, sense 5).

633-34] *All I dare hug . . .* long thin lily-streak!'   My only consolation is the remembrance of the way in which you blossomed out into your full beauty in response to me (the glove is the outer covering that enclosed the flower). Cf. 2.222, where the Elder Man referred to her as "lily-like."

635-36]   See 11.490-523.

643-46] *then the soul . . . itself in sand*   Her at first strong laugh has continued until, as the narrator says, it can be spoken of as soft and delicate, like a rivulet that trickles, then gradually disappears into sand.

645] *silvered*   "Having a clear gentle resonance like that of silver; soft-toned, melodious" (*OED*, sense 13).

669-71] *You are the Adversary! . . . Wander the World*   Cf. 1 Peter 5:8.

676] *fixed*   "Firmly resolved; constant, steadfast" (*OED*, sense 2; in 19th century rarely used of persons).

686] *Bismarck's self*   Otto von Bismarck (1815-98), following his 60th year celebration in 1875, was much praised in the liberal British press as the man who brought his separated race together (See *The Times*, 6 April 1875, 11).

Section 5

23] *bag and baggage*   The boy is punning on baggage in its literal and figurative sense ("a woman of disreputable or immoral life" [*OED*, sense 6]). It was not until the year following B's poem that Gladstone made "bag and baggage" a household phrase in his pamphlet called "Bulgarian Horrors and the Question of the East," which contained what became known as his "bag-and-baggage" policy (See *DNB*).

38] *tip-top swells* "Tip-top" was colloquial in the mid-19th century for "the very top," and "swell" was colloquial in the late 19th century for "one who had done something notable or who is an expert *at* something" (*Partridge*).

39] *Quits, I cry* I declare myself clear of you.

43-49] "Come, my boy— . . . God knows!" A loose paraphrase of what the Elder Man said in Section 2.

51-53] *Look out, Salvini!* . . . 'Here's Othello' Tommaso Salvini (1829-1916) was an Italian actor of tragedies who came to London in the spring of 1875. In *Leaves from the Autobiography of Tommaso Salvini* (London, 1893), he writes: "Drury Lane was crowded on the nights when I played *Othello*. . . . The celebrated poet Browning proved his friendship by securing my admission as a guest to the *Athenæum Club*. . . ." Between April 1 and July 16, 1875, I gave 'Othello' thirty times . . ." (169-70). On the last night of Salvini's London engagement, B wrote a congratulatory letter to the actor. B and Salvini were the principal guests for dinner at Mrs. FitzGerald's on 3 June 1875 (See *Autobiography*, 170; *Learned Lady*, 74-75).

54] 'But where's Iago?' . . . *Why, there* Although the reviewers praised Salvini highly, they always commented on the ineptness of Carboni playing Iago. In this line, the Younger Man declares the Elder Man's ability to fulfill the role of arch-villain. (See Watkins, 14; see *Saturday Review* for 22 May 1875.)

60] Art . . . concealment *Ars est celare artem*, a Latin adage; see Alfred Henderson, *Latin Proverbs and Quotations* (London, 1869), 27.

62] *scamp* Slang for "cheat" or "swindler," used mainly between 1805-40 (*Partridge*).

72] *that day* During Commemoration-week at Oxford. See 2.446n.

73-75] *And there's the key . . . mystery of humbug* An allusion to the Oxford degree-giving ceremony. One element was that the Masters of Arts granted permission for the candidates to proceed to the higher degree. The Younger Man here implies that the Elder Woman is a Master of Deceit and has allowed the Elder Man to proceed to that grade of achievement. "Mystery" is used in its archaic sense of craft or art (*OED*, sense 2a); "humbug" is spoken of as a trade.

87-91] *As him I searched . . . heart his house* I.e., as I saw into the heart of your mentor, so do I see right through to *your* inner self and am proud to report that I perceive your outer man enshrines a pristine innocence (a dewdrop) as plainly as one sees a spider imprisoned in amber. The Elder Woman is using this cliché image (insects entombed in amber during the process of fossilization were sometimes used as ornaments; see citation from Pope in *OED* under *amber*) to point up the image which she has created to express the Younger Man's purity. But the reader naturally associates the spider-in-amber image with the woman's view that the lord's polished outer covering houses something ugly and insidious in his hollow heart.

133] *embroilment* Entanglement (with the Elder Man) (see *OED*, sense 4; only citation of this sense is 1884, *Saturday Review*).

149] *emprison* Obsolete form of *imprison*.

157-58] *anticipate the snake . . . bruise heel* Cf. Genesis 3:15.

160] *Tree of Life* Cf. Genesis 2:9.

169] *interpellates* Appeals to. The word became obsolete before 1700 but was re-introduced in 19th century as a political term.

173-90] The older man receives an indication that the woman has told her husband the entire story of the Elder Man's seduction of her, but the Elder Man assumes that the husband has decided not to harm the older woman because to do so would publicize his wife's indescretion: the husband is being *mercifully-politic*.

236-38] *And you depart . . . sound at home* The Elder Man offensively describes the state of her marriage by deliberately recalling her image of 11.210-15 above.

260] *Shut up!* B's Oxford man uses a colloquial expression cited by the *OED* as being used first in *Adventures of Mr. Verdant Green, an Oxford Freshman* by Cuthbert Bede (1853).

275] *the Club* The Club was founded in 1764 by Sir Joshua Reynolds and Dr. Samuel Johnson. At first its membership was "limited in the extreme," and was "the most exclusive institution in Europe." But later "the rigour of the Club relaxed," and the numbers accepted grew. Still, in the 19th century many well-known men, including Gladstone, belonged. It is possible that B did not mean "The Club," but rather "The Athenæum Club," which in letters he sometimes referred to as "the Club." (See Neville, *London Clubs*, 263, 264, 265, 266 and 1.327n.)

'sauter la coupe' A *Times* editorial on the de Ros trial (see 1.175n) states that "the most material part of the evidence against Lord de Ros [was] that called *sauter la coupe,* which for the sake of our English readers we shall translate into *changing the turn-up card*" (14 February 1837, 5).

275-76] *cut* The word *cut* is used in two senses: first, in reference to the cutting of a pack of cards (*OED,* sense 8); second, in the colloquial sense meaning "ostracized" (see sense 33a).

278-79] *I dare say you had bets . . . doctored at the Derby* In *The Blue Ribbon of the Turf* (London, 1890), L. H. Curzon writes: "It will be well in the recollection of all race-goers that the defeat of [Macgregor by four lengths in the 1870 Derby] caused quite a sensation; and that all sorts of ugly stories circulated regarding the untoward event, which affected many thousands who had backed him . . ." (346). According to *The Sporting Times,* 4 June 1870, "it is said that Macgregor was got at, and something or other administered to him beforehand, and his liveliness and unmanageableness are quoted as confirmations of such a notion" (178). "Doctor" is a sporting term from about 1860 for "to 'dope' a horse" (*Partridge*).

308] *post* To expose to ignominy by posting a placard (rare) (*OED,* sense 5b).

316-18] *That were indeed . . . old scorpion-scourge* Cf. 1 Kings 12:11, and 2 Chronicles 10:11: "my father hath chastised you with whips, but I will chastise you with scorpions." A *scorpion* "has commonly been supposed to denote a kind of whip made of knotted cords, or armed with plummets of lead or steel spikes, so as to inflict excessive pain."

329] *launch* Rush.

333-35] *My young friend owns . . . A ready rhymer* See 1.54 above. Iago was characterized as a "ready rhymer" when he spoke the long list of rhymed aphorisms in reply to Desdemona's query, "how wouldst thou praise me?" (*Othello* 2.1.130-58).

337] boltsprit An obscure variation of *bowsprit.*

339] *Dared and done* An echo of Christopher Smart's "Determin'd, dar'd, and done" in "A Song of David."

Section 6

5] *weapon* The threat of exposure at the Club.

21] *kennel* Gutter. Cf. 1.379n.

27] *conceit* Belief (obsolete). See 2.596n and 3.82n.

31] *phyz* Variant of *phiz,* colloquial abbreviation of physiognomy: face.

32] *couched* To *couch* is to invest an eye with sight, "figuratively in reference to mental or spiritual vision" (*OED,* sense 9).

44] *out at elbows* "to have a coat worn at the elbows, to be ragged, poor, in bad condition" (*OED*), thus "down and out."

47] *took your measure*   Weighed your character, with a view of what I should expect of you (See *OED,* sense 3a of *measure*).

56] *was minded*   Obsolete for "had a mind to" (*OED,* sense 6b).

61] *Byron*   Another allusion to the Byronic hero whose pose is to be sad about life. See 4.230n.

111] *candle-crotchet*   Apparently this is a made-up term suggesting that the practice of burning candles in devine services was peculiar and unreasonable. The burning of candles was one of the ornaments which the Ritualists were attempting to restore to Anglican services, and it is therefore intolerable to the Evangelical country preacher. See 4.238n.

113] *moils*   A word often coupled with toil and meaning about the same.

125]   See 1.58 above.

134]   water-gruel   Oatmeal or fine Indian meal boiled in water.

   Roman punch   A drink made of water, citron peels, and proof spirit.

137] *spooniness*   "the condition of being sentimentally in love" (sense 2; a 19th-century term first cited in *OED* in 1864).

165] *Cape*   The Cape of Good Hope in South Africa.

172] *dragons . . . blackies*   "aggressively watchful" blacks (*blackies* is a Victorian colloquialism).

174] *cocoa-mat*   "coco-nut matting, made of the fibre of the outer husk of the coco-nut" (*OED*).

186] *Things at this issue*   Things having got to this point.

203] *crab*   "wild apple, especially connoting its sour, harsh, tart, as-tringent quality . . ." (*OED*). In *Fifine at the Fair* B speaks of "the sour / And stinted crab, [man] calls love-apple . . . (79.2-3).

   sloe   Fruit of a common thorny shrub called the blackthorn (*OED*).

205] *Hercules*   For one of his twelve labors, Hercules slew the dragon Ladon and gained the golden apples of the Hesperides, the daughters of Night.

212] *Consols*   "An abbreviation of *Consolidated Annuities,* i.e. the government securities of Great Britain" (*OED*).

Section 7

9] *undesecrate*   Undesecrated.

12-19] *Yes . . . The Adversary*   An allusion to Exodus 7:9-15, in which Aaron's rod becomes a serpent, which swallows the serpents produced by the Pharaoh's magicians. But the Elder Woman's obsessed mind appropriately turns the allusion regarding the destruction of evil into one of absorption and growth of evil, and the Elder Man stands in her vision as the snake who embodies, is representative of, all evil. See 4.669-71n.

36] 'I was not my own' Cf. 1 Corinthians 6:19.

37-38] *eyes to see . . . To hear* Cf. Matthew 13:13-17.

43] *fit such chapman's phrase* A chapman is "a merchant, trader, dealer" (obsolete or archaic). "Bargain" is not the only "chapman's phrase" used by the Elder Woman; see "consigned" (1.40).

51] *Those limes . . . College avenue* Identified as the limes of Merton College by the *Daily News,* 23 November 1875 (Watkins, 13).

63] 'Gods many and Lords many' Cf. 1 Corinthians 8:5.

72] *arms' . . . leprosy* See 4.200-01.

enwinding Winding around, surrounding as with coils.

78-79] *All love begins . . . rests at home* Cf. John Donne. "A Valediction: forbidding mourning," 11.29-32.

91] *breaks* See 4.214n.

92] *Sin no more* Cf. John 8:11.

96-97] *He, waking, whispered . . . wicked counsel* Cf. *Paradise Lost,* 4.800ff.

118-24] *Now, you see . . . Would you* Cf. B's "A Pillar at Sevzevah": "Wholly distrust thy knowledge, then, and trust / As wholly love allied to ignorance! / There lies thy truth and safety" (11.64-66). In this poem, Ferishtaw teaches that facts do not contribute to knowledge and truth, which are gained through trusting in the imagination and the intuitions of the heart. DeVane calls this concept "perhaps the most peculiar development of [B's] thought in the last fifteen years of his life" (*Hbk.* 487). Also see 11.144-49, 361-62n.

135] *himself* See 4.267n.

144-49] *Fool then . . . He can* Cf. 11.118-24n.

202] *drop like shot* A 19th-century phrase meaning "drop at once, with rapidity." The phrase is in reference to the process of making shot by dropping lead from a shot-tower into a water-cistern.

206-07] *And that shall make . . . to wait you there* The Younger Man's attitude is similar to that of the lovers in "Evelyn Hope" and "The Last Ride Together," stanzas 4-5.

233] *bib and tucker* This American term, meaning "best clothes," became colliquial in England about 1875. The term apparently referred originally to the dress of Puritan women, who wore kerchiefs, which they tucked in at the neckline.

235] *champagne and* mayonnaise Champagne and *mayonnaise* represent to the Elder Man self-indulgence, the giving in to natural desires.

The satisfaction of these desires comes after the masquerade ball (pretence of morality) is over.

248] *duffel* "A course woolen cloth having a thick nap or frieze" (*OED*).

251] *Ere Spring-time . . . ring-time* Cf. *As You Like It* 5.3.19: "In the spring time, the only pretty ring time." The song in which this line appears is sung by two pages just before the unraveling of the love triangle. It celebrates spring as the most apt time for marriage.

255] *Stand for the county* To appear as a candidate for the county seat in Parliament (*OED*, sense 12).

pink See 3.144n.

256] *Master of hounds* "usually, the member of a hunt who is elected to have the control of the kennels and of the hunting arrangements generally; chiefly equivalent to *Master of foxhounds*" (*OED*).

258] *Sons at Christ Church* B's son passed the entrance examination for Christ Church, Oxford, on 15 January 1869. Father and son argued as a result of the boy's wastefulness and lack of success there. In June 1870 Pen failed an examination and was sent down.

275] *prig* This word is used here in a more special sense than was intended in 2.192. In the late 17th and early 18th centuries, *prig* applied to "a puritanical person, a precisian in religion, *esp.* a nonconformist minister" (*OED*, sense 5).

291] *tip nor wink* B has remolded the phrase *tip the wink* ("to give a wink to a person as a private signal or warning," *OED*, sense 3) making both *tip* and *wink* nouns.

296] *Iago* See 5.54, 333-35n.

303] *Left-hands* The sinister connotation of the left hand (see 3.3n) again appears to be employed; note that, in contrast, B takes care to draw attention to the Elder Woman and the Younger Man holding right hands in 11.329-30, 333-35 below, while she displays the Elder Man's evil work (i.e., the threat he recorded in the Album) with her left hand. Also see 8.2.

310] *prelusive* Preliminary or introductory to that which is to follow.

311] *broke out* Broke out in verse (see sense 54f; last citation in *OED* is 1875, Jowett, *Plato*, 2nd ed.).

314] place aux dames Ladies first.

339] *warrant* Two senses of this word, as it is used to describe what is written in the Album, are employed simultaneously. In addition to the implication of "death-warrant," sense 8a of *OED* is employed: "Justifying reason or ground for an action . . ." (the warrant is the reason the Elder Woman has made the "till us death do part" pact with the

Younger Man, and it is also a justification of the boy's murder of the Elder Man). See 8.17.

361-62] *I did well, trusting instinct:* . . . *in fellowship* Like the Younger Man (see 11.118-24n above), the Elder Woman trusts instinct rather than reason.

369-71] *Conquer who can* . . . *vibration of the tongue* An elaborate allusion to *Macbeth* 3.2.13: "We have scotch'd the snake, not kill'd it. . . ."

379-80] *A tiger-flash* . . . *him—ugh* These lines seem to be suggested by B's reading of *The Examiner*, 10 April 1875, which describes Salvini's Othello as he is about to murder Desdemona: 'he walks savagely to and fro across the stage with a leopard-like crouch and scowl . . . then when the ill-chanced mention of Cassio's name occurs, his fury bursts all bounds, he seizes her violently . . ." ("Signor Salvini's Othello," 418). Other reviewers described this Othello as "springing at Iago like a 'wild beast,' a 'wild cat,' a 'tiger'" (Watkins, 14). See Domett 162-64. Also cf. George Eliot, *Middlemarch* (1871-72): "The slim young fellow with his girl's complexion looked like a tiger-cat ready to spring on him" (Ch. 60). On the line's last word *The Saturday Review* remarked, "The 'G-r-r-r' of the monk in Mr. Browning's *Spanish Cloister* is not out of keeping with the grim humour of the situation. The 'ugh!' . . . would in the mouth of one of [*The Inn Album's*] actors be questionable. In the mouth of the narrator it becomes ridiculous" (40 [4 December 1875], 176).

381-82] *But ne trucidet* . . . / *Horatian rule* Let not a young man slay an old man in front of the people. This is B's variation of *ne pueros coram populo Medea trucidet*, i.e., let not Medea kill the children in front of the people ("Ars Poetica," *The Epistles of Horace*, ed. Augustus S. Wilkes, [London, 1896], 185). These lines might also allude to reviews of Salvini's Italian version of *Othello*. From *The Examiner*, 10 April 1875: "the seclusion of the bedchamber where the murder [of Desdemona] is consummated might . . . seem to be a refinement, as carrying out the precept of Horace not to give offence by deeds of violence coram populo." But then the reviewer adds: "it may be questioned whether the classical rule of killing behind the scenes has the effect of softening the horrors of tragedy; a murder out of sight and within hearing is perhaps more exciting than when the actors are in full view" (418).

Section 8

2] *His right-hand* . . . *her right-hand* See 3.3n and 7.303n.
6] *himself* See 4.267n.

13] *the thing* I.e., poison.

17] *warrant* See 7.339n.

35-55] *All's ended . . . taps discreet* The Younger Woman imagines that the trial of the Younger Man carried out by the Elder Woman is over and that he has been found innocent amid cheers the judge pretends to ignore. Then the girl goes in her imagination back to the moment just before the judgment was pronounced. Alluding to *The Merchant of Venice* (wherein Portia is also a friend only briefly playing the part of the judge and is called a Daniel alternately by both Shylock and Gratiano), the girl muses: now Portia, let us hear you in your Daniel character; in the beginning you were severe, but now you have become kind. The Younger Woman's fancy produces the words of judgment that indicate the Younger Man's innocence and at the same time coyly hint that what the boy needs is a wife to bring out the best in him. The gardening image suggests that love does not grow naturally in the Younger Man but that a young woman may induce love and assure its development. At this point, the girl in the imagined courtroom waves a handkerchief in joyful assent—but she realizes that she will need the handkerchief to hide her blushes when she becomes a bride. Then she thinks of having to say good-bye to her faithful friend who she imagines to have brought about the happy union with her cousin. At this point, the Younger Woman sings, "*'Cigno fedel, cigno fedel, / Addio!'*" (Faithful swan, faithful swan, farewell!), from the "Swan Song" of Wagner's *Lohengrin* (1850). In the opera Lohengrin sings this farewell to the faithful swan whose appointed task, to deliver him to his love (Elsa), is completed whereupon it must return to the blessed land from which it came (1.3). Suddenly the Younger Woman realizes what a mistake and what an ugly omen to have such sad thoughts when she should be filled with excitement over the expected marriage to her cousin. Thus, she disregards the Wagner line and the sentiment associated with it and turns instead to a line in I, vii of Pietro Metastasio's *La Clemenza di Tito* (1737): "*'Amo te solo, te / Solo amai!'*" (I love you only, you only have I loved), a much more appropriate emotion for a bride-to-be.

The circumstances under which "*'Amo te solo . . .'*" is uttered in *La Clemenza di Tito* have significance for B's poem. A young woman called Servilia loves Annio and is loved by him, but their future seems dark because the emperor Tito also wants her to be his bride. Thus Servilia is faced with the problem of having a great love for Annio and her duty to the emperor, as the Younger Woman is faced with what now seems love for the Younger Man and her fidelity to her friend, the Elder Woman. But the just judge in each case does not impede the lovers: Tito announces that he will not stand in the way of the young couple and that Servilia and Annio shall marry, and the Younger Woman shows renewed faith that the Elder Woman will have the same wish for her and her cousin (which indeed this judge has shown in 5.145-52)—and there is also the suggestion that the affection between the Younger Woman and the Elder Woman will not interfere with the girl's happy marriage, which certain of her earlier statements would put in question (e.g., "Perhaps, / Giving you all the love of all my heart, / Nature, that's niggard in me, has denied / The after-birth of love there's some-one claims, / —This huge boy . . ." [3.121-25; also see 3.219-25]).

In 1847 a formal opera company was established at Covent Garden, the Royal Italian Opera; and it stayed until 1884. Therefore it is not at all unusual for Wagner's opera to be quoted in Italian. B probably saw *Lohengrin* when it was performed at Covent Garden in Italian on 8 May 1875, about three weeks before he started *The Inn Album,* though he would have had ample opportunity to see this opera throughout the 1875 season. It was performed at Drury Lane after leaving Covent Garden.

B owned a copy of G. B. Rolandi, *Opere Scelte dell' abate Pietro Metastasio* (1826), tomo I.

53] *cheeks . . . erewhile* The girl's cheeks are blushing.

PACCHIAROTTO AND HOW HE WORKED IN DISTEMPER: WITH OTHER POEMS

Emendations to the Text

The following emendations have been made to the 1889a text:

Of Pacchiarotto and How He Worked in Distemper, 1.109: The 1889a reading *Tongue tied* without the hyphen is incorrect; the MS-1876 reading of *Tongue-tied* is restored.

Of Pacchiarotto and How He Worked in Distempter, 1.232: 1889a omits one *c* in Pacchiarotto's name; the MS-1876 reading is restored.

Of Pacchiarotto and How He Worked in Distemper, 1.343: Both 1876 and 1889a omit comma following *description,* which terminates a subordinate clause commencing with the comma following *gained.* The MS reading is restored.

Of Pacchiarotto and How He Worked in Distemper, 1.431: Punctuation required at end of sentence apparently inadvertently dropped in 1889a; 1876 period is restored.

Of Pacchiarotto and How He Worked in Distemper, 1.449: End punctuation apparently inadvertently dropped in 1889a; exclamation mark of 1876 accords with tone and is therefore restored.

House, 1.4: Quotation mark required to close quotation. 1876 reading restored.

Fears and Scruples, 1.1: 1889a omits comma after *him,* which is followed by a parenthetical phrase; the necessary comma, found in MS-1876, is restored.

Appearances, 1.6: Punctuation, omitted in 1876 and 1889a, is called for at the stanza's end; the MS exclamation mark, which fits the tone, is restored after *heard.*

Appearances, 1.12: Punctuation at end of sentence that ends the poem is omitted in 1889a; the exclamation mark, fitting the command and which appeared in MS-1876, is restored after *mask.*

Hervé Riel, Title: The acute accent disappeared from the poem's title in 1876 and 1889a; the MS reading is restored.

Hervé Riel, 1.71: End punctuation inadvertently dropped in 1889a. Syntax and tone call for exclamation mark after *grace.* Therefore PMMS-1876 reading is restored.

Cenciaja, 1.13: A double quotation mark, absent from all texts, is required to close the quotation.

Cenciaja, 1.212: 1889a omits period at end of sentence; restored according to MS-1876.

Filippo Baldinucci on the Privilege of Burial, 1.178: Comma after the elliptical adverb clause is omitted in 1889a; MS-1876 reading is restored.

Filippo Baldinucci on the Privilege of Burial, 1.256: A single quotation mark closing the quotation is omitted in 1889a; the MS-1876 reading is restored.

Epilogue, 1.103: Syntax requires comma following *you,* dropped in 1876 and 1889a. MS reading is restored.

Epilogue, 1.180: 1889a omits the required single quotation mark at the end of the line; 1876 reading restored.

Epilogue, 1.181: 1889a omits the required single quotation mark at the end of the line; 1876 reading restored.

In *Pacchiarotto and How He Worked in Distemper,* B usually indicated divisions in discourse by line spacing rather than by indentation, though he sometimes used both. During the printing history of these poems, paragraph divisions were occasionally lost when they happened to occur between pages. I have restored all of B's paragraphs. These form a separate class of emendations to the 1889a text. Paragraphing is restored in the following instances:

A Forgiveness, 246-47

Cenciaja, 114-15, 138-39, 187-88, 212-13, 261-62.

Texts

The manuscript entitled "Pacchiarotto: and How he worked in Distemper, with other poems" which B sent to the printer is in Balliol College Library and is bound with *La Saisiaz* and *The Two Poets of Croisic* (1878) in brown morocco, with the front cover bearing the Browning family coat of arms stamped in gold. The poems together are catalogued as Balliol MS. 390. On the first page of the title poem B wrote parenthetically, "original copy / R.B." In fact, the manuscripts of all of the poems in this volume are the original ones except for the six-page MS of "Hervé Riel," which is a copy with some additional revision of the original MS in the Pierpont Morgan Library (MA 1050) or of a subsequent revision of this original. The Pierpont Morgan MS consists of three 5⅜- by 8-inch double-leaf pages in a small hand, without doubt B's. Together with the MS poem, the Pierpont Morgan has

B's letter of 6 November 1871 to Edith Story, which accompanied his presentation of the MS to her; the letter assured her that he was sending the original manuscript of the poem. The whereabouts of any proofs for any of these poems is unknown (Kelley and Coley, 424).

Except for "Hervé Riel" all of the poems at Balliol were written on the same kind of paper as *The Inn Album* (see above) and numbered and renumbered in the same way. The first two pages of the Balliol "Hervé Riel" are on a lined paper of the same size; the subsequent pages are on a paper about ¼ inch narrower, and these pages had at one time been folded to a pocket size. Another difference between this MS and the other Balliol MSS is that here B did not include the L.D.I.E. with the date. Finally, B signed "Hervé Riel" but not the other poems in the collection.

The first edition was published on 18 July 1876 by Smith, Elder, & Co. The 241 pages plus title and contents pages of the octavo volume were bound in boards of drab cloth. It sold for seven shillings, six pence, and 2500 copies were printed. A full bibliographical description of the 1876 edition is provided in Leslie N. Broughton, Clark S. Northup, and Robert Pearsall, *Robert Browning: A Bibliography, 1830-1950* (Ithaca, NY: Cornell Univ. Press, 1953), 19. In his own copy of the first edition, now at the Armstrong Browning Library, B made a number of corrections and revisions. These are recorded in my textual apparatus. *Pacchiarotto and How He Worked in Distemper with Other Poems* is in volume fourteen of the 1888-89 final edition of *Poetical Works*, together with *La Saisiaz* and *The Two Poets of Croisic*. There are 279 pages plus title and "contents" pages in the volume, which is bound in brown cloth boards (see Broughton et al., 36).

Reception

In general *Pacchiarotto and How He Worked in Distemper: with Other Poems* was condemned in the contemporary reviews—which is not surprising at all since the volume contained several poems that denounced those who wrote the reviews. As was often the case, *The Athenæum* came out with the first response to B's new poem; this critic objected to "a tendency to quarrel with his critics . . . in a manner not altogether worthy of himself." The reviewer then wondered why B had elected to "deal vicious side-strokes at his enemies" who accuse him of being "no poet" when such criticisms can in fact do no harm to B's reputation (22 July 1876, 101, 102). Edward Dowden in *The Academy* expressed mild surprise to learn that B belonged to "the *genus irritabile*" (29 July 1886, 99), and R. H. Hutton regretted that "he has wasted the larger portion of this . . . volume . . . in an angry onslaught on the common and unclean herd" of critics (*The Spectator*, 49 [26 August 1876], 107).

But it was *The Saturday Review* that first got its hackles up, asserting that in the present volume B "challenges all who presume to form and express an independent judgment of his poems in language so unprovoked, so unreasonable, and so coarse that it would be almost an act of cowardice not to answer his defiance"; and *The Saturday Review*-er proceeded to answer with his own defiance: "it is a monstrous pretension to deny the right of criticism to students who have perhaps proved the accuracy of their taste by a keen enjoyment of the best poetry of all countries, and even by their appreciation of Mr. Browning's works before he wrote *The Inn Album* and *Pacchiarotto*" (42 [12 August 1876], 205). During the next month, *The Graphic* sneered sarcastically at B's attitude towards the critics: "what a comfortable frame of mind it must be when a poet entertains a perfect belief in his own wisdom and excellence, and an utter contempt for other folks' opinion!" (14 [9 September 1876], 254). And of course there was nothing unexpected from Alfred Austin's paper, *The Evening Standard*, which began:

> The poem which gives its title to this volume is written to prove that, whatever his critics or readers may choose to the contrary, Mr. Browning himself is perfectly assured not only that he is a very great poet, but that all who think differently are fools and knaves, and he enforces this great truth by means of a parable.
>
> (19 August 1876, 3)

The Westminster Review and *The Secularist* were much more in sympathy with B's attack on his critics. Actually, *The Westminster* was alone in responding to *Pacchiarotto* just as B would have wished. Recognizing that the poem was meant to be full of humor, this reviewer also felt that it expressed a significant truth—that B's critics "have talked more nonsense about [him] than about anybody else except Shakespeare." The small fault that this reviewer finds with *Pacchiarotto* must have pleased B, for he was found to be "too good-natured" and in want of "a sharper knife and a good deal more of the ferocity of a Turk" in dealing with his critical adversaries ("Belles Lettres," 106 [October 1876], 576). Then James Thompson, writing for *The Secularist*, thought B's contempt for his critics "quite justifiable, but scarcely worth the while of so great a thinker and poet to fling at such pigmies." Nonetheless, since the thinker had done the flinging, Thompson found B's effort a thoroughgoing success: "he not only vindicates himself with a haughty and jovial self-confidence, but overwhelms his accusers with counter-charges of imbecility and humbug" (9 September 1876, 168).

Though the critics were generally hostile to those poems in which B took issue with them, they did take some pleasure in B's having provided a volume of short poems, the first since *Dramatis Personae*, published twelve years earlier. "Some of the shorter pieces are very fine, and two or three will take [their] place with his best," said *The Westminster* (168). Dowden, as well, contended that "Numpholeptos" was as good as anything in *Men and Women* or *Dramatis Personae* (100). Even *The Saturday Review* found "Fears and Scruples" to be written in B's "happiest manner" (206). All of the reviews singled out "Hervé Riel" for praise.

Having proffered B a few crumbs of commendation for some of the shorter pieces in the collection, the reviewers set about protesting against the obsurity that pervaded the volume. *The Saturday Review,* for example, accused him of representing his "own uncommunicated reflections for products of creative art" and then remarked that his "frequent and growing obscurity resembles a cypher of which the key is withheld," because, the reviewer contended, his poems too frequently "convey no meaning to the most intelligent reader . . ." (205). Hutton complained in his own peculiar way about the indigestibility of B's poems: B will not "break the bread before feeding the multitude. . . . [He] cannot have his thought broken, no, not even stripped of its hard encasement: we must bolt it whole, or not at all" (107). *The Graphic* allowed that " 'Bifurcation' and 'Numpholeptos' are almost unintelligible enough to delight the admirers of 'Fifine at the Fair,' " of which it imagined no great number (254).

PROLOGUE

Date and Composition]   No date appears on the manuscript, and the only alteration is in the title.

5]   *creepers*   Virginia creeper, a climbing plant. Mrs. Thomas Fitz-Gerald had given B a cutting that he had planted against the brick wall next to his study at 19 Warwick Crescent (*Learned Lady*, 51).

7-8]   *bricks draped . . . lappets*   The thick creeper has clusters hanging like the flaps of a garment.

OF PACCHIAROTTO, AND HOW HE WORKED IN DISTEMPER

Date and Composition]   According to the Balliol MS, the poem was begun on 15 April and completed on 1 May 1876. A letter of 25 May 1875 to George Barrett, in which B uses the language of the poem, suggests the possibility of an earlier draught of the poem—at least in part. On the other hand, B might only have composed a few phrases of the poem that he then put in the letter to his brother-in-law. Hood speculates that the final section of the poem might have been added at a later time, but his argument is based on a misinterpretation of the two dates at the end of the MS. They do not indicate two times that B finished the poem but rather the date of beginning and the date of completing it. (See Hood, *Ltrs.*, 363 and Landis and Freeman, 300.)

The Balliol MS reveals that although B worked rapidly, he immediately afterwards gave a great deal of thoughtful attention to the improvement of his original draught, and this thoughtful attention continued as he revised for the 1876 edition. During these two stages, he thoroughly reworked key passages and added lines in order to clarify meaning and action, to introduce visual and auditory images, and in various ways to sharpen his measured denunciation of his critics. He also carried out small-scale revisions that yielded smoother lines, metrical appropriateness, and simple clarity and strength of expression. Punctuation was his concern especially in the final revisions for the 1876 edition. Though he gave only slight attention to the poem when preparing for *The Poetical Works* (1888-89), these few revisions improve the text. For additional information on B's revisions of the manuscript and a fuller discussion of revisions in general, see "Browning and How He Worked in Good Temper," in Ashby Bland Crowder, *Poets and Critics, Their Means and Meanings* (1993) 139-62, originally published in *Browning Institute Studies*, 17 (1989), 93-113.

Sources]   "Of Pacchiarotto and How He Worked in Distemper," together with a number of the other poems in the *Pacchiarotto* volume, constitutes B's only sustained response to the literary critics who plagued him throughout his life as a poet. Thus the criticism of his poetry is a basic source for these poems and for "Of Pacchiarotto" in particular.

The Athenæum's complaints in 1835 about the obscurity of *Paracelsus* were a foretaste of the critical fare that B would have to endure for the rest of his life. B managed to be philosophical about the early complaints, figuring to mend his shortcomings. In this vein he wrote to his friend Alfred Domett on 13 July 1846:

> As to the obscurity and imperfect expression, the last number of my 'Bells,' which you get with this, must stand for the best I could do, *four or five month* ago, to rid myself of those defects—and if you judge I have succeeded in any degree, you will not fancy I am likely to relax in my endeavour now. As for the necessity of such endeav-

> our I agree with you altogether: from the beginning, I have been used to take a high
> ground, and say, all endeavour elsewhere is thrown away.

B then proceeded to write with the sure and certain hope that the critics would one day recognize his worth. But that day never came, and as time passed B detected a malignant intent in the critical reception of volume after volume. Following the critical and financial failure of *Christmas Eve and Easter Day* (1850), he had high hopes for *Men and Women* (1855)—which were savagely dashed, prompting the following advice of 17 December 1855 to his publisher, Edward Chapman:

> don't take to heart the zoological utterances I have stopped my ears against . . . of
> late. "Whoo-oo-oo-oo" mouths the big monkey—"Whee-ee-ee-ee" squeaks the little
> monkey and such a dig with the end of my umbrella as I should give the brutes if I
> couldn't keep my temper, and consider how they miss their nuts and gingerbread!

Although there was some insightful commentary on this collection of poems, B characterized the notices in general as "stupid and spiteful, self-contradicting and contradictory of each other"; in short, they were "rot." Kenneth Knickerbocker is right in his suggestion that the tone of this letter prefigures "Of Pacchiarotto." When B's displeasure over what he felt to be the inadequate critical reception of his wife's *Aurora Leigh* (1856) was added to his own disappointment, the mood that gave rise to "Of Pacchiarotto" grew, and he complained to Chapman of the "blackguardism from the 'Press,'" alluding to those critics who did not sign their reviews as "those night-men who are always emptying their cart at my door." B concluded this letter of 2 December 1856 with a threat that was not to be made good for twenty years: "Don't you mind them, and leave me to rub their noses in their own filth some fine day." (See F. G. Kenyon, ed. *Robert Browning and Alfred Domett* [London, 1906], 127; K. L. Knickerbocker, "Browning and His Critics," *Sewanee Review,* 43 [July-September 1935], 285, 288; DeVane and Knickerbocker, 85, 87, 97.)

Apparently B blew off enough steam in this sort of correspondence to quieten his temper for some time; but also various circumstances and events assuaged his ire: first, EBB's *Aurora Leigh* sold well in spite of the early bad reviews, and B's previous works (save *Pauline*) were published in a three-volume set (1863), which was favorably received. Further, *Dramatis Personae* (1864) met with a very encouraging response, and it required a second edition. Suddenly, it seemed, B was being recognized; his poems were in demand, additional collected editions being required in 1865 and 1868 (six volumes and including *Pau-*

line). He was writing *The Ring and the Book,* and the concern over unfair criticism appears to have diminished ("Browning and His Critics, 290).

Amidst the almost clear critical skies was one dark and threatening cloud: the response to *Sordello,* which he had revised heavily for the 1863 collection. Many jokes were made at B's expense, and there was no let up as time passed. Junius Henri Browne, judging *Sordello* to be "rhapsodical rubbish, wholly devoid of a glimmer of meaning," collected various stories about this poem of "calculating obscurity," two of which I shall mention. The first story is that *Punch* offered £100 to anyone who could explain the meaning of a single line of *Sordello,* and in a year's time no one had claimed the prize. The second is that condemned prisoners at Newgate who were "offered full pardon on condition that they would hear 'Sordello' read, went to the gallows with hilarious alacrity" (*The Galaxy,* 19 [June 1875], 766, 772, 768). The obscurity the critics found in *Sordello* was subsequently observed in everything else that he wrote: reviewers declared over and over that to enter B's poetical world was to enter a land of fogs and mists.

It must have been with much anticipation that B awaited the critical reception of his *magnum opus, The Ring and the Book* (1868-69). Reviewed in practically every journal and newspaper of any significance, this long poem did not fail to elicit a deal of praise, but it also attracted an unignorable assortment of adverse criticism. The critics complained once again of B's obscurity, of his plan of telling the same story ten times, of his crabbed English, but mostly they complained of his obscurity. *Macmillan's Magazine* said that "Mr. Browning cannot tell a plain story in a plain way; he cannot report a simple speech with simplicity. He must needs introduce everywhere comparisons and metaphors; metaphors which darken, and comparisons which obscure" (J. R. Mosley, "The Ring and the Book," April 1869, 544-45). *The Athenæum,* though generally happy with the poem, could not suppress misgivings over what it took to be "wilful *[sic]* obscurities" (41 [26 December 1868], 876); likewise, *The British Quarterly Review* saw disfiguring "obscurities that seem almost intentional" (49 [March 1969], 458).

A glimpse into B's feelings about all this is provided by Sir Frederick Pollock's *Personal Remembrances,* which records that in April of 1869 B spoke to the baronet at the Athenæum Club about *The Ring and the Book:*

> He said that he had at last secured the ear of the public, but that he had done it by vigorously assaulting it, and by telling his story four times over. He added that he

had perhaps after all failed in making himself intelligible, and said it was like bawl-
ing into a deaf man's trumpet, and then being asked not to speak so loud, but more
distinctly.

(Personal Remembrances of Sir Frederick Pollock [London: Macmillan, 1887], 2.202).

B seemed in pretty good humor here, perhaps because there were plenty
of comments about the "spiritual perfection" and "poetic achievement"
(*The Spectator*, 13 March 1869, 325, and 30 January 1869, 139) mixed in
with the critical response, although it would be inaccurate to say that
there was more praise than blame.

At any rate, B rode the crest of the best reviews that he was ever to
have and did not resume writing poetry until 1871, when he produced
Balaustion's Adventure and *Prince Hohenstiel-Schwangau*. The re-
views of these poems detected a reduction in poetic power, Sidney Col-
vin, for example, remarking that B's "true student and admirer cannot
but hold himself entitled to ask amends in the shape of something that
shall have in it more of the master's higher genius" (*The Fortnightly*, 16
[1 October 1871], 490).

Though B might have felt relieved that he had escaped the charge of
obscurity, such relief found no proof in the years that followed. Imme-
diately after *Fifine at the Fair* (1872) was published, *The Athenæum*
sounded what was to become the dominant theme in the criticism of B's
poems for the rest of his life: "At last Mr. Browning has his revenge upon
all those who voted 'Balaustion's Adventure' a May-month's amuse-
ment, and found 'Hohenstiel Schwangau' not too hard for them to grasp
the full meaning of. 'Fifine at the Fair' . . . [is] scarcely more and
scarcely less of a puzzle than 'Sordello' itself" (8 June 1872, 711). *The
Saturday Review* picked up the comparison to *Sordello* and developed it
(34 [17 August 1872], 220). But it was *The Graphic* that expressed the
strongest frustration: "To call [*Fifine*] unintelligible would be easy, and
on the whole true, but would only partly convey the sense of bewilder-
ment in which one rises from its perusal" (29 June 1872, 606).

The next year and the next poem brought more elaborate com-
plaints about B's lack of clarity. *The Illustrated London News* was
fierce:

Language, so far as the use of it is to conceal thought, has been most skilfully and
ingeniously employed in *Red Cotton Night-Cap Country*. . . . Or, perhaps, it would
be more correct to say that, though thoughts apparently abound, it is more difficult to
grasp and disencumber them than to hold and skin so many eels. Indeed, the volume is
likely to have upon most readers an effect similar to that which Persius had upon the
blessed St. Jerome. The poem, as it is called on the last page but one, is an extreme
example of what is regarded in these latter days as the art of poetry. It is a game of hide

and seek between the writer and the reader. . . . [I]t presents such a collection of involved sentences and peculiar grammatical constructions as ought to find great favour in the eyes of those gentlemen who preside over competitive examinations and delight in torturing the candidates with unprofitable puzzles contrived out of the English language.

(62 [21 June 1873], 590)

Looking at the poem from a distant shore did not enable *The Atlantic Monthly* reviewer to see any more clearly what B was about; to him the poem was merely "that strange last performance of Mr. Browning, to which, for reasons of his own, he has given the outward form and typographical mask of poetry . . ."; the reviewer could not guess "why he should have called it Red Cotton Night-Cap Country sooner than The Man in the Moon, or Ding-Dong Bell." In the end, said this reviewer, the reader "is left dancing upon nothing" and with little but a dim awareness that he has encountered something "unwholesome," a condition resulting from B's much disapproved technique: "It seems as if Mr. Browning lay in wait, and, lest any small twinkling or glimmer of meaning should reach the reader, sprang out and popped a fresh parenthesis on the offending chink that let it through" (32 [July 1873], 114-15).

Right up to 1875, the year before the publication of *Pachiarotto*, the reviewers strained to denounce B's manner and lack of intelligibility with a high degree of outrage. Even *Blackwood's Magazine,* which generally did not review B's poems, could not resist attacking the "unintelligible and unlovely rant" which is *Aristophanes' Apology:* "What has come to him in these later days? What bewildering spirit has carried him round the fatal circle and landed him once more in those wilds of confused wordiness which made Sordello the wonder and fear of all readers?" (118 [July 1875], 93, 91). On B's next poem, *The Inn Album,* John Addington Symonds complained as follows: "there are qualities in Mr. Browning's style which render the reading of his poetry a strain upon the mental faculties, and it is, perhaps, imprudent to expect that twice in one year the public will care to undergo the labour necessary for arriving at the gist of what their poet has to tell them" (*The Academy,* 27 November 1875, 543; see the account of the critical response to *The Inn Album* in the Editorial Notes to that poem, above).

It was only five months earlier that *The Galaxy* had carried a review of all of B's poetry through to *Red Cotton Night-Cap Country.* Junius Browne's judgment was that B must have possessed an "indifference to popularity" which has "rendered entire clearness of secondary consideration," and he imagined an additional price that B would have to pay for his sins: "In the new Purgatorio, they who could have written clearly, and have not, will be condemned to read the books of all who have so erred. The worshippers of Robert Browning must needs pray long and fervently for the deliverance of his unintelligible soul" (771, 774).

While it was in the context of years of such criticism that B wrote "Of Pacchiarotto and How He Worked in Distemper," an answer to all of those—in his view—ignorant and dishonest critics, his poem is also directed specifically towards one critic: Alfred Austin (1835-1913), who was also the poet who eventually succeeded Tennyson to the laureate-ship, a prize many attributed to his flattering of Lord Salisbury. He had begun a career as a lawyer, but in 1858 he turned his attention to litera-ture. Austin's first two publications, *The Season, a Satire* (1861) and *My Satire and Its Censors* (1861), were modeled upon Lord Byron's *English Bards and Scotch Reviewers* (1809). For many years a chief contributor to *The Evening Standard* of London, Austin wrote many anonymous and scathing reviews of B's poetry.

In May of 1869 Austin commenced his critical career with a searing assault in *Temple Bar* on Tennyson. Protesting against the prevailing opinion that Tennyson was near the top of the first rank of poets, Austin argued that he was nothing more than a garden and lawn poet, not one who could soar to great heights like an eagle; Tennyson's limitations relegated him to the lower portion of the scale of third-rate poets. This attack proved such a sensation that the editor of *Temple Bar* enlisted Austin to produce a series of essays on contemporary literary figures, and in the next year this series was published as a book under the title *The Poetry of the Period.*

The second poet to be placed on the rack by Austin was B. Austin began by exposing the folly of a movement to displace Tennyson and name B the foremost poet of the age. There is even less reason to place B among the first rank of poets, for "that Mr. Browning is our great mod-ern seer" is "the most astounding and ludicrous pretension ever put for-ward in literature . . ." (42). It was to prove this assertion that Austin devoted the next 34 pages of *The Poetry of the Period.*

In certain respects Austin transcends all the cavilers whose opinions I have recounted. Like them, he objected to B's obscurity of expression, but he attributed that obscurity to B's obscurity of thought. *Sordello* is not merely "rhapsodical rubbish" (see Browne above), which allows some merit, but "detestable gibberish"; it is not merely unintelligible but "shockingly unintelligible" (53). B is not just a poet with faults, as most detractors averred; his poetry was a "ludicrous mistake" (56). B is a man "interested in mental peculiarities" (43), "a mere analyst, . . . potter-ing about among the brains and entrails of the souls he has dissected . . . utterly unable to do anything with them . . ." (56-57). Such observa-tions lead to the point that B not only failed at being a poet of the first rank but also failed at being a poet of the third rank. That is because, argued Austin, he was in fact not a poet at all: "He is not a poet, and yet he would fain write poetry"; therefore, "[w]e have no right to be surprised if he is inarticulate . . ." (64). B wrote prose and then disguised it as poetry, resulting in "very bad prose" (62).

In his closing paragraphs, Austin returned to Tennyson to make a telling comparison, assuring his admirers that

> They need be in no fear lest Mr. Tennyson should be displaced by any critic in his sound senses to make way for Mr. Browning. When men desire to behold the flight of an eagle, and cannot get it, they do not usually regard the tramp of an elephant as a substitute.
>
> (75)

After asking the public to treat B's works as though they were nonexistent, Austin closed his essay with the following volley:

> It is bad enough that there should be people, pretending to authority among us, who call a man a great poet when, though unquestionably a poet, he has no marks of greatness about him [Tennyson]. But that is a venial error, and a trifling misfortune, compared to what would be the misery of living in an age which gibbeted itself beforehand for the pity of posterity, by deliberately calling a man a poet who—however remarkable his mental attributes and powers—is not specifically a poet at all. I hope we shall be spared this humiliation.
>
> (76)

B owned a copy of volume 26 of *Temple Bar,* in which Austin's essay first appeared, and B inscribed on the cover these words: "Austin's *Opinion.*"

These articles when first published in *Temple Bar* prompted much discussion in the press. *The Guardian* seemed to feel that B had been mistreated: "poor Mr. Browning is handled even more severely than the Poet-Laureate was in May. The author is a writer of some considerable poetic taste, but he allows his desire to say fierce things to override his soberer judgment . . ." ("The Magazines," *The Guardian* [Supplement] 23 June 1869, 713). B was defended more forcefully by others (see *The Spectator,* 42 [5 June 1869], 685, for example).

William Lyon Phelps believes that Austin's essay in *Temple Bar* and its subsequent re-publication in *The Poetry of the Period* prompted B to write "Of Pacchiarotto." What Austin said about him was harsher than any of B's other detractors, and B was upset by all of the attention Austin's book was attracting ("Robert Browning and Alfred Austin," *The Yale Review,* 7 [1918], 585-86).

Even so, there was more to cause B's reaction. B's friend Alfred Domett, having expressed regret over the nature of "Of Pacchiarotto," received the following explanation for the treatment of Austin in the poem: "He has been flea-biting me for many years past in whatever rag of a newspaper he could hop into. . . ." Then B included the following additional explanation for his treatment of the critics in general: "I don't mind leaving on record that I had just that fancy about the people who, 'forty years long in the wilderness' criticized my works" (Quoted in Griffin and Minchin, 260). And to Edmund Gosse, B explained,

> I had in my mind [Austin's] anonymous writings in the 'Standard' and other papers. The first of these which fixed my attention was a criticism on 'Balaustion'—wherein, undertaking to give 'specimens of Mr B's inability to write a line' (or some such phrase) the critic produced several isolated lines—seven, I remember—five of which he had altered by omission or addition: in the first were two omissions and one addition of a syllable: the remaining lines untampered with contained each a break in rhythm which the context would have justified.
>
> (Letter of 19 August 1876, Hood, *Ltrs.*, 175)

Although B was not altogether accurate in his account of Austin's handling of his lines, neither does he exaggerate. Austin had actually quoted correctly the first line, but his inaccuracy elsewhere—whether owing to carelessness or purpose—is deplorable: "Follow me!' And I wrought so with my prayer" was misquoted as "Follow me! and so I wrought with prayer." And "Since ourselves knew what happened but last year—" was transformed by Austin into "Since ourselves knew what happened last year." Austin then pronounced all the random lines, which he had misquoted and quoted out of context, not "verses of any kind" (*The Evening Standard*, 17 August 1871, 5).

Although Austin denied that he wrote the reviews to which B alluded (see *The Examiner*, 10 June 1876, 653-54, rpt. in Hood, *Ltrs.*, 359-60), B, nonetheless, remained sure that he had, and this belief provided extra fuel for his denunciation of Austin in "Of Pacchiarotto." The following passage conveys the tenor and tone of all of Austin's reviews of B's poetry in *The Evening Standard:*

> It is humiliating to think . . . that any generation, no matter how sunk in affectation and love of the grotesque, should endure the metrical tumbling which Mr. Browning would fain pass off for poetry. It would of course be a satire upon the nation at large to say that it does so; for Mr. Browning's notoriety depends exclusively, to use the language of Wordsworth, upon "the clamour of that small though loud portion of the community, ever governed by factitious influence, which, under the name of the Public, passes itself upon the unthinking for the People." Such notoriety, however, is a very transitory affair, and that must be meanwhile the comfort of all who are jealous of the honour of English literature.
>
> (6 January 1872, 1)

However one feels about the appropriateness of B's counterattack in "Of Pacchiarotto," no one can deny that Austin gave B plenty of cause. Phelps believes that B "had some fresh Austinian abuse in May, 1876, when he was correcting the proofs of his new work . . ." (585), but I am aware of no evidence to support this supposition.

It remains to suggest what the story of Pacchiarotto (1474-1540), the Sienese painter, has to do with Austin. First, the sources for the story of Pacchiarotto, of which there are several:

There are brief accounts of Giacomo di Bartolommeo Pacchiarotto in Filippo Baldinucci, *Del Notizie De' Professori del Disegno del Cimabue in Qua* (Firenze, 1767-74), 4. 236, which contains a half-page account of the painter's hiding out in the sepulchre in the Oratory of San Bernardino, and in *Biographie Universelle, Ancienne et Moderne* (Paris, 1822), a source for many of B's other poems (Irvine and Honan, 7). B's main source was Vasari's *Le Vite de' Piu Eccelenti Pittori, Scultori e Architetti* (Firenze, 1855), 11. 172-84, a book with which B had been familiar throughout his life in many editions (Kelley and Coley, 200).

B left out details of the painter's life that do not fit with his conception of an intolerant moralist, and he adds details that fill out his character as such a one. B made use of Vasari's account of the social and philosophical turmoil in Siena where Pacchiarotto operated, and he accepted Vasari's view that Pacchiarotto's downfall was owing to his ambition and vanity. Also from this source B got the idea of the painter's advancing from the fanciful reforming of persons on his painted wall to the effort at reforming real people in the political sphere. Vasari does not include an account of Pacchiarotto's speech before the Bardotti and the frenzied objection to it, and there is nothing in this source about his putting himself forward as the leader who could save his society. Vasari, rather, gives other reasons for Pacchiarotto's need to hide out in the tomb, and there is nothing about what happened to him in the convent of monks and his subsequent awakening to the foolishness of trying to reform mankind.

Although B mainly relied upon Vasari, he surely got some details for his poem from Pietro Fortini's novella about Pacchiarotto. The manuscript for this story is in the Library of Siena, and B might have seen this MS on one of his several visits to Siena from 1850 to 1859 (Mairi Calcraft, "Browning and the Good Life: A New Reading of 'Pacchiarotto'," *BSN*, 18 [1988-89], 4; DeVane and Knickerbocker, 120-21). Or he might have encountered the pamphlet entitled *Giacomo Pacchiarotto pittore, e la Compagnia dei Bardotti* (Bologna, 1858), which was printed from a Sienese newspaper, *l'Eccitamento* (Carlo Fabio Borgi, Introduction to *Tre Novelle Inedite di Pietro Fortini* [Bologna 1877]). B must have read Fortini's story in some form, because he clearly used details from it in "Of Pacchiarotto." For example, the confusion of Pacchiarotto and Pacchia to which B alludes in 1.5 is constantly made in Fortini. More significant, however, is the similarity between B's and Fortini's beginnings. The opening of the novella describes Pacchiarotto in a room that he has covered with painted figures. The description of his gestures and thoughts resemble B's poem more than Vasari does. In Fortini, Pacchiarotto thinks of being an actual leader in Siena, which is more in accord with B's depiction of the politically ambitious painter; further, he goes immediately from his painted figures to try to reform real men as he does in B's poem (Vasari makes no connection between the imaginary and the real reforming). And Fortini implies that Pacchiarotto is changed by his prolonged intimacy with the corpse, a notion absent in Vasari's account, but the important lesson learned in B's poem. Finally, Fortini tells how Pacchiarotto goes to the Observancy to be fed and to tell his story, after which he is lectured to by the Abbot—all details not in Vasari but in the poem.

B uses the story of the reforming painter Pacchiarotto as a parallel to the reforming poet Alfred Austin. As Pacchiarotto used his pencil ("paint-brush" [*OED*, sense 1a]) to create the figures of men to preach to, so did Austin use his pencil ("word-painting or descriptive skill" [*OED*, sense 1b]) to create in his poems representatives of society that he could moralize to. As Pacchiarotto "took 'Reform' for his motto," so does Austin in *The Golden Age* (1871) assert that "the author humbly aspires to be [a reformer] himself" (78); and like Pacchiarotto Austin was an intolerant reformer whose moral vision saw only black and white. B expands the scope of Pacchiarotto's reforming beyond what Vasari reports, including "King, Clown, Pope, Emperor," "an assemblage of Ladies," poets, and painters, in order to establish more fully a parallel between the Sienese painter and his Victorian re-embodiment. In *The Season: A Satire* (1861; rev. 1869), Austin attempts to reform those who participate in London's "season": in his "Preface to the Second Edition," Austin avows that his "charitable mission" is to "frighten some people into an honest recognition of what they are doing . . ." (xxi), and in the poem itself he allows that he is "A most uncompromising moralist" (15). As Pacchiarotto preaches on the "vanities" of "the Fair Sex" (155, 153), he parallels Austin's satiric lessons to the fashionable female personages of his poem:

> The world, to kindly compensation prone,
> Gives you its honour when you lose your own.
>
> (59)

As Pacchiarotto is "the censor of [his] age" (173), so is Austin the general critic of the moral hypocrisy of his day:

> Craving a respite from pursuit of pelf,
> Our age in shows seeks shelter from itself.
>
> (45)

There seems little doubt that B had Austin's *The Season* in mind when he created the earnest reformer Pacchiarotto.

Austin's other poems contributed something to the conception of Pacchiarotto as well. Austin's "vitriolic diatribe" against "the dungfly critics" (47) that plagued him, which he called *My Satire and Its Censors* (1861), was the model for B's poetical attack on his critics. Austin had mainly attacked William Hepworth Dixon, editor of *The Athenæum* from 1853 to 1869, who was responsible for much of the adverse criticism of Austin, but also others, including Wentworth Dilke, a contributor, and Henry Fothergill Chorley, a staff member. Similarly, B mainly focuses on Austin, and yet he broadens his intent as well. Austin, however, is much more relentless and personal in attacking his chief detractor than B is in taking on his. Austin directly addresses Dixon as follows:

> Boldly you tread, illiterate and rude,
> Where scholars scarcely venture to intrude:
> Unskilled in science, language, art, you maul
> The Life of Him, supremely skilled in all. . . .
> Doff these false feathers, you transparent fool!
> Back to your scissors, lexicon, and stool.
>
> (26, 27)

B must have felt that such invective provided warrant for him to take aim at Austin, and he might as well have felt a degree of obligation to strike back on behalf of the editor of the journal that had over the years been friendlier than most towards his poems. And so it is no accident that in "Of Pacchiarotto" B takes up the outlandish couplet and the occasional even more outlandish triplet that was employed by Austin in *My Satire* (on p. 9, for example, Austin rhymes *ulcerate, state,* and *prate*) and exaggerates that style, shortening the line and employing the triplet much more frequently.

There are yet other ways in which B found "inspiration" in Austin's poetry and even his life. Pacchiarotto gives up the vain hope of reforming society by lecturing to the representatives of society that he has created for his frescoes and enters practical politics only to fail miserably. Likewise, at the end of *The Season,* Austin laments:

> Who think by verse to better make the bad,
> I grant it freely, must be vain or mad.
> From Horace downward, monitory rhymes
> Have but amused, and mended not the times.
>
> (71)

Therefore, four years later, with great confidence in his oratorical powers, he made a brief sortie into the political sphere, standing for Parliament as a Tory candidate from Taunton. Like Pacchiarotto, he asked the people to make him their leader, and they rejected him resoundingly (apparently he failed even to hold the votes purchased with bribes [see 1.272-73n and Crowell, 11). Furthermore, the view touted in *The Golden Age* (1871) that an unequal distribution of wealth accounts for the chief ills of society accords with the speech that Pacchiarotto makes to the Bardotti.

B's frequent references to Byron in "Of Pacchiarotto" are owing, in large measure, to Austin's connection to Byron. Austin's imitation of Byron in *My Satire,* his holding up in *The Poetry of the Period* of Byron as the ideal that contemporary poets cannot approach, his reviews in *The Evening Standard* that put B's "crabbed and crooked inharmoniousness" next to Byron's "delicious stanzas" (6 January 1872, 1), and his devoted advocacy on Byron's behalf in *A Vindication of Lord Byron* (London: Chapman and Hall, 1869)—all this surely influenced B to refer to Austin in his poem as a "Banjo Byron" and to mock Byron's poetry at every opportunity as yet another means to strike at Austin.

One final note on a likely influence on B's style in "Of Pacchiorotto": DeVane (*Hbk.,* 398) and Irvine and Honan (481) have remarked on the similarity in style between B's poem and Butler's *Hudibras.* In this connection, it is interesting that B has used a number of words illustrated in Johnson's *Dictionary* with quotations from Butler's poem; among them are *confutation, doublet, caitiff, besotted,* and *noddle.* It would appear that B's conscious imitation of *Hudibras* was in response to the following criticism in *The Laughter of the Muses: A Satire on the Reigning Poetry of 1869* (Glasgow, 1869):

> His rhyming he hath learned from HUDIBRAS,
> Where such rhymes answer well; but what we pass

> In BUTLER, has in BROWNING not a grace,
> For when he jokes, he turns awry his face.
>
> (19)

See 1.528n.

Title] The Italian name *Pacchiarotto* means literally "fond" (-rotto) of wine, good food, and company (Pacchia); it is also the appellation of a "silly young fellow." The word *Distemper* is a pun meaning "A method of painting, in which the colors are mixed with some glutinous substance soluble in water, as yolk of egg mixed with water, etc., executed usually upon a ground of chalk or plaster mixed with gum (*distemper-ground*): mostly used in scene-painting, and in the internal decoration of walls." The word is chiefly encountered in such phrases as "to paint in distemper." In its second sense, the term refers to "ill humour, ill temper," and in this second sense it applies both to Giacomo Pacchiarotto and to Alfred Austin (see *OED* and Calcraft, 6).

2] *crotchet* A peculiar notion (*OED*, sense 9a).

5] *Fungaio* Bernardino Fungai (1460-1516), a native of Siena, was the teacher of Pacchiarotto. Though his paintings seem dry and stiff in manner, he was during Pacchiarotto's tutelage considered the best artist in Siena. Among his most important works in Siena are *Coronation of the Virgin, The Virgin and Child with Saints, The Annunciation, Christ Between St. Francis and St. Jerome,* and *Madonna,* the latter with the assistance of Pacchiarotto who also assisted with *The Nativity of Christ,* which is in Chiusi.

7] *Pacchia* Girolamo Pacchia (1477-1535) was a contemporary of Pacchiarotto who was, to the detriment of his reputation, often confused with Pacchiarotto. B probably saw the two confused in Pietro Fortini's novella about Pacchiarotto, which he might have read in the library of Siena during one of his visits to that city in 1856, 1857, or 1859. Or he might have seen one of the published versions, for example, *Giacomo Pacchiarotto pittore, e le Compagnia dei Bardotti, Novella storica di Pietro Fortini* (Bologna, 1858), a pamphlet of 26 pp. printed from a Sienese newspaper, *l'Eccitamento.* B would have been reminded of Fortini's novella by a footnote on p. 181 of Vasari's *Le Vite.*

12] *Kirkup* B addresses Baron Seymour Stocker Kirkup (1788-1880) as a fellow connoisseur of Italian art. Kirkup was an artist, antiquarian, and authority on Italian art, who uncovered some important lost paintings. He lived in Florence and was a friend of the Brownings.

San Bernardino One of the numerous oratories in Siena, the Franciscan Oratory of San Bernardino was erected in 1423 by San Bernardino beyond the Porta Ovile, one of the gates to the city; the oratory was rebuilt according to the designs of Giacomo Cozzarelli in 1485. It was decorated by Pacchia (see 1.5n), Bazzi (see 1.17n), Beccafumi (see 1.17n), and Pacchiarotto, who contributed *The Annunciation* and *The Nativity of the Virgin* (*Murray's Hand-book for Travellers in Central Italy* [London, 1875], 343).

14] *Siena* Fifty-nine miles south of Florence, this "ancient city occupies the irregular summit of a hill of tertiary sandstone, rising on the borders of the dreary and barren track which forms the S. province of Tuscany" (*Murray's Handbook,* 331). Significant in the development of Renaissance painting, the Sienese school was in decline during the 15th century. The 16th century saw a revival led by Antonio de' Bazzi and Domenico Beccafumi (see 11.17-19n). Once a rival to Florence, with 200,000 inhabitants, the city had declined in population to about 22,000 by B's day. The story that B narrates takes place in 1533, the year of a serious famine, and at this time Siena was ruled by the Spanish. This political arrangement was the result of the city's inviting Charles V's protection from the Florentine pope, Clement VII. The Spanish garrison sent to defend Siena soon took over and ruled on its own. With the help of the French, the Sienese—after much turmoil and insurrection, in which Pacchiarotto participated—eventually threw off the Spanish rulers in 1552.

17-19] *Bazzi . . . Razzi* Giovanni Antonio de' Bazzi, called Sodoma (?1477-1549), was from Lombard but became a resident of Siena in 1501 and worked there for the rest of his life. For The Oratory of San Bernardino (see 1.12n), he painted *The Visitation, The Presentation in the Temple, The Assumption,* and *The St. Louis.* A minor artist, he is known especially for the erotic *Marriage of Alexander and Roxana* (c. 1517), a bedroom fresco in Villa Farnesina, Rome; in B's day he was known especially for *Christ at the Column,* "one of the finest frescoes in Italy," which is in the Church of San Francesco (*Murray's Handbook for Travellers in Central Italy* [London, 1843], 186). He also painted *St. Catherine Receiving the Stigmata* for the House of St. Catherine of Siena. Bazzi was indeed miscalled Razzi for many years, for example, by Vasari and by *Murray's Hand-book for Travellers in Northern Italy* (London, 1847), and even by B himself in a letter to William Allingham: "How you would like Siena! I have seen this morning half a dozen of the finest things in their way by men whose names are all but unknown in England. Razzi's 'Christ at the Column' and his

'Eve.' . . . Razzi's women—faces more lovely than Raphael's" (Letter of 9 October 1859, in *Letters to William Allingham*, eds. Helen Allingham and E. Baumer Williams [London: Longman, 1911], 105).

Beccafumi   Domenico Beccafumi (1485-1551) was one of the finest Sienese painters. He is most well known for his *Stigmatization of St. Catherine* (c. 1518) and *Fall of the Rebel Angels*, an altarpiece meant for the Church of the Carmine, Siena. He also painted *Sposalizio* for the Oratory of San Bernardino. B had praise for Beccafumi, especially for his *St. Catherine* and *Michael*, in his letter to Allingham (see note for Bazzi above).

20-44]   B means to establish a parallel between the reforming Pacchiarotto and the reforming Alfred Austin. These lines also suggest Austin's moral vanity, illustrated in *The Season: A Satire* where he boasts, ". . . I am, I must insist, / A most uncompromising moralist . . ." (London: Robert Hardwick, 1861), 15, and in *My Satire* where he puts himself forward as a "literary athlete" willing to devote "all [his] life to giv[ing] a tongue to Truth" (13, 14). In *The Golden Age*, Austin once again pictures the foibles and evils of mankind, and his technique, in part, is to depict imaginary individuals that he seeks to reform—which is what Pacchiarotto goes on to do.

sopra-sotto   Upside down.

Giotto   Giotto di Bondone (c. 1266-1337), a Florentine painter of enormous significance, equal in fame to his friend Dante Alighieri. Vasari's *Le Vite* begins with Giotto.

60]   *pearls to the swine*   Cf. Matthew 7:6.

63]   *mazzard*   The head (jocular archaic); *OED* cites this line.

66]   *Stalloreggi*   The quarter of Siena in which Pacchiarotto lived, south of the Campo, the historic center of the city.

71]   quiesco   I rest.

74]   *Noble in cap and feather*   This phrase, taken with the "Beggar barefoot" of the previous line, plays upon the expression "from head to foot."

75]   *sorts and conditions*   From the "Prayer for All Conditions of Men," *The Book of Common Prayer*.

77]   *hail fellow well met*   One on familiar terms. Cf. Swift's "My Lady's Lamentation" "Hail fellow, well met, / All dirty and wet; / Find out, if you can, / Whose master, whose man . . ." (11.165-68).

78]   *Priest armed . . . book and candle*   The priest is pictured with the equipment for the ceremony of excommunication, at the end of which a bell is rung, a book is closed, and a candle is extinguished. Cf. Shakespeare, *King John*, 3.3.112.

80] *distemperer* "One who paints in distemper" (This line is the only one cited in *OED*).

83] *pinched* Straightened in means.

85] *Which work done . . . rested him* Cf. Genesis 2:2.

87] frescanti Painters of frescoes.

93] *Taught its duty . . . station* See 11.20-44n.

94-95] *The Pope . . . warrant* In like manner Austin had been critical of the papacy. He had covered the Ecumenical Congress in 1870 for *The Evening Standard* and, though he was a Roman Catholic, objected strongly to an underhanded and successful effort to have the pope declared infallible: The consequence of the Church's decision will be that "for the future neither scholar nor theologian, neither statesman nor man of science, can be bred and retained in the Roman communion. . . . Henceforth no Roman Catholic can take part in the practical administration of government; no Roman Catholic scholar can write history with truth and honesty; no Roman Catholic student can cultivate physical or moral science without bringing himself almost immediately in collision with the teachings and under the anathema of the Papacy. . . . There will be, therefore, an irreconcilable quarrel and a permanent divorce between the Roman faith and the practical work of life . . ." ("The Vatican Council," *The Evening Standard*, 10 January 1870, 1).

96-102] *The Emperor . . . fooling* Probably these lines refer to Napoleon III, whom both B and Austin had written about. B's dramatic method in *Prince Hohenstiel-Schwangau* (1871) allows the Emperor to say "what I imagine the man might, if he pleased, say for himself" (Letter of 19 January 1872 to Isa Blagden, *Dearest Isa*, 372). By Austin, on the other hand, Napoleon is judged harshly as being subject to "the lust of glitter" and "Splendour's follies," and those who followed him are "shallow" and "base" (*The Golden Age*, 92).

98] *"Shear sheep but nowise flay them!"* Napoleon is imagined to be ignorant of another emperor's maxim, that of Tiberius Caesar, the second Roman emperor, who reigned from 37-14 B.C.; he "answered some governors who had written to recommend an increase in the burden of provincial taxation, with: 'A good shepherd shears his flock; he does not flay them'" (Suetonious, *The Twelve Caesars*, trans. Robert Graves).

103] *Pooh-pooed* An expression originating in the Victorian period meaning made "light of, dismiss[ed] as unworthy of notice" (*OED*); see "At the Mermaid," 1.128n and "Filippo Baldinucci on the Privilege of Burial," 1.458n.

104] *Poets . . . lewd ditties* B might be ironically alluding to

Austin himself, who in *The Season* writes of ". . . propped-up bosoms bare / To catch some boyish buyer unaware . . ." (16), which couplet he omitted from the poem's second edition owing to its indecency (Crowell, 46). Other lines that might well have been considered lewd by the Victorians remained, for example: "Now love-struck boys transfer their fickle eyes / From Mary's trinkets to Morlacchi's thighs . . ." (41). On the other hand, *The Season* preaches against the immorality of *La Traviata* (see 33-37); still, B is more likely to have in mind Austin's suggestion that there is coarseness in Mrs. Browning's *Aurora Leigh* (see *The Season*, 4-5).

105] *Painters . . . nudities* B's son Robert Wiedeman Barrett Browning was one of those painters who "pester[ed] with nudities!" However, B not only approved of his son's paintings of nudes and endeavored to get them accepted in London galleries but he vehemently expressed his outrage at those who objected to Pen's nudes. See "With Francis Furini" (11.144-73), in *Parleyings with Certain People of Importance in Their Day* (1887) and DeVane, *Browning's Parleyings* (New Haven: Yale Univ. Press, 1927), 179-84.

106] *rater* "One who reproves or scolds" (*OED*).

117-22] *As you see . . . opponent to mincemeat* When Pacchiarotto is "baulked by a mere spectator" (1.107), he is moved to counterattack his assailant in these lines, which are an obvious allusion to *My Satire*, in which Austin counterattacks Hepworth Dixon, the critic credited with an unhappy review of *The Season* (see Crowell, 112-13).

123-35] *So, off from his head . . . defence of the injured* A clear reference to Austin, who after satirizing the aristocracy in *The Season*, later became a Tory and a defender of the aristocracy. This passage also alludes, perhaps, to Austin's vociferous denunciation of all of the poets of his day and then his later suppression of those opinions (see Crowell, 114, and 11.165-83n below).

127] *hop, skip and jump* An allusion to Austin's small stature; see 11.170, 469n, and 529n.

132] *out-roared Boanerges* Boanerges is the name Christ gave to the sons of Zebedee, meaning "sons of thunder" (Mark 3:17). The term is proverbial for a "loud, vociferous preacher or orator" (*OED*). Cf. Austin, *The Golden Age*: "Boänerges bawl" (85).

133] *minikin-* Dainty, affected, mincing (used contemptuously).

134] *gingered* Full of mettle and spirit, a sense first employed by Disraeli in 1849 (*OED*). *Gingered* is thus used contradistinctively with *gentled* to provide a sense of the range of Pacchiarotto's tone.

136] *O call him . . . Pontiff* See 11.94-95n.

137-39] *Be hard on this Kaiser . . . attend elevation* As a correspon-

dent for *The Evening Standard,* Austin was permitted by the King of
Prussia and Bismarck to frequent their headquarters. He was a German
sympathizer in the war against France and even rode with the victo-
rious German army as it entered Paris. There can be little doubt, then,
that B had Austin in mind when he wrote this passage.

154-56] *How much . . . falsehood* In *The Season* Austin catalogues
what he sees as the female vanities, moralizing as he does so:

> The softest ribbon, pink-lined parasol,
> Screen not the woman, though they deck the doll.
> The padded corsage and the well-matched hair,
> Judicious jupon spreading out the spare,
> Sleeves well designed false plumpness to impart,
> Leave vacant still the hollows of the heart.
> Is not our Lesbia lovely? In her soul
> Lesbia is troubled: Lesbia hath a mole;
> And all the splendour of that matchless neck
> Consoles not Lesbia for its single speck.
> Kate comes from Paris, and a wardrobe brings,
> To which poor Edith's are "such common things."
> Her pet lace shawl has grown not fit to wear,
> And ruined Edith dresses in despair.
>
> (22)

And then he puts these faults in the context of men's shortcomings:

> . . . by severe induction may we guess,
> If yours are great, our faults will scarce be less.
>
> . . .
>
> So are our manly virtues, be assured,
> But female vices only more matured.
>
> (24)

156] *poll's-hood* A covering for the head worn by women.
158] *. . . trumpets* B's ellipsis encourages the reader to supply the
"s" to make "trumpets" into "strumpets." Alternatively, the reader
might hear the sound of a woman's blowing her own trumpet, that is,
sounding her own praises.
159] *How kind . . . dumb pets* The kindness to "dumb pets" that
Pacchiarotto seems to praise leaves undefended the general charge of
unkindness on the part of women.

160] *Of their charms . . . venal* The very idea that a charm can be venal is startling, even if only a few of them are.

161] *Juvenal* The great Latin poet (c. A.D. 60-c.130) was the author of *Satires*, Satire IV being a denunciation of every manner of female vice and vanity—preoccupation with beauty, licentiousness, and pretentiousness, to name but a few.

162-63] Quæ nemo . . . illoto Which no one would have said in totality, unless (by Pollux) with a filthy mouth. Pollux is the twin brother of Castor; known together as the Dioscuri, they were especially honored and worshipped in Rome.

164] Apage Go away.

165-83] *Then, cocking . . . lay converted* These lines make further reference to Austin's transformation from one who attacked the privileged to one who stood by and with the privileged. See 11.123-35n.

165] *a-gee* Awry, to one side.

166] *doublet* "The waistcoat: so called from being double for warmth" (Johnson's *Dictionary*).

168] *gestion* Conduct (*OED* cites this line).

170] *Hop, skip, jump* See 1.127n.

190] non verbis sed factis Not by words but by deeds. Cf. Shakespeare, *King Henry VIII:* "'Tis well said again, / And 'tis a kind of good deed to say well, / And yet words are no deeds" (3.2.152-54).

198] *Siena* See 1.14n.

199] *fetch grain out of Sicily* Most of the land area of this largest of the Mediterranean islands was used for agriculture, and wheat was Sicily's main crop.

200] *bakehouse* A house or apartment for baking bread (*OED*).

204] *recency* "quality of being recent" (common in 19th century [*OED*]).

207] *fescue* Teacher's pointer.

213] *hornbook* "A treatise on the rudiments of a subject; a primer" (*OED*).

217] *Siena, both province and borough* The city of Siena is the capitol of the province of Siena.

223] *"Freed Ones"—"Bardotti"* Pacchiarotto was "a conspicuous member" of the Bardotti, "a society of uncommissioned reformers, whose occupation was to cry down abuses, and prescribe wholesale theoretical measures for removing them." (Hence their title; which signifies 'spare' horses or 'freed' ones: they walk by the side of the wagon while others drudge at, and drag it along). The only actual policy of the historical organization was to fly in the face of respectability; it was broken up by the government in 1535 (Orr, *Hbk.,* 279).

224] *"Spare-Horses"* See 1.223n.
227] *paid scot and lot* Paid out thoroughly (*OED*).
229] *Bailiwick* "The office or jurisdiction of a ballie or a bailiff" (*OED*).
233-34] *These Spare-Horses . . . citizens trembled* See 1.223n.
235-36] *Square by / The Duomo* The Cathedral (the Duomo), as well as the Palazzo Pubblico, the seat of civil government, stands along one side of the Piazza del Campo.
251] *Bailiwick* See 1.229n.
252] *paly* Pale (poetic *[OED]*).
253-54] *If wealth . . . superfluous* In several places in his poetry, Austin argues that wealth should be *inter*fluous, which means *interfluent:* "Flowing into each other, intermingling; in which there is an interflow" (*OED*, sense 2. Earliest citation in *OED* is 1872; it also cites this line). In *The Season*, for example, Austin presents the immorality of the unequal distribution of wealth:

> What is the spell that 'twixt a saint and sinner
> The diff'rence makes? a sermon? bah! a dinner.
> The odds and ends our silken Claras waste,
> Would keep our calico Clarissas chaste.
> Celia! the lace from off your parasol
> Had held Celinda's sunburnt virtue whole:
> A hundred pounds would coy have made the nude,
> A thousand pounds the prostitute a prude,
> A little more expenditure of pelf
> Fanny a bigot bitter as yourself!
>   Hence! flimsy sophists! who with fasts and cries
> Would fain compel Omniscience to be wise!
> What if, instead of craving sun or rain,
> You built a reservoir or delved a drain?
> Instead of looks and platitudes demure,
> Diffused the wealth that keeps peers' daughters pure?
>   (37-38)

Austin's proposal is here typical of Tory socialism in general: "odds and ends" are sufficient to fill in the material lacunae of the poor. But in *The Golden Age* Austin presents a stark contrast between wealth and poverty that represents a more serious attitude:

> Secure in glaring opulence, [the wealthy of London] scan
> With placid eyes the miseries of man;

Fat units, watch the leanness of the whole,
And gag remonstrance with a paltry dole:
Mid harrowing want, with conscience unafraid,
Die on the golden dirt-heaps they have made.
Here Plenty gorges gifts from every zone,
There thankful Hunger gnaws its meagre bone;
Profusion here melts more than pearls in wine,
There craves gaunt Penury some shucks from swine;
And whilst rich rogues quaff deep round roaring fires,
At Dives' portal Lazarus expires!

(68-69)

258] kai ta loipa The Greek equivalent of *et cetera*.

259] kappas, taus, lambdas The initial letters of *kai ta loipa* (see 1.258n).

265] Amalfi The Duke of Amalfi.

266] clotpoll A blockhead, dolt (*OED* cites this line).

272-73] *If this done . . . right place* Pacchiarotto's proposal that the Bardotti establish him as the practical-minded chief magistrate capable of leading the city out of its difficulties parallels Austin's political aspirations. After offering himself as a parliamentary candidate to the Conservative party, he was sent by Disraeli to Tiverton to stand for election; he retired after another Conservative asserted prior claim. Then on his way back to London he heard from the only other occupant of his railway compartment that Taunton needed a candidate, and so Austin put himself forward there. In spite of paying £480 in bribes, he finished last among the four candidates (Alfred Austin, *Autobiography* [London, 1911], 1.183-88; Crowell 11).

276] *Spare-Horse* See 1.223n.

277] *pother* Commotion.

278] *fleering* Sneering.

280] *caitiff* A villain.

284] *discomfiture* "Defeat . . . or frustration of plans or hopes; utter disappointment" (*OED*, sense 2a).

289] *tristful* Sorrowful. Only citation in *OED* after 18th century is to B's use of this term in *Dramatic Idylls*, Series II (1880).

293] *tow* Flax with which the fire is rekindled.

295] *Horace . . . per ignes incedis* In the original: *incedis per ignes*, which means "you are walking through the fires"; from Horace, *The Odes*, 2.1.7.

298] *purlieu*   A "mean, squalid, or disreputable street or quarter" (*OED*, sense 4).

308] *situate*   A participial adjective, meaning "situated."

309] *St. John's Observance Observance*   is a rare term for monastery (*OED* cites this line, the only instance after 1486).

316] *conterminous*   Coexistensive (*OED*, sense 3b; in this sense first used during the Victorian period).

319] *retail*   Recount.

329] 'haud in posse sed esse mens'   Mind as it is, not as it might be.

330] *As it was . . . shall be for ever*   Cf. *Gloria Patri, The Book of Common Prayer:* "Glory to the Father, and to the Son: and to the Holy Ghost; / As it was in the beginning, is now, and ever shall be: world without end."

336] *maundered*   B must mean the obsolete sense "grumbled" (*OED*, sense 1), especially since he uses it with *rambled*, the common Victorian meaning for *maundered* (see sense 3).

344] *Observancy*   "A house of the Observant order" (*OED* cites only this instance). The Observants are the stricter Franciscans.

348] *Superior*   Head of the monastery.

351] *rincing*   *Rince* is an obsolete or dialectic spelling of *rinse*.

353] *pestiferous*   Noxious.

358-95] *Ah, Youth . . . man's mute*   In the Abbot's speech, which is a serious expression of B's own views, the rhymes are much less outrageous than they are in the rest of the poem.

368] *leaven*   "To permeate with a transforming influence" (*OED*, sense 2).

375-76] *A spare-Horse . . . mill-horse*   The horse metaphor gives clarity and force to the Abbot's urgent advice to Pacchiarotto that he should abandon the Bardotti (the Spare-Horses) and become a shaft-horse, one that works, or even a mill-horse, one that, following a mill-track, has no freedom but nonetheless accomplishes useful work. Cf. *The Inn Album* 4.257n.

377] *mufflers*   Blindfolds (obsolete; *OED*, sense 1b).

379] *lugging*   Pulling.

382] *mill-post*   "The post on which a windmill was formerly often supported" (*OED*, sense 1).

387] *hopper*   "In a corn or other grinding mill, a receiver like an inverted pyramid or cone, through which grain . . . to be ground passes into the mill . . ." (*OED*, sense 3).

390] *daub-brush*   Brush for daubing, i.e., painting in an inartistic manner.

daub-pot   Pot for paint.

393]   *fray*   Irritate by rubbing (*OED*).

403]   *a non-sequence*   A non-sequitur.

421]   Piece   A play.

Induction   An old term for "introduction" and in Renaissance plays signifies particularly the prologue that provides the framework for a play.

431]   All's well that ends well   The corpse continues the "drama" imagery with this allusion to Shakespeare's title.

442]   besotted   "Intellectually or morally stupefied or blinded" (*OED*).

444]   imposthume   "A purulent swelling or cyst in any part of the body; an abscess" and figuratively "with reference to moral corruption, . . . the 'swelling' or pride, *etc.*" (*OED*).

447]   *mahlstick*   Variant of *maulstick,* a "light stick used by painters as a support for the right hand, and held in the left. The upper end is surmounted by a ball of cotton-wool covered with soft leather" (*OED*).

451-52]   saeculorum / In saecula   For ever and ever.

452]   *jorum*   "A large drinking-bowl" (*OED*).

455]   Benedicte   Blessing.

456-57]   *I have . . . harsh analytics*   B breaks in on the story of Pacchiarotto to point out to his critics that he has not engaged in "analytics," which is what Austin had accused him of only doing; in *The Poetry of the Period,* Austin writes: "He remains a mere analyst to the end of the chapter . . ." (56). B of course is being ironical, for he has done a thorough job of analyzing Pacchiarotto.

459]   *Who greeted . . . uprising*   This line has two meanings: first, it refers to the critical reception of B's poetry when he was first starting out as a poet; second, it refers to the critics now before him, who greeted him immediately upon his arising. B's habit was indeed to rise early (Orr, *Life,* 301).

460]   *I knew . . . disguising*   B refers to the critics who hid behind unsigned reviews of his poems.

462]   *This Monday . . . May-day*   In 1876, 1 May was indeed on a Monday. The London chimney sweeps, donning ribbons and flowers, traditionally participated in their own May-day festival. English May-day celebrations were originally consecrated to Robin Hood (and Maid Marian) because he is supposed to have died on 1 May. The day is spent in morris and May-pole dancing.

463]   *drabs, blues, and yellows*   *The Saturday Review,* 43 (12 August 1876), says that these colors represent the *Quarterly,* the *Edinburgh,* and other literary journals containing criticism of B. *Drab* is a particularly apt term because it refers to several shades of light brown, from light olive to grayish yellowish brown. *Drab* in the plural was Victorian usage for clothing of a drab color, and so this term strengthens the image of the incongruously dressed assemblage below the poet's window. *OED* cites Dickens's *Nicholas Nickleby* for "old gentlemen in drabs and gaiters."

465] *saltbox . . . bellows* "In burlesque music, the salt-box has been used like the marrow-bones and cleaver, tongs, and poker, etc." (*An American Dictionary of English Usage*, 1847).

469] *critics . . . chimbly* Since chimney sweeps were usually small children, this seems one of B's many allusions to Alfred Austin's diminutive stature. B had alluded to Austin's size n *Balaustion's Adventure* (1871):

> Even when I told the play and got the praise,
> There spoke up a brisk little somebody,
> Critic and whipper snapper, in a rage
> To set things right.
>
> (11.305-08)

Lord Byron had established the precedent of speaking of critics as diminutive, referring in "English Bards and Scotch Reviews" to the critic's pen as "That mighty instrument of little men!" (1.10). And it is traditional to be*little* objects of satire; for example, in Aristophanes' *The Clouds*, Socrates is "little Socrates," and he has a "little house" with a "little door." *Chimbly* is a dialectal variant of *chimney*.

470] *flue* B's poetic flue.

471] *Who spares . . . sir* Obviously the kitchen is where B cooks his poetry; the line appears to refer to the rapid production of poetry, which the critics had begun to complain about. For example, *The Saturday Review* opened its commentary upon *Fifine at the Fair* as follows: "Panting Time, as Dr. Johnson said of Shakespeare, and panting Space, as he threatened to say, toil after Mr. Browning in vain: Within twelve months he has published three poems of considerable length . . ." (34 [7 August 1872], 220). In its review of *Pacchiarotto* itself, this journal complained of B's "unparalleled and increasing rapidity of production" (42 [12 August 1876], 205).

472-73] *neighbours . . . smoke, sir* This appears to be an allusion to B's obscurity, which the critics thought B ought to eliminate. In particular, B is probably responding to the reviewer for *The Guardian* (Supplement), who complained of the poet's obscurity as follows: "Mr. Browning is apt to keep his own genuine poetical fervour in the state familiar to a gardener's bonfire. Just as it is beginning to produce clear flames, he throws a fresh mass of allusions on it; and it can do nothing better than smoke and smoulder" (Rev. of *Aristophanes' Apology*, 9 June 1875, 741). B also might have had in mind a passage from *The Laughter of the Muses:* "[B] would / Burn up the earth with language, if he could, / And be with rolling words, like smoke from chimney curled . . ." (30).

474-80] *Ah, rogues . . . the packet* B alludes to his critics' accusations of immorality and points out that they bring more filth to his poetry than they find in it. *The Guardian* (Supplement) judged *The Inn Album* to be "an advanced specimen of criminal literature," objecting especially to B's treatment of seduction and adultery (1 December 1875, 1537)—and *The British Quarterly Review* termed the poem "retrograde and perverted" (63 [January 1876], 236). And see B's letter of 2 December 1856 to Edward Chapman wherein he refers to the "blackguardism from the 'Press,'" saying that the reviewers are "all like those night-men who are always emptying their cart at my door" (DeVane and Knickerbocker, 97).

481] *dust my jacket* Beat me soundly (colloquial).

482] *Bang drum . . . blow fife* B throws back to his critics the very image employed against his poetry; cf. *The Laughter of the Muses:* "Still 'Bang, whang, whang,' resounds the poet's drum, / And 'Tootle-te-tootle' his fife . . ." (23), quoted from "Up at a Villa—Down in the City," 1.53.

484-85] *Don't trample . . . my snowdrop and crocus* Early on B thought of his poetry as the garden produced by his mind and trampled upon by the critics; to EBB he wrote on 11 February 1845: "I force myself to say ever and anon, in the interest of the market-gardeners regular, and Keats's proper,—'It's nothing to *you*,—critics & hucksters, all of you, if I *have* this garden and this conscience,—I might go die at Rome, or take gin and the newspaper, for what *you* would care'!" (RB-EBB, ed. Kintner, 1.19). EBB alluded to B's garden analogy in her response: "Yes—and it does delight me to hear of your 'garden full of roses and soul full of comforts'" (24).

490-93] *Whereby, tap-tap . . . contrapuntist* B's most telling defense of his own poetry is against the common charge that he has a "tough-gristled" ear (1.494) and thus cannot produce a musical or rhythmically satisfying line (e.g., "Poor Mr. Browning is both muddy and unmusical to the last degree. . . . He has no voice, and yet he wants to sing" [Austin, *Poetry of the Period*, 64]; "music is . . . distant from his ears" [*Laughter of the Muses*, 21]). B's defense is based on a comparison between himself and two famous composers. In the first instance, he makes the deaf Ludwig Van Beethoven (1770-1827) and himself fellow rule-breakers, set well above the "tap-tap, chink-chink" of the measuring critics who base their judgments solely upon formula. Next B establishes a parallel between himself and his innovative and much-misunderstood contemporary Robert Alexander Schumann (1810-1856). In fact, a real-life critic for the *Pall Mall Gazette* had already noted a parallel between B and Schumann; reviewing *Aristophanes' Apology* he had said: "perhaps a parallel between Schumann's music and Mr. Browning's poetry might be found not too fanciful if anyone chose to pursue it" (22 [15 July 1875], 203-04). Here B picks up on the suggestion to bolster his defense of his own prosodic methods. Unimpressed, *The Saturday Review* quipped: "In other words, every defect which can be imputed to the poet represents some mysterious and unattainable excellence" (42 [12 August 1876], 205).

497] *My story, the largest . . . all* The largess is B's lesson offered to his critics in the form of the story of Pacchiarotto.

498] aubade Sunrise music, sometimes an open-air concert, used ironically of the critics' rattling, tinkling, and jangling music.

505] *zany* "One who plays the fool for the amusement, or so as to be the laughing-stock, of others" (rare or obsolete, *OED*).

512] *quit-rent* "A rent, usually of small amount, paid by a freeholder or copyholder in lieu of services which might be required of him" (*OED*).

518-20] *treading down . . . homunculus* The contrast between the enduring nature of B's utterance and the fleeting song of the critics is emphasized here. B has turned the title of the popular Victorian song "Tommy Make Room for Your Uncle" into a verb that emphasizes the meanness and outrageousness of what the critics have been doing: they have produced a low-quality song themselves, and they in general possess powers of discrimination so meagre as to make it impossible for them to tell the difference between good music or poetry (a rose) and undistinguished music or poetry (a ranunculus, which is a wild flower). Then B points to Austin's small stature again in calling him "a homunculus" (Latin for a diminutive man). Cf. 1.469n and 11.485-86n.

The lively ballad "Tommy Make Room for Your Uncle" was sung with immense success by the comic vocalist W. B. Fair in London during 1876; the song was composed by Thomas S. Lonsdale, author of other popular songs as well. The song begins as follows (punctuation is according to the sheet music):

Fred Jones hatter of Leicester Square,
Presents himself to you,

By courtesy of the British Library

Cover of the sheet music for "Tommy Make Room for Your Uncle" by Thomas S. Lonsdale, a popular music hall song in 1876.

> And you may guess; when he is dressed,
>> Of girls he knows a few,
> A Widow fell in love with him,
>> While riding in a train,
> She had a blessed Boy with her,
>> Who caused us both much pain!

(SPOKEN.) Yes, the confounded young urchin caused me a great deal of pain, and sorrow; and the Widow his Mother introduced me to him as his Uncle? Fred Jones was never an Uncle before, and will never be again, not if he knows it—and the whole of the journey the Mother said to the boy—

> (*Chorus*)—Tommy make room for you Uncle,
>> There's a little dear,
> Tommy make room for your Uncle,
>> I want him to sit here,
> You know Mamma has got a *bun,*
>> And that she'll give to you;
> So don't annoy, there's a good Boy,
>> Make room for your Uncle do!

This particular song annoyed B (Harold Scott, *The Early Doors: Origins of the Music Hall* [London: Nicholas and Watson, 1946], 212).

521] *Xanthippe* This is the name of Socrates' shrewish wife. B has made her his housemaid and the muse of this poem that dumps abuse on his critics.

523] skoramis Chamber pot, amusingly identified as "a vessel of dishonour" by Edward Berdoe in *Browning Cyclopaedia* (London, 1916), 307. According to Chaucer's Wife of Bath, Xanthippe used a skoramis upon her husband:

> No thyng forgat he the care and the wo
> That Socrates hadde with his wyves two;
> How Xantippa caste pisse upon his heed.
> This sely man sat stille as he were deed;
> He wiped his heed, namoore dorste he seyn,
> But 'Er that thonder stynte, comth a reyn!
>> (The Wife of Bath's Prologue, 727-32)

Writing to his publisher Chapman on 2 December 1856, B had said of his critics: "Don't you mind them, and leave me to rub their noses in their own filth some fine day" (DeVane and Knickerbocker, 97). Here then B's muse empties verse-slops in Austin's own manner upon his head. And in *The Examiner* of 5 August 1876, responding to Austin's letter of 10 June 1876 to *The Examiner* in which he disclaimed responsibility for reviews in *The Evening Standard*, B has a poem that concludes with the following stanza:

> You would like, no doubt, to knock and ring,
> To be just hail fellow well met, with me,
> But I've slops dirtier still to fling
> About you, and I shall, you'll see!
>
> > (Hood, *Ltrs.*, 360)

Also cf. *Aristophanes' Apology*, when Aristophanes imagines Euripides' attitude towards his critics:

> There, pillared by your prowess, he remains,
> Immortally immerded. Not so he!
> Men pelted him but got no pellet back.
> He reasoned, I'll engage,—'Acquaint the world
> Certain minuteness butted at my knee?
> Dogface Eruxis, the small satirist,—
> What better would the manikin desire
> Than to strut forth on tiptoe, notable
> As who so far up fouled me in the flank?'
> So dealt he with the dwarfs. . . .
>
> > (11.1669-78)

Immerded means "cover[ed] with ordure" (*OED*).

527] *Jack-in-the-Green* "A man or boy inclosed in a wooden or wicker pyramidal framework covered with leaves, in the May-day sports of chimney-sweepers . . ." (*OED*). The term might also refer to the green covering of a volume that had attacked B, an interpretation that seems especially likely in view of 1.463n. Though green-backed books were not uncommon, it is likely that B had *Laughter of the Muses* in mind. Anonymous, it was divided into two parts, one satirizing B and the other Tennyson. The section on B contains 30 pages of heroic couplets that list all of his so-called faults; they are identical to the criticisms made by Austin in *The Poetry of the Period*. And there is evidence that B did in fact associate Austin with the sentiments expressed in this volume dressed in green. *Laughter of the Muses* contains the following suggestion about what should be done to B:

> . . .'twould be wrong to spare the stripe,
> And he may say again, tied to the mast,
> 'Surely the bitterness of death is past;'
> Then with indignant energy well grogged,
> Let our rough quartermaster see him flogged.

(34-35)

In B's letter to Alfred Domett in which he complained of Austin's flea-biting him over the years, he says, "there was talk of 'administering castigation to poor Mr. Browning,' which I have never brought myself to acquiesce in, even in metaphor . . ." (Griffin and Minchin, 260). Nonetheless, B must not have been sure that Austin was the author of *Laughter of the Muses,* for he considered its author, Jack-in-the-Green, a companion of Austin's.

529] *Quilp-Hop-o'-my-thumb*   Here B points specifically to Austin's smallness. Daniel Quilp is the evil dwarf in Dickens's *Old Curiosity Shop* (1841), and *Hop-o'-my-thumb* has been the generic name for a dwarf since the 16th century. B was criticized in the reviews for such allusions to Austin's size. *The Examiner* roundly rebuked him for "taunt[ing] Mr. Austin with personal deformity. 'Mr. Browning is an analyst rather than a poet,' says Mr. Austin. 'Hold your tongue, Quilp,' retorts the angry bard, 'you are a saucy dwarf' ". In response to this criticism, B wrote: "If the 'Examiner' can conceive of a gentler name than littleness for tricks of this kind [Austin's criticizing lines of poetry that he had tampered with] persisted in up to the present time—*I* cannot. One particular piece of blackguardism headed 'Men of Letters: R. B.'—could only save its author from a kicking by the charitable hope that he was too small for the treatment. I never was unlucky enough to set eyes on the man: if he *is* physically as well as morally and intellectually a dwarf—you may be sure I should have considered him a pygmy had his stature been that of Goliath." But Edmund Gosse has handed down "from Browning's lips" the following anecdote about a dinner party: "The guests were assembled round the fire at the end of the room, most of which was occupied by an unusually large table. The butler threw open the door to announce *Mr. Alfred Austin.* 'And I give you my word of honour,' said Browning, '*nothing* whatever came into the room.' A moment later the tiny form of the future Poet Laureate was seen to be trotting round the edge of the table which was just on a level with the top of his head." (See Hood, *Ltrs.,* 363, 175; Edward Marsh, *A Number of People, a Book of Reminiscences* [New York: Harper, 1939], 109.)

530] *Banjo-Byron . . . there*   This reference points to Austin, who made himself out to be the "literary heir of Byron," though he was never thought to have played his "inherited lyre" very well (Crowell, 29). Reviewing *The Season, The Athenæum* referred to Austin as "a youthful satirist, who is on the most flattering terms with himself as he stands smirkingly before the mirror of consciousness, and traces his likeness to Byron" (34 [20 April 1861], 528). *The Season* was modelled upon Byron's *English Bards and Scotch Reviewers*.

B is not here merely suggesting the absurdity of Austin's trying to be a Byron; well before 1876 B had become disillusioned with Byron, though this disillusionment is bound to be associated to some extent with Austin's attack on B and Austin's subsequent fierce defense of Byron in *A Vindication of Lord Byron* (London, 1869). Also *The Times*, 6 October 1871, in a review of *Balaustion's Adventure*, held up Byron as the "translucent" model that the obscure B ought to try to emulate (8). Cf. *The Inn Album*, 4.230n and 6.60n.

The *strum-strum* is a "rude stringed instrument" (obsolete or rare; last citation in *OED* is for 1728).

531] *pickle* A real mess (colloquial). As colloquial as B's poetry often is, he never elsewhere used *pickle* in this sense, and so it seems highly likely that he is here alluding to Byron's use of the term in *Don Juan* (8.43).

532] *I've discharged . . . own verses* In his confusion Austin will think that B's imitation of Austin's abusive and crude verse is in fact Austin's own verse.

533-34] *"Dwarfs are saucy," says Dickens . . . own sauce, . . .*[1] The statement that B attributes to Dickens does not appear elsewhere in print, though the remark might well have been made in conversation in response to Austin's attack on Dickens in *My Satire*, which accuses him of being a bed-fellow of the critics:

> O Dickens! Dickens! yours this flimsy brood:
> They kept by you, and you by them kotoued.
> They call you Demi-god: you think it true:
> First you feed them, and then they slaver you. . . .
> Can you not see collected round your chair,
> These base Delilahs cutting off your hair?
>
> (40)

Then Austin accuses Dickens of making his "heart and brain . . . lacqueys to the lust of gain," especially scoring him for writing serialized fiction (*Little Dorrit* was the most recent novel Dickens had published in this form) and for having cheapened his art by taking to the stage, which he had begun to do in 1858 (John Forster, Dickens's friend and biographer, had himself objected to the novelist's readings as undignified):

> Write, print, and publish, when ye've nought to say,
> Like what must not be even named for pay.
> Weigh out the monthly shilling's worth of wit,
> And measure if the length of grief be writ.
> Nay—as if not enough by these you sank—
> Degrade the Author to the montebank!
> Enter the lists of grinning showmen with
> A Paul, a Woodin, or an Albert Smith.
> Do all you can to lower in our eyes
> The noblest calling underneath the skies.
>
> (42-43)

Austin puts Dickens into the category with other popular Victorian showmen, Howard Paul, who with his wife Isabella Paul, gave entertainments "in town and country in 1860 and successive years" (*DNB*) and Albert Richard Smith, a prolific novelist and dramatist, who turned to show business with a program involving anecdote, impersonation, and song. His "Ascent of Mont Blanc" packed them into the Egyptian Hall, Piccadilly, in the early 1850's. Woodin remains unidentified.

The ellipsis following the comma in B's l.534 makes it clear that "Alfred Austin" is to be supplied by the reader—to rhyme with "sauced in" in the line above.

B's footnote is attributed to "Printer's Devil," which is an apprentice in a printing shop. That which is here attributed to the Printer's Devil actually appeared about a year before the poem was begun in one of B's letters to George Barrett: "Whenever there is a funny piece of raving against me in a newspaper you may be sure my little bug of an Austin is biting his best: this is the third instance within as many weeks—and I suppose he has written above a dozen such things. 'Dwarfs,' Dickens tells us, 'are mostly sarcy—' and if this particular Quilp gets any good, beside the penny-a-line, out of his 'sarce,' he has my full leave: but even dwarfs need not be blackguardly: and this one has a trick of 'giving an instance of Mr. Browning's unintelligible stuff' which he makes so indeed by altering my words to his own,— leaving out a whole line, for instance, and joining two broken ends! He did this in the 'World' a fortnight ago. . . . All this bugjuice from a creature . . . whose scribblings, except when they related to myself, I never read a line of! But—as the poet sings—

> Who would be satirical
> On a thing so very small?"

(Letter of 25 May 1875, Landis and Freeman, 300). B slightly alters two lines from Jonathan Swift's "Dr. Delany's Villa": "For who would be satirical / Upon a thing so very small?" (11.3-4).

Cf. Austin, *My Satire:* "Propriety and printers' devils call: / Pluck your own quill and plunge it in your gall" (10; also see 13).

535] *Knight of the Pencil* B's version of common jocular usage of the term *knight* along with the name of some tool associated with a trade or profession, as *knight of the cue,* for a billiard-player (*OED*). B is referring to Pacchiarotto, *pencil* being "An artist's paint-brush of camel's hair . . . or other fine hair, gathered into a quill" (*OED*).

536] *stencil* Suggests that Pacchiarotto is an inferior artist—perhaps merely a decorator needing to use pattern designs in his fresco.

540] *crown cracked . . . bloodied* Hotspur says to Lady Hotspur, ". . . This is no world / To play with mammets and to tilt with lips. / We must have bloody noses and crack'd crowns . . ." (*Henry IV, Part I*, 2.3.91-93).

547] karterotaton belos The strongest dart. An allusion to Pindar's *Olympian Odes* (1.115): ". . . for me the Muse is rearing to full strength the mightiest thunderbolt of song." B had copied this passage in Greek on the fly-leaf of the *Old Yellow Book*.

548] melos Mode.

552] *kidney* Temperament or disposition.

554] *"grammar" . . . "coach" me* Sidney Colvin was one of those who found fault with B's grammar: "the characteristic of Mr. Browning's grammar is—shall we say its absence? Nay, but so unrecognizable is it that often it might as well be absent. . . . [T]houghts, of some perplexity to begin with, are still further and wantonly perplexed for want of grammatical smoothing and jointing . . ." (*The Fortnightly Review*, 10, N. S. [October 1871], 488). Cf. *The Inn Album*, 2.13n.

557] *clog at your fetlocks* A *clog* is a heavy object fixed to the leg of a beast to impede motion; a *fetlock* is "that part of a horse's leg where the tuft of hair grows behind the pastern-joint" (*OED*).

559-70] *Was it "clearness . . . easily uttered* B had been defending himself against the charge of obscurity (see "Sources," above) for many years; for example, to John Ruskin he had written on 10 December 1855: "For your bewilderment . . . how shall I help *that?* We don't read poetry the same way, by the same law; it is too clear. I cannot begin writing poetry till my imaginary reader has conceded licenses to me which you demur at altogether. I *know* that I don't make out my conception by my language, all poetry being a putting the infinite within the finite. You would have me paint it all plain out, which can't be; but by various artifices I try to make shift with touches and bits of outlines which *succeed* if they bear the conception from me to you. You ought, I think, to keep pace with the thought tripping from ledge to ledge of my 'glaciers,' as you call them; not stand poking your alpenstock into the holes, and demonstrating that no foot could have stood there;—suppose it sprang over there? In *prose* you may criticize so—because there is the absolute representation of portions of truth[,] . . . but in asking for more *ultimates* you must accept less *mediates*, nor expect that a Druid stone-circle will be traced for you with as few breaks to the eye as the North Crescent and South Crescent that go together so cleverly in many a suburb (W. G. Collingwood, *Life and Work of John Ruskin* [Boston, 1902], 164).

560] *enswathe* To wrap in a swathe or bandage.

565] *noddle* "The head as the seat of the mind or thought." This colloquial term carries with it a "contemptuous suggestion of dullness or emptiness" (see *OED*, sense 3).

566] *goose* It is natural for B to make an analogy between critic and goose, for in 1875 he had named "two hissing and snapping pet geese 'Edinburgh' and 'Quarterly'" (Irvine and Honan, 479). It is interesting to note that B had originally referred to the "quack-quack" of the goose-critic. It might seem odd that a man who kept geese would attribute to them the sound of a duck. Austin's *My Satire* supplies a clue; in this poem he portrays the critics as being addressed by their bosses as follows:

> Wake, snoring scribes! Ye varlets! do ye hear?
> Up from your straw each drowsy garreteer!
>
> . . .
>
> Extend your neck, each interrupted goose,
> And quack me quick five shillings' of abuse.
>
> (10, 11; also see 33)

Perhaps B at first meant to allude to Austin, both in referring to the critics as geese and in having them quack. If he did mean to do this in 1876, when he revised "Of Pacchiarotto" in 1889, that intention must have been supplanted by his concern over some criticism put forth by *The Saturday Review* (42 [12 August 1876], 205): "Mr. Browning, in his dreary and laboured jocosity, has apparently confounded geese with ducks." It is ironic, then, that B would appear to take into account the quibbling of the critics in revising a poem about how he has no intention of taking into account the quibbling of the critics—especially in view of his obstinacy in refusing to correct a subject-verb agreement error pointed out by *The Saturday Review* a year earlier (see *The Inn Album*, 2.12-13n).

568] os frontis The forehead.

572] *my birth-day* B was born on 7 May 1812.

573-76] hebdome, hieron emar—/ . . . / —Tei . . . Leto The seventh is a holy day, on which Leto bare Apollo with the blade of gold (Hesiod, *Works and Days* [11.770-71]). B has *egeinato* where Hesiod has γεινατο (Hood, "Classical Sources," 133).

580] *Leave snoring . . . Pheidippides* It does not appear that B means the Pheidippides (or Phidippides) who is famous for the run to Sparta and who, as John Pettigrew and T. J. Collins remark, "had little time for snoring" (*Robert Browning, The Poems* [New York: Yale, 1981], 2: 1045). The sense of the line, rather, suggests a Phidippides who had indeed plenty of time for snoring—the one in Aristophanes' *The Clouds*, which begins at night in a sleeping-room in Strepsiades' house where he and his son Phidippides are in bed. The father, awake and worrying about the debts accrued by his extravagant playboy son, complains about Phidippides "who never wakes the whole long night" but "farts" and "snore[s]" "to his heart's content" (W. J. Oates and Eugene O'Neill, Jr., eds., *The Complete Greek Drama* [New York, 1938], 2.541).

581] *We'll up . . . Euripides* B links himself with his favorite Greek dramatist, who was treated with hostility by his critics. B implies that the criticism keeps him up and working as it had kept Euripides up and working.

AT THE "MERMAID"

Date] According to the Balliol MS, the poem was finished on 15 January 1876.

Title] The Mermaid Tavern, which once stood in Bread Street with an entrance in Friday Street, is the setting for this poem. The Friday Club, started by Sir Walter Ralegh and with Ben Jonson, John Donne, John Selden, Thomas Carew, Francis Beaumont, John Fletcher, and probably Shakespeare as members, met at the Mermaid.

Epigraph] Adapted from Ben Jonson's lines "To the Reader," which appear opposite the portrait of Shakespeare in the First Folio edition of his works (1623):

This Figure, that thou here seest put
It was for gentle Shakespeare cut,
Wherein the Graver had a strife
With Nature, to out-do the life:
O, could he but have drawn his wit
As well in brass, as he hath hit
His face, the Print would then surpass
All, that was ever writ in brass.
But, since he cannot, Reader, look
Not on his Picture, but his Book.

Jonson's verse exhibits B's theme: that readers ought to look at his poems and not concern themselves with him as a person.

Source] This poem, together with the title poem, "House," "Shop," and "Epilogue," is B's response to the sort of misinterpretation of his poetry represented by R. H. Hutton in his review of *Fifine at the Fair*. Hutton does not seem to understand that the speaker in the poem is not B himself, in spite of all of the poet's efforts to tell the world that his poems are dramatic. For example, Hutton says, "Mr Browning preaches that what men believe only because they desire it, is all human—the falsehood through which Truth at last manifest[s] itself . . . ." (*The Spectator*, 45 [6 July 1872], 854. Further, *Temple Bar*, also taking the speaker of *Fifine* to be B, says that the poem "presents itself as a confession of faith, and . . . we are clearly intended to believe that that faith is Mr. Browning's own"; this reviewer complains especially of B's "direct advocacy of free love" (see *Temple Bar*, 37 [February 1873], 315, 326). B must have been livid! He wrote "At the Mermaid" to set his critics straight.

"At the 'Mermaid'" is also a response to Austin's great concern over the question of "Next Poet" (see l.1). In *Poetry of the Period*, Austin contended that although Tennyson had many admirable qualities, he was but a "Pegasus without wings": "he never soars" (29, 30), and therefore it was absurd for critics to pretend that Tennyson is the great poet of the age. Then at the outset of his chapter on B, Austin claimed that there is a movement afoot to displace Tennyson from his position of exaggerated recognition and to replace him with B: "our Poet Laureate is beginning to totter on his throne. The signs of mutiny against his long unchallenged supremacy are unmistakable. I have already expressed the opinion that, as far as work done is concerned, he is unquestionably at the head of living English poets. But in the quarters whence first issued, and where was long stoutly maintained, the preposterous theory that he is a really great poet, voices scarcely ambiguous proceed, intimating not only that there is perhaps some doubt upon that point, but that in any case one greater than he has long been dwelling amongst us. . . . The same coteries . . . who by dint of persistence imposed upon the unreflecting crowd the exaggerated estimate of Mr. Tennyson against which I have protested, are now striving to induce them to abandon their idol and set up another. Where they have long put Mr. Tennyson, they now want to place Mr. Browning" (39-41).

1] *Next Poet* The ostensible speaker of this poem is Shakespeare, but of course B is giving to Shakespeare his own position, which is that he has no interest in being the "next poet" (see note for *Source*). The main reason that B selected Shakespeare as his mask is that in *Essay on Shelley* he had identified Shakespeare as the epitome of the objective poet, who had an unknown existence that was separate from his imaginative creations: "The man passes, the work remains. The work speaks for itself . . . [,] and the biography of the worker is no more necessary to an understanding or enjoyment of it, than is a model or anatomy of some tropical tree, to the right tasting of the fruit we are familiar with on the market-stall . . ." (*Essay on Shelley,* 5:138 of this edition; cf. "House," 11.37-40). The other possible reason that B makes Shakespeare his representative is that the favorable reviews of B's work had the habit of putting him on an equal footing with Shakespeare. For example, *The Athenæum* for 20 March 1869 called *The Ring and the Book* "the supremest poetical achievement of our time [and] . . . the most precious and profound spiritual treasure that England has produced since the days of Shakespeare" (399).

2] *nor . . . nor* Neither . . . nor.

fain Willingly.

4] *revolt* Go over (Last citation in *OED* for this sense is for 1692).

5-8] *I, forsooth, sow . . . You joke* B was probably thinking of himself in relation to Tennyson and might have had in mind John Morley's defense of *The Ring and the Book:* "we have this long while been so debilitated by pastorals, by graceful presentation of the Arthurian legend for drawing-rooms, by idylls, not robust and Theocritean, but such little pictures as might adorn a ladies' school, by verse directly didactic, that a rude burst of air from the outside welter of human realities is apt to spread a shock, which might show in what simpleton's paradise we have been living" (*Fortnightly Review,* 2 [1 March 1869], 331ff). Tennyson, then, might well be the "bubble-king" indirectly alluded to.

9] *sherris* Archaic for *sherry* and the term Shakespeare gives to Falstaff in the Henry IV plays. See, for example, *Henry IV, Part II* 4.3.113.
  mantling A suffusion of color.
10] *mayhap* Archaic for perhaps.
11] *scantling* Modicum.
16] *dead king* See note for *Source*.
17] *discover* "To disclose or expose to view" (rare, *OED*).
39] *rout* "A large number or collection of things" (According to *OED*, poetic; last citation is for 1624).
48] *brass we took for gold* See Jonson's "To the Reader" in note on Epigraph. Cf. "Ponte Dell'Angelo," 11.35-36.
50] *orichalc* "Some yellow ore or alloy of copper, highly prized by the ancients; perhaps brass" (*OED*). This is surely one among many words that B must have taken delight in using as an irritant to those critics who objected to his unusual vocabulary.
58] *last king* DeVane suspects that B, speaking behind the mask of Shakespeare, has Wordsworth in mind (*Hbk.*, 399; and see "The Lost Leader" [4:183]). Joseph Devey, *A Comparative Estimate of Modern British Poets* (London, 1873), compares B unfavorably to Wordsworth (400), concluding that B held "a respectable place among the third-class poets of our literature" (421), and this might have disposed B to refer to Wordsworth in a derogatory manner. Cf. the review of Devey's book in *The Illustrated London News* (21 June 1873, 591) in which the issue of B's rank as a poet was further discussed. Byron, on the other hand, is the poet that the unfriendly critics of B most often held up as the great poet of the past that B could not equal. In *Poetry of the Period*, Austin contrasted the clarity of Byron with the obscurity of B (64). Also see *The Evening Standard*, 6 January 1872, 1.
  loth Unwilling (frequently *loath*).
59] *pointed moral* William Allingham, in "The Proposed Byron Memorial," *Fraser's Magazine*, 13 (February 1876), says that Byron "has nothing to say to us but this . . . : a moment ago this was a human being, full of pain, pleasure, passion, agitation; now it is a piece of clay, food for worms" (255). B approved heartily of Allingham's essay: "Browning asks me about Byron article in *Fraser*, and praises it most warmly. 'Shouldn't mind if my name were at the bottom of it'" (*William Allingham: A Diary*, eds., H. Allingham and D. Radford [London, 1907], 246, entry for 10 March 1876).
61-64] *Out rushed sighs . . . king and you* Behind his mask, B here presents Byron's imitators, the most objectionable of which was Alfred Austin, the "Banjo-Byron" of "Of Pacchiarotto" (see 1.529n).
  cater-cousins Persons on terms of intimate familiarity and accord

who are not related by blood. It is a "traditional expression . . . chiefly from Shakespeare" (*OED*).

64] *king* See 1.58n.

66] *sherris* See 1.9n.

67] *no jot nor tittle* Not the least bit (*OED*). Cf. Matthew 5:18: "For verily I say unto you, Till heaven and earth pass, one jot or one tittle shall in no wise pass from the law, till all be fulfilled."

72] *plague* Affliction.

74] *smack* Taste (According to *OED*, with adjectival complement first used by Disraeli in 1847).

81] *your Pilgrim* Byron; B is apparently alluding to "Childe Harold's Pilgrimage" wherein Harold is obviously Byron himself, who, as Arnold puts it, bore "The pageant of his bleeding heart" throughout Europe ("Stanzas from the Grande Chartreuse," 11.135-36).

82-88] *This our world . . . throw away* These lines are B's summary of Byron's philosophy.

92] *Balaam-like* Balak, king of the Moabites, sent messengers to Balaam, saying, "Behold, there is a people come out from Egypt: behold, they cover the face of the earth, and they abide over against me: Come now therefore, I pray thee, curse me this people; for they are too mighty for me . . . : I wot that he whom thou blessest is blessed, and he whom thou cursest is cursed. . . . God said unto Balaam, . . . thou shalt not curse the people: for they are blessed" (Numbers 22:4-6, 12). Because B is Balaam-like, he cannot be Byron's heir.

101] *Scan the near high . . . far low* I. e., give full attention to the lofty people near at hand; dismiss scornfully those of lesser merit.

103] Simpletons? . . . Marlowe I. e., what if simpletons advance on me? "My match" (obsolete for *companion* [*OED*, sense 2]) is Christopher Marlowe (1564-93), closest to Shakespeare in inventive powers of all the Renaissance literary figures.

104] *Sciolists . . . Ben* I.e., if sciolists (pretenders to knowledge, wiseacres) confront me, my friend is Ben Jonson (1572-1637), known as a man of enormous learning. B's use of *sciolists* suggests that Arnold's "Stanzas from the Grande Chartreuse" (see 11.99, 102) was fresh in his mind.

105-12] *Womankind . . . breaking hearts* Renaissance poetry is replete with complaints about female fickleness and vanity—and so is Byron's poetry.

113] *fortune* The goddess "supposed to distribute the lots of life according to her own humour" (Johnson's *Dictionary*).

114] *threw Venus . . . expound* It would appear that *threw Venus* means "rejected the goddess of love," but another sense of the term alternatively applies: "The highest or most favourable cast or throw in playing with huckle-bones," a 17th-century game in which the player that turns up the figure of Venus, which is on one side of the bone, wins, while he who turns up the dog loses (see *OED*). The call for Ben Jonson, a 17th-century figure, to explain the term gives the nod to the second alternative.

117]   *my benefactress*   Fortune of 1.113.

118-20]   *Cursings suit . . . turn her—so*   These lines refer to the critics who were always trying to turn around B's good Fortune. B supplies the appropriate "cursings" in "Of Pacchiarotto."

128]   *poohed and pished*   Depreciated. See "Of Pacchiarotto," 1.103n and "Filippo Baldinucci on the Privilege of Burial," 1.458n.

132]   Welt-schmerz   "Sorrow or sadness over the present or future evils or woes of the world in general; sentimental pessimism" (*Webster's New International Dictionary*), an obvious parting dig at Byron.

133]   *shelly*   A word first used by Shakespeare in *Venus and Adonis* and meaning "shell-like" (*OED*).

134]   *Cuirass*   A piece of armour consisting of breast- and back-plate.

137]   *sherris-brewage*   See 11.9n and 66.

138]   *quotha?*   An archaic term meaning "'said he?,' used with contemptuous or sarcastic force" (*OED*).

144]   *Ben*   See note for Title, 1.104n, and 1.114n.

HOUSE

Date]   According to the Balliol MS, the poem was completed on 1 February 1874.

Sources]   B is no doubt responding both to those reviewers who yearned for a direct encounter with him ("He seldom speaks to us in his own [character]. His verse does not tell us . . . what he aims at . . ." (*Contemporary Review*, 4 [January 1867], 6) and to those who assumed that in the reading of his dramatic poems they were nonetheless having a personal encounter with him and thus identified B with, for example, Prince Hohenstiel-Schwangau ("That is what Mr. Browning would have thought, had *he* been 'Saviour of Society'. . . . [He is] painting his own thoughts . . ." [*The Spectator*, 44 (30 December 1871), 1607]) —or with Don Juan of *Fifine*, who "is not a man, but a congeries of pegs on which Mr. Browning hangs his miscellaneous imaginings" (*The Guardian*, 27 [25 September 1872], 1216).

The title "House," according to DeVane, suggests that the poem is as well a response to Dante Gabriel Rossetti's series of sonnets of a very personal nature, *The House of Life* (1870). DeVane's suggestion does not conform to the fact that, in B's poem, the front of the house is dislodged by an earthquake; but there are several striking parallels. Richard Altick suggests an earlier source for "the house of life" that is scrutinized by those who have no business doing so. It is John Greenleaf Whittier's "My Namesake" (1857):

> Let Love's and Friendship's tender debt
> > Be paid by those I love in life.
> Why should the unborn critic whet
> > For me his scalping-knife?
>
> Why should the stranger peer and pry
> > One's vacant house of life about,
> And drag for curious ear and eye
> > His faults and follies out?—
>
> Why stuff, for fools to gaze upon,
> > With chaff of words, the garb he wore,
> As corn-husks when the ear is gone
> > Are rustled all the more?

It is likely that B knew this poem, since he and Whittier had recently been corresponding. B owned a copy of Whittier's *The Panorama, and Other Poems* (1856), which had been presented to him and EBB by the author, but it does not contain "My Namesake." (See DeVane, *Hbk.*, 400-01; Richard Altick, "Memo to the Next Annotator of Browning," *VP*, 1 [January 1963], 67-68; *The Writings of John Greenleaf Whittier* [Boston, 1886], 2.116-17; Kelley and Coley, 207.)

3] *pelf* Wealth, "filthy lucre" (*OED*).

4] *Unlock . . . sonnet-key* A reference to Wordsworth's *Miscellaneous Sonnets*, Part II, sonnet I:

> Scorn not the Sonnet; Critic, you have frowned,
> Mindless of its just honours; with this key
> Shakespeare unlocked his heart. . . .
> > > (11.1-3)

B obviously disagrees with Wordsworth's views on the sonnet and on Shakespeare.

5] *my betters* An ironic reference to those poets devoted to the sonnet as a form for personal expression, especially Wordsworth and Rossetti.

6-9] *Take notice . . . the Publisher* These lines represent B's understanding of Rossetti's purpose in writing *The House of Life*. The phrase "suites of reception" is clearly a direct reference to Rossetti's sonnet sequence, which invites the reader into the poet's "private apartment" to see him in bed with his wife (see "The Kiss" and "Nuptial Sleep"). This practice was anathema to B, who did everything in his power to protect the private life of his wife as well as himself and was outraged whenever anyone wished to publish a biography of EBB or an edition of her letters (Ryals, 133). B could possibly also be thinking of Donne's "Canonization": "We'll build in sonnets pretty rooms" (1.32).

22-23] *Odd tables . . . old books about*   In *The Wife of Rossetti: Her Life and Death* (New York, 1932), Violet Hunt describes the strange second-hand furniture that Rossetti purchased for Chatham Place, where he lived with his wife, and that he removed to the Chelsea House after Elizabeth died; for example: "Knock-kneed couches and commodes stained deep with the crusted rime of ages. . . . Lamps, statuettes, bas-reliefs were propped on spindly *étagères* or corner cupboards whose keys had long been lost so that the doors, after being carefully 'put to,' would yawn open suddenly at you." Hunt also refers to an "ill-lit passage full of dusty book-shelves" (52).

24] *He smoked . . . lost his health*   Although Rossetti did not smoke, his physical and mental health were poor for many years, worsened by his mixing of laudanum and whisky.

25] *I doubt . . . he dressed*   Rossetti was notorious for his slovenliness.

26] *brasier . . . perfumes*   B uses an obscure form of *brazier*, a flat pan for burning charcoal upon which incense might be applied. When Rossetti lived at Chatham Place, he burned incense to mask the "smell of the river—awful and insistent . . ." (Hunt, *Wife of Rossetti*, 273).

28] *His wife . . . separate rooms*   According to Hunt, Rossetti and his wife slept apart, he often spending the night with Fanny Hughes, a model (see *Wife of Rossetti*, 280-81).

29] *goodman*   Master of a house (archaic; *OED*).

36] *No optics like yours*   A reference to B's critics.

37] *Hoity toity*   "An exclamation expressing surprise with some degree of contempt, especially at words or actions considered to show . . . undue assumption" (*OED*).

38-39] *With . . . unlocked his heart*   See 1.4n. B adds the word *same* to the first of these lines from Wordsworth.

40] *Shakespeare*   In his *Essay on Shelley*, B had made Shakespeare his supreme example of the objective poet in opposition to Shelley, the arch subjective poet (see 5:137 of this edition and "At the 'Mermaid,'" 1.1n.).

SHOP

Date]   Written ten days after "House" (11 February 1874), this poem takes up where the former left off.

5]   *Sheet*   Cylinder-glass, which is "made by blowing glass into the form of a cylinder which is then cut open and flattened" (*OED*, sense 9c).

6-10]   *What gimcracks . . . catalogue*   Reminiscent of Romeo's description of an apothecary's shop in *Romeo and Juliet:*

> And in his needy shop a tortoise hung,
> An alligator stuffd, and other skins
> Of ill-shap'd fishes, and about his shelves
> A beggarly account of empty boxes,
> Green earthen pots, bladders, and musty seeds,
> Remnants of packthread, and old cakes of roses
> Were thinly scattered, to make up a show.
> (5.1.42-48)

Gimcracks are slight, flimsy ornaments.

12]   *vastitude*   Unusual largeness (*OED* cites this instance as earliest usage).

20]   *traffic-groove*   Rut of doing business in his shop.

23]   *City chaps*   Colloquial for businessmen (*city* refers to that part of greater London within the original boundaries which has long been the commercial center).

26]   *parked about*   Surrounded with a park (*OED* cites only this instance of *parked* in this sense).

29]   *seat*   Country-seat, the residence of a nobleman.

30]   *the rail*   The railway.

35]   *Rothschild*   Probably a reference to Nathan Mayer Rothschild (1840-1915) of the London house of the banking family that controlled finance in Europe. B's uncles Reuben and William were associated with Rothschilds' bank in Paris.

36]   *Mayfair*   The "smart," exclusive area of London, north of Piccadilly.

38]   *Hampstead*   Formerly a village standing upon one of the highest hills near London. About mid-19th century, there was a great deal of residential development for the wealthy. Although many areas remained wild and unpopulated, the area had become part of the metropolis by 1875.

40] *country-box*   A small country house, often a temporary residence used while one is engaged in hunting, shooting, or fishing.

53] *great shakes*   Apparently a colloquial term first appearing in the 19th century; Partridge lists "no great shakes": "Nothing remarkable or very important or unusually able or clever."

54] *fizzes*   Makes a hissing or sputtering sound.

58] *Receipt of Custom*   A place for receiving money. Cf. Matthew 9:9.

59] *outworld*   Outside world (B apparently revived this word—previously out of use since the 17th century—when he used it in *Sordello*).

63] *darkling*   Proceeding in the dark (*OED*, sense 1).

70] scud   Hurry.

78] *Solomon's sceptre*   The ornamental rod that was the symbol of Solomon's authority as king of Israel in the 10th century B.C.

79] *coral*   "The piece of coral which children have about their necks, imagined to assist them in breeding teeth" (Johnson's *Dictionary*).

84] *Times*   B found the *Times* of London a source for his poetry. Cf. *The Inn Album*, note for *Sources*, and "How It Strikes a Contemporary" (5:274-77) where B presents the poet as one who studies the life around him.

swang   Obsolete past tense of *swing*.

94] *Chaffer*   Dealing.

101-05] *I want to . . . upon the flute*   B probably alludes to the original version of the nursery rhyme in which some tradesmen require relief from their work and find it at "a dubious side-show at the local fair":

> Hey! rub-a-dub, ho! rub-a-dub, three maids in a tub
> And who do you think were there?
> The butcher, the baker, the candlestick-maker,
> And all of them gone to the fair.

> (Iona and Peter Opie, eds.
> *The Oxford Dictionary of Nursery Rhymes*
> [Oxford, Clarendon Press, 1951], 376).

109-10] *From where . . . our hearts be*   For where your treasure is, there will your heart be also (Matthew 6:21).

PISGAH-SIGHTS I

Date]   According to the Balliol MS, the poem was written on 28 December 1875.

Title]   Pisgah was the mountain height from which Moses saw the

Promised Land upon which he would never set foot (see Deuteronomy 34:1-5).

19] *aye* Variant spelling of *ay*, which means *ever*.

PISGAH-SIGHTS II

Date] According to the Balliol MS, the poem was written on 19 February 1876.

Title] See note for *Title* for "Pisgah-Sights I."

9] *Soft* An archaic "exclamation with imperative force either to enjoin silence or deprecate haste" (*OED*, sense 8).
10] *Three-score . . . years* Cf. Psalms 90:10.
12] *deniers* French coins used to signify a very small sum.
13] *dazed* "Dazzled with excess of light" (*OED*, sense 1b).
47] *Glowworm* An insect, the female of which is wingless and emits "a shining green light" (*OED*).

FEARS AND SCRUPLES

Date] According to the Balliol MS, the poem was finished on 26 February 1876.

Title] The title comes from Banquo's speech after the news of Duncan's murder:

> And when we have our naked frailties hid,
> That suffer in exposure, let us meet
> And question this most bloody piece of work,
> To know it further. Fears and scruples shake us.
> In the great hand of God I stand, and thence
> Against the undivulg'd pretense I fight
> Of treasonous malice.
> (Macbeth, 2.3.126-32)

2] *unseen friend* God (see 1.48).
5] *his letters* Holy scripture.
18] *experts* The "Higher Critics"—David Strauss, in *Das Leben Jesu* (1835-36); Ernest Renan, in *La Vie de Jesus* (1860); and others—discredited the authority of holy scripture.
33] *All my days . . . softlier, sadlier* Cf. Isaiah 38:15: 'I shall go softly all the years in the bitterness of my soul."

NATURAL MAGIC

Composition] This poem, together with its companion "Magical Nature," was pasted on lightly-lined paper, like that on which the other poems in the Balliol MS volume were written; the titles of these two poems were written on the paper to which the poems were pasted. Although there is no date on "Natural Magic," the second poem, "Magical Nature," is dated 4 March 1876, and it is presumed that they were written at the same time, for both poems are written on the same kind of darkly-lined paper and apparently with the same pen.

5] *Nautch* A professional East Indian dancing girl (*OED*). B was the first to use the word to refer to the dancer instead of to the dance (see *Fifine at the Fair*, 1.31).
6] *bolt* Of the lock.

MAGICAL NATURE

Composition] See note on *Composition* of "Natural Magic."

BIFURCATION

Date] According to the Balliol MS, the poem was completed on 29 November 1875.

Title] "Bifurcation," division into two parts, in the figurative sense, came into use in the mid-19th century (see *OED*).

Source] The love triangle in this poem is similar to the one in *The Inn Album* and thus might depend upon some of the same sources (see above). Also cf. "The Statue and the Bust," 5:261-71 of this edition.

17] *broadway* "A wide open road or highway, as opposed to a narrow lane or byway" (*OED*).
19] darkling Lying in darkness (*OED*, sense 2).
24] *greensward* "Turf on which grass is growing" (*OED*).
26] sward "A growth of grass" (*OED*).

NUMPHOLEPTOS

Date] According to the Balliol MS, the poem was completed on 25 April 1876.

Title] B wrote to F. J. Furnivall in June 1889: "Is not the key to the meaning of the poem in its title—*νυμφοληπτος* [caught or entranst by a Nymph], not γυναικεραστηζ [a woman-lover]? As allegory, that is, of an impossible ideal object of love, accepted conventionally as such by a man who, all the while, cannot quite blind himself to the demonstrable fact that the possessor of knowledge and purity obtained without the natural consequences of obtaining them by achievement—not inheritance,—such a being is imaginary, not real, a nymph and no woman: and only such an one would be ignorant of and surprised at the results of a lover's endeavour to emulate the qualities which the beloved is entitled to consider as pre-existent to earthly experience, and independent of its inevitable results" (Peterson, 160). As DeVane, *Hbk.*, suggests, B's explanation is not so clear as the poem.

B's manner of rendering the Greek into English might be understood as a defiant gesture in keeping with the tone of many other poems in this volume. Many critics objected strenuously to B's English versions of Greek; for example, in reviewing *Aristophanes' Apology,* the *London Quarterly Review* complained about his turning the traditional *Athens* into *Athenai, Thebes* into *Thibai,* and *Sparta* into *Sparte:* "we object emphatically to the alteration of such common nouns of Hellenic origin as have passed into the fabric of the language and are in common use . . ." (44 [July, 1875], 37-75). It is no surprise, then, that in reviewing the Pacchiarotto volume *The Saturday Review* remarked: "It would probably be regarded as unpardonable presumption to suggest to Mr. Browning that 'nymph' is more euphonious as well as more familiar than 'numph'" (42 [17 August 1876], 206).

Nymphs, according to Greek myth, were inferior divinities of nature who dwelt in groves, forests, caves, fountains, beside springs, streams and rivers; they were the benevolent spirits of these places.

Source] Hood finds the origin of the poem in B's study of Plutarch. In *Aristides* Plutarch explains the origin of the term *nympholepti* and in *Numa Pompilius* provides a tale that seems to accord with B's letter to Furnivall (see note on *Title*): "Numa, after the death of his wife, frequented the groves, fields, and desert places, and was admitted to celestial wedlock in the love and converse of the goddess Egeria—goddesses being capable of intermixture by the body with mortal men" ("Classical Sources," 170).

11] *prime* The first hour of the day (*OED*).
20-21] *Spirit-Seven . . . lamp before* When Furnivall inquired about the meaning of "Spirit-Seven," B replied: "The 'seven-spirits' are in the Apocalypse, also in Coleridge and Byron: a common image" (Peterson, 160). B used the Greek name *Apocalypse* for the book of Revelation because he read the New Testament in Greek. The allusion would

seem to be to Revelation 4:5: "And out of the throne proceeded lightnings and thunderings and voices: and there were seven lamps of fire burning before the throne, which are the seven Spirits of God" (also cf. Revelation 1:4). According to *The Oxford Annotated Bible* (New York: Oxford Univ. Press, 1965), the Seven Spirits are "likely a symbolic reference to the manifold energies of the Spirit of God" (1491), but there is the possibility that the term refers to angelic beings. The context of the term in this poem suggests that B might well have understood "Seven Spirits" to refer to the seven arch-angels that headed the celestial hierarchy. And his reference to Coleridge and Byron confirms this view. In the 1796 version of "Religious Musings," Coleridge writes:

> Yea, and there,
> Unshudder'd unaghasted, he shall view
> E'en the Seven Spirits, who in the later day
> Will shower hot pestilence on the sons of men. . . .
>   (11.78-81)

Also see Byron, "Heaven and Earth":

> Seraph!
> From thy sphere!
> Whatever star contain thy glory;
> In the eternal depths of heaven
> Albeit thou watchest with "the Seven,"
> Though through space infinite and heavy
> Before thy bright wings worlds be driven,
> Yet hear!
>   (Part 1.36-43)

Cf. Revelation 15 and 16.
   lamp Shine; cf. *Aristophanes Apology*,1.5345.
23-24] *moon / Which smiles* Cf. "Love Among the Ruins," 1.1.
24] *boon* "The matter prayed for or asked" (obsolete or archaic, *OED*).
49] *erst* Before (obsolete, *OED*).
51] *unembued* Embue is an obsolete variant of *imbue (OED)*.
60] *Centuply-angled* Angled a hundred-fold; this is the only instance cited by the *OED*.
61] *hearted* Fixed or established in the heart (17th-century usage revived in Victorian period).
73-74] *blank pure soul . . . prismatic glow* "Cf. 'My Star.'"
   blank White (obsolete).

76] *flamelet* A small flame; according to *OED*, first used by Henry Wadsworth Longfellow in 1849.

78-79] *Sulphury hint . . . rage* Cf. "Bishop Blougram's Apology": "While certain hell-deep instincts, man's weak tongue / Is never bold to utter in their truth / Because styled hell-deep . . ." (11.990-93). Sulphur has long been associated with hell and its fires.

79] *stint* Limit.

80] *yellow* Sulphur is a greenish-yellow.

84] *bow* Poetic for *rainbow* (*OED*).

93] *trode* Archaic form of *trod* (*OED*).
 tinct Poetic for *tint* (*OED*).

101] *bickers* Poetic for "flashes, gleams, quivers" (*OED*). Cf. "A Forgiveness." 1.256.

118] *drear* A poetic shortening of *dreary* (*OED*).

121] *smatch* Slight indication (*OED*, sense 2).

126] *sulphur-steeped disguise* See 11.78-79n.

133] *petrific* Stony (*OED*, sense 2).

134] This line stands alone in a poem of couplets with a few triplets.

142] *bulrush-spear* The bulrush, actually very fragile, gives the "delusive appearance of strength" (*OED*).

APPEARANCES

Date] According to the Balliol manuscript, the poem was completed on 6 April 1876.

ST. MARTIN'S SUMMER

Date and Composition] B finished the poem on 27 March 1876 according to the Balliol manuscript. Stanza 17 is written on the back of p. 52 of the MS.

Title] St. Martin's Summer is "a season of fine mild weather occurring about Martinmas," which is 11 November (*OED*).

Source] Kenneth L. Knickerbocker shows that the poem is "a fairly transparent account of part of Browning's unfortunate affair with Lady Louisa Ashburton" (see "An Echo from Browning's Second Courtship," *Studies in Philology*, 32 [April 1935], 120-24).

4] *serest* *Sere* is poetic for "dry, withered" (*OED*).

29] *obscurely* Inconspicuously (*OED* cites this line).

35] *Many . . . oft* From *The Merchant of Venice*, 1.3.106.

46] *shady* B uses the adjective form of "shade" in order to achieve the rhyme with "lady" (43).

50] *My hands . . . or nearly* About EBB, B wrote on 19 August 1871, "All is best as it is—for her, & me too: I shall wash my hands in a minute, before I see her, as I trust to do" (*Dearest Isa*, 365). The "or nearly" probably refers to B's half-hearted proposal to Lady Ashburton, which he felt soiled his hands.

58] *mansionry* B apparently takes this word from *Macbeth:*

> This guest of summer,
> The temple-haunting marlet, does approve,
> By his lov'd mansionry, that the heaven's breath
> Smells wooingly here. . . .
>
> (1.6.3-6)

This passage is the only citation under "mansionry" in *OED* other than B's line, and the meaning is uncertain. The context in B suggests that the word designates a lasting dwelling.

59] *I weave but trellis-work* I.e., I aim for a less substantial love than the "Durable mansionry" (58) that his first love was.

71-72] *Ask else Penelope . . . in youth* Penelope, wife of Odysseus (Ulysses) in Homer's *The Odyssey* and representative of enduring faithfulness in married love, says to her husband after he has proved his identity: "the gods have given thee toil, who envied that we, remaining near one another, should be delighted with youth, and reach the threshold of old age" (*The Odyssey*, 23.210-12).

86] *avaunt* Obsolete term meaning *depart* (last citation in *OED* was for 1601).

89] *clipped* Archaic term meaning *embraced* (*OED*).

coyed Touched soothingly (*OED*, sense 2), or perhaps the obsolete sense 3: won over by "caresses or coaxing."

HERVÉ RIEL

Composition] According to the original MS in the Pierpont Morgan Library, the poem was finished on 30 September 1867 in Croisic, which is on the coast of Brittany. It was first published in the *Cornhill Magazine*, 23 (March 1871), 257-60. George Smith of Smith, Elder and Co., who was editor of the magazine at this time, paid B £100 for the poem, and B contributed the entire sum to the French Relief Fund. (There was much suffering in France as the result of a Prussian invasion.) The poem was included in the *Pacchiarotto* volume at Smith's request. But

Alfred Austin's being a German sympathizer in the war against France might have made a poem first published in support of the French seem to B a fitting inclusion. (See Hood, *Ltrs.*, 145, 173, 178 and "Of Pacchiarotto," 11.137-39n.)

Title]   Hervé Riel (born 12 April 1654, died 23 November 1729) was the Breton sailor who, after the English victory in the Battle of La Hogue in 1692, piloted the remaining 22 French ships to safety. B's source refers to this "signal service" as a "deed [that] had completely fallen into oblivion."

Source]   The main source is four pages copied in Sarianna Browning's hand from p. 67 of *Notes sur le Croisic* (Nantes, 1842), a guide-book by Caillo Jeune (Sarianna's MS is in the Armstrong Browning Library). B follows this source faithfully, varying from it in one detail, the result of a misreading of the French phrase *congé absolu*. B has the hero request only a day's vacation to see his wife as reward for his heroic service instead of having him request a permanent discharge; F. J. Furnivall pointed out to B the error, which the poet acknowledged: "You are undoubtedly right, and I have mistaken the meaning of the phrase . . . : an absolute discharge seems to approach in importance a substantial reward" (Letter of 20 December 1881, Peterson, 43-44). Then at the end of the material that Sarianna copied is an extract in B's hand, about half a page, from Gustave Grandpré's *Promenade au Croisic, suivie d'Iseul et Almanzor, ou la Grotte à Madame* (Paris, 1828), 3. 186, which refers to a French governmental commission formed to investigate Riel's role in the aftermath of the Battle of Hogue. The investigation found no evidence of Riel's heroic actions and thus concluded that the story was "only a fable." The next sentence in B's notes is not complete but concludes with "c.c" and connects in thought and syntax with Sarianna's notes. B includes Grandpré's source as Alexis Rochon's *Voyage à Madagascar, à Maroc et aux Indes orientales* (Paris, an x), 2. 38. B did not consult Rochon himself, for he would have noticed that Grandpré cites the wrong page number in his source.

1]   *the Hogue*   *La Hogue* is the cape at the northwestern tip of Normandy.
2]   *English fight . . . woe to France*   Fifty-six French vessels had been sent by Louis XIV in support of James II's bid to regain the English throne. The battle raged from 19 May to 24 May 1692. The French fleet was soundly defeated by 90 English and Dutch ships, thus securing William of Orange on the English throne. B does not mention the role of the Dutch.

5] *Saint-Malo . . . Rance* St.-Malo is a seaport in Brittany across the Gulf of St.-Malo from the Hogue and is the place of safety to which Hervé Riel guided the French ships not destroyed by the English (and the Dutch). The River Rance empties into the Gulf.

8] *Damfreville* Lieutenant General Marquis D'Amfreville was captain of the *Gaillard,* one of the ships destroyed at *La Hogue* (Philip Aubrey, *The Defeat of James Stuart's Armada* [Totowa, New Jersey: Rowman and Littlefield, 1979], 178). The notes that Sarianna copied refer to the 22 ships that Hervé Riel saved as the Damfreville division.

18] *'Formidable'* Sarianna's and B's notes refer to this as the ship of 92 guns that General Damfreville commanded, but according to Aubrey (see 1.8n) there was in fact no French ship by this name (see ship lists in Aubrey's Appendix).

20] *ticklish* Risky (*OED,* sense 5); perhaps the context also should bring to mind sense 2: "easily capsized."

30] *Plymouth Sound* A harbor on the coast of Devon.

32] *Damfreville* See 1.8n.

Breton Native of Brittany.

43] *pressed* "Forced to enlist" (*OED*).

Tourville Anne Hilarione de Constantin, Chevalier de Tourville, was admiral of the French fleet (Aubrey, 36, 84).

44] *Croisickese* A person from Le Croisic, a Breton village on a peninsula north of the River Loire.

46] *Malouins* Persons from St.-Malo.

49] *offing* "Position at a distance off the shore" (*OED*).

Grève The sandbanks at the mouth of the River Rance (see 1.5n).

disembrogues Flows into the open sea.

53] *Solidor* Sarianna's notes from Jeune refer to the port of Solidor at St.-Malo, and B's notes from Grandpré refer to "Port Solidor [as] a shelter against the attack of the enemy," but the name generally refers to a tower at St. Servan-sur-Mer, now in south St.-Malo.

56] *line* A "row of ships in a certain order" (*OED,* sense 21).

58] *'Formidable'* See 1.18n.

61] *Solidor . . . Grève* See 11.49n and 53n.

66-83] *Not a minute . . . too late* *The Athenæum* remarks on these lines: "To properly enjoy this, as is indeed the case with almost all that Mr. Browning has ever written, we must read it aloud, and then—to use a phrase as abominable as 'numpholeptos' or 'Aischulos'—the 'onomatopœa,' or lilt of the thing, becomes not so much evident as infectious" (22 July 1876, 101).

75] *profound* Vast depth.

86] *Grève* See 1.49n.

92] *rampired Solidor . . . Rance* *Rampired* is an archaic term meaning fortified by a rampart (*OED*). See 11.53n and 5n.

104, 113] *Damfreville* See l.8n.

108] *the King* Louis XIV, King of France from 1643 to 1715.

120] *Malo Roads to Croisic Point* The distance is about 100 miles.

124] *Belle Aurore* Jeanne Jubel, the daughter of a "Notary Royal" (solicitor), was Riel's second wife, whom he married on 23 October 1691, two years after the death of his first wife and cousin, Julienne Legal. Riel is buried with his second wife in the cemetery of the Church of Notre Dame de la Pitié in Le Croisic.

127-31] *Not . . . the man* Years after the publication of B's poem, however, the citizens of Le Croisic erected "an heroic bronze effigy of the Breton at his helm . . . on a high pedestal near the entrance to their . . . harbor" (Irvine and Honan, 421).

    head "The fore part of a ship . . ." (*OED*, sense 21).

    fishing-smack "A single-masted sailing-vessel, fore-and-aft rigged like a sloop or cutter . . ." (*OED*).

131] *wrack* Obsolete for *ruin* (*OED*).

132] *bore the bell* Took first place; the "phrase refers to the bell worn by the leading cow or sheep . . . of a drove or flock" (*OED*).

135] *Louvre* *Musée du Louvre*, the art museum in Paris that contains the most significant paintings and sculptures of France, including the collections of the kings of France.

A FORGIVENESS

Date] According to the Balliol manuscript, the poem was finished on 5 February 1876.

Title and Sources] The MS title, "Komm Spanisch!," which is Flemish for "How Spanish!," was meant to draw attention to the Spanish attitude in the poem, about which more later. The parenthetical name "Egmont," which on the MS appears just to the right of this original title, signifies one of the great families of Flanders. B must have intended to suggest that the protagonist was Flemish yet conducted himself as a Spanish aristocrat might have done. The name "Egmont" might also have been meant to suggest a prominent figure who was devoted to serving his society, which is true of the poem's chief character. The original MS title also appears on the MS table of contents; this suggests that B did not change the title until he was reading the page proofs.

    All efforts to find a historical basis for the poem's narrative have been unsuccessful. DeVane suggests that B might have heard such a story in 1875 when he travelled to Antwerp to visit his son, who was studying painting and sculpting there. In Antwerp B might have seen a statue of Lamoral Egmont, done by Charles-Auguste Fraiken (1817-93) in 1865 (see *Hbk.*, 409).

Literary sources for "A Forgiveness" are evident. B owes much to the honor tragedies of the Spanish dramatist Calderón de la Barca (1600-81), especially to his *El Medico de su Honra (The Physician of His Honor* [1635]), which like "A Forgiveness" begins with a husband's entering his house by an unexpected way and observing his wife's "lover" escaping through a garden. In Calderon's plays honor is "the private banner or escutcheon that a man hung up in the temple of his ego, the symbol of his pride and self-respect." It was axiomatic that the Spanish aristocrat of the 17th century allow no sullying of his honor, either real or imagined; any offence required the death of the offender. In *The Physician of His Honor*, Gutierre, the wronged husband, remarks: ". . . men like me / do not require to see it; it is enough to imagine, / to suspect . . . ," and later on he adds: ". . . honor / can only be washed with blood." The code of *pundonor* or *puntillo* prescribed "the finest points of conduct or etiquette," especially in sexual offences. "To preserve his honour, a man might feel authorized to kill both his wife and the person he suspected of being her lover, whether he had proofs of her infidelity or not" (Gerald Brenan, *The Literature of the Spanish People* [New York: Meredian, 1957], 280, 281). The main character in "A Forgiveness" obviously acts in accord with the provisions of *pundonor*.

That B was in fact familiar with Calderón is confirmed variously. Norman Maccoll dedicated his edition of Calderón's *Select Plays* (London, 1888) to B, and Archbishop Trench presented a copy of Richard Trench's *Essay on the Life and Genius of Calderón* (London, 1880) to B. Finally, B's quotation from Calderón that precedes his "Scene in the Building of the Inquisitors At Antwerp" suggests that he was very familiar with the Spanish dramatist at least as early as 1872 and further establishes a Flemish-Spanish connection in B's mind.

"A Forgiveness" owes something as well to Dante Gabriel Rossetti's "A Last Confession" (1870), which is also a dramatic monologue. Though there are obvious differences between these two poems, there are certain elements in B's poem that seem likely to be derived from Rossetti's: the speaker in each is a man devoted to serving the state to the neglect of the woman he loves; one woman proves to be and the other pretends to be an unfaithful wife; each speaker kills the woman he loves; each poem takes place in a confessional where the murder is confessed; and in each case the murder weapon is a finely crafted knife.

5] *monk* This monk is also a priest, since he is administering sacramental confession.

14] *in heaven's behoof* The use of *in* with *behoof* is apparently a result of confusion with *behalf*.

22] *silvery* With a "silvery sound" (*OED*).

clockhouse An obsolete term for a house built for a public clock or the steeple that contains such a clock (*OED*).

23] *postern-gate* A side way.

29] *porphyry vase* One made of a costly purple stone and highly polished.

31] *in ambuscade* Lying in ambush.

35] *closelier* Not in *OED*.

38] *thrids* Variant of *threads*.

41] *you know* This phrase is more than an expletive here, because the priest, we later find out, is the man whose actions the speaker is describing.

44] *train* Sequence of events.

74] *toils* Nets to entrap (*OED*).

91-96] *I concern . . . such* Although duelling was the usual way to restore one's good name under the Spanish system of honor, a man of high standing could not duel with a person of inconsequential social status (Brenan, 281), such as the intruder here is depicted as being.

97-100] *Hidalgo . . . Mambrino's helm* The speaker told his wife that marrying her was like Don Quixote's (Hidalgo's) taking a brass barber's basin for Mambrino's helmet, the magic helmet of a pagan king in the *Orlando Furioso* by Ariosto. The speaker is, however, different from Don Quixote in that he has awakened from his mistaken perception (see *Don Quixote*, Book 1, Ch. 21).

101] *God's . . . cup* The chalice used in the Mass.

102-03] *Why should . . . as gold* The husband asked his wife why he should blame her baseness when she could be polished up to look like gold to everyone but himself and thus still be useful in keeping him from being embarrassed before the world.

105-07] *Hidalgo . . . the basin's worth* See 11.97-100n.

110-13] *Still should . . . I meant* The husband repaired his honor by punishing his wife with absolute silence until death, a refined cruelty in keeping with *pundonor*.

124-32] *The world had . . . sympathetic rapture* There is an analogue to this pretense of affection between man and wife and the sudden dropping of the pretense in John Dryden's *Marriage a La Mode* (1672) 3.2. B's character's use of the terminology of the theater encourages the reader to see the parallel to Dryden's play.

126]   *enarming*   Variant of *inarming* (embracing).

137]   *a place like mine*   I.e., a position of leadership in government.

163]   *saloon*   A variant of *salon*, a large and lofty apartment serving as one of the principal reception rooms in a palace or other great house, used only with reference to continental countries (*OED*).

183]   *annoy*   Poetic for *annoyance* (*OED*).

190]   *bower and hall*   A bower is "an inner apartment . . . as distinguished from the 'hall' or large public room, in ancient mansions . . ." (*OED*).

194]   *bestowment*   In the sense of "gift conferred," first used in the Victorian period (*OED*).

195]   *deck*   Adorn with ornamental garments.

   golden-fleeced   Invested into the Order of the Golden Fleece, an order of knighthood instituted at Bruges in 1430 by Philip the Good, Duke of Burgundy. By B's time the right of investiture belonged to the kings of Spain and Austria. The knights wear a golden fleece.

197]   *symbolled*   A Victorian form meaning "symbolized" (see *OED*).
   chain   Chain of office or other mark of distinction.

201]   *arquebuss*   Spelt *arquebas* or *harquebus in OED*: "The early type of portable gun, varying in size from a small cannon to a musket, which on account of its weight was, when used on the field, supported upon a tripod, trestle, or other 'carriage,' and afterwards upon a forked 'rest.' The name in German and Flemish meant literally 'hook-gun,' from the hook cast along with the piece, by which it was fastened to the 'carriage' . . ." (*OED*). Johnson's *Dictionary* spells the word *arquebuse* or *harquebuss*.

223]   *What physician shrinks*   A direct reference to Calderón's *The Physician of His Honor* (see note at *Title and Sources*). Like Calderón's Gutierre, B's wronged husband prescribes the proper course of treatment for the removal of the stain upon his honor.

248-77]   *Horror coquetting . . . right to aim*   The description of these "arms of Eastern workmanship" is based upon the collection of 27 weapons bequeathed to B by his friend Ernest Benzon. Kelley and Coley catalogue this collection, which includes a weapon with "Green jade hilt carved as a bird pecking at fruit," a dagger with "damascened blade, and ivory grip damascened and jewelled," a Nepalese kukri with "[d]ouble fluted and engraved blade, hilt inlaid with mother-o'-pearl," and others apposite to this passage (see 11.504-07).

250]   *Yataghan*   "A sword of Mohammedan countries, having a handle without a guard and often a double-curved blade" (*OED*).
   kandjar   Variant of *khanjar*, an Eastern dagger.

256]   *bicker*   See "Numpholeptos," 1.101n. *OED* cites this line.

265]   *diapered*   Surface decoration composed of a small repeated pattern such as lozenges or squares.

269]   *water-purlings*   Decorative motif like the curls made by the motion of water.

281]   *statesfolk*   Obsolete term, meaning "person of (great) estate or position" *(OED)*.

295]   *At instance of*   Archaic term meaning "at the instigation of" *(OED)*.

299-304]   *As no leap . . . Was quietly apparent*   The speaker coolly calculates the precise way to follow the formula dictated by *pundonor.*

305]   *porphyry vase*   See 1.29n.

308]   *Double-dyed*   Deeply stained.

312]   *to your cost*   To your detriment.

334]   *broidered*   Ornamented with needlework.

335]   *emblazoned*   Decorated with an armorial device.

336]   *scutcheon*   Escutcheon; in heraldry a term sometimes employed to express the entire coat of arms, sometimes only the field (i.e., the whole surface of the shield or escutcheon, which is the ground upon which tinctures, furs, ordinaries, and charges are presented), upon which the arms are emblazoned.

348]   *ropes of sand*   A rope of sand is "something having no coherence or binding power" *(OED)*.

372]   *poignard*   Variant of *poniard,* dagger.

387]   *erst*   Earlier (obsolete).

396]   *grate*   Of the confessional.

CENCIAJA

Date and Composition]   According to the Balliol MS, the poem was finished on 28 April 1876. Kenneth L. Knickerbocker argues that B probably wrote the poem in three days' time, beginning on the day after he finished "Numpholeptos" ("Browning's *Cenciaja*," *Philological Quarterly,* 13 [October 1934], 390).

Title]   The title alludes to Shelley's play *The Cenci.* B explained in a letter to Buxton Forman that the "depreciative termination" makes a word that means "a bundle of rags: a trifle" (Hood, *Ltrs.,* 174).

Epigraph]   B explained to Forman that the Italian proverb means " 'every poor creature will be for pressing into the company of his betters,' and I used it to deprecate the notion that I intended anything of the kind" (Hood, *Ltrs.,* 174). Mrs. Orr translates the quotation as follows: "every trifle will press in for notice among worthier matters" (*Hbk.*, 269).

Sources] "Cenciaja" focuses on the case of Paolo Santa Croce, who killed his mother on the last day of Beatrice Cenci's trial for the murder of her father in 1599. Paolo's action affected the outcome of the trial upon which Shelley's *The Cenci* (1819) was based. B's poem explains why the Pope, who had been expected to pardon Beatrice, resolved suddenly to condemn her to death. B's letter to Forman suggests that he consulted *The Old Yellow Book*, which "has a reference to the reason given by Farinacci, the advocate of the Cenci, of his failure in the defence of Beatrice . . ." (Hood, *Ltrs.*, 174). Korg suggests that B also consulted Farinacci's *Dissertation on the Statutes of the Cities of Italy*, ed. George Bowyer (1838), and B might have obtained a few details for his poem from a MS on the Cenci affair that he had borrowed from Sir John Simeon. But the main source is a manuscript in the British Library, *Giustizia fatta da Onofrio Santa Croce per aver acconsentito at Matricidio commesso da Paolo Suo Fratello in persona della Signora Costanza loro Madre* (MS. Add. 19884). B must have had this MS open before him as he wrote "Cenciaja," for he uses almost every detail of it. See Kenneth L. Knickerbocker, "Browning's *Cenciaja*," *Philological Quarterly*, 13 (October 1934), 390-400, which provides a table that illustrates B's use of this MS. In spite of the letter to Buxton Forman (Hood, *Ltrs.*, 174-75) that suggests otherwise, Sir Simeon's pamphlet, *Contemporaneous Narrative of the Trial and Execution of the Cenci*, published in *Miscellanies of the Philobiblon Society* (1857-58), is not a source for "Cenciaja."

1-14] *Shelley . . . fulfilled* In Shelley's *The Cenci*, the evil Count Francesco Cenci had committed innumerable crimes against society and his family. In 4.4 of the play, the legate of Clement VIII, pope from 1592-1605, arrived with orders for the immediate execution of the Count, only to find that he had just been murdered. Beatrice, who had apparently been raped by her father, had, in alliance with her brother Giacomo and her step-mother Lucretia, killed the Count. The three were tried and sentenced to death by the Pope. Beatrice's brother Bernardo and Cardinal Camillo sought to obtain a pardon from Clement, but another case influenced his decision. B's poem quotes in part and inaccurately Camillo's account of the pope's response to his and Bernardo's importunings:

And he replied: "Paolo Santa Croce
Murdered his mother yester evening,

> And he is fled. Parricide grows so rife
> That soon, for some just cause no doubt, the young
> Will strangle us all, dozing in our chairs.
> Authority, and power, and hoary hair
> Are grown crimes capital. You are my nephew.
> You come to ask their pardon; stay a moment;
> Here is their sentence; never see me more
> Till, to the letter, it be all fulfilled.''
>
> *(The Cenci, 5.4.18-27)*

15-16] *verbosity / That lies before me* The Italian manuscript that was B's source (see note above).

22] *Titian* Painting by Titian, also known as Tiziano Vecellio (c. 1488-1576), the most famous painter of the Venetian School.

27] *She wears . . . displays the palm* There is no known painting by Titian that fits this description. The display of a palm frond, however, refers generically to depictions of martyrs.

33] *Marchese dell' Oriolo* Or Onofrio Santa Croce, the innocent elder brother of Paolo Santa Croce. *Marchese* in Italian means *marquis.*

37] *those three words—she must die* In *The Cenci*, Cardinal Camillo recounts that after his appeal on behalf of Beatrice and her family, the Pope

> . . . turned to me then, looking deprecation,
> And said these three words, coldly: 'They must die.'
>
> (5.4.13-14)

42] *Vicar-upon-earth* Title applied to the pope.

49] *Marchesine Costanza* Paolo Santa Croce's mother, whom he murdered.

66] *Hydroptic* A term unused since the 17th century for *dropsical,* until B revived it for "A Grammarian's Funeral" (1.95).

80] *primogeniture* The first-born's right of succession and inheritance.

82] *Subiaco* An Italian town in Rome Province, Lazio region, on the Aniene River.

91] *coëtaneous* Contemporary.

97] *Basilicate* An ancient kingdom of southern Italy.

106] *Count Francesco Cenci's death* See 11.1-14n.

110] *Princes Massimi* Of one of the four branches of the ancient and princely Roman family Massimo.

113] *Beatrice's pardon* See 11.1-14n.

117] *Cardinal Aldobrandini* Giovanni Francesco Aldobrandini, 21-year-old nephew of Pope Clement VIII, had just prior to the time of the action of this poem been promoted to general of the papal army. In 1598 Giovanni Dolfin, Venetian Ambassador to the Court of Clement VIII, described Aldobrandini as "of very noble nature, and as amiable and gracious as words can tell. The whole court follows his lead, and with good reason, for he is of utmost authority with the Pope and by him most tenderly loved" (Corrado Rice, *Beatrice Cenci*, trans. Morris Bishop and H. L. Stuart [London: William Heinemann, 1926], 1.241, 243).

123] *perquisition* An official domiciliary search for a person, incriminating documents, or other evidence.

132] *lynx-eyed* Keen-sighted.

142] *the Orsini* An old, illustrious, and powerful Roman family, first taking on great significance with the election of Giacinto Orsini as Pope Celestine III in the 12th century. With him began the family's territorial fortunes.

143] *Monte Giordano* The legendary medieval fortress of Giordano Orsini stands on this small, artificial hill. The castle was in the Orsini family until 1688.

145] *Barigel* A *barigello* or *baregello* is a chief constable.

148] *Taverna* Ferdinando Taverna was a Milanese who was appointed Governor of Rome on 1 May 1599 and then was made Cardinal on 9 June 1604 by Clement VIII (Rice, *Beatrice Cenci*, 2.28, 248).

150] *president* The chief judge of court.

153] *keep the bench* Conduct the court of justice.

156] *by-work* "An obsolete term for accessory and subsidiary work" (*OED*, sense 2).

158] *connivency* Connivance (*OED* cites this line as the only instance since 1689).

161] *The Hat and Purple* A cardinal's hat. In early usage *purple* signified various shades of red; here it refers to the scarlet color of the official dress of a cardinal in the Roman Church (see *OED*).

162] *diligence* An obsolete term meaning "an act of diligence" (Last citation of this sense in *OED* is 1652).

164] *Purple and the Hat* See 1.161n.

176] *Tordinona-prison* This prison is on the left bank of the Tiber between the river and the street that still bears the name Tordinona. The tower, built in the 13th century by the Orsini (see 1.142n), was converted to a prison in the 14th century and by the beginning of the

15th century was known as "the pope's prison." Buildings grew up around the original tower and eventually formed a vast *palazzo* with a central court (Rice, *Beatrice Cenci*, 1.270).

177] *a vault . . . is ice* The secret inner section of Tordinona-prison reserved for the custody of a person arrested for a grave offence (Pasquale Adinolfi, *Il canale di Ponte e le sue circostanti parti* [Narni, 1860], 12).

183] *nuthatch Sitta europaea* is a small bird that has an unusual way of cracking nuts: he places the nut in a crevice in the bark of a tree and then hammers with his bill till the shell breaks.

203] *jot and tittle* The least part or point. Cf. Matthew 5:18: "For verily I say unto you, Till heaven and earth pass, one jot or one tittle shall in no wise pass from the law, till all be fulfilled."

220] *Advocate* The technical title in countries that retain the Roman law for one "whose profession it is to plead the cause of any one in a court of justice . . ." (*OED*).

227] *Who sins must die* Cf. Marlowe, *Doctor Faustus* (1604), 1.1: "The reward of sin is death" (1.40); "Why then, belike we must sin, and so consequently die" (1.45); and Romans 6:23.

228] *Marchese* See 1.33n.

229] *concourse* Gathering of people (*OED*, sense 1).

230] *Place Saint Angelo . . . Bridge* An open area beside Castle Sant' Angelo, originally the Mausoleum of Hadrian and later, in the middle ages, made the citadel of Rome, adjacent to the Ponte Sant' Angelo, which was built by Hadrian as the approach to his mausoleum; the usual place for executions.

242] *privity* "The fact of being privy to . . . ; participation in the knowledge of something . . . secret, usually implying concurrence or consent . . ." (*OED*).

249] dotation Endowment.

257] *Taverna* See 1.148n.

260] Taverna's cap See 11.148n and 161n.

266] *Marquisate* The status of a marquis.

280] *gage* Pledge.

288] *wight* Archaic for *person.*

296-98] *So ends . . . delinquency* B quotes directly from *Giustizia fatta da Onofrio Santa Croce per aver acconsentito at Matricidio . . .* (see note at *Source* above).

300] *Victor rules . . . in Rome* On 17 March 1861 Victor Emmanuel II was proclaimed by Parliament King of all Italy after leading his army through papal territory and annexing Marches and Umbria.

FILIPPO BALDINUCCI ON THE PRIVILEGE OF BURIAL

Date and Composition]   According to the Balliol manuscript, B fin-
ished this poem on 19 May 1876. A letter of 25 July 1876 to Edmund
Gosse indicates that this poem was the last in the *Pacchiarotto* volume
to be written; it was in fact composed in a hurry "while the earlier
sheets were passing through the press . . ." (Hood, *Ltrs.*, 174). B wrote
the following in the right margin: "Print this poem *the last but one* in
the volume"—i.e. immediately before "Cowslip Wine," which was the
original title of "Epilogue."

Title and Source]   Filippo Baldinucci (c. 1624-96) was an Italian art
historian and author of *Delle Notizie de' professori del disegno da
Cimabue in qua* (1681-1728), a work useful to B on many occasions as a
supplement to Vasari. But B also used Baldinucci as an object of satire:
in this poem he satirizes the man for his anti-Semitism. Specifically, B
draws upon Baldinucci's treatment of Lodovico Buti, a Florentine
painter (see *Notizie* [Firenze, 1846], 3.420-24), for the first part of the
poem (stanzas 1-36); and stanzas 37-58 are "his own invention."

Subtitle]   The reminiscence is that of Baldinucci's uncle.

1-3] *No, boy . . . good old man*   The dramatic device involving
Baldinucci and his uncle is not in *Notizie.*
10] *Florence*   Having been since the middle ages a center for intellec-
tual life, Florence is an ironical setting for the ignorance and prejudice
of the poem's speaker.
11] *scathe*   Harm.
12] *crew*   A derogatory term for persons classed together according to
common characteristics (*OED*, sense 4).
14] *Arno's pranks*   The Arno is the main river in Tuscany and flows
through Florence; it has a long history of overflowing its banks.
22-24] *laws . . . wholly unmolested*   After the Reformation, Jews
were treated more severely than before. In 1555 Pope Paul IV issued a
bull "imposing certain disabilities upon them." In 1584 Pope Gregory
XIII required Jews to attend conversion sermons. It was not until the
19th century that all of the anti-Jewish laws were abolished (Korg, 133).
26] *San Frediano*   Porta San Frediano, at the junction of Viale Pe-
trarca, Via Pisana, and Via San Frediano, is one of the old gates still in
use today.
27] *Blessed Olivet*   About a quarter of a mile from Porta San Frediano
on the Via di Monte Oliveto is the Monastery of Monte Oliveto, which
gets its name from the Monte Oliveto Maggiore near Siena, which was

itself named after the Mount of Olives running north and south on the east side of Jerusalem. The beautiful church was erected in 1472; it has a fresco of *The Last Supper* by Sodoma, but most of the pictures were removed to Florence before the monastery became a military hospital in B's day (Edward Hutton, *Country Walks About Florence* [London: Methuen, 1908], 90-91).

28-29] *A wayside ground . . . Jews* The Jewish cemetery, Cimitero Israelitico, was at the foot of Monte Oliveto (Orr, *Hbk.,* 281).

48] *Grew corn . . . grapes for vat* The Christian farmer grows the basic natural requirements for the Mass.

53] *Buti* Lodovico Buti or Butti (c. 1550-1611) was a Florentine painter responsible for many frescoes at Rome and at Florence. Also at Pisa he painted for the Conventual Church *The Miracle of the Loaves and Fishes* (about 1590) (John Murray, *Handbook for Travellers in Northern Italy* [London, 1847], 462).

54-56] *A holy picture . . . sky by angels* According to Baldinucci, *Notizie,* this painting is one of many copies that Buti made of the painting by Andrea del Sarto (3.420-21).

57-62] *Which shrine . . . Mary's triumph* "A path ascending [Mount Oliveto] skirted [the] upper end [of the Jewish burial ground], and at an angle of this stood a shrine with one side blank, the other adorned by a painting of the Virgin Mary. The painting was intended to catch the eye of all believers who approached from the neighbouring city-gate . . . and was therefore so turned that it overlooked the Jewish cemetery at the same time" (Orr. *Hbk.,* 281). Actually B's speaker has the picture away from the public way and situated so as to annoy the Jews on purpose.

63] *mummeries* Religious rituals regarded as silly (*OED,* sense 2).

73] *phyz* Variant of *phiz*, colloquial abbreviation for physiognomy: face.

74] *brave* Splendid (Apparently a literary revival in the 19th century [*OED*])

80] *Pilate* Pontius Pilate (d. after A.D. 36), Roman procurator of Judaea who oversaw the death sentence of Christ.

96] *dotes* Talks foolishly or stupidly.

114] fare Archaic for *travel* (*OED*).

137] kind What is natural (obsolete, except as a conscious archaism [*OED*]).

143] ducats Coins, sometimes gold and sometimes silver, used in Italy.

144] Avouch Obsolete term for *declare*.

152] *cut up* Censured, criticized (*OED,* sense 59g).

166] Master Buti's brush See 1.53n.

176] *Esaias* Alternate spelling of Isaiah.

stiff-necked A Hebrew idiom literally translated "hard of neck," found in Exodus 32:9, 33:3 and 5, and Deuteronomy 9:6 and 13. A forceful variation of the set phrase is found in Isaiah 48:4: "Because I knew that thou are obstinate, and thy neck is an iron sinew. . . ."

178] *poke* "A pocket worn on the person" (obsolete and archaic [*OED*]).

195] *hoarding* Fencing made of boards.

198] *sluices over* Drenches and scours.

206] *High Priest* Referring to the discussion following Percy A. Barnett's paper of 25 November 1887 delivered before The Browning Society, B wrote to F. J. Furnivall as follows: "It was remarked that I mistook a Rabbi for a High Priest! This comes of forgetting that one writes dramatically. The speaker, Baldinucci, is a typically ignorant Tuscan, and makes the gross mistake already noted in Arbuthnot's *Martinus Scriblerus*—of whom it is said, at the very beginning: 'Those who had never seen a Jesuit took him for one, while others thought him rather to be some High Priest of the Jews' " (Letter of 12 February 1888, Peterson, 150). B slightly misquotes John Arbuthnot's *Martinus Scriblerus* (1741). There is, in fact, only one Jewish High Priest, and he is in authority at the temple in Jerusalem (L. F. Hartman, *Encyclopedic Dictionary of the Bible* [1963]).

The account of the burial of the "High Priest's" wife that follows was not in B's source, *Notizie*. Baldinucci merely remarks that the Jews discovered Buti's *Crucifixion*, and he records their response.

222] *pully-hauly* The action of pulling and hauling.

223] *quick* Field-grasses and weeds (*OED*).

231] *phyz* See l.73n.

242-43] *to make quit / Of* Obsolete expression meaning "to dispose of" (*OED*).

243] *Christ the Crucified* In *Notizie* Baldinucci writes, "[Buti] was . . . commissioned to do the figure of Christ crucified which we now see in a corner of the wall outside the door of the Church of San Friano" (3.422).

244] *biters bit* A biter is "one who amuses himself at another's expense; a sharper" and in this sense is obsolete except in "the biter bit," a traditional quotation (*OED*).

246] *shooting* Jutting (*OED*, sense 10).

248] *verjuice* "The acid juice of green or unripe grapes, crab-apples, or other sour fruit" (*OED*).

250-51] *A-top af wall . . . rare* In *Notizie*, Baldinucci says nothing of the farmer's and the painter's lying in wait to abuse the Jews.

252] *rates* Chides.

264] glut Gratify to the full (*OED*, sense 2).

268] Ghetto "The quarters in a city, chiefly in Italy, to which the Jews were restricted" (*OED*).

270] chaps Colloquial for "a person of whom a contemptuous opinion is entertained" (see *OED*, sense 2).

288] *my Book* Baldinucci does not record it in his *Notizie.*

289ff.] *For, next day* . . . The episode that begins with this line was not in Baldinucci's *Notizie.*

295] *he-Jew* This formation is contemptuous and is usually used of lower animals, as in *he-goat* (see *OED*).

baulks Variant of *balks,* meaning *frustrates* (*OED*).

307] *tub* B anticipates the vulgar colloquialism for a corpulent person.

311] *speeds* Furthers (archaic [*OED*]).

334] nor . . . thews Neither bone nor muscular development.

352] *Saul changed to Paul* Saul of Tarsus, who had persecuted the followers of Christ, was converted on the road to Damascus and then acquired the name Paul (Acts 9:1-8).

353] dog-Jew Cf. Shakespeare, *The Merchant of Venice:* 'You call me misbeliever, cut-throat dog, / And spit upon my Jewish gaberdine . . ." (1.3.111-12; also see 1.129).

364] *in a trice* In an instant (obsolete [*OED*]).

370] trow Suppose (*OED*, sense 4b [obsolete]).

377] I remembered me This reflexive form meaning "I reflected upon myself" is obsolete (*OED*, sense 5).

385] issue join Proceed to argument on a particular point (*OED*, 13b).

397-400] Leda, Ganymede . . . Jupiter in every shape In Greek mythology, Leda (daughter of Thestius), Ganymede (son of Tros), and Antiope (daughter of the river-god Asopus) were all raped by Zeus (Jupiter) who appeared to them in various shapes—to Leda as a swan, to Ganymede as an eagle, and to Antiope as a satyr. (There, of course, is no story in which Zeus appears as an ape.) These Greek stories were depicted in Renaissance art (e.g., Andrea del Sarto's *Leda* in the Borghese Gallery and Leonardo da Vinci's *Leda and the Swan* in the National Gallery, London).

402] *Eminence* A cardinal's title of honor, granted by Pope Urban VIII in 1630.

402-08] *though Titan's . . . called his god* Appreciation by artists, patrons, and collectors for pagan as well as Christian paintings was characteristic of the Renaissance. The mixing of pagan with Christian images was a practice strenuously objected to by A. W. N. Pugin in *Contrasts* (1836, 1841). Titian (c. 1488-1576), the Venetian master, for example, painted both *Bacchanal* and *Christ Crowned with Thorns;* and see B's "The Bishop Orders His Tomb at Saint Praxed's Church" (4.189).

The Name God, according to the ancient Jewish mode of expression (see *OED*).

419-21] *Leda . . . Jupiter* Titian did not paint a Leda, though his *Danae* bears many similarities to *Leda and the Swan* after Michelangelo. Another Leda and the Swan, almost a miniature and which must have been meant for a jewel box or toilet box, painted on one of two panels (the other panel holds *Girl with a Baby and a Youth*), has been wrongly attributed to Titian (see *All the Paintings of Titian* [1965]).

434-37] *Your picture . . . as a picture* Ryals says, "Browning's point is that a work of art must not be viewed in a limited context of traditional 'meaning' and 'instruction' but should be valued for itself" (140). This view runs counter to the prevailing Victorian aesthetic that made subject-matter a crucial issue in judging the artistic merit of a painter, as in Ruskin's *Modern Painters:* "The Habitual choice of sacred subjects, such as the Nativity, Transfiguration, Crucifixion (if the choice be sincere), implies that the painter has a natural disposition to dwell on the highest thoughts of which humanity is capable; it constitutes him so far forth a painter of the highest order . . ." (Vol. 3, Part 4, Ch. 3).

439-40] *Master Buti's . . . flaws ought* The rabbi's son underscores the point that paintings do not derive artistic value from their "sacred subjects" by allowing that the flaws in Buti's religious painting will be laughed at as they ought to be.

452] *Or . . . or* Used in the sense of "either . . . or" (poetic).

458] *pishes* Depreciates by saying "pish" (*OED*). Cf. "At the Mermaid," 1.128n.

poohs Expresses contemptuous disdain for.

462] *In Mary's . . . one more sword* As *Our Lady of Dolours* Mary is represented in Christian art with seven swords, emblems of her seven sorrows, piercing her breast. The seven sorrows are Simeon's Prophecy, the Flight into Egypt, Christ Missed, the Betrayal, the Crucifixion, the Taking Down from the Cross, and the Ascension, when she was left alone. Cf. "Up at a Villa—Down in the City," 11.51-52.

464] *O Lord . . . Lord* Cf. Thomas Babington Macaulay's "The Marriage of Tirzah and Ahirad":

> From all the angelic ranks goes forth a groan,
> 'How long, O Lord, how long?'

> The still small voice makes answer, 'Wait and see,
> > O sons of glory, what the end shall be.'

Also cf. Zechariah 1:12; Psalms 6:3, 9:5; Isaiah 6:11; Habakkuk 1:2; and Revelation 6:10. This line in B's poem might be understood as Baldinucci's inadvertent self-inflicted jab at his own anti-Semitism.

EPILOGUE

Date] According to the Balliol MS, the poem was completed on 24 April 1876.

Title] The change in title from "Cowslip Wine" to "Epilogue" was a last-minute one. The original title remained in the MS table of contents after B had changed the title on the poem's MS.

Subtitle] From 1.807 of Aristophanes, *The Plutus*, spoken by Cario: "and filled are the jars of wine, dark and fragrant."

Source] The idea of identifying poetry with wine is a long-standing literary convention. More specifically B draws upon EBB's "Wine of Cyprus" (1844), and he begins "Epilogue" with the 108th line of his wife's poem, omitting the initial conjunction and the punctuation: "And the poets poured us wine?" B pursues the metaphor of poetry as wine throughout the poem. And, as EBB's poem is a survey of the Greek poets, so is B's a survey of the varieties of English poetry.

Another source might be the sort of criticism that B received in *The Graphic*, 4 (23 September 1871), 302, which in reviewing *Balaustion*, observed that B "has no gift to make him a lyrical poet. It is power and not sweetness, massive strength and not tenderness, grandeur and not grace, which are the distinct and distinguishing attributes of his mind. . . . Whenever Mr. Browning has attempted to render literally the choral utterances of Euripides he has given us brass for gold in exchange." In "Epilogue," B makes an argument for the incompatibility of strength and sweetness in poetry.

6] *screw* Screw-press, for extracting the juice of the grape. The analogy being made between wine and poetry suggests that the term also refers to a screw-type printing press.

9] *cup—stark strength* Powerful poetry, according to B's metaphor.

19] *rathe* Early. Cf. Milton's "Lycidas," 1.142.

20] *grass in swathe* Mown grass lying on the ground.

35] *potable* Drinkable.

37] *smatch* Taste.

42] *ticket* Label.

55]   *purled*   Bubbled up.

61]   *Pindar and Aeschylus*   Pindar (c. 523-442 B.C.) was a Greek lyric poet who gained tremendous recognition early on in his life. Many victors in the Olympic Games employed Pindar to celebrate their accomplishments in poetry. Aeschylus (525-456 B.C.) was one of the most acclaimed Greek tragedians, having written *Prometheus Bound, Agamemnon,* and many others.

63]   *bloomy*   "Blooming, in the beauty or flower of youth" (*OED*).

67]   *attar-gul*   The full Persian for the "fragrant, volatile, essential oil obtained from the petals of the rose," first used by Byron in *The Bride of Abydos* (1813). The only citation in *OED* other than Byron is to B's use here.

70]   *Shakespeare and Milton*   See 11.82n and 90n.

73-74]   *paid myself . . . French say well*   The French phrase is *payer quelquun de paroles, de mots,* which means "to put someone off with fine words."

75]   *bowsed*   Variant of *boused:* guzzled (*OED* cites this line).

77]   *pottle-deep*   Of the depth of a pottle, which is half a gallon.

78]   *toped*   Drank.

82]   *forty barrels with Shakespeare's brand*   These barrels are probably the 37 plays (not including *The Two Noble Kinsmen,* which has only recently been included in collected editions of Shakespeare's works), *Venus and Adonis, The Rape of Lucrece,* and the sonnets.

83]   *abroach*   Pierced so as to yield liquor (*OED*).

90]   *four big butts . . . Milton's brew*   These butts (casks for ale with a capacity of about 108 gallons) surely allude to *Paradise Lost, Paradise Regained, Samson Agonistes,* and the fourth is probably *Comus.*

94]   *Embellied*   B's coinage contributes to the alliteration of "butts" and "bungs" (see 1.90). Not in *OED*.

95]   *fig*   Something of little value.

98]   *the deuce*   A slang term used as an intensifier (see *OED*, sense c).

101]   *gust*   Flavor.

102]   *racy*   Said of wine, referring to excellent taste, flavor or quality (*OED*).

108]   *for the nonce*   For the time being.

116]   *tun*   Large cask of wine.

117]   *chaps*   "The jaws as unitedly forming the mouth," ordinarily used of animals and humorously of human beings (*OED*).

124]   *Frothed flagon*   Caused the flagon's contents to foam up.

126]   *spilth*   That which is spilled.

133]   *dwarf's-lap*   Slang for a small, weak drink (*OED*).

135]   *smutch*   Smudge.

143] *Koh-i-noor* A large and magnificent diamond, from the famous Indian diamond that became one of the British Crown jewels when Punjab was annexed in 1849 (*OED*).

145] *pulse in might* Cf. "The Bishop Orders His Tomb at St. Praxed's Church" (1.30), where the bishop speaks of a "red wine of a mighty pulse." *OED* does not contain the term *pulse* in B's sense; James F. Loucks (*Robert Browning's Poetry* [New York: Norton, 1979]), however, defines it as "Pulp of the grape."

146] *must* "New wine; the juice of the grape either unfermented or before the fermentation is completed" (*OED*).

150] *proof* "The standard of strength of distilled alcoholic liquors" (*OED*).

153] *Man's thoughts . . . hates* These are the "grapes" from which B makes his strong wine.

158] *Earth's yield . . . the Dark Blue Sea's* B expresses scorn for those who prefer poetry like Byron's. Cf. *The Corsair,* which begins:

> O'er the glad waters of the dark blue sea,
> Our thoughts as boundless, and our souls as free. . . .
>
> (11.1-2)

159] *lay, pray, bray* In ridiculing those who prefer a poetry of the sea rather than of the earth, B alludes to the poor grammar of Byron's "Childe Harold's Pilgrimage" (1818), Canto 4, stanza 180, which concludes with the ocean's being apostrophized as the force that sends man

> . . . shivering in thy playful spray
> And howling, to his Gods, where haply lies
> His petty hope in some near port or bay,
> And dashest him again to earth:—there let him lay.

Cf. B's *Fifine at the Fair* (1872), where the speaker also attacks Byron's philosophy and grammar in a long passage that contains this same line of Byron's: "Go curse, i' the poultry yard, his kind: 'there let him lay' . . ." (67.1125). *The Times* felt

> compelled to notice [this] most ill-advised sneer which Mr. Browning turns out of his way to bestow upon Byron. The stanzas of the address to the ocean at the end of *Childe Harold* jar with Mr. Browning's philosophy, and he derides it in terms which come ill from any poet to another, and very ill from the author of these crabbed couplets, which few will ever read, to the singer of those grand verses that have stirred the souls of millions of Englishmen. . . . It is both a pity and a mistake that Mr. Browning should with hard words and small jokes so assail another poet, throwing petty darts at a passage of poetry which, for all its bad grammar, teaches us

that in every word and in its sublimest flights the English tongue may be so written that it can be read and understood, not merely by students and experts but by ordinary Englishmen.

("Two Poems By Robert Browning," 2 January 1873, 5)

Also see "Robert Browning's Attack on Lord Byron," *Public Opinion,* 23 (11 January 1873), 47. It would appear that such criticism prompted B to make this renewed assault upon Byron's poetry in "Epilogue," referring to the same passage containing Byron's misuse of *lay.*

In a letter of 16 August 1873 to Annie Egerton Smith, B wrote:

In the Spectator which came yesterday, somebody repeated that foolish lie that I called Lord Byron "a flatfish." Those are the practices of your more lively article-mongers, who tell these lies, like Austin, for the malice rather than the fun of the thing. I never said nor wrote a word against or about Byron's poetry or power in my life; but I did say, that, if he were in earnest and preferred being with the sea to associating with mankind, he would do well to stay with the sea's population; thereby simply taking him at his word, had it been honest—whereas it was altogether dishonest, seeing that nobody cared so much about the opinions of mankind, and deferred to them, as he who was thus posturing and pretending to despise them.

(Hood, *Ltrs.,* 159)

addle-pates Stupid bunglers.

167] *cowslip* The field flower is a metaphor for "fanciful images of a pleasing kind" that are "plentiful and easily gathered" (Drew, 53).

179-82] *Thoughts . . . children's-feast* A poet might produce a cowslip wine, i.e., a pseudo-Romantic poetry about the insignificance of man next to nature, as Byron did in "Childe Harold's Pilgrimage," which contrasts the abiding power of the sea with the transience and smallness of man (see B's satire of Byron in *Prince Hohenstiel-Schwangau:* "O littleness of man! . . . // O grandeur of the visible universe . . ." [11.517-19ff]); he might write a sentimental love poetry about parted lovers (B does not seem to have any particular poet in mind here); or he might make a light, ironic, and charming poetry such as Alexander Pope's Epistle "To a Lady" (1717), written first to Teresa Blount and later transferred to her younger sister, Martha—all of which kinds of poetry B suggests are more suitable for children than for men.

197] *ginger-pop* "A colloquial term for ginger-beer," a non-alcoholic drink similar to ginger ale (*OED*).

217] *nettles . . . broth* Nettle-broth is a Victorian term for the soup made from the nettle plant, which is known for the stinging property of the leaf-hairs. B uses it as a metaphor for his "astringent verse" (Drew, 53).

219] *Maws* Stomachs.

222-24]   *The sick . . . nettle-broth*   B uses the intransitive sense of *posset* as a transitive verb: apparently he means that he will make for the sick a posset (a remedy for various afflictions) of nettle-broth with which he will, ironically, *cosset* (a 19th-century literary term for "indulge, pamper") them.

   loth   Unwilling (frequently *loath*).